D1583546

80 DALES WALKS

PAUL HANNON'S HILLSIDE GUIDEBOOKS

YORKSHIRE DALES
- Malhamdale
- Nidderdale
- Wharfedale
- Three Peaks Country
- Howgill Fells
- Swaledale
- Wensleydale
- Dales Way Companion

FREEDOM OF THE DALES
Exploring Yorkshire Dales on foot
218 colour photographs
Hardback
NOW ONLY £9.95

NORTH YORK MOORS
- Western Moors
- Southern Moors
- Northern Moors
- Cleveland Way Companion

WALKING COUNTRY TRIVIA QUIZ
1000 questions on the great outdoors

LAKE DISTRICT
- Over Lakeland Mountains
- Over Lakeland Fells
- The Westmorland Way
- The Furness Way
- The Cumberland Way

SOUTH PENNINES
- Ilkley Moor
- Bronte Country
- Calderdale

BIKING COUNTRY
YORKSHIRE DALES CYCLE WAY
130 miles waymarked route
(Richard Peace)

LANCASHIRE
- Bowland
- Pendle and the Ribble
- North Bowland Traverse (David Johnson)

NORTH PENNINES
- Teesdale

NORTH COUNTRY
- The Coast to Coast Walk
- Lady Anne's Way (Sheila Gordon)

YORKSHIRE PUB WALKS
- Harrogate and the Wharfe Valley (Valerie Yewdall)
- Haworth and the Aire Valley (Valerie Yewdall)

80 DALES WALKS

A comprehensive walking guide to the Yorkshire Dales

Paul Hannon

Photographs by Paul Hannon and Van Greaves

CORDEE - LEICESTER

First published 1989

Reprinted 1992

Reprinted 1995 with revisions

The maps in this book are based upon
Ordnance Survey 1:10,560 maps
1895 - 1934

British Library Cataloguing in Publication Data

Hannon, Paul
80 Dales Walks: a comprehensive walking guide to the Yorkshire Dales.
1. North Yorkshire. National Parks: Yorkshire Dales National Park - Visitors' guides
I. Title
914. 28' 404858

ISBN 0-904405-99-0

CORDEE
3a De Montfort Street
Leicester LE1 7HD

Ask for a copy of our complete catalogue of outdoor recreation/travel books and maps

Printed in Great Britain by
Joseph Ward + Co.
Dewsbury
West Yorkshire

CONTENTS

Colour plates - facing page numbers

INTRODUCTION

The Yorkshire Dales is the third largest of the ten National Parks in England and Wales, being designated as such in 1954. With an area of some 680 square miles, it encompasses the bulk of the central Pennines between the Aire Gap in the south and the Stainmore Gap in the north. While one's first impression of the Yorkshire Dales may be of sweeping green valleys, it might equally be the wonders of limestone country, or the charming, tightly packed stone villages: such is the diversity of the Yorkshire Dales.

The limestone region in the south and west of the park is internationally renowned for its caves, waterfalls and gleaming white pavements and scars, while the south-eastern and northern parts are crowned with heather moors, where the call of the grouse is regularly heard. The higher fells are broad tracts of lonely country scattered throughout the park, some with rugged gritstone caps, others permanently sodden quagmires, with endless miles of rough-grass walking. As for the dales themselves, lush pastures may carpet the valley bottoms, but almost everywhere they very soon give way to steep slopes suitable only for sheep. Naturally all the villages are to be found strung along the dale-floor, just safely above the flood level.

Each valley has its own individual character, its own speciality, including Swaledale with its meadows, parallel with Wensleydale and its waterfalls. Not surprisingly the walks are equally varied, and within these pages riverside paths alternate with hill climbs. A wealth of ancient routeways are traced, including packhorse, corpse and Roman roads, and old access tracks to long defunct mines, quarries and peat and coal pits. Modern routes are also encountered, with short sections of the Pennine Way, Dales Way and Coast to Coast Walk followed: though none begin or finish in the park, they all traverse it from end to end.

Having praised the delights of the Dales, it is perhaps fair to see the other side of the coin.... threats to this delicately balanced district abound, some obvious, others less so. They include, in no particular order, holiday homes, footpath erosion, quarrying, low-flying aircraft, the demise of public transport, timeshare plans, the plight of small hill farms, and the pitiful government funding for our treasured landscapes.

Finally, when appreciating the condition of paths, stiles and waymarking, we must be grateful to be in the area of an authority that places a high priority on such matters.

ORDNANCE SURVEY MAPS

The strip-maps illustrating each walk are intended to guide one safely around, but cannot show anything of the surrounding countryside. An Ordnance Survey map remains the best possible companion, the relevant sheets being these:

1:50,000 Landranger

92 97 (1 walk only!) 98 99 103 104

1:25,000 Outdoor Leisure

2 10 30 (with Pathfinder 617 they cover all but 3 walks)

While the Landranger series may complement this guide better, the 1:25,000 (2½") maps are more detailed for seeking out further paths not included in the guide.

TRANSPORT

The availability of public transport varies enormously. Currently, trains serving the Dales run from Skipton to Carlisle or Lancaster, but hopes for the future are not high. Buses run the length of most major valleys, with Wensleydale being most regularly. Numerous seasonal services operate, and all services are liable to changes. Main operators are listed on page 14.

ACCOMMODATION

There is a wide range of accommodation for every taste, though in the height of the season vacancies can be few. The National Park Authority produces a useful booklet, and some information centres provide lists. Youth hostels are spread fairly uniformly throughout the district, being located at

Aysgarth Dentdale Ellingstring Grinton
Hawes Ingleton Keld Kettlewell
Linton Malham Stainforth

As most of these serve one of the long-distance paths, they too can become fully booked.

Camping and caravan sites can be found in numerous locations, along with an increasing number of 'bunk barns'. As 'stone tents', they bridge the gap between camping and hostelling.

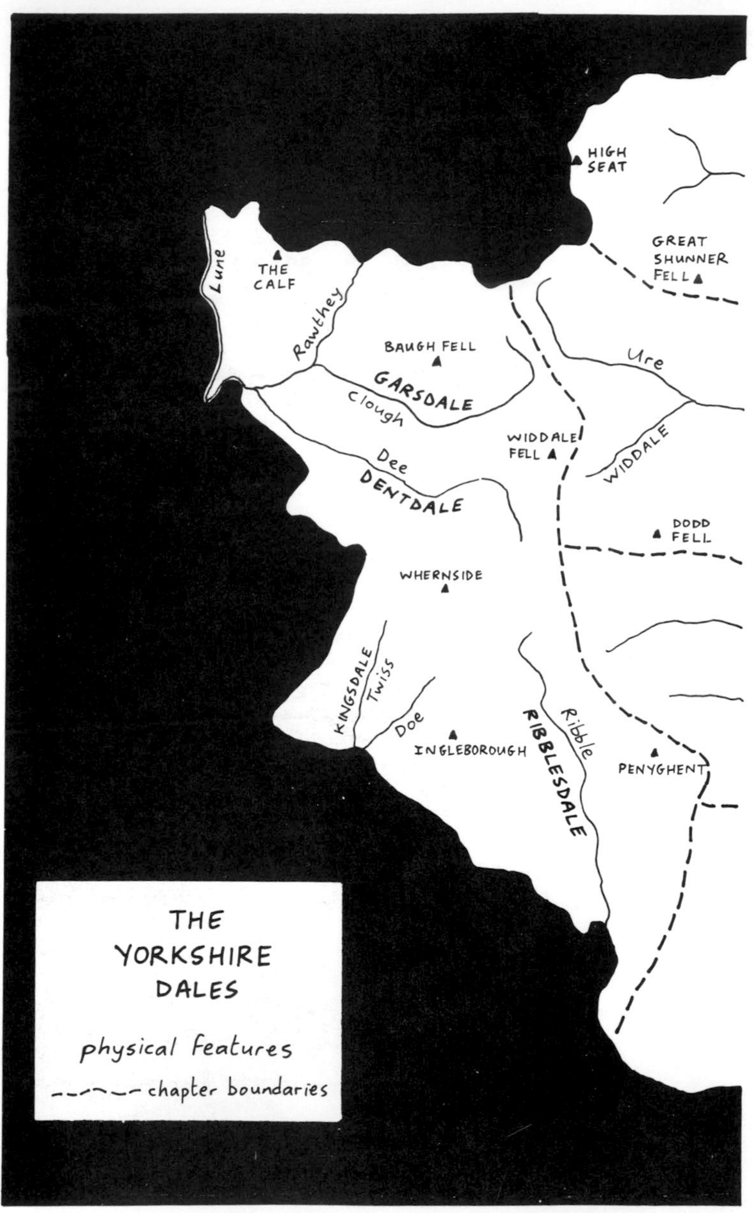
HIGH SEAT
GREAT SHUNNER FELL
Lune
THE CALF
Rawthey
BAUGH FELL
GARSDALE
Clough
Ure
WIDDALE FELL
WIDDALE
Dee
DENTDALE
DODD FELL
WHERNSIDE
KINGSDALE
Twiss
Doe
INGLEBOROUGH
RIBBLESDALE
Ribble
PENYGHENT
THE YORKSHIRE DALES
physical features
chapter boundaries

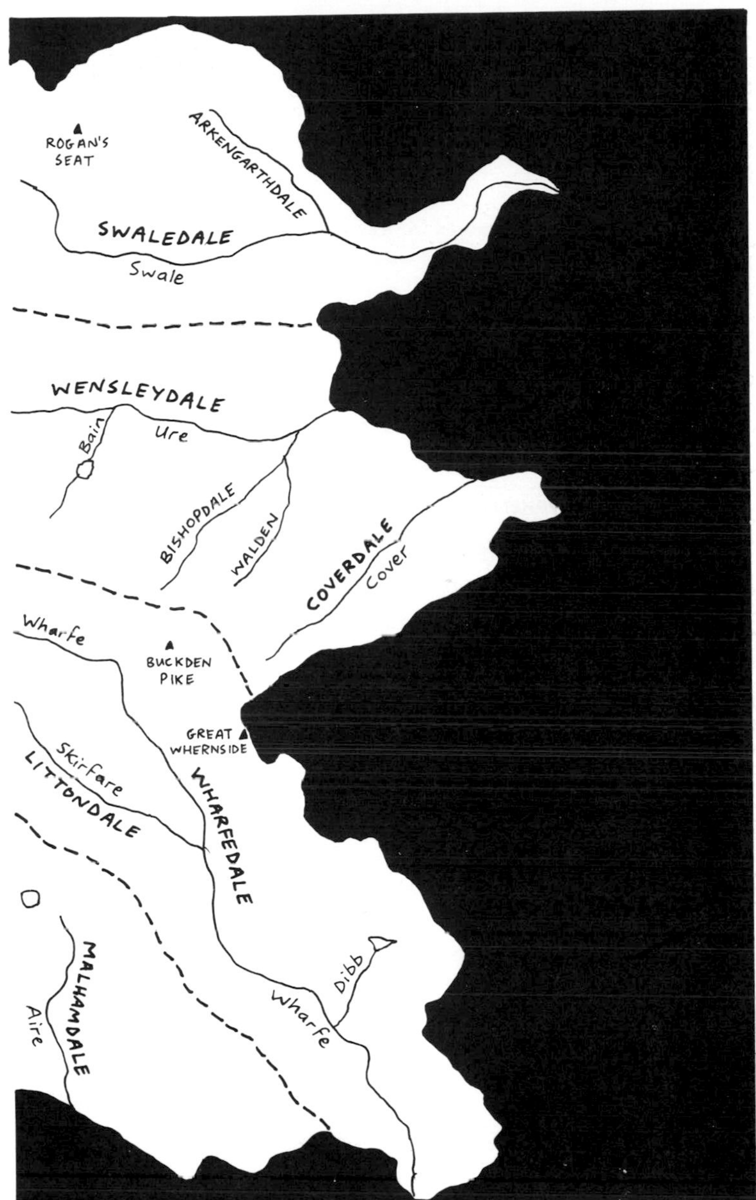
ROGAN'S SEAT
ARKENGARTHDALE
SWALEDALE
Swale
WENSLEYDALE
Ure
Bain
BISHOPDALE
WALDEN
COVERDALE
Cover
Wharfe
BUCKDEN PIKE
GREAT WHERNSIDE
Skirfare
LITTONDALE
WHARFEDALE
MALHAMDALE
Aire
Dibb
Wharfe

THE WALKS
and their starting points

CHAPTER FOUR WENSLEYDALE

CHAPTER FIVE SWALEDALE

74	AROUND KISDON AND THWAITE	Keld
75	SLEI GILL AND BOOZE MOOR	Langthwaite
76	A CIRCUIT OF OXNOP GILL	Ivelet
77	HARKERSIDE MOOR AND APEDALE	Grinton
78	THE ENVIRONS OF LOW ROW	Low Row
79	MUKER SIDE AND THWAITE	Muker
80	ARKENGARTHDALE	Langthwaite
81	MARRICK PRIORY AND THE SWALE	Reeth
82	BIRKDALE AND WHITSUNDALE	Hoggarths
83	THE ENVIRONS OF GUNNERSIDE	Gunnerside
84	WHITCLIFFE SCAR AND THE SWALE	Richmond

Keld
Reeth
Richmond
Sedbergh
Hawes
Aysgarth
Horton
Kettlewell
Ingleton
Malham
Settle
Skipton

SOME USEFUL ADDRESSES

Ramblers' Association
1/5 Wandsworth Road, London SW8 2XX
Tel. (0171) 582 6878

Youth Hostels Association
Trevelyan House, St. Albans, Herts. AL1 2DY
Tel. St. Albans (01727) 55215

Yorkshire Dales National Park
Information Service, Colvend, Hebden Road,
Grassington, Skipton, N. Yorkshire BD23 5LB
Tel. Grassington (01756) 752748

Yorkshire and Humberside Tourist Board
312 Tadcaster Road, York YO2 2HF
Tel. York (01904) 707961

Yorkshire Dales Society
Otley Civic Centre, Cross Green, Otley
West Yorkshire LS21 1HD (01943) 607868
(an organisation concerned with the well-being of the area, providing an important 'watchdog' service.)

The National Trust
36 Queen Anne's Gate, London SW1H 9AS
Tel. (0171) 222 9251

Dales Connections
Elmtree Press and Distribution, The Elms,
Exelby, Bedale, N. Yorkshire DL8 2HD
Tel. (01677) 424298

Cumbria County Council (Transport)
Tel. (01228) 812812

North Yorkshire County Council (Transport)
Tel. (01609) 780780

British Rail, Leeds
Leeds : Tel. (0113) 244 8133
York : Tel. (01969) 642155

INFORMATION SERVICES

NATIONAL PARK CENTRES
(open April - October, except * winter weekends also)

AYSGARTH FALLS, Leyburn, N. Yorkshire DL8 3TH
Tel. Aysgarth (01969) 663424

CLAPHAM, via Lancaster, Lancashire LA2 8ED
Tel. Clapham (015242) 51419

GRASSINGTON* Skipton, N. Yorkshire BD23 5LB
Tel. Grassington (01756) 752774

HAWES, Station Yard, Hawes, N. Yorkshire DL8 3NT
Tel. Hawes (01969) 667450

MALHAM*, via Skipton, N. Yorkshire BD23 4DA
Tel. Airton (01729) 830363

SEDBERGH, 72 Main Street, Sedbergh, Cumbria LA10 5AD
Tel. Sedbergh (015396) 20125

TOURIST INFORMATION CENTRES (varied opening times)

HORTON, Penyghent Cafe, Horton-in-Ribblesdale, N. Yorkshire
BD24 0HE Tel. Horton (01729) 860333

INGLETON, Community Centre Car Park, Main St, Ingleton,
N. Yorkshire Tel. Ingleton (015242) 41049

LEYBURN, Thornborough Hall, Leyburn, N. Yorkshire
Tel. Wensleydale (01969) 23069

REETH, Swaledale Folk Museum, Reeth, N. Yorkshire DL11 6QT
Tel. Richmond (01748) 84373 (evenings only)

RICHMOND, Friary Gardens, Victoria Rd, Richmond, N. Yorks,
DL10 4AJ Tel. Richmond (01748) 850252

SETTLE, Town Hall, Settle, N. Yorkshire
Tel. Settle (01729) 825192

SKIPTON, Sheep Street, Skipton, N. Yorkshire
Tel. Skipton (01756) 792809

SOME USEFUL FACILITIES

This and the following two pages list all known facilities at the start points and villages encountered. *It is a general guide only.*

relevant chapter		accommodation	inn	car park	bus service	rail service	Post office	other shop	payphone	WC
2	Airton	•			•		•		•	
5	Angram				•				•	
4	Appersett									
1	Appletreewick	•	•		•		•		•	
1	Arncliffe	•	•		•		•		•	
4	Askrigg	•	•		•		•	•	•	•
3	Austwick	•	•		•		•		•	
4	Aysgarth	•	•	•	•		•	•	•	•
4	Bainbridge	•	•		•		•		•	
2	Bell Busk	•					•			
1	Bolton Abbey	•	•	•	•		•	•	•	•
1	Buckden	•	•	•	•		•	•	•	•
1	Burnsall	•	•	•	•		•	•	•	•
4	Burtersett	•						•	•	
4	Carlton	•	•		•		•		•	
4	Carperby	•	•		•		•		•	
4	Castle Bolton			•			•		•	•
3	Cautley	•								
3	Chapel le Dale	•	•	•	•		•		•	
3	Clapham	•	•	•	•	•	•	•	•	•
1	Conistone						•		•	
4	Countersett	•								
4	Coverham				•					
3	Cowgill/Dent Head	•	•			•			•	

relevant chapter		accommodation	inn	car park	bus service	rail service	Post office	other shop	payphone	wc
1	Cracoe	●	●		●			●	●	
1	Cray	●	●		●					
3	Deepdale Foot	●								
3	Dent	●	●	●	●		●	●	●	●
2	Eastby	●	●		●					
2	Embsay	●	●	●	●		●	●	●	●
2	Eshton	●			●					
2	Gargrave	●	●	●	●	●	●	●	●	●
3	Garsdale Head	●			●	●			●	
3	Gawthrop	●						●	●	
4	Gayle	●			●				●	
1	Grassington	●	●	●	●		●	●	●	●
5	Grinton	●	●		●		●		●	
5	Gunnerside	●	●	●	●		●	●	●	●
4	Hardraw	●	●					●	●	
4	Hawes	●	●	●	●		●	●	●	●
1	Hawkswick	●								
5	Healaugh				●		●		●	
1	Hebden	●	●		●		●		●	●
3	Helwith Bridge	●	●		●				●	
2	Hetton	●	●		●				●	
4	Horsehouse	●	●		●		●		●	
3	Horton	●	●	●	●	●	●	●	●	●
1	Howgill	●			●			●	●	
1	Hubberholme	●	●							
3	Ingleton	●	●	●	●		●	●	●	●
5	Keld	●			●				●	●
1	Kettlewell	●	●	●	●		●	●	●	●

relevant chapter		accommodation	inn	car park	bus service	rail service	Post office	other shop	payphone	wc
2	Kirkby Malham	●	●		●				●	
3	Langcliffe	●	●	●	●		●		●	
5	Langthwaite	●	●				●	●	●	●
1	Linton	●	●	●	●		●		●	●
1	Litton	●	●				●		●	
5	Low Row	●	●		●		●		●	●
2	Malham	●	●	●	●		●	●	●	●
5	Marrick	●							●	
5	Marske						●		●	
5	Muker	●	●		●		●	●	●	●
5	Reeth	●	●	●	●		●	●	●	●
3	Ribblehead	●	●		●	●				
5	Richmond	●	●	●	●		●	●	●	●
2	Rylstone				●					
5	Satron				●				●	
3	Sedbergh	●	●	●	●		●	●	●	●
3	Settle	●	●	●	●	●	●	●	●	●
2	Skipton	●	●	●	●	●	●	●	●	●
3	Stainforth	●	●	●	●		●	●	●	●
1	Starbotton	●	●		●				●	
2	Stirton	●	●							
4	Thornton Rust	●			●		●			
1	Thorpe	●								
1	Threshfield	●	●		●				●	
5	Thwaite	●			●			●	●	
4	West Burton	●	●		●		●		●	
4	West Witton	●	●		●		●	●	●	
4	Worton	●	●		●				●	

USING THIS GUIDE

The 84 walks described range in length from 3½ to 11 miles, and the terrain covered is equally varied, giving a walk to suit almost any mood, be it personal, or of the oft-changing weather. All walks are circular, and with an average distance of 6 miles are ideal for half-day rambles. Each walk is given its own mini-chapter consisting of 'immediate impression' diagram, detailed narrative and strip-map, and illustrations and notes of features of interest along the way. The walk number is the key to easy location in the guide.

KEY TO THE MAP SYMBOLS

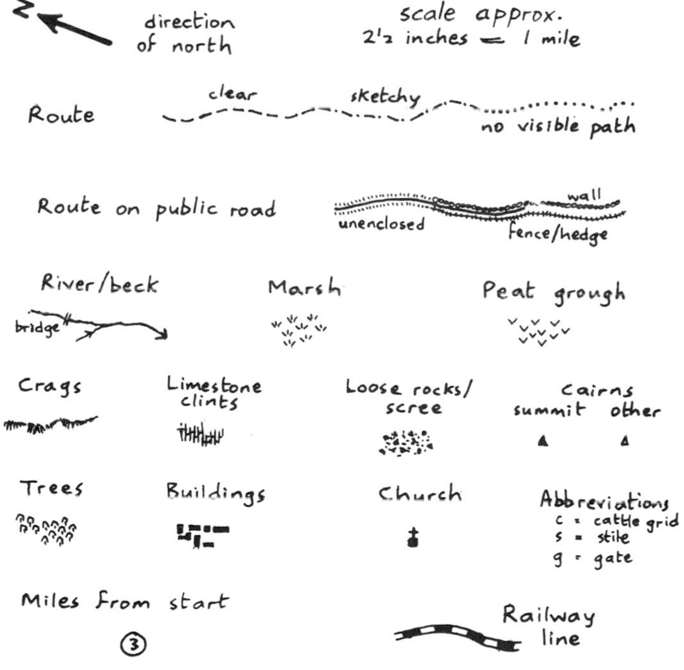
N
direction of north
scale approx. 2½ inches = 1 mile
Route
clear
sketchy
no visible path
Route on public road
unenclosed
wall
fence/hedge
River/beck
bridge
Marsh
Peat grough
Crags
Limestone clints
Loose rocks/scree
Cairns
summit
other
Trees
Buildings
Church
Abbreviations
c = cattle grid
s = stile
g = gate
Miles from start
3
Railway line

For ease of reference, this key is duplicated on the final page.

CHAPTER ONE

WHARFEDALE

Linton-in-Craven   opposite: Bolton Priory

WHARFEDALE

The subject of this chapter is the upper valley of the river Wharfe, from the boundary of the Yorkshire Dales National Park at Bolton Bridge to beyond Buckden: included is the quieter side-valley of Littondale. Wharfedale is the most popular valley in the Dales, this being attributable not least of all to its accessibility. The West Yorkshire cities of Leeds and Bradford and their surrounding towns are but a modest distance away, and on summer weekends the banks of the river see as many sun-worshippers as ramblers.

The Wharfe's name originates from the Celtic meaning 'swift water', and this lovely river races for almost 30 miles from Beckermonds to Bolton Bridge before a rather more sedate run to join the Ouse near Selby. At Beckermonds the Wharfe is made by the confluence of Oughtershaw and Green Field Becks, which have themselves already covered some distance from the lonely heights of Cam Fell.

The Wharfe's major tributary is the Skirfare, which flows through – and sometimes beneath – its own dale, Littondale to lose its identity near the famous landmark of Kilnsey Crag. Though Littondale has many characteristics of its big brother, it is separated by steep-sided fells and its seclusion gives it an intimate, possibly even greater charm.

North of Kilnsey the valley floors are dead flat and never more than half a mile wide, and at a very clearly-defined boundary the fells begin their majestic rise to numerous 2000-foot summits. At regular intervals their slopes are scored by crystal clear mountain becks which have a short-lived but very joyful journey. While the higher tops display the gritstone features of peat groughs and never-dry terrain, the lower slopes show off the ever-fascinating scars of gleaming limestone.

Lower down the dale meanwhile, gritstone dominates in the huge forms of Barden Moor and Fell. These extensive areas of rolling heather moorland face each other across the Wharfe, and together are valued grouse shooting country. Happily they are the subject of a negotiated access agreement with the landowner (the Duke of Devonshire's estates) and walkers are free to roam over the upland areas subject to various restrictions.

The main point is that the moors can be 'closed' on certain days when shooting takes place, though not Sundays. Although notices are posted at the access points (along with a list of all restrictions) disappointment can be avoided by ringing the estate office beforehand (Bolton Abbey 227). Also worth knowing – dogs are not allowed. *Walks 1 and 15 take advantage of this facility.*

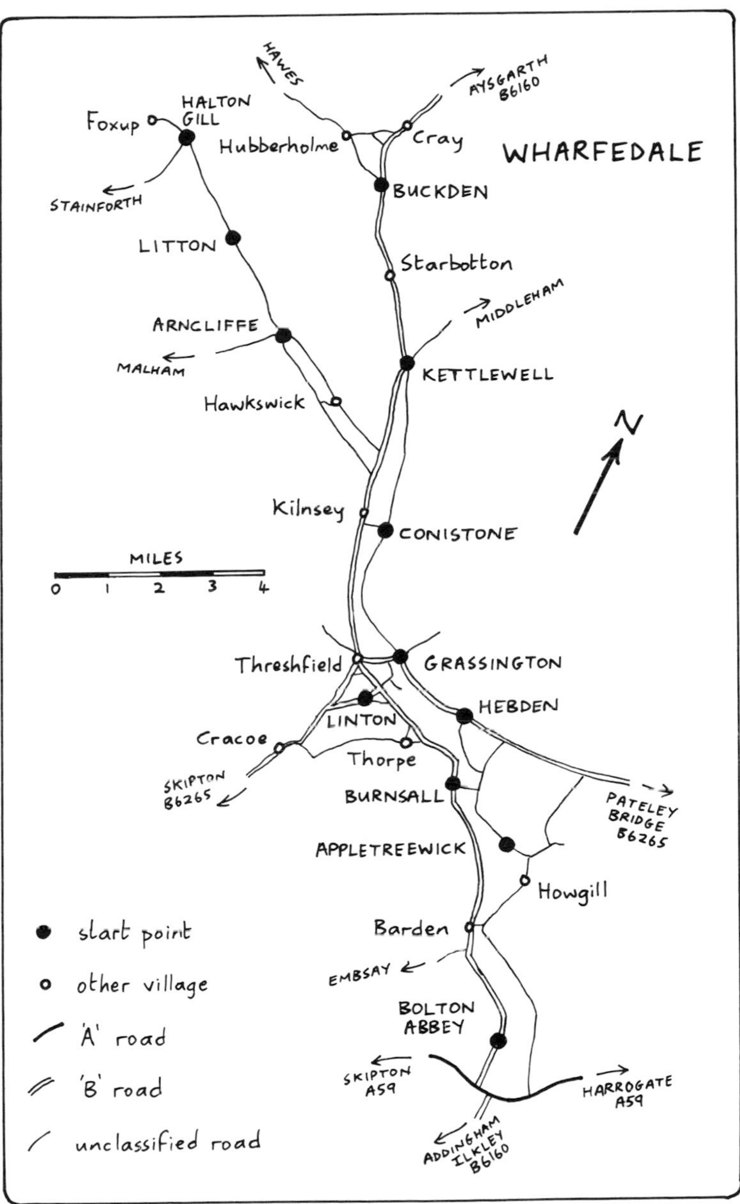
WHARFEDALE
HAWES
AYSGARTH B6160
HALTON GILL
Foxup
Hubberholme
Cray
BUCKDEN
STAINFORTH
LITTON
Starbotton
MIDDLEHAM
ARNCLIFFE
MALHAM
KETTLEWELL
Hawkswick
N
Kilnsey
CONISTONE
MILES
0 1 2 3 4
Threshfield
GRASSINGTON
LINTON
HEBDEN
Cracoe
Thorpe
SKIPTON B6265
BURNSALL
PATELEY BRIDGE B6265
APPLETREEWICK
Howgill
Barden
EMBSAY
BOLTON ABBEY
SKIPTON A59
HARROGATE A59
ADDINGHAM ILKLEY B6160
start point
other village
'A' road
'B' road
unclassified road

WALK 1

THE ASCENT OF SIMON'S SEAT

8½ miles

from Bolton Abbey

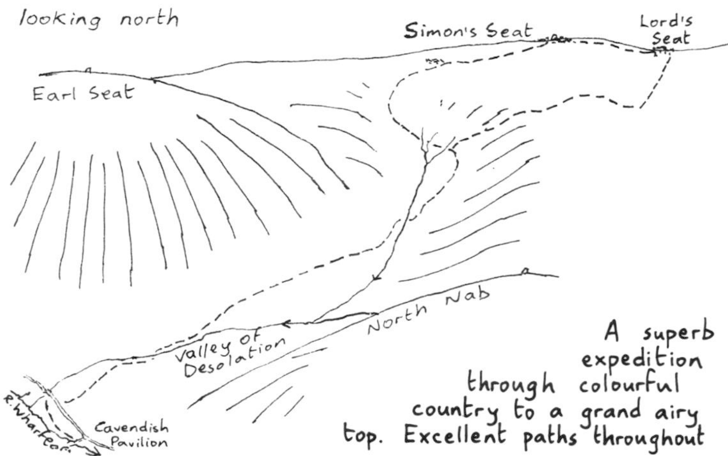
looking north
Simon's Seat
Lord's Seat
Earl Seat
North Nab
Valley of Desolation
R. Wharfe
Cavendish Pavilion

A superb expedition through colourful country to a grand airy top. Excellent paths throughout

This is the only walk in the book to return by what is largely the same route.

The most suitable starting point is the Cavendish Pavilion. It is signposted off the B6160 just north of Bolton Abbey, turning off by the large memorial fountain.

THE WALK

Leave the Pavilion by crossing the wooden bridge over the river and immediately taking a path upstream. Entering some trees it soon emerges onto a narrow road at Posforth Bridge. Double back up the hill to a clearing at the top, and forsake the road for a gate on the left by an access notice. Head half-left across the pasture past some hoary oaks to a gate, from where a good track crosses to reach Posforth Gill. While the main path turns right to run along the rim of the drop to the beck, a detour down to it will be well repaid with a close-up view of the waterfall.

Having witnessed the spectacle the beck might be forded and the north bank followed upstream, though the usual path remains on the same side to cross by a tiny footbridge a little further up. Soon a fork is reached: although our way rises to the left, another brief diversion is recommended, simply continuing upstream to enjoy an equally lovely waterfall. The main path, meanwhile, rises to a stile to enter Laund Pasture Plantation. A wide track leads rapidly to the far end of the trees, where a gate admits onto the open moor.

A good, clear track heads directly away, and leads unerringly to the summit of Simon's Seat. On the way there it fords Great Agill Beck prior to a short, steep section. Beyond a stone table a shooter's track branches off to the right: this is where we rejoin the outward route on returning from the top. Our ascending path crosses the headwaters of the beck before swinging right to pass Truckle Crags, and the large grouping of rocks atop Simon's Seat are only a couple of minutes away.

The environs of the summit are a source of potential confusion in bad visibility, but the presence of a footpath sign at the nearby path junction helps avoid this possibility. The unmistakeable form of an Ordnance Survey column adorns the highest rocks, and to add interest to the final few feet, hands must be used to attain it.

To vary the return take the sketchy path heading east to the prominent outcrops of Lord's Seat, then turn right alongside the wall immediately behind. After a short half-mile of gradual descent turn sharp right along a shooter's track. This wide track undulates across the moor and leads unfailingly back to the outward route near the stone table. Steps can now be happily retraced all the way back to the Pavilion.

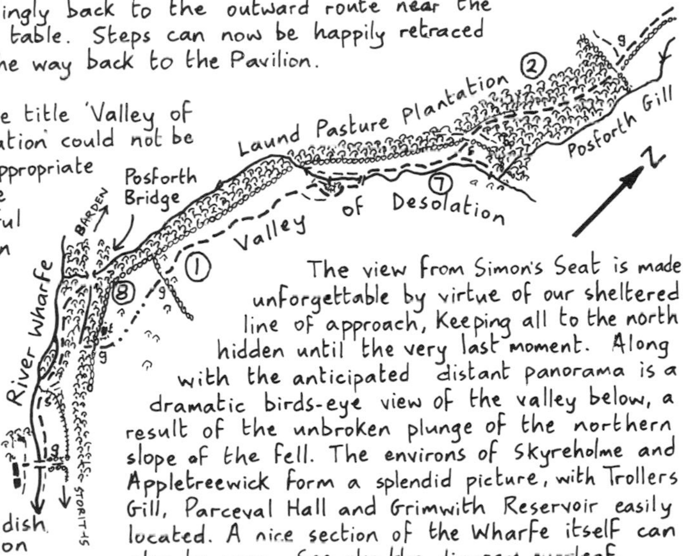

The title 'Valley of Desolation' could not be less appropriate to the colourful terrain here.

The view from Simon's Seat is made unforgettable by virtue of our sheltered line of approach, keeping all to the north hidden until the very last moment. Along with the anticipated distant panorama is a dramatic birds-eye view of the valley below, a result of the unbroken plunge of the northern slope of the fell. The environs of Skyreholme and Appletreewick form a splendid picture, with Trollers Gill, Parceval Hall and Grimwith Reservoir easily located. A nice section of the Wharfe itself can also be seen. See also the diagram overleaf.

1

The giant boulders of Simon's Seat and Lord's Seat make an ideal playground for scramblers.

※ From this stone table Truckle Crags and more distantly Simon's Seat come into view.

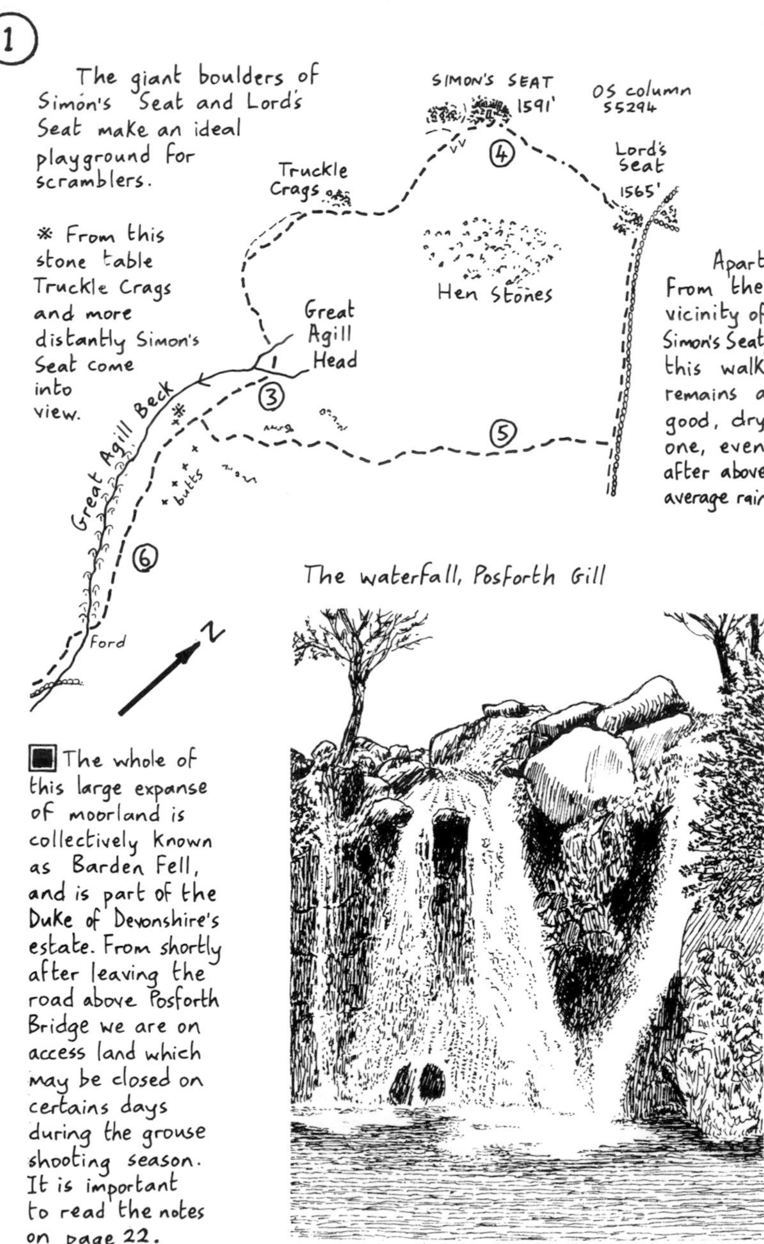

SIMON'S SEAT
1591'
OS column
S5294
Lord's Seat
1565'
Truckle Crags
Hen Stones
Great Agill Head
Great Agill Beck
butts
Ford
N
4
3
5
6

Apart from the vicinity of Simon's Seat, this walk remains a good, dry one, even after above average rain.

■ The whole of this large expanse of moorland is collectively known as Barden Fell, and is part of the Duke of Devonshire's estate. From shortly after leaving the road above Posforth Bridge we are on access land which may be closed on certains days during the grouse shooting season. It is important to read the notes on page 22.

The waterfall, Posforth Gill

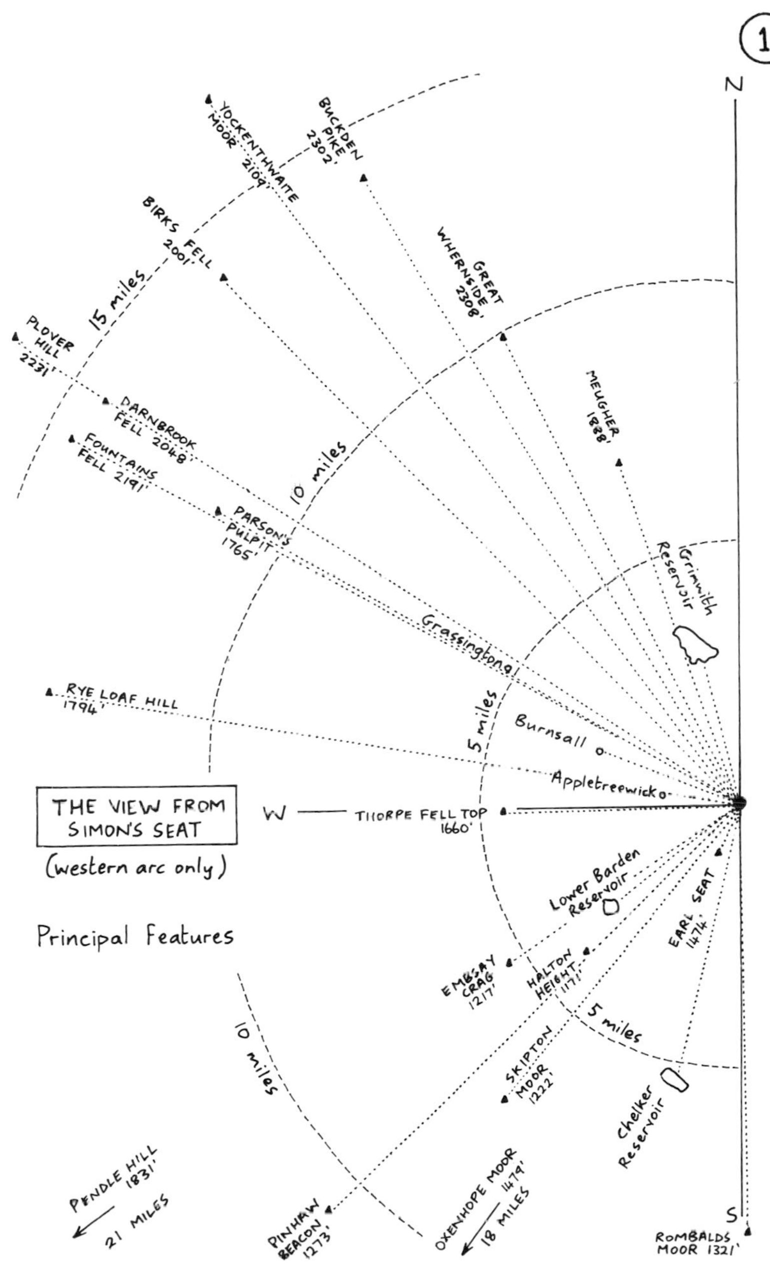
1
N
YOCKENTHWAITE MOOR 2109'
BUCKDEN PIKE 2302'
BIRKS FELL 2001'
15 miles
PLOVER HILL 2231'
GREAT WHERNSIDE 2308'
DARNBROOK FELL 2048'
FOUNTAINS FELL 2191'
MEUGHER 1888'
10 miles
PARSON'S PULPIT 1765'
Grimwith Reservoir
Grassington
RYE LOAF HILL 1794'
5 miles
Burnsall
Appletreewick
THE VIEW FROM SIMON'S SEAT
W
THORPE FELL TOP 1660'
(western arc only)
Lower Barden Reservoir
EARL SEAT 1474'
Principal Features
EMBSAY CRAG 1217'
HALTON HEIGHT 1171'
5 miles
10 miles
SKIPTON MOOR 1222'
Chelker Reservoir
PENDLE HILL 1831'
21 MILES
OXENHOPE MOOR 1479'
18 MILES
PINHAW BEACON 1273'
S
ROMBALDS MOOR 1321'

(2)

WALK 2 — THRESHFIELD AND LINTON

3½ miles — from Linton Falls

A mere stroll through the fields, with a host of interesting features.

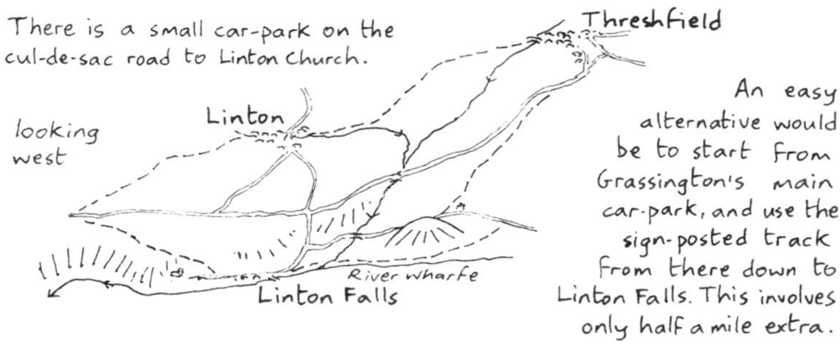
Threshfield
Linton
looking west
River Wharfe
Linton Falls

There is a small car-park on the cul-de-sac road to Linton Church.

An easy alternative would be to start from Grassington's main car-park, and use the sign-posted track from there down to Linton Falls. This involves only half a mile extra.

THE WALK

From the car park head back along the road for a short distance, and after the last house turn down to the right in a ginnel leading to the footbridge across the Wharfe. After surveying the turbulent falls immediately downstream, turn back a few yards to cross the little pack-bridge over a similarly tiny stream. Now pass to the right of the cottage to accompany the Wharfe upstream, soon being channelled up to a stile onto a road. Now turn left the short distance to Threshfield school. Take a gate immediately after the schoolyard and head up the field on a track which swings right to a bridge across the former railway line. It then continues away from it to run a little sketchily to a gate onto another road. Turn right then first left to enter the centre of old Threshfield.

At the end of the road turn left to join the main road as it descends to Threshfield Bridge. Immediately after the buildings on the other side escape by a stile on the left to rise diagonally up the field to a gateway. Follow the wall away from it to pass through a tree-fringed wall, then continue straight across the next field to a footbridge back over the former railway line. Bear half-right down the field to a wall corner shrouded in trees, where a gate gives access to an enclosed track. Running parallel with Linton Beck to the left, it leads unfailingly to the road through Linton village.

Turn briefly right and then sharp left between

the green and the whitewashed inn. A choice of beck-crossings conveys us to the opposite lane, which is followed to the right to within yards of its demise. Here turn left in front of a barn and along a short enclosed track. Soon it breaks free, and is rapidly vacated by means of a stile on the left. Stay with the left-hand wall until it begins to drop away, then contour round to the right: down to the left now is the former Linton residential school. On reaching a cross-wall, the first of four stiles on virtually the same contour is encountered. After the last of these - a fine old work of art hidden in a corner - drop down to the left to a gate onto the Threshfield-Burnsall road again.

Turn right along the road for a few yards only to a gate on the opposite side, then head diagonally across two narrow fields with gap-stiles. Continue the direction to near the top corner of a plantation, but remain above the steep drop towards Linton church and the river, instead going across to the far corner of the field. A stile will be found to the right of a barn: from it continue on through a meadow to its far corner, there joining a short, enclosed way emerging back onto the road. Before returning to the car park, turn right to visit the church, now only two minutes away.

The Church of St. Michael and All Angels, Linton

Linton is generally accepted as being one of northern England's most attractive villages, and not without good reason. A rich assortment of limestone buildings stand in very laid-back fashion, none wishing to crowd the spacious green. Nearest is the whitewashed little hostelry, whose name recalls a local benefactor: Richard Fountaine made his money in London, but in his will he remembered Linton by paying for the 'hospital' at the end of the green. This 18th century building is still in use as almshouses. Through the green runs Linton Beck, crossed in quick succession by a road bridge, a ford, a clapper bridge and most strikingly, a packhorse bridge.

(2)

Threshfield is a disjointed village scattered in various directions around the junction of the Skipton-Grassington road with the main up-dale road. The 'new' part of the village - with its striking Catholic church of modern design - is along the road towards Grassington, but it is the more interesting old corner we visit. Solid stone cottages and farm buildings overlook a quaint, triangular green, enclosed by walls and shrouded in trees. Inside are some stocks and the flowers of spring.

On turning alongside the green note the stone lintel of the old post office, dated 1651. Just across the main road is the popular inn, whose title serves to indicate its original purpose.

Passed earlier in the walk is the village school, which was built in the 17th century as a grammar school.

The former railway was a branch line from Skipton to Grassington, and was in use from 1902 to 1969. It still comes within a couple of miles, but only to serve a quarry.

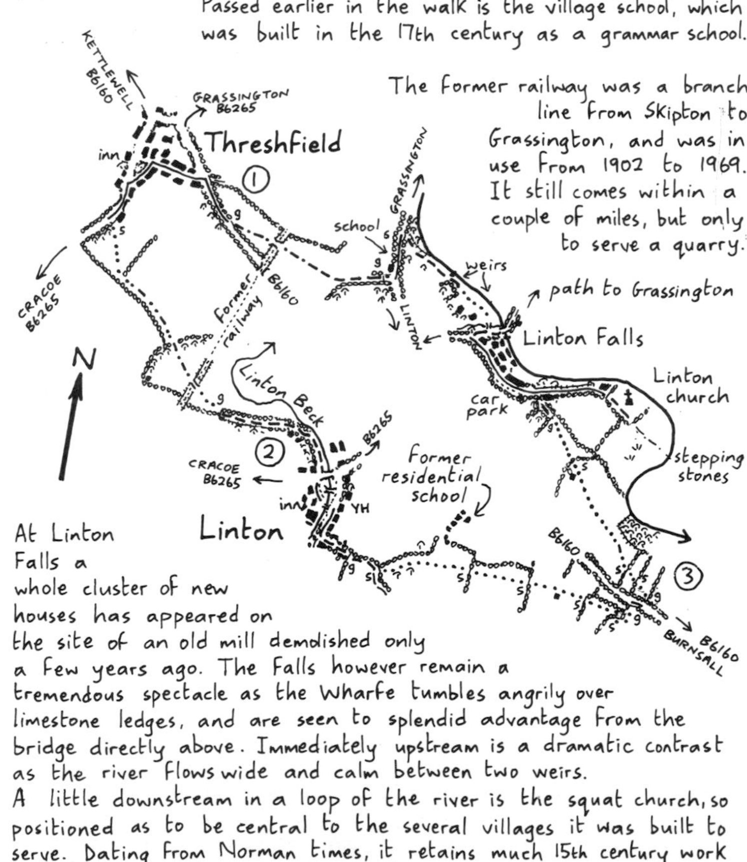
KETTLEWELL B6160
GRASSINGTON B6265
Threshfield
inn
1
school
GRASSINGTON
weirs
path to Grassington
Linton Falls
Linton church
car park
stepping stones
CRACOE B6265
Former railway
B6160
N
Linton Beck
2
B6265
CRACOE B6265
inn
YH
Linton
Former residential school
LINTON
B6160
3
B6160 BURNSALL

At Linton Falls a whole cluster of new houses has appeared on the site of an old mill demolished only a few years ago. The Falls however remain a tremendous spectacle as the Wharfe tumbles angrily over limestone ledges, and are seen to splendid advantage from the bridge directly above. Immediately upstream is a dramatic contrast as the river flows wide and calm between two weirs.

A little downstream in a loop of the river is the squat church, so positioned as to be central to the several villages it was built to serve. Dating from Norman times, it retains much 15th century work and its lovely interior lives up to its idyllic setting.

WALK 3 — HUBBERHOLME, CRAY AND SCAR TOP

5 miles

from Buckden

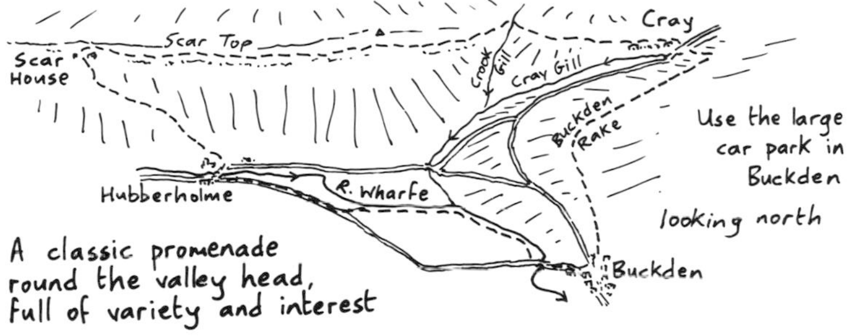
Cray
Scar Top
Scar House
Crook Gill
Cray Gill
Buckden Rake
Hubberholme
R. Wharfe
Buckden

Use the large car park in Buckden

looking north

A classic promenade round the valley head, full of variety and interest

THE WALK

Leave the car park not by its usual exit, instead use a gate at its northern end from where a stony track gently rises up Buckden Rake. At the end of the surround of trees it turns right through a gate to commence a pleasant, level section. On drawing level with the buildings of Cray down to the left, take a gate in the adjacent wall and drop down a steep field to another gate from where Cray Gill is forded to join the road right next to the inn.

To leave Cray take the farm track immediately behind the hostelry and follow it up to the left, keeping to the right of the various farm buildings. Having passed through a gate above the last building the way remains level through several fields, becoming indistinct but aiming for a barn just ahead. Go to the left of it to then swing right to a tiny footbridge over Crook Gill.

From the footbridge swing left to commence a long, easy mile above the well-defined escarpment cloaked in trees on the left: part-way along, the stately Wharfedale Cairn beckons just up to the right. All too soon the path arrives just above Scar House. Turn down between the buildings to accompany the stony access road down the hillside into Hubberholme, emerging alongside the church.

For the final leg of the walk cross the bridge over the Wharfe to the inn, and if not delayed there turn to the left along the road. After about half a mile take a gate on the left to rejoin the river, which is now accompanied downdale to soon reach Buckden Bridge. Join the road to recross the river and so arrive back in Buckden village.

3

Buckden is the first sizeable settlement encountered by the Wharfe, and stands at the meeting place of two high roads from Wensleydale to the north. The good quality B6160 comes via Cray to take over as the valley road from the narrow, winding road that reaches nearly 2000 feet on its way over Fleet Moss from Hawes, before running through Langstrothdale to get to Buckden. In medieval times Buckden was the centre of a vast hunting forest, and its hostelry recalls its former importance in its name. The village stands high above the river on the slope of Buckden Pike, and swift-flowing Buckden Beck carves a deep defile down from the summit.

Buckden Pike from the Wharfedale Cairn

Though barely even a hamlet, Hubberholme boasts two famous buildings and a shapely bridge which connects them. The church of St. Michael is a gem, its tower showing Norman traces. Its best feature is a 500 year old oak rood loft, one of only two remaining in Yorkshire, while some pews bear the famous trademark of 'Mousey' Thompson. Carving therefore - both ancient and modern - dominates the interior of this highest church in the dale. Outside, meanwhile, the sparkling Wharfe runs almost past its very door.

Across the river is the whitewashed and homely George Inn in an idyllic setting. Formerly housing the vicar, its flagged floors continued to be the scene of the New Year 'land-letting' when proceeds of a 'poor pasture' go to needy parishioners.

(3)

Restored last century, the isolated Scar House was the scene of early Quaker gatherings.

Situated at over 1000 feet above sea level, the farming hamlet of Cray is the last outpost of Wharfedale on the high road over to Bishopdale and ultimately Wensleydale. This crossing of the fells is known as the Kidstones Pass, and is the easiest motorable escape out of the valley north of Grassington. Cray's one amenity is the White Lion, an uncomplicated and welcoming hostelry with a flagged floor.

The walk from Crook Gill to Scar House is along short-cropped turf above a steep drop through ancient woodlands, the scarp being marked by limestone scars and sections of pavement. The slopes to the north rise more steadily to the height of 2109 feet on the largely unfrequented Yockenthwaite Moor.

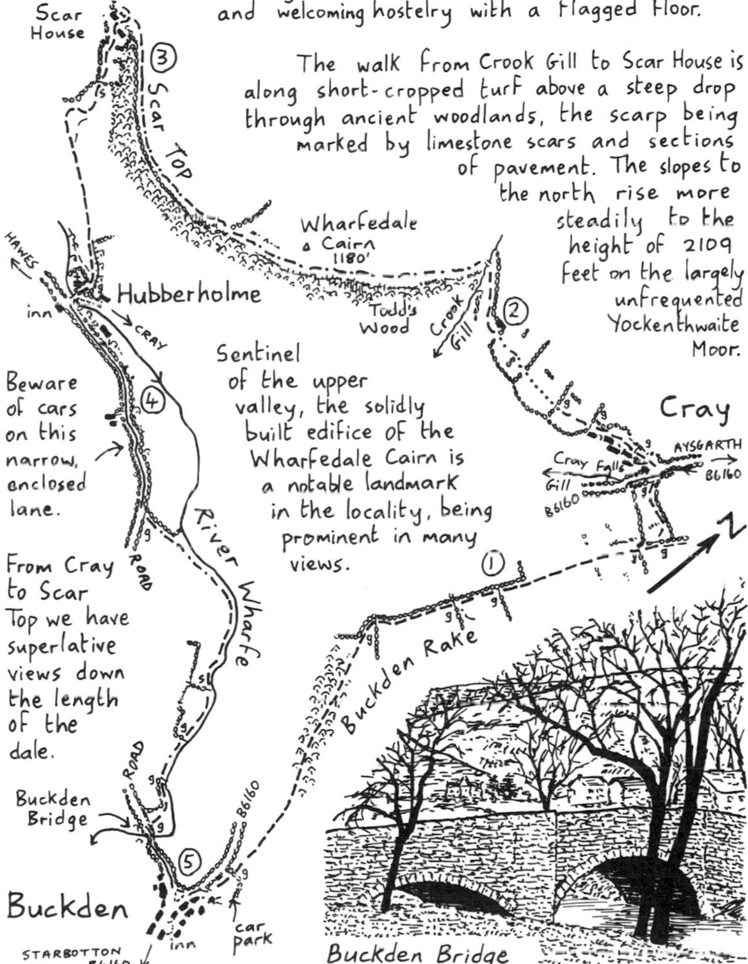
Scar House
3
Scar Top
S
HAWES
Hubberholme
inn
CRAY
Wharfedale Cairn 1180'
Todd's Wood
Crook Gill
2
Cray
g
AYSGARTH
B6160
Cray Falls
Cray Gill
B6160
N
1
4
ROAD
River Wharfe
Buckden Rake
ROAD
Buckden Bridge
B6160
5
Buckden
inn
car park
STARBOTTON B6160

Sentinel of the upper valley, the solidly built edifice of the Wharfedale Cairn is a notable landmark in the locality, being prominent in many views.

Beware of cars on this narrow, enclosed lane.

From Cray to Scar Top we have superlative views down the length of the dale.

Buckden Bridge

WALK 4 GRASS WOOD AND GHAISTRILL'S STRID

5½ miles from Grassington

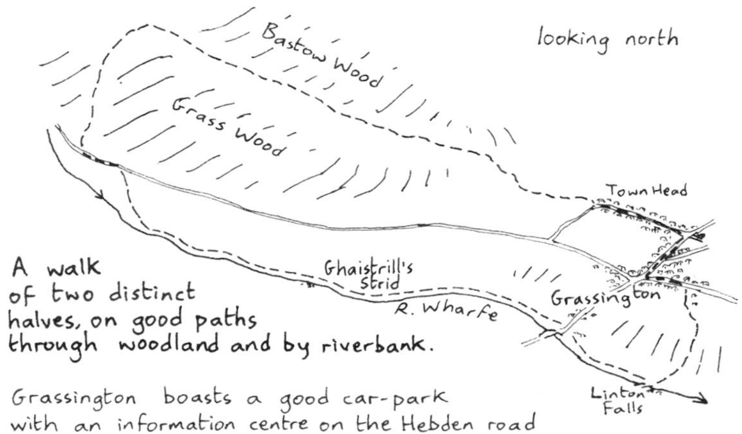

Bastow Wood
looking north
Grass Wood
Town Head
Ghaistrill's Strid
Grassington
R. Wharfe
Linton Falls

A walk of two distinct halves, on good paths through woodland and by riverbank.

Grassington boasts a good car-park with an information centre on the Hebden road

THE WALK

Leave the car park by the road into the centre of Grassington, then head up the main street past the cobbled square and the Devonshire Arms as far as a crossroads next to the institute. Here turn left along Chapel Street, and when it eventually turns sharp left, leave it by turning right into a farmyard. Bear round to the right of the main buildings to find a gate beyond the last one. A track across the field is soon vacated in order to reach a narrow gap-stile in the wall opposite, and a larger field is likewise crossed to a stile onto an enclosed track. Accompany it to its demise then take the right-hand of two facing gates to follow a wall in the same direction. At the field-end cross to a ladder-stile which admits to Grass Wood.

A good path heads up through the trees, rising steadily for about half a mile. After levelling out, two narrower paths branch right in quick succession, followed by a slight descent to a flat clearing where several tracks meet. Although this widest track we are currently on will drop down to meet the definitive path, our route proper involves retracing the few yards back to the second of those aforementioned narrower branches passed on the way to the clearing. It maintains a level course through the trees with a moss-covered limestone pavement on the left, before dropping down towards the far end of the wood. After a sharp left turn it descends more gently, merging into the wide track forsaken earlier before emerging at a stile onto Grass Wood Lane.

Head left along this quiet back road for a short distance and then take a stile into the trees on the right. The main path sets a course for the Wharfe's bank, which is accompanied downstream firstly through trees and then green pastures to the cluster of trees marking the position of the Ghaistrill's Strid. From here a string of stiles in quick succession precede more green pastures to arrive at Grassington Bridge.

Cross the road here to pass below a row of houses before regaining the same bank of the river to very soon reach the Tin Bridge at Linton Falls. After surveying the scene conclude the walk by turning up the narrow snicket from our bank, which returns us very quickly to the main car park.

Grassington Bridge

Grassington is the undisputed 'capital' of the upper Wharfedale area, a thriving community with a good range of facilities. The fine, cobbled square is the focal point but is really only the shop window: hidden away is enough interest for a day's leisurely exploration. Historically, Grassington boasted an 18th century theatre and a lead mining industry of which its nearby moor still displays much evidence. The many buildings of character include the Old Hall and the former Town Hall-cum-institute. Here also is the Upper Wharfedale Folk Museum and the headquarters of the fell rescue organisation and the National Park.

④

Although graced with much wooded beauty, Grass Wood is also of major importance in the botanical world, a bewildering variety of flowers being found here. It is run by the Yorkshire Naturalists' Trust. Its counterpart Bastow Wood reaches greater altitudes to the right of our path.

Where we rejoin the road stood the gibbet that hung Tom Lee, local blacksmith turned notorious murderer two centuries ago.

The large building high on the opposite bank is Netherside Hall, now a school.

In our two miles by the Wharfe we are treated to two of its rougher sections, the first being at Ghaistrill's Strid. The main feature of this loop in the river is a narrow gorge near our bank, though in times of spate it will be smothered in the general turbulence.

Beyond Grassington Bridge we pass two weirs before arriving at the less uniform delights of Linton Falls. Here the Wharfe drops loudly over a tangle of rock ledges and boulders, and is viewed dramatically from the Tin Bridge just above. New houses have replaced the former mill.

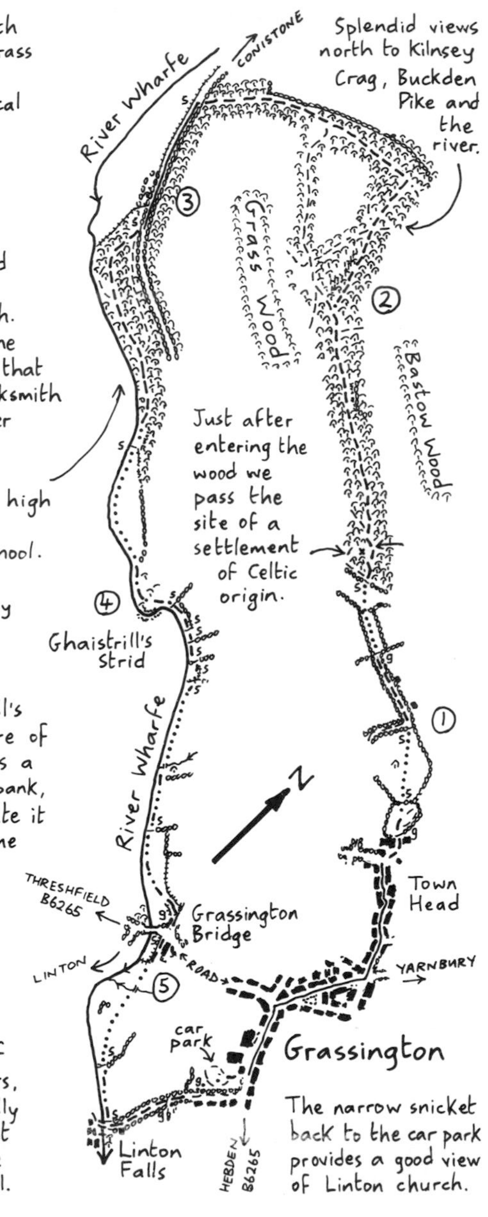

CONISTONE
Splendid views north to Kilnsey Crag, Buckden Pike and the river.
River Wharfe
Grass Wood
Bastow Wood
Just after entering the wood we pass the site of a settlement of Celtic origin.
Ghaistrill's Strid
River Wharfe
N
THRESHFIELD B6265
Grassington Bridge
Town Head
LINTON
ROAD
YARNBURY
car park
Grassington
Linton Falls
HEBDEN B6265
The narrow snicket back to the car park provides a good view of Linton church.

WALK 5 BETWEEN SKIRFARE AND WHARFE

6½ miles from Arncliffe

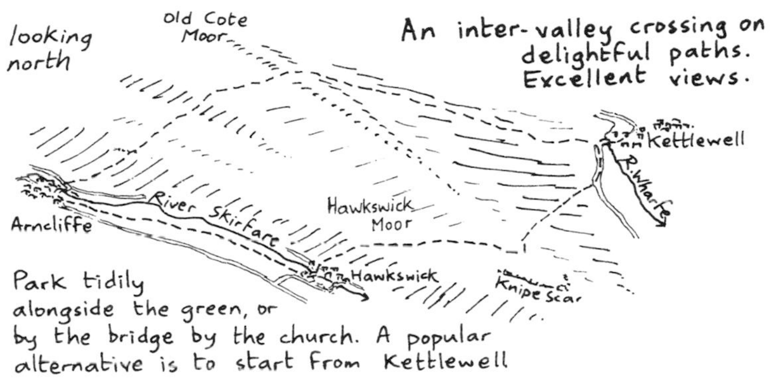
looking north
Old Cote Moor
Kettlewell
R. Wharfe
River Skirfare
Arncliffe
Hawkswick Moor
Hawkswick
Knipe Scar

An inter-valley crossing on delightful paths. Excellent views.

Park tidily alongside the green, or by the bridge by the church. A popular alternative is to start from Kettlewell

THE WALK

From the village green take the Litton (up-dale) road, past the church and across the bridge over the Skirfare. At once leave the road by a stile on the right to accompany the river downstream, but only a short distance to another stile onto a narrow road. From the stile opposite a good path rises diagonally through two fields to enter a wood, continuing up through the trees to leave by negotiating a limestone scar at the top.

Still maintaining the same course, the path resumes in easier vein: at a gateway in a collapsing wall a short level section precedes the final pull, and at the second of a pair of neighbouring stiles the ridge-wall on Old Cote Moor is gained. The descent to Kettlewell commences immediately, the slightly less clear path inclining to the right to eventually locate a stile in a wall descending from the moor-top. Continuing down at a similar angle a plateau briefly interrupts the drop before squeezing through 'The Slit', a well-used way through a narrow band of limestone. The path then drops down to merge with another before reaching a gate onto the road at the entrance to Kettlewell.

The route now lies along to the right, though this opportunity to break the journey may well be snatched first. On leaving the village return over the bridge and follow the road a short distance as far as a gate and footpath sign pointing up to the right. A good path heads away, bearing right at a

(5)

Fork and then rising through trees to a level enclosure. Bearing up to the right beneath a pinewood a stile will be found in the top corner of the field, with another one just above it. The path then rises through a low scar and continues climbing steadily to a cairn marking the highest point of this crossing.

From the cairn the path undulates across to a stile in the ridge-wall. Just beyond is another cairn from where the path turns sharply right to begin its descent into Littondale. A nice, easy drop down concludes by entering Hawkswick enclosed by walls. Turn right past the houses to arrive at a footbridge, and on crossing it take a stile on the right to accompany the Skirfare upstream.

This level return to Arncliffe is fairly straightforward, with an assortment of stiles and gates to point the way. For the most part the river keeps its distance, but it returns for the last third of a mile to usher us back into the village, a gate by a barn preceding a short drive to emerge by the church.

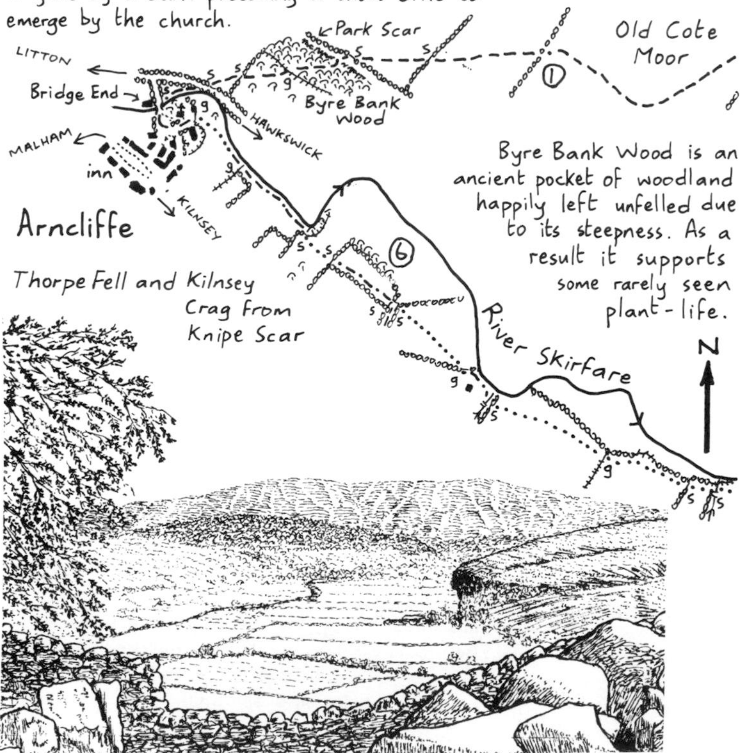
Park Scar
Old Cote Moor
LITTON
Bridge End
Byre Bank Wood
HAWKSWICK
MALHAM
inn
KILNSEY
Arncliffe
River Skirfare
N

Byre Bank Wood is an ancient pocket of woodland happily left unfelled due to its steepness. As a result it supports some rarely seen plant-life.

Thorpe Fell and Kilnsey Crag from Knipe Scar

Arncliffe is one of the most attractive yet least spoilt villages in the Dales, and is regarded as the 'capital' of Littondale. A variety of characterful greystone houses stand back in relaxed manner from a spacious green. The unpretentious inn maintains this mood, and is in fact the only hostelry in the area to serve its ale in that unrivalled fashion, directly from the barrel.

Out of sight of the green is the church of St. Oswald, which has found its own niche, embowered in trees in a truly beautiful riverside setting. Though largely rebuilt last century, the solid tower dates back 500 years. Inside is a list of the Littondale men who marched off to fight at Flodden Field in 1513.

Across the shapely bridge, the house at Bridge End played host to Charles Kingsley during his 'Water Babies' period.

Kettlewell
(see Walk 10)
B6160 BUCKDEN
Old Cote Moor
1600'
The Slit
2
CONISTONE
River Wharfe
KILNSEY B6160
3
ARNCLIFFE
5
ROAD
Hawkswick
KILNSEY
River Skirfare
Hawkswick Moor
1240'
4
Knipe Scar
N

Less than two miles below Hawkswick the Skirfare merges with the Wharfe, and during this walk we are treated to unparalleled vistas of substantial lengths of these twin-like dales immediately above their confluence. In both cases flat valley floors give way to equally well-defined slopes.

Above Arncliffe a major feature is the deep-cut Cowside Beck just behind the village, while on gaining the moor-top Buckden Pike dominates the scene with uniform-looking villages at its foot. Great Whernside rises above Kettlewell, while the lower ridge crossing permits more intimate views down Wharfedale.

On the climb from Kettlewell note the chapel at Scargill House, somehow managing to blend into the scene.

Hawkswick is the Skirfare's last village, and being the only one off the 'main' up-dale road it remains wonderfully undisturbed.

6

WALK 6 CAPPLESTONE GATE AND CONISTONE DIB

7½ miles

from Conistone

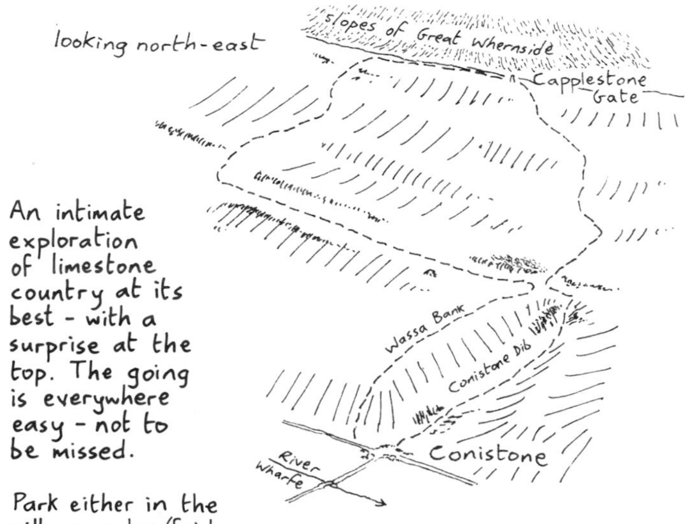
looking north-east
slopes of Great Whernside
Capplestone Gate
Wassa Bank
Conistone Dib
Conistone
River Wharfe

An intimate exploration of limestone country at its best - with a surprise at the top. The going is everywhere easy - not to be missed.

Park either in the village centre (fairly limited) or on the wide section of road towards the bridge. Alternative start: the B6160 at Kilnsey, across the valley.

THE WALK

From the road junction outside the post office set off along the Kettlewell road, and immediately turn right on a track across a wide 'green'. From the gate at the far end bear right between two old caravans, a clear path materialising and becoming stony underfoot as it heads up the dry valley of the Dib. After being tightly confined by the imposing buttresses of Gurling Trough the path emerges into the open to pass through a long, green pasture. When the slopes close in again stay with the wall for a short, stony climb to the head of the valley.

At the very top the wall is crossed by a stile as it abuts onto a cliff: just above take a stile on the right, and then turn left on a track to a gate which gives access to the wide track known as Bycliffe Road. Turn right along here, and shortly after becoming enclosed leave it by a gate on the left just as it bends sharp right. A tractor-track crosses the field towards a small plantation, passing to the right of it before rising to the far end of a prominent scar. From a gateway the

path rises a little more gently to approach the white Ordnance Survey column at Capplestone Gate.

After a well-earned rest resume the walk by taking the stile by the gate and turning left along a sketchy path which remains close to the wall running along the bottom edge of the moor. An area rich in relics of the mining industry is encountered, followed by some modest gritstone outcrops. When the wall rejoins us a solid cairn is passed, and a little further a stile in the wall is used to leave the moor. After an initially steep descent the path drops leisurely through a collapsed wall and on through a long pasture. At a sketchy fork bear left; remaining in the same pasture, bear right near the bottom to leave by a gate near the corner. A track then descends half-right towards a gate into a plantation.

Do not enter the trees however, but instead turn sharp left on a path which bears to the right of an increasing scar to commence a long, level section. A stile in a cross-wall is the first of five, and although the path is not always clear underfoot, the route is in no doubt. The final stile is adjacent to Conistone Pie, beyond which another scar materialises to usher us back to rejoin the Bycliffe Road above Conistone Dib.

Now turn right along it, soon descending Wassa Bank past the T.V. mast which has been in sight at various stages of the walk. Soon becoming surfaced, the access road leads down to join the Conistone-Kettlewell road, with the village only minutes along to the left.

In Conistone Dib

(6)

Conistone is an attractive little village fortunately avoided by the main road which heads updale just half a mile distant, across the river at Kilnsey: even from this distance the famous crag loses none of its grandeur. Every piece of stone in Conistone's cottages matches the natural landscape of the village's hinterland. Though restored a century ago, the hidden church retains some Norman features.

St. Mary's, Conistone

After the wonders of dazzling limestone it comes as quite a surprise to meet the sombre gritstone of Capplestone Gate. If our goal had been a hundred feet lower we would not have left limestone, but this dramatic transformation at the 1600 foot contour gives us a stroll among boulders and old mine workings in complete contrast to the rest of the journey.

As might be expected Capplestone Gate is a highly extensive viewpoint, and could well qualify as the best all-round vantage point for the varied Wharfedale scene. The fell country to the west includes, clockwise; Simon's Seat, Thorpe Fell Top, Cracoe Fell, Pendle Hill, Parson's Pulpit, Fountains Fell, Penyghent, Plover Hill, Birks Fell, Yockenthwaite Moor, Buckden Pike and Great Whernside, of which our viewpoint is a shoulder.

N
KETTLEWELL
(7)
Wassa Bank
River Wharfe
KILNSEY
Gurling Trough
GRASSINGTON
Conistone

※ From the gate at the end of the long pasture comes the first real valley view of the walk, with the environs of Kettlewell prominent.

On surmounting the stile to leave the moor, the whole world seems to appear at one's feet.

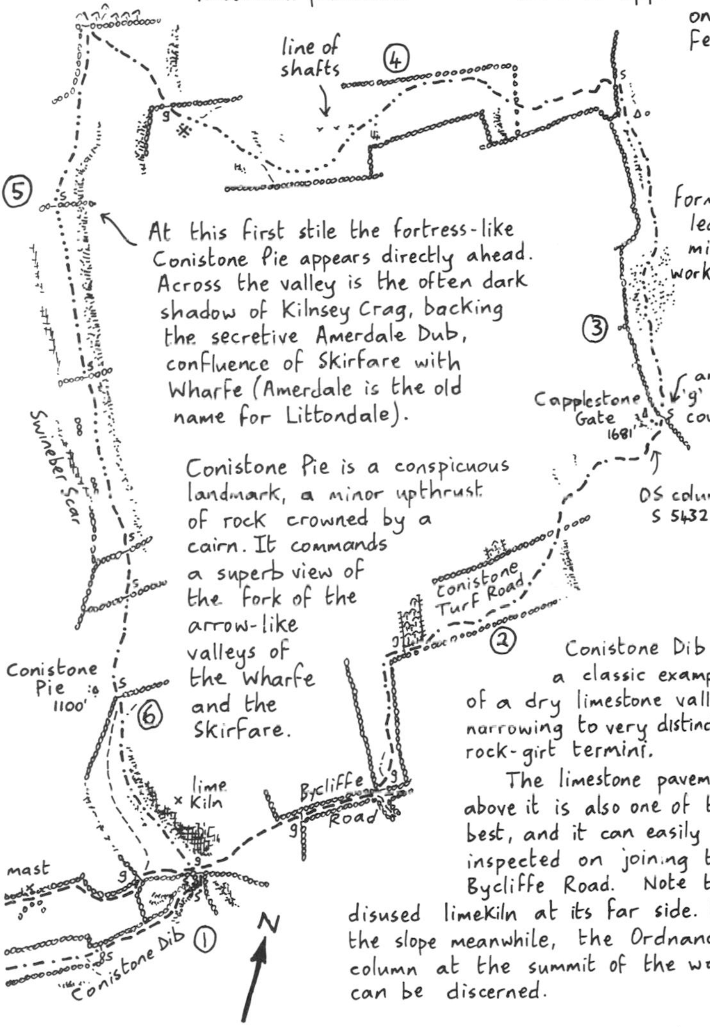

At this first stile the fortress-like Conistone Pie appears directly ahead. Across the valley is the often dark shadow of Kilnsey Crag, backing the secretive Amerdale Dub, confluence of Skirfare with Wharfe (Amerdale is the old name for Littondale).

Conistone Pie is a conspicuous landmark, a minor upthrust of rock crowned by a cairn. It commands a superb view of the fork of the arrow-like valleys of the Wharfe and the Skirfare.

Conistone Dib is a classic example of a dry limestone valley, narrowing to very distinctive rock-girt termini.

The limestone pavement above it is also one of the best, and it can easily be inspected on joining the Bycliffe Road. Note the disused limekiln at its far side. Up the slope meanwhile, the Ordnance column at the summit of the walk can be discerned.

The Bycliffe Road continues to lonely Mossdale, then crosses bleak moors to Middlesmoor in Nidderdale.

WALK 7 **LANGERTON HILL AND DIBBLE'S BRIDGE**

6 miles

from Burnsall

A circuit of Barben Beck over gently rolling hills, with a fine stretch of the Wharfe to finish

Burnsall has a sizeable car park at the entrance to the village, added to which a riverside meadow is often opened up to supplement it. (fee at both)

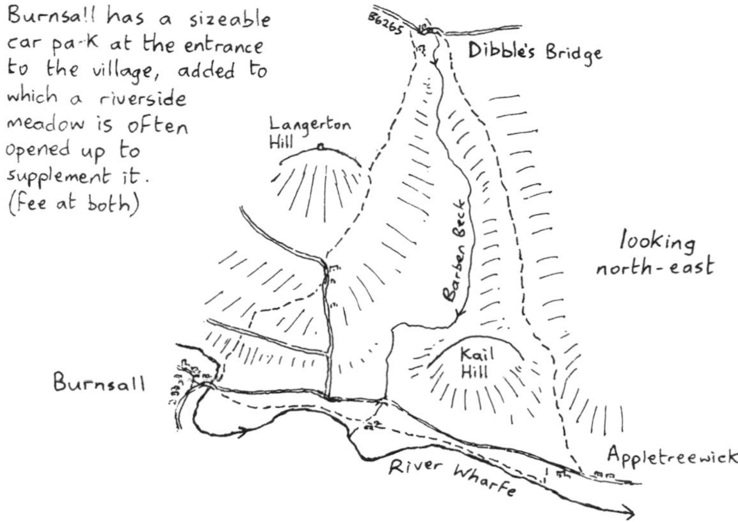
B6265
Dibble's Bridge
Langerton Hill
Barben Beck
looking north-east
Kail Hill
Burnsall
Appletreewick
River Wharfe

THE WALK

Leave Burnsall by crossing the bridge and using the steps on the left to descend to the river. After two stiles near the river climb directly up the very steep field to a stile onto the narrow Skuff Road. From the stile opposite climb another field to a stile and on to another in the very corner ahead. Now rise diagonally across a large field to a stile onto another road. Turn up it only as far as a sharp bend, and then leave by a stile directly ahead. After a continual rise up the sides of two fields, the brow of Langerton Hill is gained just below its highest point.

Our route, meanwhile, resumes its original direction from the last stile and continues to follow the right-hand wall away to a stile in it. Remain near the wall to descend a large field to a tiny stream at the far end. From the stile behind it rise half-right to a stile near a barn, then accompany the right-hand wall up to another barn. From two neighbouring stiles continue with the wall now on the left to arrive at Turf Gate

Farm. Head straight on past all the buildings to follow its access road out onto the Grassington-Pateley Bridge road.

Turn right along the road which very soon drops down to cross Dibble's Bridge, immediately after which a stile gives access to a beckside area of limestone outcrops. Vacate it by a stile in the far top corner, and continue along to a gate directly ahead. Continue straight across to a stile ahead to enter a large expanse of untamed pasture sloping down to Barben Beck. A tiny beck across our path is followed by a long, level section on a reasonably clear route high above the beck.

When a wall appears in front the path fades, but simply deflect left of it to suddenly be confined by stone walls. Escape along a short, narrow passage on the left, and on emerging turn right with the wall to eventually join an enclosed track across our way. Cross straight over to enter another long, narrow pasture, and by the opposite corner a wide track has materialised. It now gets enclosed by walls to soon drop down onto the road at one end of Appletreewick village, rather conveniently adjacent to one of its two hostelries.

From here turn right (away from the village) past Low Hall to locate an enclosed path leading down to the river. Turn right to follow the Wharfe upstream. When the river takes a big swing to the left, we are deflected right by an intervening wall to enter the farmyard at Woodhouse. When its access track turns right to join the road, go straight ahead to a footbridge and on again to a stile. The river is rejoined and soon leads back to Burnsall, omitting a final loop to cross the last field to a stile at the start of the bridge.

For its modest altitude Langerton Hill is an extensive viewpoint. At the top end of Wharfedale are the summits of Buckden Pike and Great Whernside, with Simon's Seat and Burnsall Fell dominating the immediate vicinity. To the west are the heights beyond Malham and those of Malham Moor. Note also the dam of Grimwith Reservoir.

Ordnance Survey column, Langerton Hill

⑦

A mile north of Dibble's Bridge is the recently enlarged Grimwith Reservoir, which supplies Bradford.

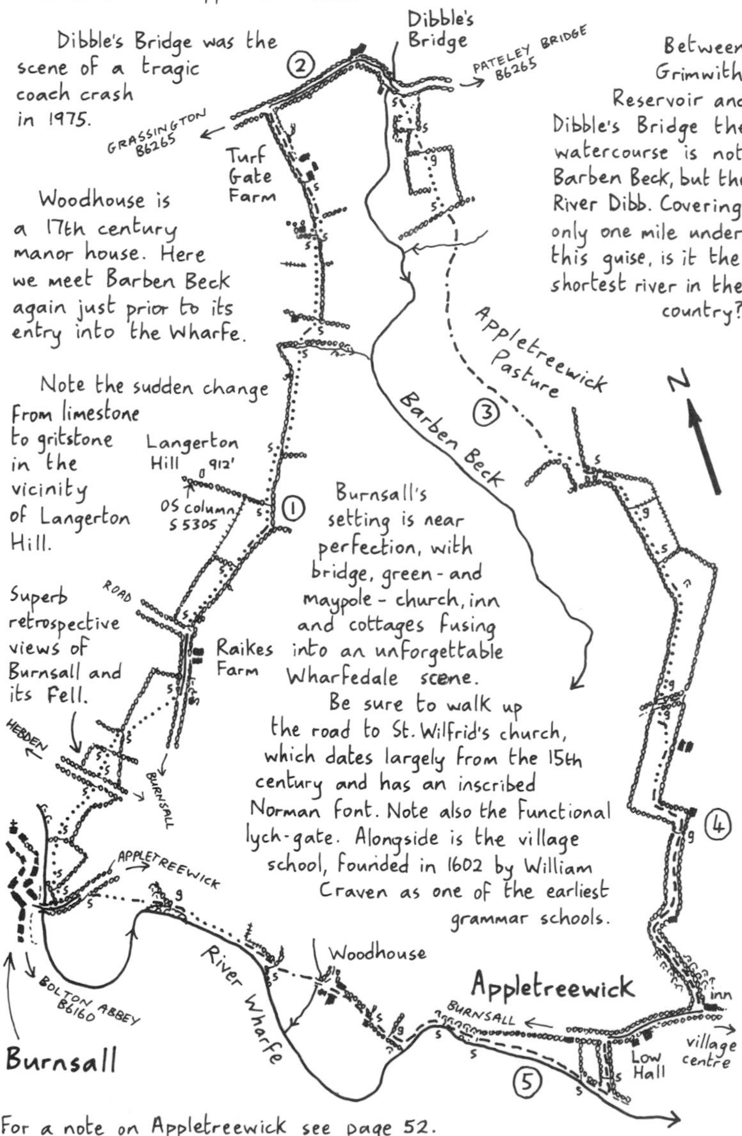

Dibble's Bridge was the scene of a tragic coach crash in 1975.
Dibble's Bridge
PATELEY BRIDGE B6265
GRASSINGTON B6265
Between Grimwith Reservoir and Dibble's Bridge the watercourse is not Barben Beck, but the River Dibb. Covering only one mile under this guise, is it the shortest river in the country?
Turf Gate Farm
Woodhouse is a 17th century manor house. Here we meet Barben Beck again just prior to its entry into the Wharfe.
Appletreewick Pasture
N
Barben Beck
Note the sudden change from limestone to gritstone in the vicinity of Langerton Hill.
Langerton Hill 912'
OS column S 5305
Burnsall's setting is near perfection, with bridge, green - and maypole - church, inn and cottages fusing into an unforgettable Wharfedale scene.
Be sure to walk up the road to St. Wilfrid's church, which dates largely from the 15th century and has an inscribed Norman font. Note also the functional lych-gate. Alongside is the village school, founded in 1602 by William Craven as one of the earliest grammar schools.
Superb retrospective views of Burnsall and its Fell.
ROAD
Raikes Farm
HEBDEN
BURNSALL
APPLETREEWICK
River Wharfe
Woodhouse
Appletreewick
inn
BURNSALL
village centre
Low Hall
BOLTON ABBEY B6160
Burnsall

For a note on Appletreewick see page 52.

WALK 8 — AROUND PENYGHENT GILL

8 miles — from Litton

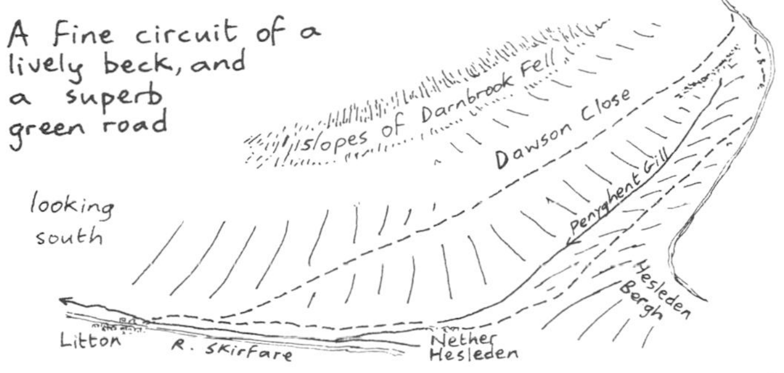

A fine circuit of a lively beck, and a superb green road
slopes of Darnbrook Fell
Dawson Close
Penyghent Gill
looking south
Hesleden Bergh
Litton
R. Skirfare
Nether Hesleden

Park on the roadside either in the vicinity of the inn, or further along the road in the village 'centre'.

THE WALK

From the inn head west through the village and leave the road just beyond the 'phone box, down a drive to the left immediately before two barns usher the road out of Litton. Bear left of a short wall to a narrow wooden footbridge across the river Skirfare, then head for a gapstile just to the right. Two fields are then diagonally crossed to a pair of barns in the corner of the second. From a gate by the main barn turn right to join an enclosed track, which is then followed along to the right to arrive alongside New Bridge.

Without crossing the bridge keep straight on to a gate in front, from where a rough track climbs the hillside. This is to be our return route, but for the moment make use of only a few yards of it then break off across the field to locate a footgate in the wall ahead. After the next field a pleasant walled section returns us to the water's edge, though it is no longer the Skirfare but Hesleden Beck just short of its confluence with the river. As Nether Hesleden is approached a bridge conveys us over the beck, then turn sharp left through a gate onto the access road to the farm.

Keep left to pass between the buildings to a gate from where a track climbs to another gate. From the adjacent stile a narrow trod accompanies a fence as it rises unceasingly above the beck, eventually swinging sharp right to join the fell-road out of Halton Gill. Turn left along it as far as the first cattle-grid (a matter of a few yards), and beyond it turn down to a gate in the wall below. Drop a little further and then turn right on an increasingly clear trod, parallel with the gill throughout a splendid length.

Eventually the enclosures below Penyghent House are skirted to arrive at a mini-ravine beneath a cave entrance. On entering a larger pasture maintain the same course, closing in on the head of the gill and crossing a rocky tributary to arrive at a gate back onto the road. Turn left again for about five minutes to reach a guidepost indicating a bridle-road to Litton.

With full steam ahead this wonderful track transports us unerringly back to New Bridge, and the opening half-mile then leads equally clearly back to the village.

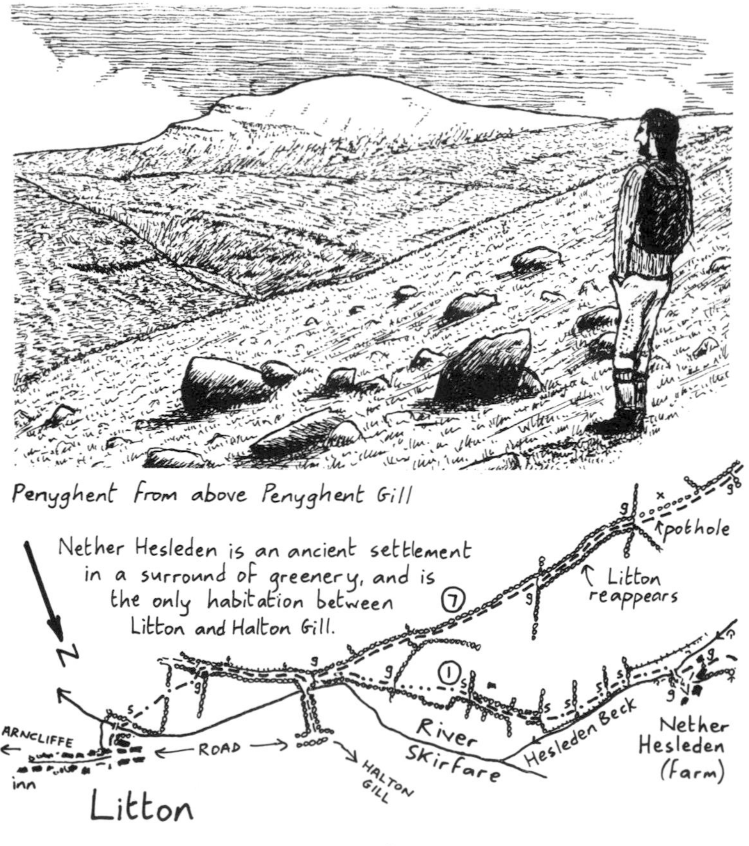
Nether Hesleden is an ancient settlement in a surround of greenery, and is the only habitation between Litton and Halton Gill.
pothole
Litton reappears
7
1
N
ARNCLIFFE
ROAD
HALTON GILL
River Skirfare
Hesleden Beck
Nether Hesleden (Farm)
inn
Litton

Penyghent from above Penyghent Gill

8

The bridle-road across Dawson Close is an outstanding example of a green road which, fortunately, like many packhorse routes escaped being surfaced, to remain as one of the most distinguishable features of the Yorkshire Dales. Evidence of its road status can be found on signposts at either end - where it meets the valley road beyond New Bridge a forlorn roadsign of not-too-distant origin points the seven miles to Stainforth.

Needless to say it provides some splendid views, firstly to Halton Gill and the head of Littondale, and later down to Litton and beyond.

Another major feature of the walk is the extended opportunity to survey Penyghent from a lesser known angle. At 2273 feet this crouching lion looks over half of the walk.

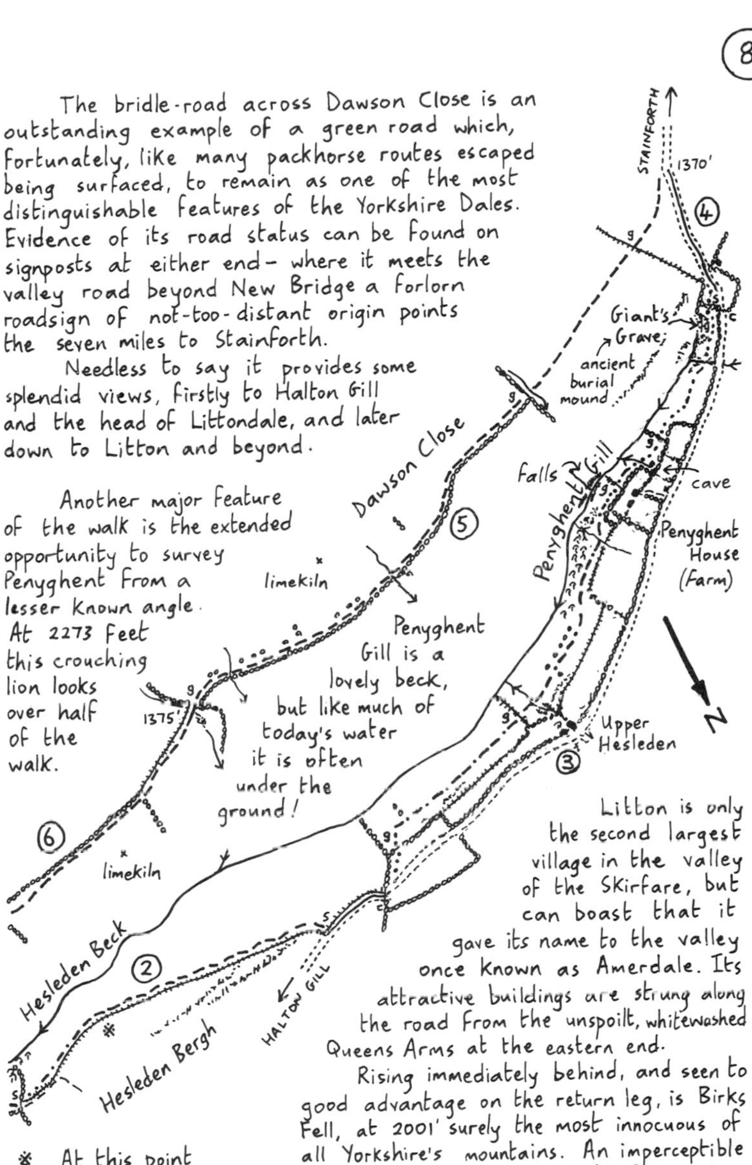

STAINFORTH
1370'
4
Giant's Grave
ancient burial mound
Dawson Close
5
limekiln
Falls
Penyghent Gill
cave
Penyghent House (Farm)
Penyghent Gill is a lovely beck, but like much of today's water it is often under the ground!
N
1375'
Upper Hesleden
3
6
limekiln
Hesleden Beck
2
HALTON GILL
Hesleden Bergh

Litton is only the second largest village in the valley of the Skirfare, but can boast that it gave its name to the valley once known as Amerdale. Its attractive buildings are strung along the road from the unspoilt, whitewashed Queens Arms at the eastern end.

Rising immediately behind, and seen to good advantage on the return leg, is Birks Fell, at 2001' surely the most innocuous of all Yorkshire's mountains. An imperceptible rise marks the highest point of a ridge stretching over 11 miles from Knipe Scar in the east to an arbitrary conclusion in Ribblesdale, beyond the wilds of Cosh.

* At this point Penyghent appears, soon followed by Fountains Fell up to the left, above our return route.

(9)

WALK 9 — SKYREHOLME AND TROLLERS GILL

7½ miles — from Appletreewick

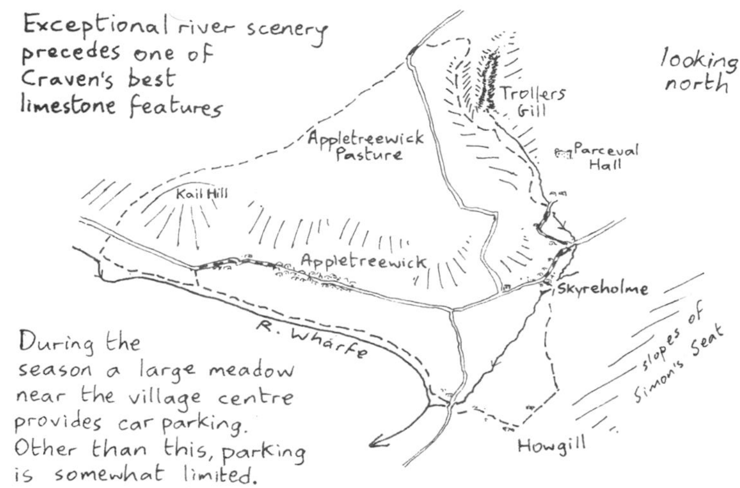
Exceptional river scenery precedes one of Craven's best limestone features
looking north
Trollers Gill
Appletreewick Pasture
Parceval Hall
Kail Hill
Appletreewick
Skyreholme
R. Wharfe
slopes of Simon's Seat
Howgill
During the season a large meadow near the village centre provides car parking. Other than this, parking is somewhat limited.

THE WALK

Leave Appletreewick by heading west out of the village on the Burnsall road, past the two inns and Low Hall to reach a walled path leading down to the Wharfe. Turn left alongside the river, though almost immediately deflected away from it, albeit breifly, through a succession of gates. On regaining the riverbank it is now clung to faithfully, through a couple of pastures before entering a delightfully wooded section. At its far end forsake the river by striking half-left across a field to join a track out onto a narrow road at a bridge.

Cross the bridge and leave the road in favour of an enclosed track up to the left. At the top a rough lane is joined alongside the farm at Howgill: turn left along it past the caravan site at Howgill Lodge. A little beyond a barn go through a gate on the left opposite an old milestone, and head away alongside the wall, first on its right, then its left. After a gateway slope down the field to a stile in the next wall, and continue down to cross a tiny beck behind which is another stile. Remain close to the main beck on the left now to soon arrive at a footbridge. Cross it and rise through a housing development to emerge onto the road at Skyreholme.

Turn right along this quiet road, forking left at a bridge to the road end at the entrance to Parceval Hall. Take the gate just before the wooden bridge to follow Skyreholme Beck upstream, a good path encountering three stiles before forking in the amphitheatre in front of Trollers Gill. The high wedge of Middle Hill divides the gorge from its parallel valley to the left: it is through this deep side-valley that the walk continues, for unfortunately the inviting entrance to Trollers Gill just across to the right is not actually on a definitive right-of-way.

Trollers Gill

Our path therefore is the nonetheless still attractive green one which rises very gently to enter the environs of a former lead-mining site. Here the way becomes a wider track (the old access road), climbing more steeply away from the mine. When it makes a sharp turn right, leave it by continuing straight ahead (left) past the deep pothole of Hell Hole. Skirting a marshy area, swing left to approach the wall in front, soon reaching a stile onto the back road from Appletreewick up to the Pateley Bridge road.

Follow this road to the left, and a little beyond a bend take a gate on the right. A wide stony track takes us across the moorland of Appletreewick Pasture, eventually dropping gently down through two stiles by gates to the bottom corner of a field. Here leave the track in favour of a gate across to the right, from where a short walled section leads down to a crossroads of paths.

At this junction (unless time is pressing) ignore

(9) the Appletreewick sign and take the gate directly ahead to run alongside a wall to two prominent barns. Initially enclosed by walls a track runs along to the right, soon descending to join the Appletreewick-Burnsall road. Cross straight over and down the access track to Woodhouse Farm, turning to the left between the buildings to then make a bee-line for the riverbank.

All that now remains is to accompany the Wharfe downstream, to return fairly shortly to the enclosed path by which we gained the river at the start of the walk. Retrace those early steps to therefore conclude the jaunt.

Appletreewick has several claims to fame, even though many visitors may best remember its delightful name. Here are three halls and two inns in amongst a wonderful assortment of cottages. All stand on or about the narrow road wandering through the village, from High Hall at the top - note the tiny church nearby - to Low Hall at the very bottom. Probably the oldest however is the curiously named Mock Beggar Hall, a fine little edifice that once went by the title of Monk's Hall.

Of the two hostelries, one takes its name from the family of William Craven, a Dick Whittington character who found his fortune in London, becoming Lord Mayor in 1611. Not forgetting his beginnings he became a worthy local benefactor, having Burnsall's grammar school and a number of bridges in the district built. The New Inn, meanwhile, achieved national fame in recent years thanks to the enterprising 'no-smoking' policy of a previous landlord. Today it is equally enterprising in its extensive range of fascinating beers from abroad.

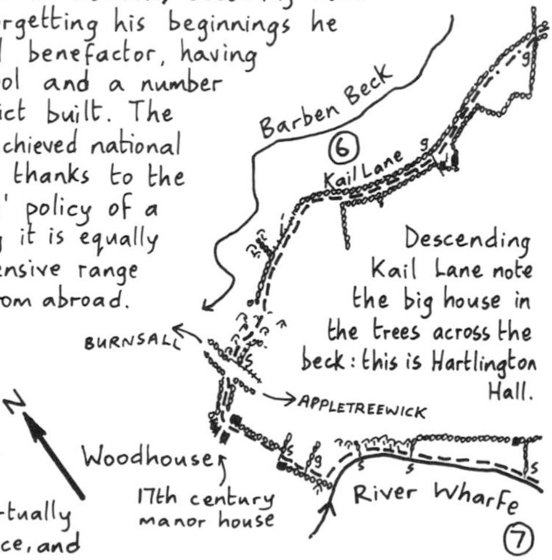

Descending Kail Lane note the big house in the trees across the beck: this is Hartlington Hall.

Trollers Gill is a magnificent limestone gorge, often known as the 'Gordale of Wharfedale'. Though not particularly tall, the cliffs remain virtually unbroken for some distance, and the narrow passage between is usually dry and safe. It is renowned as the home of the legendary 'Barguest', a spectral hound with eyes like saucers.

9

Northward views to Fancarl Crag

TO B6265

Hell Hole

875'

Middle Hill

Trollers Gill

(4) old lead mine

Appletreewick Pasture

990'

APPLETREEWICK

Skyreholme Beck

Parceval Hall

Parceval Hall is probably the grandest house in upper Wharfedale. Built over 300 years ago, its beautiful stonework looks out across Skyreholme to Simon's Seat, which totally dominates this corner of the valley. Now used as a diocesan retreat centre, the extensive gardens and intermingled woodland are open to the public from Easter to October (small fee payable).

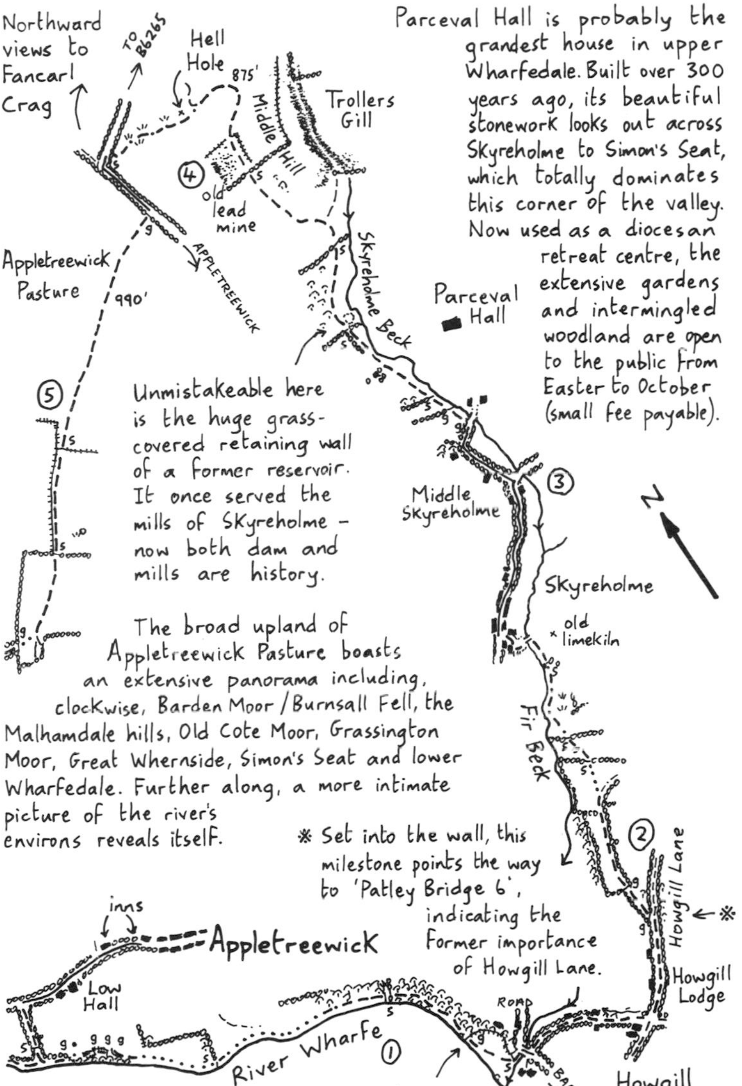

(5)

Unmistakeable here is the huge grass-covered retaining wall of a former reservoir. It once served the mills of Skyreholme - now both dam and mills are history.

(3)

Middle Skyreholme

Skyreholme

old limekiln

N

The broad upland of Appletreewick Pasture boasts an extensive panorama including, clockwise, Barden Moor / Burnsall Fell, the Malhamdale hills, Old Cote Moor, Grassington Moor, Great Whernside, Simon's Seat and lower Wharfedale. Further along, a more intimate picture of the river's environs reveals itself.

Fir Beck

(2)

※ Set into the wall, this milestone points the way to 'Patley Bridge 6', indicating the former importance of Howgill Lane.

Howgill Lane ※

inns

Appletreewick

Low Hall

Howgill Lodge

ROAD

River Wharfe

(1)

BARDEN

Howgill

The Appletreewick-Howgill-Skyreholme triangle is a popular caravanners' haunt.

Before leaving the river note the simple but touching memorial plate set into a rock.

WALK 10 ABOVE THE WHARFE TO STARBOTTON

5 miles from Kettlewell

After an early climb this is an easy walk circling the river and giving fine views both up and down the valley

Use the village centre car park

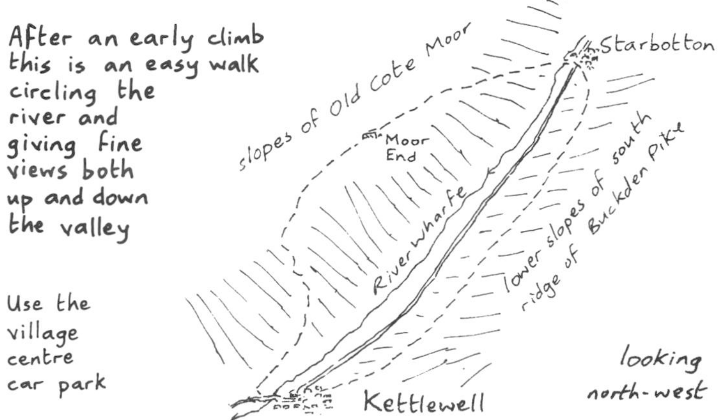

Starbotton
slopes of Old Cote Moor
Moor End
River Wharfe
lower slopes of south ridge of Buckden Pike
Kettlewell
looking north-west

THE WALK

Leave Kettlewell by crossing the main bridge at the southern entrance to the village, then almost immediately forsake the road for the second (higher) of two gates on the right. From it a good level path heads away, ignoring the Arncliffe branch which starts climbing to the left almost at once. The path on which we remain is the access track for Moor End: after a level section it bears left in front of a clump of trees, crosses a tiny beck and then commences a well graded climb up the hillside. In no time at all it resumes its level course to run pleasantly along to Moor End.

Enter the farmyard and turn left to accompany the wall rising away from the main building. From the gate at the end continue on the level alongside a right-hand wall, using a gap part-way along before resuming the same course. From another gap at the far end keep on to a stile, and stay with the right-hand wall to a stile and gate in it. Within yards the path begins its straightforward sloping descent to the valley bottom, passing through a wood on the way. By a barn at the bottom it swings right to a footbridge over the Wharfe, a track then leading onto the road on the edge of Starbotton.

Walk a yard or two to the right and then up the lane opposite, using a gate on the right to commence a return to Kettlewell. Follow a track up through three small pastures to enter one with a barn in it, then take a gate just to its left. Now turn right alongside the wall to begin a long, easy march through innumerable pastures, punctuated by a succession of stiles in intervening walls. Throughout its course the path remains virtually level and clear, with a line of unsightly telegraph poles playing their part in pointing the way.

When Kettlewell finally appears just ahead the path descends a little towards it, and the village is entered by a turn down to the right to a stile onto a short-lived enclosed path. This debouches onto a back road in the village : turn right for the quickest way back onto the main road through Kettlewell.

Fox and Hounds, Starbotton

Kettlewell is the hub of the upper dale, a junction of roads and natural halting place. It stands on what was a major coaching route to Richmond, and the two inns at the entrance to the village would have serviced the weary travellers. The route in question is now a surfaced road, but still provides a tortuous way over Park Rash and into Coverdale. Shops, tearooms a third inn and plentiful accommodation - including a youth hostel - add more life to a village being steadily engulfed by holiday homes.

Kettlewell straddles its own beck which largely drains the slopes of Great Whernside, very much Kettlewell's mountain. These slopes bear the scars of lead mining, the one-time main industry now replaced by tourism as a partner to farming. Some delectable cottages and gardens line the beck as it races through the village.

Footpaths positively radiate from Kettlewell to all points of the compass, and one could spend a richly-varied holiday week here without the need of any transport. Just set off in a new direction!

(10)

Situated midway between the better known villages of Kettlewell and Buckden, tiny Starbotton witnesses all that passes through the dale, even though only a small number pause here. The usual reason for halting is to visit the attractive and welcoming whitewashed hostelry. Off the main road are some lovely corners with 17th century cottages.

Starbotton nestles beneath the slopes of Buckden Pike, and like its neighbours stands away from the river on its own swift-flowing beck. Here it is Cam Gill Beck, which cuts a deep groove in the flank of the Pike. In 1686 this stream was swollen by a deluge which caused disastrous flooding in the village.

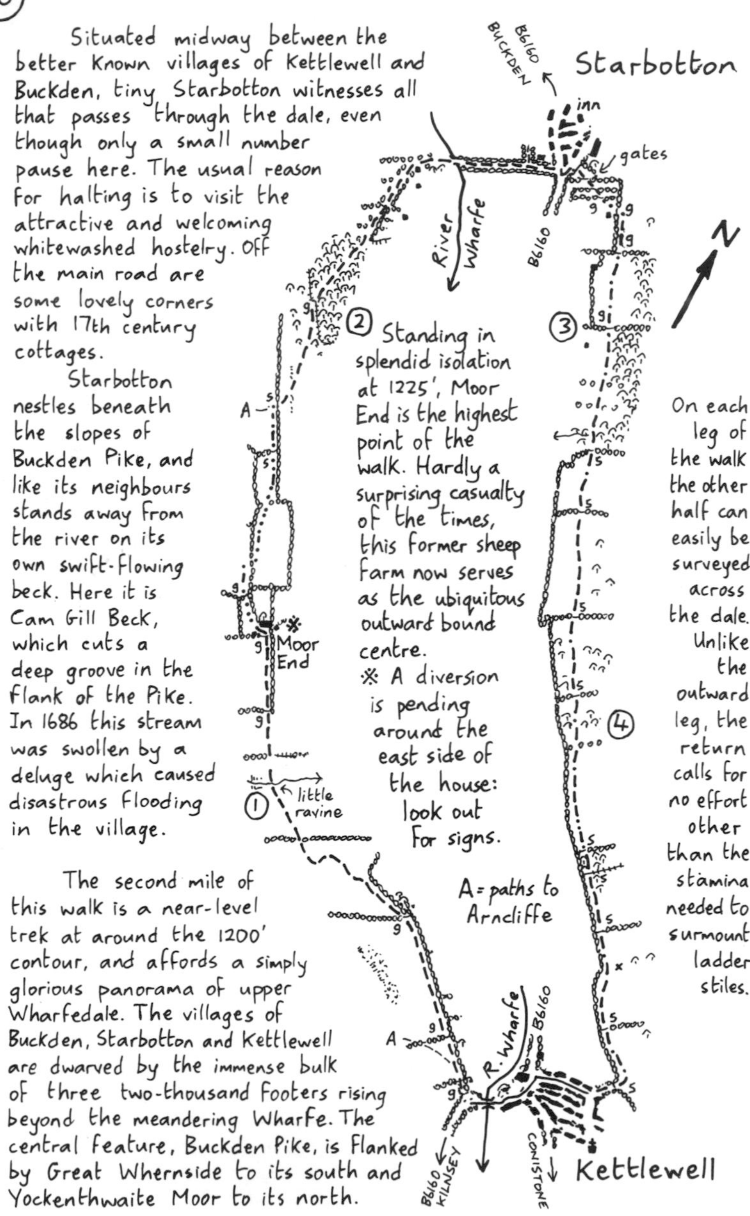
Starbotton
B6160
BUCKDEN
inn
gates
River Wharfe
B6160
N
A
Moor End
little ravine
A = paths to Arncliffe
R. Wharfe
B6160
B6160
KILNSEY
CONISTONE
Kettlewell

(2) Standing in splendid isolation at 1225', Moor End is the highest point of the walk. Hardly a surprising casualty of the times, this former sheep farm now serves as the ubiquitous outward bound centre.

※ A diversion is pending around the east side of the house: look out for signs.

On each leg of the walk the other half can easily be surveyed across the dale. Unlike the outward leg, the return calls for no effort other than the stamina needed to surmount ladder stiles.

The second mile of this walk is a near-level trek at around the 1200' contour, and affords a simply glorious panorama of upper Wharfedale. The villages of Buckden, Starbotton and Kettlewell are dwarved by the immense bulk of three two-thousand footers rising beyond the meandering Wharfe. The central feature, Buckden Pike, is flanked by Great Whernside to its south and Yockenthwaite Moor to its north.

WALK 11 THE WHARFE AT BOLTON ABBEY

4½ miles from Bolton Abbey!

A simple riverside stroll on good paths in splendid surroundings. The central feature, in sight for much of the walk, is the hoary old ruin of Upper Wharfedale's most famous building.

looking north-east

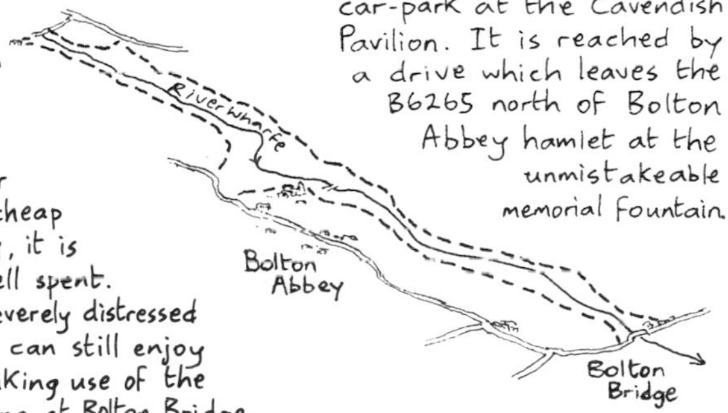

Cavendish Pavilion
River Wharfe
Bolton Abbey
Bolton Bridge

The starting point is the large car-park at the Cavendish Pavilion. It is reached by a drive which leaves the B6265 north of Bolton Abbey hamlet at the unmistakeable memorial fountain.

Although car parking is not cheap at Bolton Abbey, it is usually money well spent. However, those severely distressed by the prospect can still enjoy the walk by making use of the wide verge parking at Bolton Bridge.

THE WALK

From the Cavendish Pavilion set off back along the drive, but from the gate by the cattle-grid go left into the car park and follow the extended car park access track along the bank of the Wharfe. When the track ends keep company with the river until the pasture abruptly ends, then climb to a stile to emerge onto the road at the Cavendish Memorial.

Turn left for only a couple of minutes to a gate into the priory grounds: the most direct route back towards the river is down through the graveyard, but surely few will not halt to explore the ruins and the priory church. On arriving at the wooden footbridge and its adjacent stepping stones do not be tempted to cross, but instead follow the river downstream again. A long, pleasant pasture now leads all the way to Bolton Bridge, the river being crossed in safety by a footbridge in its shadow.

After only a few yards by the road turn into the yard of Red Lion Farm, and leave by a gate at the far end. As the river is neared we are deflected around a steep, wooded area before dropping back down to cross three pastures, parallel with the nearby Wharfe. After a tiny beck and a step-stile a field is climbed, remaining with the left-hand fence to a stile and a superb high-level vantage point.

From the stile a good path runs along to the right, being joined by another as it heads through the trees a fair way above the river. The path ends on meeting a narrow road as it prepares to ford Pickles Beck: a footbridge caters for dry-shod pedestrians. On the other side a stile gives access to the riverbank for the final few minutes back to the Pavilion bridge.

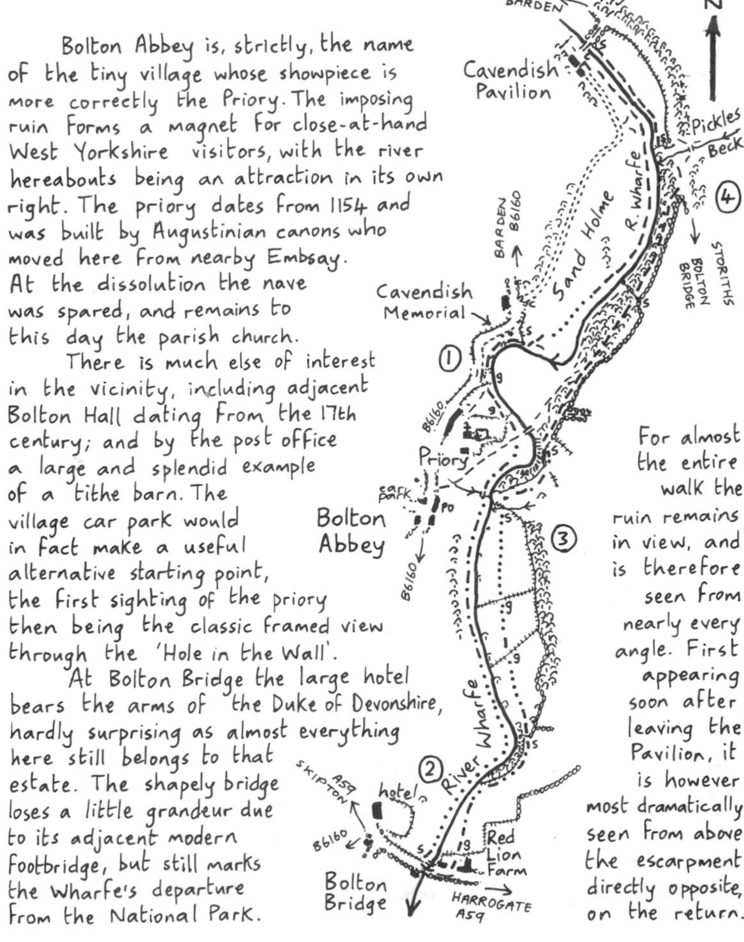
BARDEN
N
Cavendish Pavilion
Pickles Beck
R. Wharfe
Sand Holme
4
BARDEN B6160
STORITHS
BOLTON BRIDGE
Cavendish Memorial
1
B6160
Priory
car park
PO
Bolton Abbey
3
B6160
River Wharfe
2
hotel
SKIPTON A59
B6160
Red Lion Farm
Bolton Bridge
HARROGATE A59

Bolton Abbey is, strictly, the name of the tiny village whose showpiece is more correctly the Priory. The imposing ruin forms a magnet for close-at-hand West Yorkshire visitors, with the river hereabouts being an attraction in its own right. The priory dates from 1154 and was built by Augustinian canons who moved here from nearby Embsay. At the dissolution the nave was spared, and remains to this day the parish church.

There is much else of interest in the vicinity, including adjacent Bolton Hall dating from the 17th century; and by the post office a large and splendid example of a tithe barn. The village car park would in fact make a useful alternative starting point, the first sighting of the priory then being the classic framed view through the 'Hole in the Wall'.

At Bolton Bridge the large hotel bears the arms of the Duke of Devonshire, hardly surprising as almost everything here still belongs to that estate. The shapely bridge loses a little grandeur due to its adjacent modern footbridge, but still marks the Wharfe's departure from the National Park.

For almost the entire walk the ruin remains in view, and is therefore seen from nearly every angle. First appearing soon after leaving the Pavilion, it is however most dramatically seen from above the escarpment directly opposite, on the return.

Bolton Bridge

Tithe Barn, Bolton Abbey

WALK 12 **THE HEAD OF LITTONDALE**

5½ miles from Halton Gill

Easy walking, with good beck scenery in typically bleak Pennine surroundings

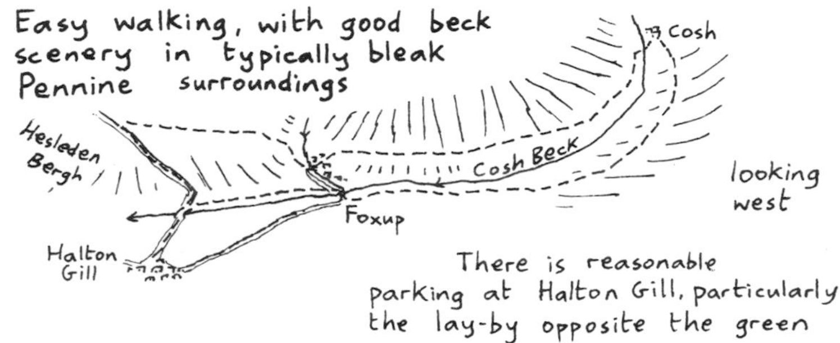
Cosh
Cosh Beck
Hesleden Bergh
Foxup
Halton Gill
looking west

There is reasonable parking at Halton Gill, particularly the lay-by opposite the green

THE WALK

From the road junction by the green turn down the Stainforth road as far as the bridge, and immediately after it leave by a stile on the right to descend to the riverbank. Now simply accompany the Skirfare upstream, taking in several gates and stiles before a new path squeezes between pens and river to emerge onto the road at Foxup Bridge. Turn right over the said structure and then immediately left on a wide track. This rough farm road heads unerringly up the valley, gradually rising above Cosh Beck to eventually arrive at Cosh, the first building since Foxup.

Without entering the confines of Cosh, turn off the track to commence the return journey by descending towards the beck, but only as far as the brink of the steeper drop to the water's edge. Maintaining this level, head downstream as far as a sizeable sheepfold which was probably seen from the outward journey. At this point descend to the beck, fording it and continuing downstream to an immediately intervening wall. From the stile in it rise very slightly across the large pasture to locate a stile in the next wall.

From here on a string of several further stiles lead through pathless fields, virtually parallel with the beck below. Eventually Foxup appears ahead, and from a gateway descend a field to the nearest buildings. A stile and gate between them give access to a track which drops down to Foxup Beck, crossing it to the road terminus and Foxup Bridge Farm.

Do not continue to Foxup Bridge again, but take a gate opposite the farm and a track up the field. After a

Cosh is Remote: geographically it stands at the very heart of the National Park, but it couldn't be further from the centre of things! A thriving farmstead earlier this century, it spent many unoccupied years, though it has now undergone restoration. Interestingly, Littondale's highest building is only a five mile walk from Horton-in-Ribblesdale's railway station, a trek that was undertaken by its former occupants.

The name Cosh is of Norse origin, and was also at one time a grange of Fountains Abbey.

THE WALK (continued)

second gate the track bears across to a gate in the right-hand wall: do not use it but continue up the field, soon levelling out to arrive at a gate in the far-left corner. Remaining level a large pasture is crossed to another gate, the path then running on through low outcrops of limestone to merge with the Stainforth road.

Turn left for a straightforward descent back into Halton Gill, a clear target in the valley bottom.

Charming scene of tiny arched bridge, lively beck and limestone ledges.

Foxup is a farming hamlet marking the upper limit of the valley's surfaced road. At Foxup Bridge the two hitherto moorland becks combine to create the Skirfare.

Halton Gill is the first sizeable settlement in Littondale. Its cluster of grey buildings include a former chapel and a former school, late 16th/early 17th century and now serving as private dwellings.

The last couple of miles provide grand views both down the dale and also across to Halton Gill nestling beneath Horse Head Moor.

(13)

WALK 13 — THE ENVIRONS OF HEBDEN GILL

3½ miles

from Hebden

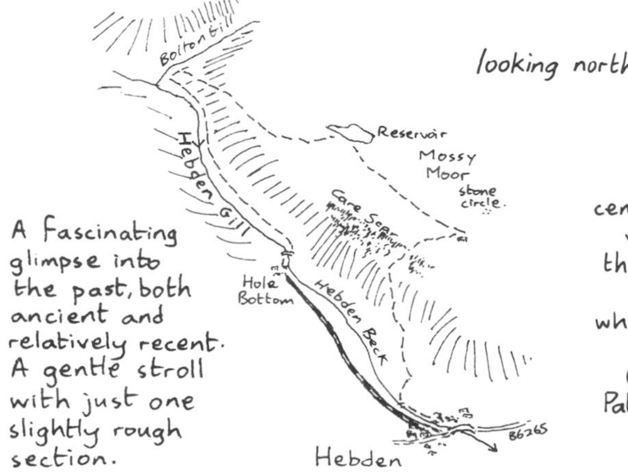

Bolton Gill
Reservoir
Mossy Moor
stone circle
Care Scar
Hebden Gill
Hole Bottom
Hebden Beck
B6265
Hebden

looking north-east

A fascinating glimpse into the past, both ancient and relatively recent. A gentle stroll with just one slightly rough section.

Park in the centre of the village, near the top of the main street where it joins the B6265 Grassington–Pateley Bridge road.

THE WALK

The walk begins from the top end of the village, where the main road crosses Hebden Beck just down from the inn. Take the surfaced road up the west (left) side of the beck, and remain on it for about three-quarters of a mile until arrival at the hamlet of Hole Bottom signals its demise.

The lane is replaced by a good track which forks right through a gate to drop down to cross a small bridge over Hebden Beck. This former miners' track now accompanies the beck upstream, rising gently alongside as evidence of the former lead mining industry appears. After a third gate we enter an area of spoil heaps and ruinous buildings: after the fourth and final gate the devastation is all but left behind.

A little beyond the site of a tiny reservoir on the right, the main track drops down to ford the beck before the inflowing Bolton Gill joins it. This is the turning point of the walk, so without crossing either beck, turn up an inviting path beckoning us up the slope to the right. Looking up the deep cleft of this side-valley, a dark shadow will be seen near to the top: it is a former winding shaft that has undergone a restoration.

Our return route, however, forsakes the inviting path at the first opportunity, in favour of an equally pleasant green path which curves back up to the right through the bracken. It is narrow but easy to follow, passing an old mine level before reaching a gate. This admits to an area of rough pasture, and a sketchy path maintains a near level trod through this and two further pastures, finding the exit from the third by being deflected left of a ruinous section of wall.

From the gate the path continues by the right-hand wall to the next gate ahead, but a short detour can be made to the conspicuous level outline to the left: it is the retaining wall of Mossy Moor Reservoir, another relic from the mining days. When traversed to the right, its little embankment points back to the gate ahead. Open moorland is now reached, and a good track skirts the sea of heather as we continue by the wall.

At the point where the wall turns sharp right to accommodate the access road to Scar Top House, a short section of collapsed wall strikes away towards a small stone circle, just out of sight from where we are standing. After having perhaps puzzled a little why our ancestors should ever have felt the urge to construct such a permanent feature out there, turn with the wall to follow the track in towards Scar Top House. Note that a wall-stile beyond the cattle-grid marks the actual right-of-way.

Do not enter the private yard of the house but follow its enclosing wall around to the right to arrive at a gateway, immediately beneath which is a sudden drop back into Hebden Gill. A short, steep section therefore ensues: from the gap descend by a wall on the left, on a clear path which skirts the greater part of the tangle of boulders of Care Scar just to the right - it is advisable to stand still when viewing this prospect. The descent is soon complete and the path continues through another gateway to more relaxed surroundings.

The path now becomes unclear in this grassy pasture - bear a little to the left to drop down to join the left-hand wall, and on levelling out, go left with it to a gate in the corner. Once through it go with the collapsing wall for a few yards, then cross it and the field behind it to a stile in the bottom corner. Rather cleverly it conveys us into the diagonally-opposite field, from where a path soon materialises to lead in similar direction down to rejoin Hebden Beck.

From a stile there either cross the footbridge to the road on which we began, or preferably remain on this bank down to a row of cottages and thence the road bridge in Hebden.

13

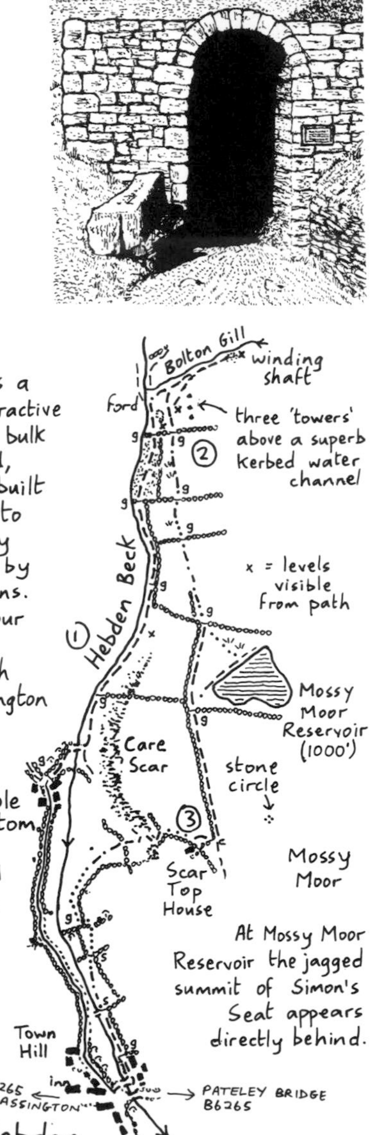
Bolton Gill
winding shaft
ford
three 'towers' above a superb kerbed water channel
2
x = levels visible from path
1
Hebden Beck
Mossy Moor Reservoir (1000')
Care Scar
stone circle
Hole Bottom
3
Scar Top House
Mossy Moor
N
At Mossy Moor Reservoir the jagged summit of Simon's Seat appears directly behind.
Town Hill
inn
B6265 GRASSINGTON
PATELEY BRIDGE B6265
Hebden

Winding shaft, Bolton Gill

This survivor from the lead mining days dates from around 1856, and was restored by the Earby Mines Research Group.

Hebden is a small village divided by the Grassington–Pateley Bridge road. North of the road - where our walk starts - is Town Hill, obviously named as the top end of the village. Here is a highly photogenic grouping of attractive cottages and an old bridge. The bulk of Hebden stands below the road, including the church which when built saved the parishioners the walk to Linton. The Wharfe is a long way below the village, and is crossed by a suspension bridge for pedestrians.

Hebden, like its bigger neighbour Grassington, grew with the once thriving lead mining industry, with Hebden Gill, and above it Grassington Moor, abounding in evocative reminders of those hard days.

Mossy Moor's stone circle is a fairly basic affair almost hidden in thick heather. It consists of four major stones, and eight in total.

Above Hole Bottom the beck is in sparkling form.

On arrival at Scar Top the dramatic view includes the bulk of Burnsall Fell and the distant outline of Pendle Hill.

(14)

WALK 14 | THE ASCENT OF BUCKDEN PIKE

8½ miles | from Buckden

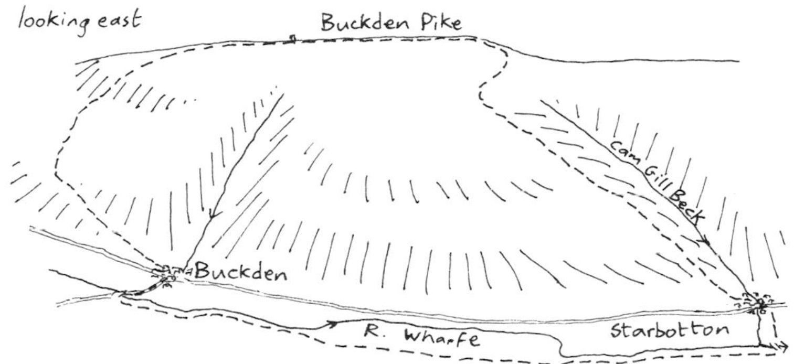
looking east
Buckden Pike
Cam Gill Beck
Buckden
R. Wharfe
Starbotton

A well-graded and popular climb to Wharfedale's second highest summit, with the bonus of a beautiful riverside return.

Buckden has a large car-park.

THE WALK

Leave the car park not by its usual exit, but instead by a gate at its northern end, from where a stony track makes its way gently up Buckden Rake. When the surround of trees disappears, the track turns right through a gate and onto the level. From the next gate however, our chosen path forks right to resume the upward push. This generally clear path rises diagonally through five pastures, and beyond the small gate after the last of them it heads more directly up the open fell. A little sketchily it crosses to a wall on the left, to then accompany it up to the cairn and Ordnance Survey column on the summit of Buckden Pike.

To leave the top use the stile to cross the boundary wall and turn right to follow it along the broad ridge of the Pike, losing little height until passing a memorial cross. At the foot of the slope behind it the track known as the Walden Road is met at a sharp angle in the wall. Use the bridle-gate there to re-cross the wall and commence the descent to Starbotton. The way is fairly clear throughout: after sloping down across two large, rough pastures linked by a little mining debris, a cracking pace can be adopted as the track descends parallel with Cam Gill Beck to our left.

The Walden Road is a former packhorse route which continues over the fell to drop down to the head of the lonely Walden valley and ultimately Wensleydale.

The path linking the summit and the Walden Road is not currently recorded as a definitive right-of-way.

Penyghent and Ingleborough across Birks Fell

Buckden Pike's virtues as a viewpoint are in its distant prospects, which are truly extensive. Most of the major Dales' summits are visible in the western sector, while to the east, moors give way to the flat plains. On a clear day the Cleveland Hills can be seen rising beyond the void.

Buckden Rake is one of the few confirmed sections of the Roman road that connected the forts at Ilkley and Bainbridge. It remains an excellent route to this day, and provides a perfect picture of the dale-head scene, looking beyond Hubberholme's church tower into Langstrothdale. As we leave it to climb, note the hamlet of Cray below.

14

THE WALK continued

Starbotton is entered via a bridge onto a lane, which leads to the right and onto the main road by the Fox and Hounds. Turn left through the village, and after the last building leave the road by an enclosed track on the right, which leads to a footbridge over the Wharfe. Cross it and turn right to follow the river upstream to commence the return to Buckden.

When the Wharfe temporarily parts company the path continues straight ahead alongside a wall on the left: several stiles and gates interrupt the journey. As the river returns a wide track is joined, but as the Wharfe bends away again this time go with it to remain on its bank until Buckden Bridge is encountered. Here leave the river and cross the bridge to re-enter the village.

For a note on Starbotton see Walk 10

The Memorial Cross

This noble structure was erected by a Polish airman, lone survivor of a second world war plane crash on the fell.

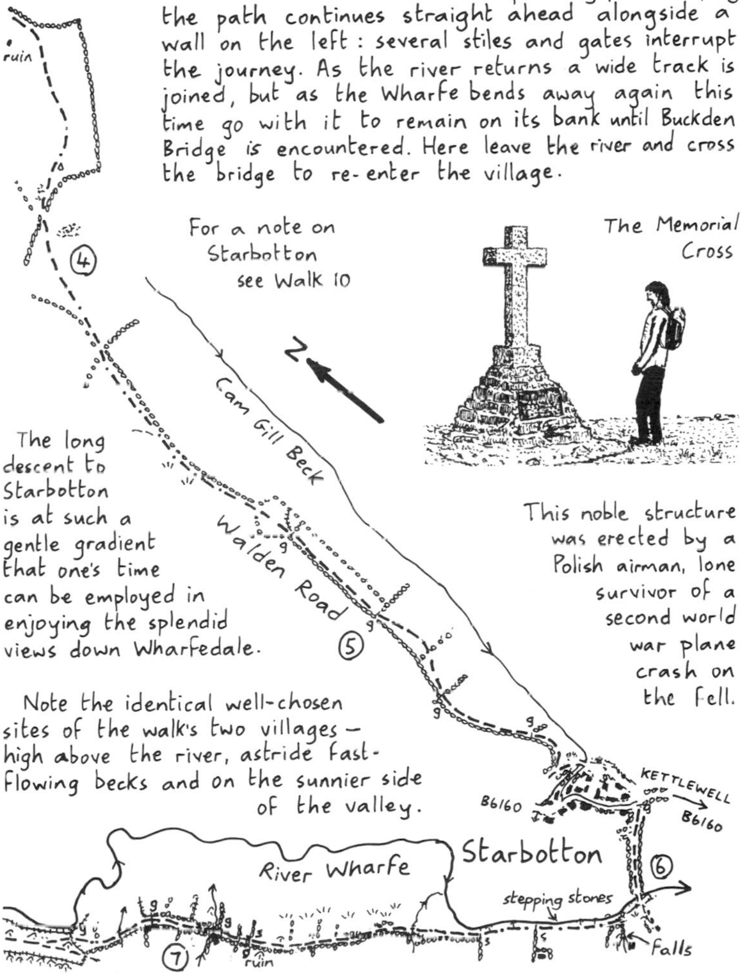

The long descent to Starbotton is at such a gentle gradient that one's time can be employed in enjoying the splendid views down Wharfedale.

Note the identical well-chosen sites of the walk's two villages – high above the river, astride fast-flowing becks and on the sunnier side of the valley.

(15)

WALK 15

THORPE FELL AND CRACOE FELL

9 miles

from Linton

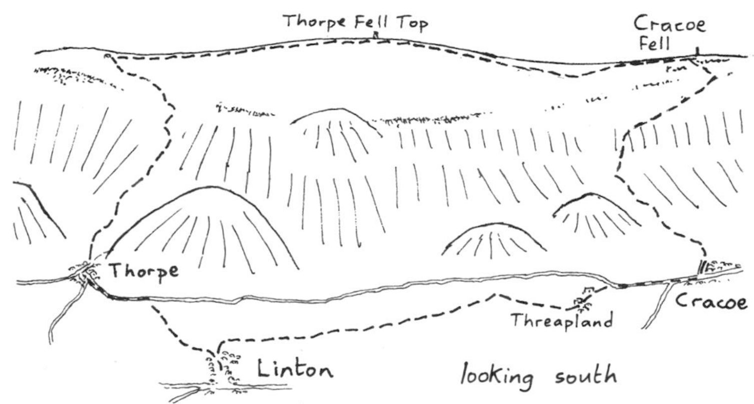

Thorpe Fell Top
Cracoe Fell
Thorpe
Cracoe
Threapland
Linton
looking south

A fine stretch of moorland rambling, contrasting well with the tiny villages under the steep slopes

Park in the village centre, either by the green or on the road through the village.

THE WALK

From the inn cross the green and the beck and follow the lane along to the right to its imminent demise at a farm. Turn left in front of a large barn and along a briefly enclosed track. At the end it climbs with the left-hand wall, and though it peters out remain with the wall to negotiate three intervening stiles. From the third head away in the same direction, rising through a large field and going left of a line of trees to a ruinous barn. A stile to the left of the barn admits onto a roughly surfaced lane. Turn left to follow its narrow course into the hamlet of Thorpe.

Bear right at the triangular junction in the centre and keep on until the road dissolves into a couple of rough tracks. Opt for the left one which climbs steeply between walls to emerge onto the open moor. Two sunken tracks head directly away from the gate, and it is the right-hand one which is to be preferred. It swings up to the right to terminate at the remains of a small quarry: here turn up to the left to head in a southerly direction, a track reappearing at a cairn. On rounding the beginnings of a beck the track regains its groove, though loses it briefly again at a faint fork. Keep right to rise up a gentle slope, and as the groove disappears for good a stone shooting house appears ahead, and is soon reached.

At the shooting house our track ends and a wider track is encountered, but unfortunately it is of little use to us. Though it can be followed a short distance to the right, it must then be forsaken in order to climb the modest slope directly behind the building. Though pathless, a short half-mile will lead to the Ordnance Survey column on Thorpe Fell Top.

After admiring the view it is necessary to engage in a further bout of heather-bashing by aiming in a south-westerly direction for the conspicuous monument on Cracoe Fell. At an inscribed boundary stone just short of the depression between the fell-top and the monument, swing right in front of a row of grouse-butts to join the substantial wall along the top of the escarpment. Now turn left on a path by the wall for an easy walk up to the monument: a stile provides access to it.

At our feet, just to the north, is Cracoe, which is the next objective. On locating the nearest group of trees this side of the village, a walled lane can also be seen running from the end of the rough pasture beneath us to the village itself. Descend the virtually pathless slope-initially with care where rocks abound- to reach the rough lane which leads unerringly into Cracoe.

Turn right along the busy main road and leave it at the first opportunity along a much pleasanter back road. This too is left at the first chance in favour of a short track to Threapland Farm on the left. After crossing the beck turn right in front of the main buildings to a gate from where an initially enclosed track heads away. When faced by a fence the track forks, and our now pathless course follows the fence around to the right to a stile. From the tiny beck behind it aim directly across two fields, then bear a little to the left above a small wood to locate the next stile.

Two narrow fields are then crossed to descend the next one to a tiny beck and an access road in front of a barn. Cross them both to a stile just left of the barn, and from the next stile follow the right-hand wall across a larger field. From the gate at the end a tractor-track leads across the final field to rejoin the track by which we left Linton. Turn left to re-enter the village and end the walk.

(15)

■ Along with Barden Fell on the opposite bank of the Wharfe, Barden Moor is also part of the Duke of Devonshire's estate, and the moorland walking between the points marked thus ✻ (ie the Fell lanes out of Thorpe and Cracoe) is on access land which may be closed on certain days during the grouse shooting season. It is important to read the notes at the foot of page 22.

The little settlement of Cracoe marks the barely discernable watershed between Wharfedale and neighbouring Airedale. Its long, low, whitewashed inn has a good few years history behind it, and like several others in the vicinity it bears the arms of the family on whose moor we have just been tramping.

On departing the untidy environs of Threapland, one's eyes cannot fail to be drawn by the scene of utter devastation presented by the quarry to the left.

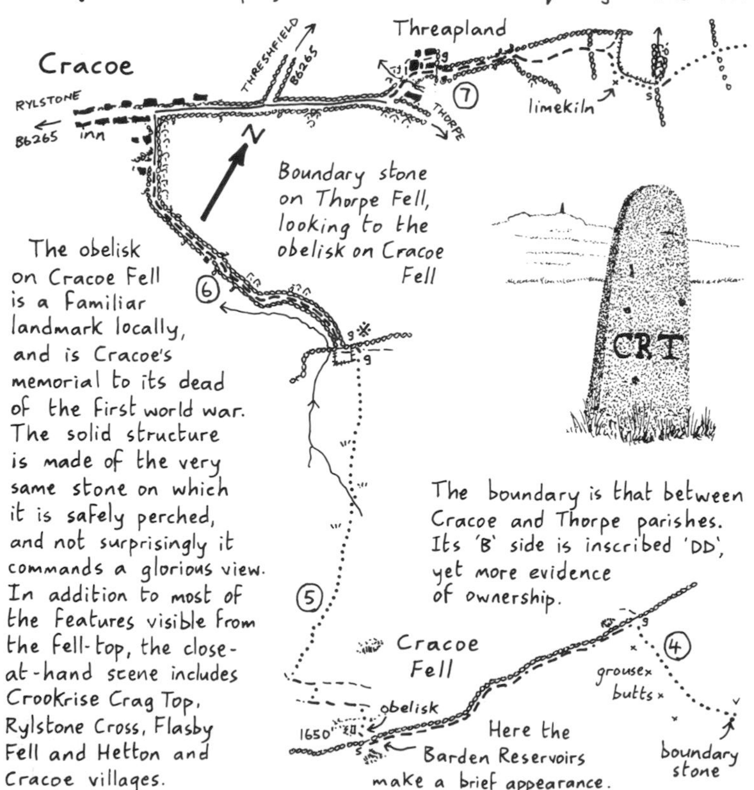
Cracoe
RYLSTONE
B6265
inn
THRESHFIELD
B6265
Threapland
THORPE
limekiln
7
6
5
4
CRT
Cracoe Fell
obelisk
1650'
grouse butts
boundary stone
Here the Barden Reservoirs make a brief appearance.

Boundary stone on Thorpe Fell, looking to the obelisk on Cracoe Fell

The obelisk on Cracoe Fell is a familiar landmark locally, and is Cracoe's memorial to its dead of the First world war. The solid structure is made of the very same stone on which it is safely perched, and not surprisingly it commands a glorious view. In addition to most of the features visible from the fell-top, the close-at-hand scene includes Crookrise Crag Top, Rylstone Cross, Flasby Fell and Hetton and Cracoe villages.

The boundary is that between Cracoe and Thorpe parishes. Its 'B' side is inscribed 'DD', yet more evidence of ownership.

The farming hamlet of Thorpe is known for its elusiveness which allegedly kept it hidden from the marauding Scots. Romantically titled 'Thorpe in the Hollow' it shelters between reef knolls and below the overpowering Thorpe Fell. Note the triangular little enclosed green.

Most prominent in the Linton and Thorpe scene are the rounded hills known as reef knolls. Of limestone with a grass covering, they are relics of underwater mounds, since exposed by the eventual erosion of overlying rocks. Immediately west of Thorpe is Elbolton, probably the best example.

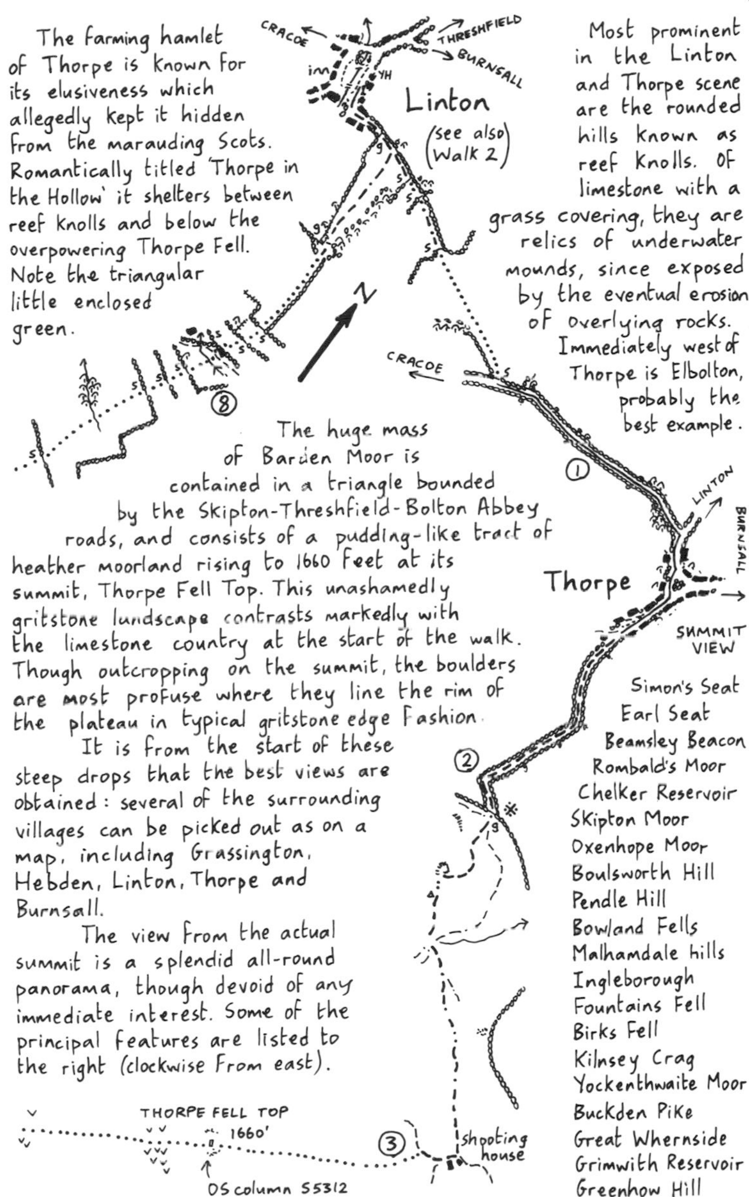

CRACOE
THRESHFIELD
BURNSALL
YH
Linton
(see also Walk 2)
N
CRACOE
8
1
LINTON
BURNSALL
Thorpe
2
3
THORPE FELL TOP
1660'
OS column S5312
shooting house

The huge mass of Barden Moor is contained in a triangle bounded by the Skipton-Threshfield-Bolton Abbey roads, and consists of a pudding-like tract of heather moorland rising to 1660 feet at its summit, Thorpe Fell Top. This unashamedly gritstone landscape contrasts markedly with the limestone country at the start of the walk. Though outcropping on the summit, the boulders are most profuse where they line the rim of the plateau in typical gritstone edge fashion.

It is from the start of these steep drops that the best views are obtained: several of the surrounding villages can be picked out as on a map, including Grassington, Hebden, Linton, Thorpe and Burnsall.

The view from the actual summit is a splendid all-round panorama, though devoid of any immediate interest. Some of the principal features are listed to the right (clockwise from east).

SUMMIT VIEW

Simon's Seat
Earl Seat
Beamsley Beacon
Rombald's Moor
Chelker Reservoir
Skipton Moor
Oxenhope Moor
Boulsworth Hill
Pendle Hill
Bowland Fells
Malhamdale hills
Ingleborough
Fountains Fell
Birks Fell
Kilnsey Crag
Yockenthwaite Moor
Buckden Pike
Great Whernside
Grimwith Reservoir
Greenhow Hill

WALK 16 THE ASCENT OF GREAT WHERNSIDE

6 miles

from Kettlewell

A charming beckside ramble precedes a short and easy fellwalk to Wharfedale's highest top

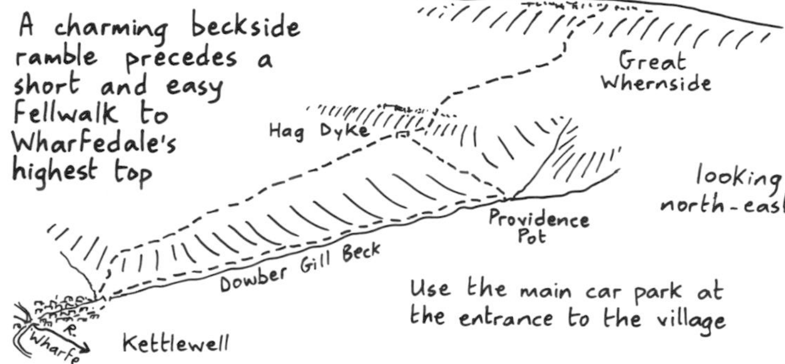
Great Whernside
Hag Dyke
Providence Pot
Dowber Gill Beck
R. Wharfe
Kettlewell
looking north-east

Use the main car park at the entrance to the village

THE WALK

From the car park head into the village and leave the main road immediately before the bridge by the two hotels, turning along the road to the right. Fork left at the maypole to pass the church, and at the third inn turn sharp right on a lane alongside the beck. At a shapely bridge and chapel the lane becomes a track, and just a little further it crosses Dowber Gill Beck: here leave it by turning up the little beckside path to a gate in the adjacent wall. Now turn right to begin a long mile and a quarter keeping very close company with the beck. Several stiles are encountered and little height gained until the unmistakeable site of Providence Pot is reached, crossing the beck just before it.

Directly behind is the meeting of twin becks, but our path is the very clear one up the left-hand slope immediately next to the pothole. Recross the beck then, and climb the path which soons levels out to approach Hag Dyke. Do not enter its confines but climb the wide path up the steep scarp to a line of cairns at the top. The summit now appears directly ahead, and the path crosses a damp plateau before a steady climb to the highest point.

To return to Kettlewell retrace steps to Hag Dyke and enter its yard by a stile by the main building. Follow the access track out to a gate, then leave it to drop half-left to eventually meet a left-hand wall. Keep parallel with the beck far below, and a sketchy path works its way back to the track over Dowber Gill Beck. The finish can be varied by crossing the bridge by the chapel.

Great Whernside is not only the highest of Wharfedale's fells, it is by far the bulkiest. Only from Kettlewell is there anything like easy access. To the east innumerable square miles of bleak moorland fall to the upper reaches of Nidderdale, indeed the Nidd is born within a mile of the summit. Atop the line of Long Crags - large 'scrambling' boulders - stands an immense pile of stones, a cairn and a half. The National Park boundary runs along this summit ridge.

The view is largely one of fells, from the nearby mass of Buckden Pike to the distant Three Peaks, of which Penyghent looks particularly distinguished. A short but lovely section of Wharfedale can be seen from Kilnsey Crag to Grass Woods.

The final mile to the summit is not a definitive right-of-way, nor is the path between Providence Pot and Hag Dyke.

At 1525 feet, Hag Dyke is one of the highest buildings in the country. It is now put to use as a scout outdoor centre.

Providence Pot is one of the Dales' better known potholes, and is well-sited in the centre of the beck. An incongruous manhole cover guards the vertical entrance.

For a note on Kettlewell see Walk 10.

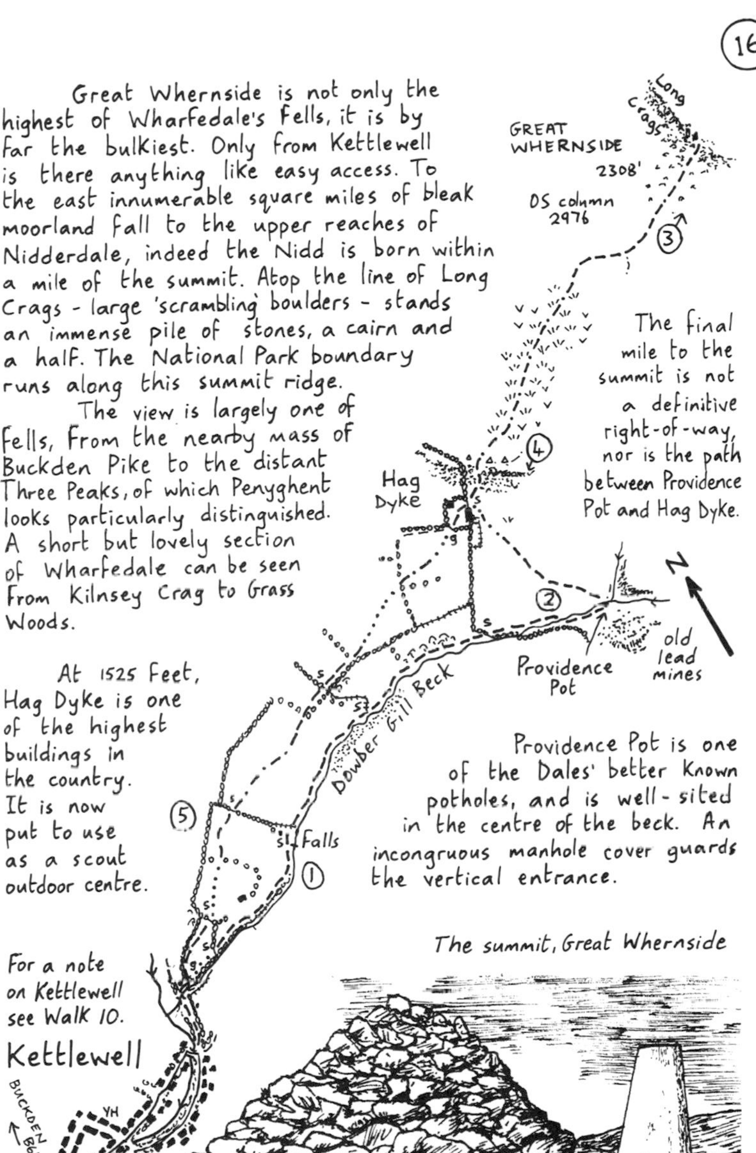
Long Crags
GREAT WHERNSIDE
2308'
OS column 2976
3
4
Hag Dyke
2
N
Providence Pot
old lead mines
Dowber Gill Beck
5
Falls
1
Kettlewell
YH
BUCKDEN B6160
R. Wharfe
B6160
CONISTONE

The summit, Great Whernside

CHAPTER TWO

THE VICTORIA
FREE HOUSE

MALHAMDALE

The Aire at Gargrave   opposite: Kirkby Malham

MALHAMDALE

The Aire is one of the major rivers of Yorkshire, yet unlike its neighbours which also rise high on the hills of the Dales, the Aire has but a brief existance in these tranquil pastures before heading into the heart of industrial Yorkshire. Fortunately its time inside the National Park is a well-spent one, and along with its numerous tributary becks provides a highly compact area to which this chapter is dedicated.

Not only is this a compact region, it is a richly contrasting one. The western half needs little introduction, for the Malham district is renowned for its stunningly impressive scenery, with Malham Cove and Gordale Scar the feathers in the cap. The uplands above these major features contain a wealth of limestone delights, with Malham Tarn in the heart of things. Downstream from Malham the valley becomes immediately pastoral, with several attractive villages nestling along the river down to Gargrave.

East of the Aire, the surroundings undergo a dramatic change: here is typical gritstone country, with rocky outcrops, bracken-covered slopes and some splendid heather moorland. The various becks flowing off the moors all meet the Aire by Skipton, some having emerged from rather attractive reservoirs.

The boundary of this chapter is clearly defined by the watersheds with the Ribble, Skirfare and Wharfe to the west, north and east respectively, and the limits of the National Park boundary to the south. Standing at this boundary is Skipton, a fascinating market town known as the 'Gateway to the Dales'. It makes an ideal base for the Craven area, and its many attractions include the Castle (a must), the parish church, the High Street, the Craven Museum and the Leeds-Liverpool Canal.

In the very east of the area rises Barden Moor, highly valued grouse-shooting country which most happily has been the subject of a negotiated access agreement with the landowner (the Duke of Devonshire's estates) and walkers are free to roam over the upland areas subject to various restrictions.

The main point is that the moors can be 'closed' on certain days when shooting takes place, though not Sundays. Although notices are posted at the access points (along with a list of all restrictions) disappointment can be avoided by ringing the estate office beforehand (Bolton Abbey 227). Also worth knowing-dogs are not allowed. *Walks 21 and 30 take advantage of this facility.*

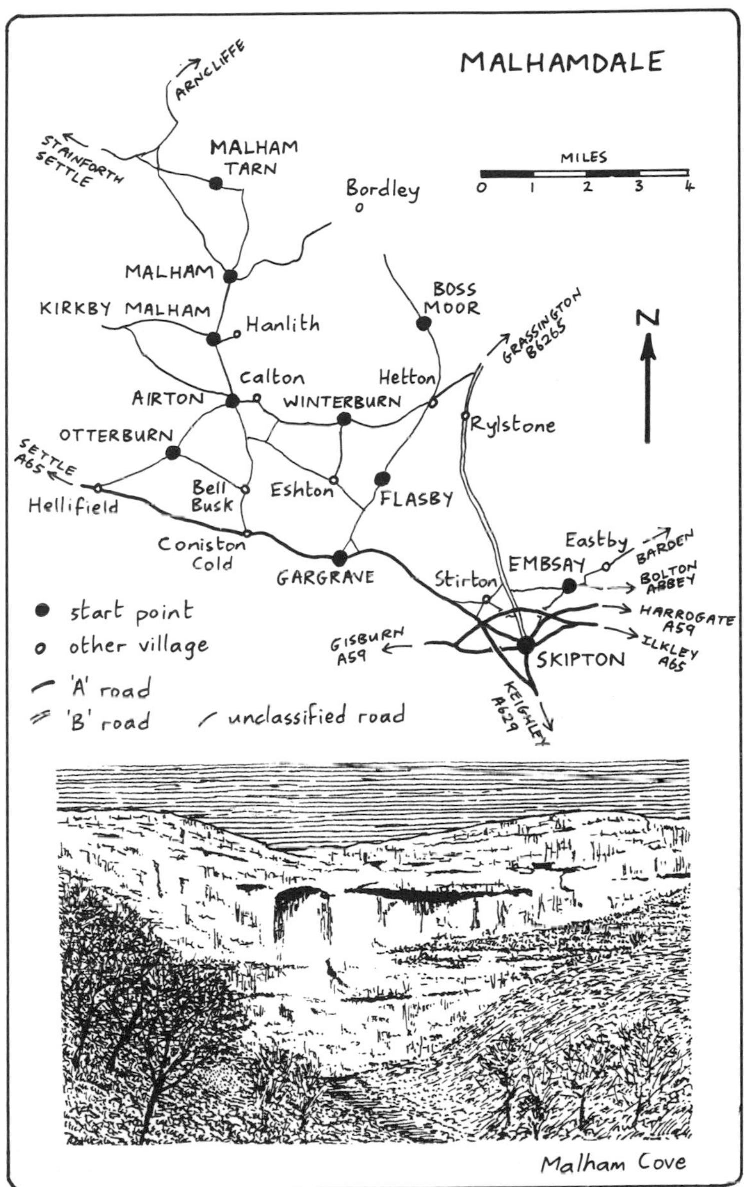
MALHAMDALE
ARNCLIFFE
STAINFORTH
SETTLE
MALHAM TARN
MILES
0 1 2 3 4
Bordley
MALHAM
BOSS MOOR
KIRKBY MALHAM
Hanlith
N
GRASSINGTON B6265
Calton
Hetton
AIRTON
WINTERBURN
Rylstone
OTTERBURN
SETTLE A65
Bell Busk
Eshton
FLASBY
Hellifield
Coniston Cold
GARGRAVE
Eastby
BARDEN
EMBSAY
Stirton
BOLTON ABBEY
HARROGATE A59
GISBURN A59
SKIPTON
ILKLEY A65
KEIGHLEY A629
start point
other village
'A' road
'B' road
unclassified road

Malham Cove

WALK 17

OVER FLASBY FELL

10 miles

from Skipton

Sharp Haw
Rough Haw
Flasby
Stirton
by-pass
Skipton

A lengthy march from the 'gateway to the Dales' to the colourful and shapely fells watching over it

looking north-west

Use one of the central car-parks in Skipton

NB: the walk can be substantially reduced by starting from the vicinity of Tarn House, Stirton

THE WALK

From the war memorial-roundabout at the top of the High Street, take the Grassington road past the church and the Castle Inn, and over a bridge. Turn immediately right along a lane (Chapel Hill) which climbs steeply to end at a gate and stile: thus we have made an exceptionally rapid escape from the town to the country. Climb straight up the field to a stile at the very top, close by the site of the old battery. From here continue in the same direction towards the by-pass, which is gained by crossing a farm-lane parallel with it. Cross with care and from a stile on the other side head directly away again, to a stile which admits to Skipton golf-course.

Continue straight across, passing a short section of wall to arrive at the wall ahead, with a small length protruding our way. Take the stile on the left and follow the fence away, crossing one final stile before accompanying a left-hand fence down onto Brackenley Lane. Turn left up the lane to its junction with the Skipton-Grassington road, and cross to a stile directly opposite. Aim for a stile at the far side of the field, then head away from it alongside a fence which soon falls into disrepair: continue up the gentle slope to reach a gate onto a lane just above Tarn House.

Turn right along the lane and at the third sharp bend reached, take a gate on the left to follow a wide, gently-rising track. After two more gates open country is entered: when the accompanying wall breaks off to the left, leave the track by bearing off to the right. On climbing the slope a faint path materialises, and improves as the top of Sharp Haw is neared and the going steepens a little. A stile in the wall across the top admits to the trig. point on Sharp Haw's airy summit. Neighbouring Rough Haw is across the depression to the north, and is our next objective. Follow the path along the short ridge for a few yards, then it drops to the right to a gateway in the wall there. The path heads straight down the slope and across the depression to a gate, from where the main path heads left. The short scramble onto Rough Haw is worthwhile though, and involves climbing the steep path directly ahead, to pass through an outcrop of rocks before levelling out to reach the cairn.

On returning to the gate, take that path heading away; it soon descends gradually through bracken, past a wood and across a tiny beck to a gate in the bottom corner. Continue along the edge of the field to another gate, from where an enclosed track winds down to the farmyard of Flasby Hall Farm. The rest of Flasby lies across the bridge over the beck, but our return route starts before the first barns on the left, along a wide track heading left.

This track runs by a wood then climbs left to a farm, running along the front of it. From the bridge beyond, it rises through a field to enter Crag Wood at a gate. A good path heads away from it, soon swinging up to the left to a footpath sign indicating a fork to the right. Take this path, which descends a little then heads left for a few sketchy yards to emerge through a gap onto the sharp bend of a wide forest road. Take the branch to the left, which heads away on a generally level course. Follow this track all the way to the point where it swings left to be seen to leave the trees for open country. Do not follow it to the gate however, but take a path forking to the right to leave the wood by a gate after a few yards.

Head across the field, over the beginnings of a beck to a stile beyond. Follow the wall away to a gate, then cross a fence and follow it away again to another gate, just beyond which a final gate leads onto a lane. Turn right for a short distance, then from a stile on the left head half-right across the field (two trees in the centre guide the way) to a kissing-gate onto another lane. Go right for just a short distance on a footpath alongside the lane, and at the end of the caravan park it branches left to a stile. From it head

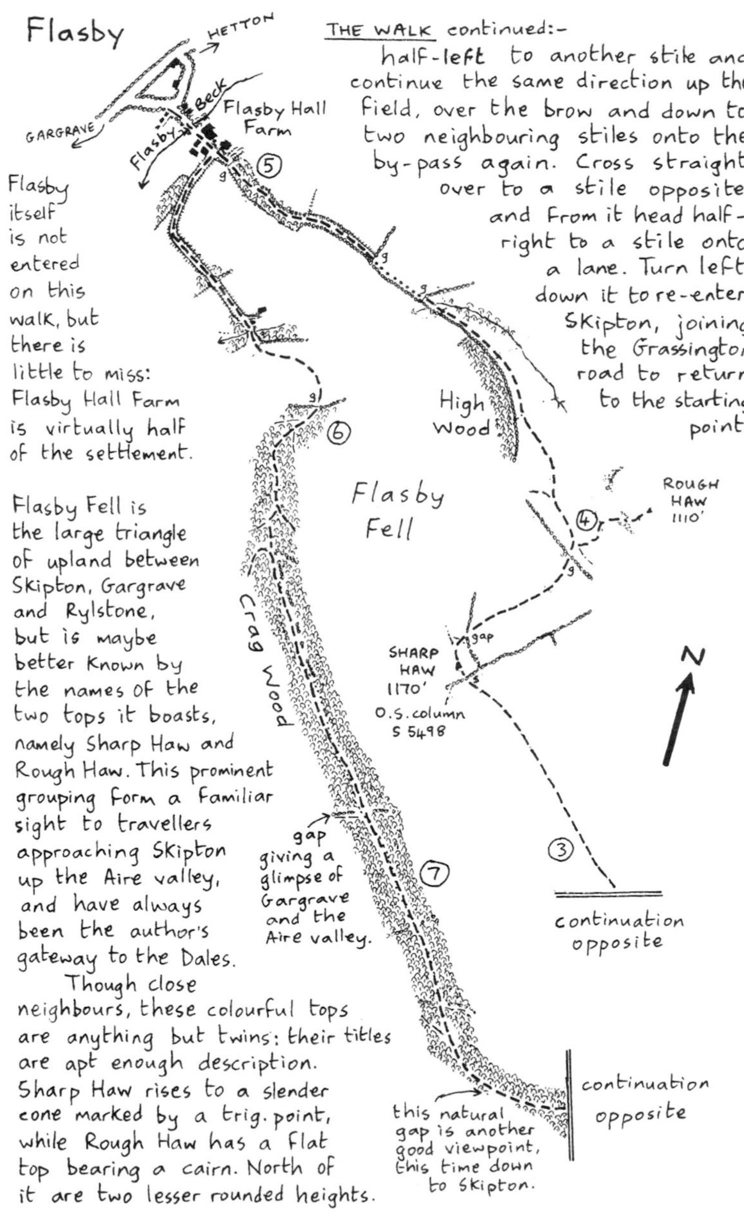
Flasby
HETTON
GARGRAVE
Flasby Beck
Flasby Hall Farm
5
g
g
g
High Wood
6
Flasby Fell
ROUGH HAW 1110'
4
g
gap
SHARP HAW 1170'
O.S. column S 5498
s
N
Crag Wood
gap giving a glimpse of Gargrave and the Aire valley.
7
3
continuation opposite
this natural gap is another good viewpoint, this time down to Skipton.
continuation opposite

THE WALK continued:-
half-left to another stile and continue the same direction up the field, over the brow and down to two neighbouring stiles onto the by-pass again. Cross straight over to a stile opposite and from it head half-right to a stile onto a lane. Turn left down it to re-enter Skipton, joining the Grassington road to return to the starting point.

Flasby itself is not entered on this walk, but there is little to miss: Flasby Hall Farm is virtually half of the settlement.

Flasby Fell is the large triangle of upland between Skipton, Gargrave and Rylstone, but is maybe better known by the names of the two tops it boasts, namely Sharp Haw and Rough Haw. This prominent grouping form a familiar sight to travellers approaching Skipton up the Aire valley, and have always been the author's gateway to the Dales.

Though close neighbours, these colourful tops are anything but twins: their titles are apt enough description. Sharp Haw rises to a slender cone marked by a trig. point, while Rough Haw has a flat top bearing a cairn. North of it are two lesser rounded heights.

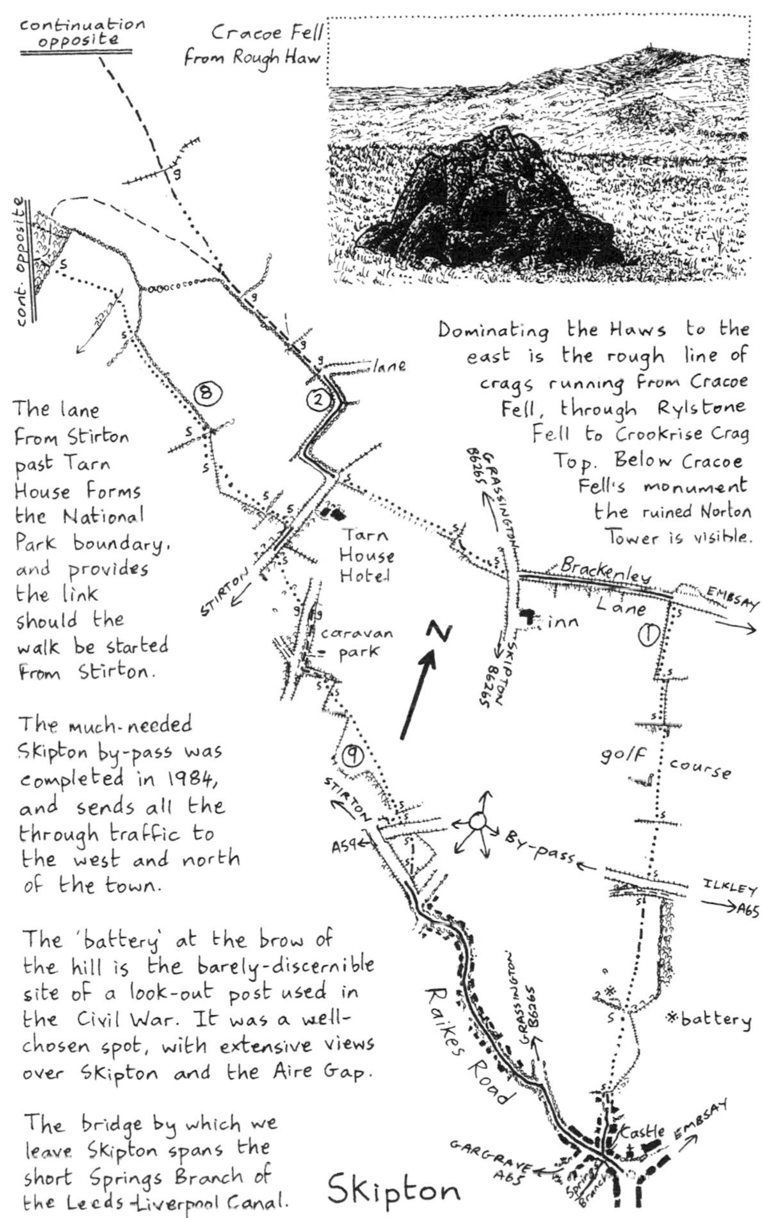
Cracoe Fell from Rough Haw
continuation opposite
cont. opposite
lane
Tarn House Hotel
caravan park
STIRTON
GRASSINGTON B6265
SKIPTON B6265
Brackenley Lane
EMBSAY
inn
N
golf course
By-pass
ILKLEY
A65
A59
battery
Raikes Road
GRASSINGTON B6265
Castle
EMBSAY
GARGRAVE A65
Springs Branch
Skipton

Dominating the Haws to the east is the rough line of crags running from Cracoe Fell, through Rylstone Fell to Crookrise Crag Top. Below Cracoe Fell's monument the ruined Norton Tower is visible.

The lane from Stirton past Tarn House forms the National Park boundary, and provides the link should the walk be started from Stirton.

The much-needed Skipton by-pass was completed in 1984, and sends all the through traffic to the west and north of the town.

The 'battery' at the brow of the hill is the barely-discernible site of a look-out post used in the Civil War. It was a well-chosen spot, with extensive views over Skipton and the Aire Gap.

The bridge by which we leave Skipton spans the short Springs Branch of the Leeds-Liverpool Canal.

WALK 18

MALHAM COVE AND BEYOND

5 miles

from Malham

A very easy walk through stunning limestone scenery
A must!

looking north-east

Use the large car-park in the village

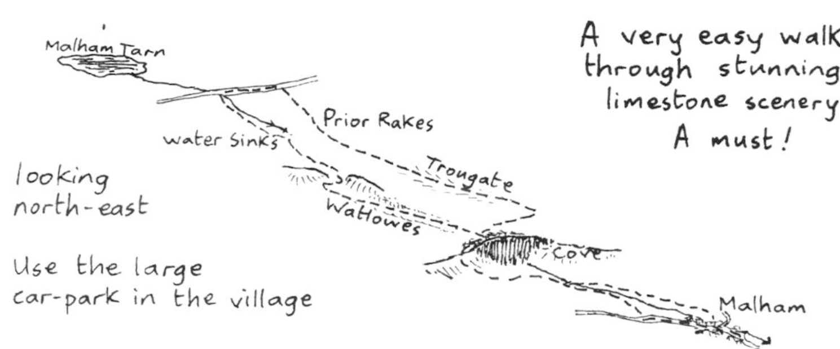
Malham Tarn
Prior Rakes
Water Sinks
Trougate
Watlowes
Cove
Malham

THE WALK

From the car-park pass through the village, keeping left at the junction by the bridge. After the cluster of buildings at Town Head the lane begins to climb: we soon leave it by a gate signposted on the right, with the majestic Cove already in full view directly ahead. A path leads to the very foot of the cliffs, but to go further, retrace steps a little to climb the man-made steps round the left side of the Cove. A stile at the top leads to the limestone pavement covering the Cove-top. Great care must be taken on crossing it, for the grikes in between have a great leg-damaging capability.

Having reached the centre of the Cove-top a wall is met: ignore both the stile and the gate however, and follow our side of the wall away from the Cove. After a stile in an intervening wall the crags on either side close in as we proceed along the floor of Watlowes, the Dry Valley. At the dramatic valley-head the path escapes by climbing to a stile in front, from where we swing sharp right alongside a fence to round a ledge under Dean Moor Hill. Soon the outcrops are left behind and a wall provides company across the open moor to lead unerringly to Water Sinks.

A line of telegraph-poles indicate the proximity of the road across the moor, and is soon reached at a gate by following the beck upstream. Turn right along the road as it starts to run freely across the moor, and soon a footpath sign indicates the Pennine Way crossing at right-angles to the road. Follow its course to the right, and we now make use of the Way to return to the Cove. Beyond a wall the extensive

Prior Rakes is crossed, then three more walls are encountered as we pass through the well-defined trench of Trougate between low outcrops. On meeting another path follow it back down to the right to return to the wall at the top of Malham Cove.

Re-cross the limestone pavement and return to the foot of the Cove. Use the path back to Malham as far as the first gate, and then cross the beck by means of a footbridge of stone slabs. Turn right up the slope, and a faint path rises towards the first of three stiles in cross-walls. Continue on to a gap in a collapsing wall, and then follow the wall to the right to reach a stile. After a few enclosed yards, head away in the same direction with a wall now on the left. On reaching a small shelter, the way becomes enclosed again, and remains so to re-enter Malham in fine style. Debouching onto a back-lane, continue straight down past the youth hostel into the village centre.

Malham Cove

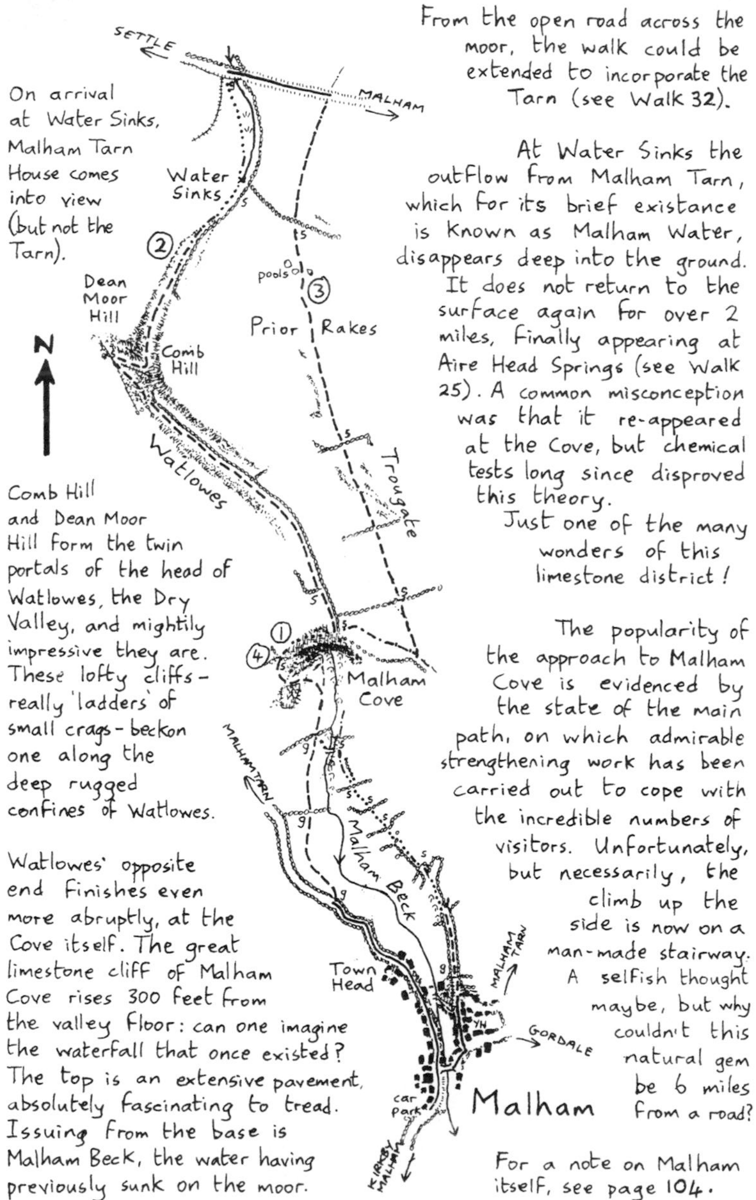
SETTLE
MALHAM
Water Sinks
Dean Moor Hill
Comb Hill
pools
Prior Rakes
N
Watlowes
Trougate
Malham Cove
MALHAM TARN
Malham Beck
Town Head
MALHAM TARN
YH
GORDALE
car park
Malham
KIRKBY MALHAM

On arrival at Water Sinks, Malham Tarn House comes into view (but not the Tarn).

Comb Hill and Dean Moor Hill form the twin portals of the head of Watlowes, the Dry Valley, and mightily impressive they are. These lofty cliffs - really 'ladders' of small crags - beckon one along the deep rugged confines of Watlowes.

Watlowes' opposite end finishes even more abruptly, at the Cove itself. The great limestone cliff of Malham Cove rises 300 feet from the valley floor: can one imagine the waterfall that once existed? The top is an extensive pavement, absolutely fascinating to tread. Issuing from the base is Malham Beck, the water having previously sunk on the moor.

From the open road across the moor, the walk could be extended to incorporate the Tarn (see Walk 32).

At Water Sinks the outflow from Malham Tarn, which for its brief existance is known as Malham Water, disappears deep into the ground. It does not return to the surface again for over 2 miles, finally appearing at Aire Head Springs (see Walk 25). A common misconception was that it re-appeared at the Cove, but chemical tests long since disproved this theory.
Just one of the many wonders of this limestone district!

The popularity of the approach to Malham Cove is evidenced by the state of the main path, on which admirable strengthening work has been carried out to cope with the incredible numbers of visitors. Unfortunately, but necessarily, the climb up the side is now on a man-made stairway. A selfish thought maybe, but why couldn't this natural gem be 6 miles from a road?

For a note on Malham itself, see page 104.

WALK 19

WINTERBURN RESERVOIR

6¼ miles

from Winterburn

An easy circuit of a lovely sheet of water, returning via a splendid old house

looking north-east
Reservoir
Winterburn
Friars Head

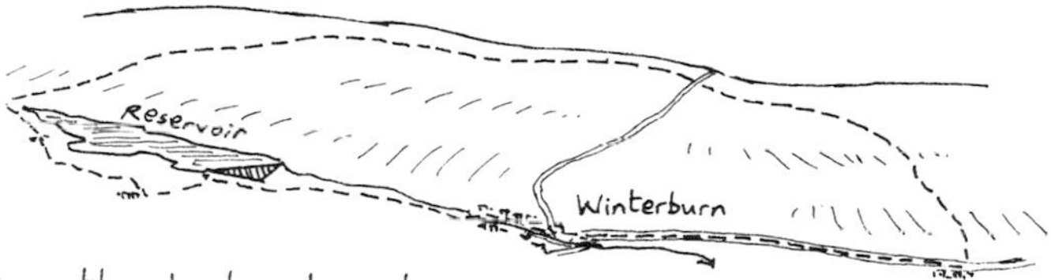

Park on the dead-end road just off the road skirting the hamlet

THE WALK

From the T-junction head up the dead-end road through the heart of the hamlet: on reaching a cattle-grid it becomes a private farm-road, crossing a length of pasture by the beck to arrive at a bridge. Cross it and follow the road along to the right, still alongside the beck. After a while it gradually climbs above the beck to arrive at the reservoir-keeper's house, with the top of the dam being easily accessible through the gate in front. Our route however does not quite reach the house, for we turn up the farm-road branching left at a right-angle, before another branch even nearer the house. Climb the farm-road which leads circuitously but unerringly to Way Gill Farm.

Without entering the confines of the farm, turn to the right, and pass along the field-top to a gate just right of the farm. Now head half-right down the field to a stile onto the farm road to High Cow House. Turn left along it, but well before reaching the farm, take a stile in the wall on the right.

Descend the field-side to approach the reservoir, then go left with a fence above the shore. Keep to this line through an intervening gate, and just beyond a stile a track down from the farm is joined. Continue on to reach the bridge at the head of the reservoir.

Across the bridge is a large expanse of rough pasture, and an improving path heads up it, half-left for a few yards only and then turning right to rise gradually. The path remains sketchy throughout, levelling out to arrive at a gate in a wall descending towards the right. The gate marks the end of a walled track, but once on it leave immediately by a gate on the right, to head over another rough pasture to a conspicuous gap in the line of trees ahead A path leads through the narrow plantation, then leaves us in an immense tract of rough pasture. Head directly away from the trees, aiming for a small cluster of trees which, on nearing, surround a farmhouse. As we converge with the wall across to the right, two barns are passed: stay outside the farm's confines and after a gate continue behind the farm itself to another gate.

A large dome-like pasture is entered, without a path or sign of exit. Panic not however, but aim diagonally away from the gate, and straight over the brow of the field using the graceful peak of Sharp Haw as an infallible guide. Passing a wall corner on the right, descend to the far corner and use a gateway a few yards to the right. From it follow the wall on the left, passing two barns and remaining with the same wall to emerge onto the Hetton-Winterburn road.

Cross to the gate immediately opposite and head straight down to a gate in the corner, then continuing by the wall to eventually reach another gate at the far end. Head away again with the wall now on the right, and from a gate in a fence bear right to drop to a gate in the corner. Now simply accompany the wall on the right down onto the lane, directly opposite Friars Head. Turn right along the lane for a short level walk back into Winterburn.

Winterbeck Beck
Winterburn
AIRTON
old chapel
HETTON
6
Friars Head
GARGRAVE
5

Winterburn is a small farming community set in an attractive location between the hills. Here is a former chapel of 1703, one of the first Independent chapels. It was restored early this century.

Friars Head is a superb 17th century house, the most interesting in the district. Here was a grange of the monks of Furness Abbey, and farm-life still thrives.

An excellent viewpoint for a last look at the rugged skyline from Cracoe Fell to Flasby Fell

Winterburn Reservoir is a substantial finger-like sheet of water, and one could be forgiven for believing it, at first glance, to be natural. Even the dam with its grass cover seems to blend in well. A clue to the reservoir's purpose is seen just prior to reaching the bridge at it's head: by the path a stone inscribed 'LLC' indicates that the reservoir was constructed to supply the Leeds-Liverpool Canal at Gargrave. Now, there is a strong air of neglect: the keeper's house is boarded up and a variety of bird-life take advantage of this peaceful setting.

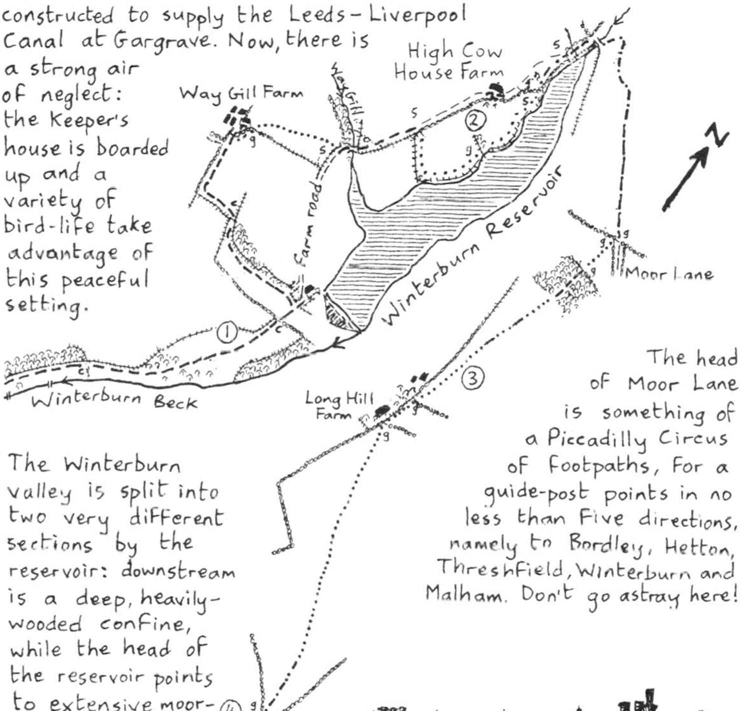

The head of Moor Lane is something of a Piccadilly Circus of footpaths, for a guide-post points in no less than five directions, namely to Bordley, Hetton, Threshfield, Winterburn and Malham. Don't go astray here!

The Winterburn valley is split into two very different sections by the reservoir: downstream is a deep, heavily-wooded confine, while the head of the reservoir points to extensive moor-like terrain.

NB: if time is pressing, this lane will cut off the last corner of the walk, but you'll forfeit this

Friars Head

WALK 20 — KIRKBY MALHAM AND THE AIRE

4¼ miles — from Airton

A gentle ramble over rolling hills and along the riverbank

looking north-west

Kirkby Malham
Hanlith
River Aire
Airton

Parking can be found alongside, but not encroaching on, Airton's green, or on the main road above.

THE WALK

Leave Airton's green by the telephone-box at the south-west corner, crossing straight over the main road and up the lane opposite, signposted to Hellifield. Shortly after the last buildings take a gate on the right, with another one just behind it. Head away from it along the field-edge to a gate at the far end, and then continue to a gate by a barn to follow a short track out onto the Settle-Airton road. Take this pleasant lane up to the left, encountering a more level section before reaching two stiles directly opposite each other.

Opt for the one on the right and climb by the wall, passing a small plantation to a stile on its left. Continue down by the wall leading away, to a stile at the bottom beyond which is a tiny beck. From it follow the wall no longer, but instead bear across the field along a conspicuous groove sloping left. At the fence at the far end go left to a stile, crossing straight over a farm-track and descending steeply alongside a fence: Kirkby Malham is now at our feet. From the stile in the corner head half-right to the next one, continuing the direction to a small gate to enter the trees below. Steps descend to a footbridge spanning Kirkby Beck, then up onto a lane by the church.

Turn right, over the crossroads by the inn and down the lane opposite to Hanlith Bridge. Cross it to a stile on the right and accompany the river downstream. The Aire is clung to, through a gate then two neighbouring stiles to arrive at a footbridge. Cross it and make for a stile

in the wall downstream, continuing on to the start of the old leat, which is also a footbridge. The path is now sandwiched between mill-leat and river, remaining like this to wind round to the converted mill. Pass round to the right of the mill, into the car-park and out onto a lane: Airton village green is just up to the right.

From Scosthrop Lane to entering Kirkby Malham, our walk follows an old way known as Kirk Gait. This, as its name suggests, is the route taken by the good folk of Otterburn (see Walk 23) to reach the parish church at Kirkby Malham. A glimpse at an O.S. map will confirm the practical, direct way they chose.

For more on Kirkby Malham see Walk 25

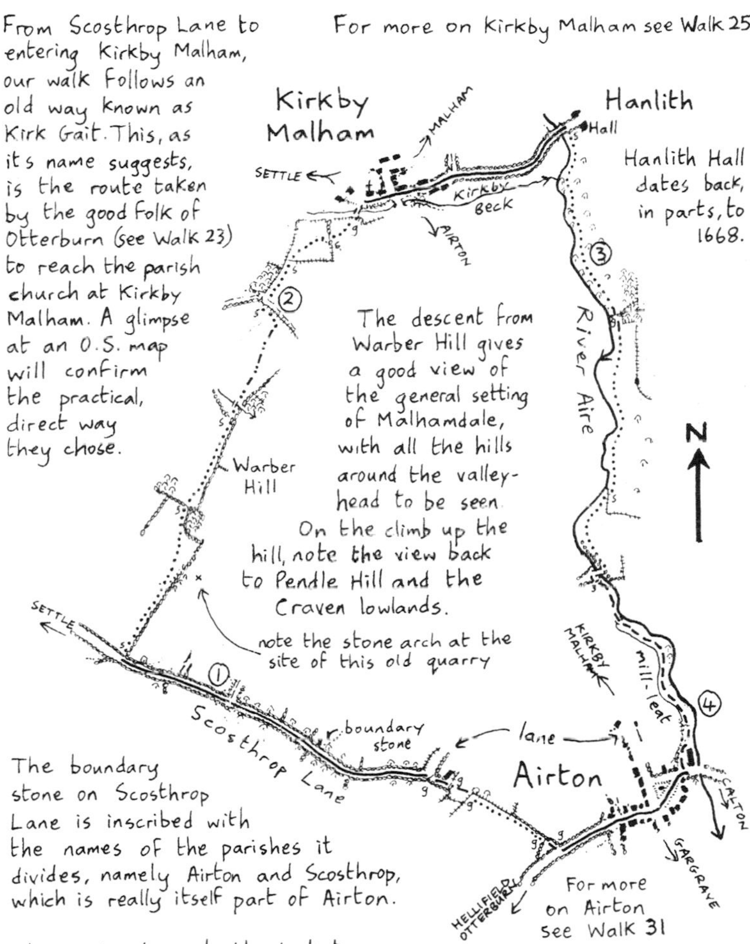
Kirkby Malham
Hanlith
Hall
MALHAM
SETTLE
Kirkby Beck
AIRTON
River Aire
N
Warber Hill
SETTLE
Scosthrop Lane
boundary stone
lane
Airton
mill-leat
KIRKBY MALHAM
CALTON
GARGRAVE
HELLIFIELD OTTERBURN
1
2
3
4

Hanlith Hall dates back, in parts, to 1668.

The descent from Warber Hill gives a good view of the general setting of Malhamdale, with all the hills around the valley-head to be seen. On the climb up the hill, note the view back to Pendle Hill and the Craven lowlands.

note the stone arch at the site of this old quarry

The boundary stone on Scosthrop Lane is inscribed with the names of the parishes it divides, namely Airton and Scosthrop, which is really itself part of Airton.

For more on Airton see Walk 31

The walk alongside the leat to Airton Mill is an interesting mini-history trail. The imposing mill, which once spun cotton, is well-preserved as individual flats.

WALK 21

CROOKRISE CRAG TOP

8½ miles

from Embsay

looking north-east

Crookrise Crag Top
Embsay Moor
Embsay Reservoir
Embsay

A sharp contrast between moorland and field-paths. The scenery on the outward leg is simply superb

Use the car-park at the top end of the village, just past the Elm Tree Inn

THE WALK

From the car-park return to Elm Tree Square and leave the main road by continuing along Pasture Road, which after passing a mill and its old pond climbs to the dam of Embsay Reservoir. On approaching the reservoir it becomes a rough track, passing along the edge of the water (not across the dam). At the end it's confining walls break away and a stile gives access to the open moor. From it keep left on a path which meets another from the farm across to the left before accompanying the wall uphill. Staying near the wall the path further improves and passes through some characterful bouldery scenery before levelling out. Soon a stile in the wall is reached: use it to attain the top of the cliffs of Crookrise, a breathtaking moment. Now confined in the narrow space between the steep drop and the wall, continue northward, straight towards the white trig. point which soon comes into sight. At 1361 feet, this is Crookrise Crag Top.

After surveying the extensive panorama, take the stile there to return to the moorland side of the wall, and once again continue northward. On reaching Hellifield Crags (the second and much more substantial rock outcrops met) the steep drop to Waterfall Gill is encountered. The worst of this is avoided as a sketchy path slopes across to the right, past the lower boulders of Hellifield Crags to meet the beck without having lost too much height. Just before reaching the beck a fine waterfall should be seen from up above: don't miss it. Once across, accompany the crumbling wall as it climbs the bank, the gradient soon eases and the wall eventually leads to a gateway where the Rylstone - Bolton Abbey track passes through. Our route takes advantage of this way, and we turn through the gateway to follow it down the fell. After two gates a small plantation is reached: here the right-of-way forks left of the trees, leaving the main track. Both however join the same enclosed track at the foot of the pasture.

Turn left along this pleasant by-way and on reaching a gate continue alongside the remaining wall, doing similar when the wall switches to our right at the next gate. At the far end a walled track is again joined but after another gate it swings right to approach Sandy Beck Bar along a modest avenue of trees. From the gate there the track passes the large house to join the Skipton to Grassington road. A short mile of road-walking in the Skipton direction is unfortunalely the low-spot of this walk as this tends to be one of the busier of 'B'-class roads. The first building we meet is None-Go-Bye Farm, and with sighs of relief turn down the track just past it.

This track heads down the field away from the farm. Keep straight on past a barn on the left, rising up to meet the railway line. Once across, leave the track and bear right to a wall-stile just above the line. Cross a tiny stream and along to another stile just short of the wall corner. Advance along the narrowing field, with a stile at the end, by the railway. Just ahead is a gate, from where cross the field (collapsed wall midway) to arrive at Hagg Farm. Pass between the buildings and into the field beyond, to locate a stile in the very far top corner.

Our way is now straightforward, for although pathless we simply accompany the wall on the left through numerous pastures with stiles or gates in between, but always remaining on the same contour. On reaching Oddacres Farm the buildings are avoided by a gate in the wall to the right. Continuing on, the cluster of farm buildings at Hill Top are next encountered. A stile by a blocked gate leads into the yard: go straight on to a gate ahead, then drop to a footbridge which leads back onto the lane to Embsay Reservoir. A right-turn takes us back into the village.

21

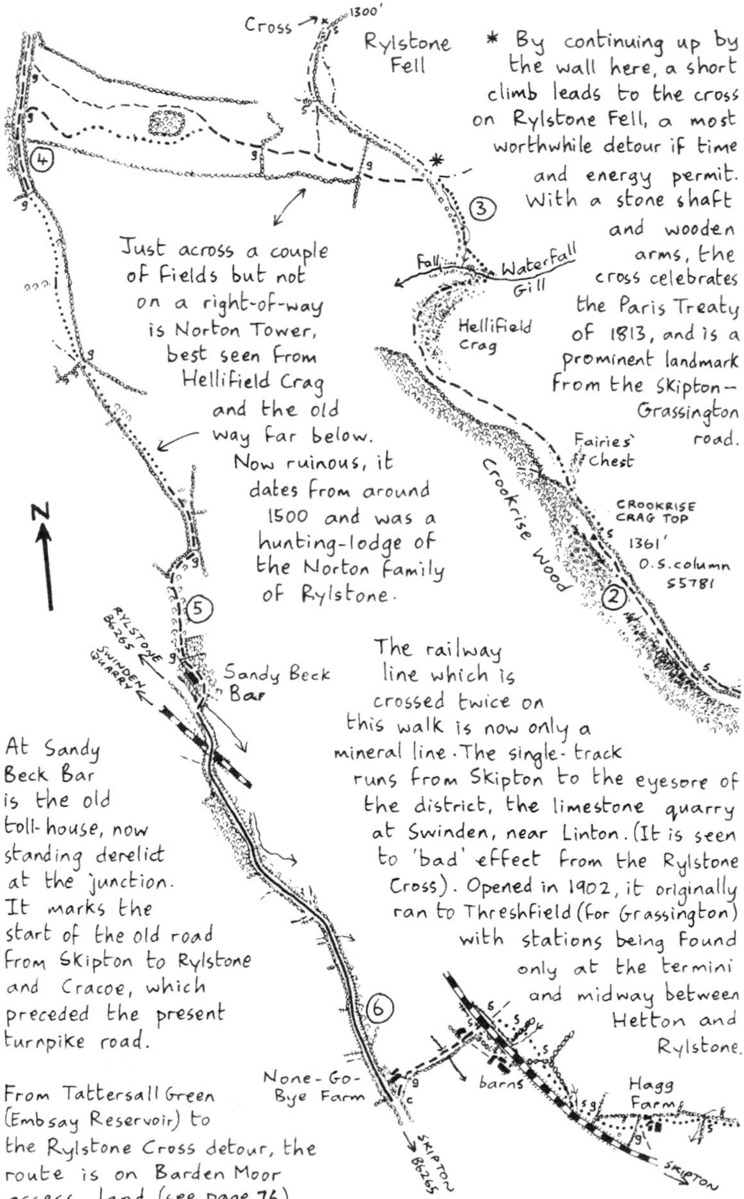

* By continuing up by the wall here, a short climb leads to the cross on Rylstone Fell, a most worthwhile detour if time and energy permit. With a stone shaft and wooden arms, the cross celebrates the Paris Treaty of 1813, and is a prominent landmark from the Skipton–Grassington road.

Just across a couple of fields but not on a right-of-way is Norton Tower, best seen from Hellifield Crag and the old way far below. Now ruinous, it dates from around 1500 and was a hunting-lodge of the Norton family of Rylstone.

The railway line which is crossed twice on this walk is now only a mineral line. The single-track runs from Skipton to the eyesore of the district, the limestone quarry at Swinden, near Linton. (It is seen to 'bad' effect from the Rylstone Cross). Opened in 1902, it originally ran to Threshfield (for Grassington) with stations being found only at the termini and midway between Hetton and Rylstone.

At Sandy Beck Bar is the old toll-house, now standing derelict at the junction. It marks the start of the old road from Skipton to Rylstone and Cracoe, which preceded the present turnpike road.

From Tattersall Green (Embsay Reservoir) to the Rylstone Cross detour, the route is on Barden Moor access land (see page 76).

Looking west from Crookrise Crags

In the middle distance is Flasby Fell, with Sharp Haw and Rough Haw to the left. In the background are the slopes rising to Rye Loaf Hill and Kirkby Fell.

The vast expanse of heather-clad upland known as Barden Moor comes to an abrupt halt at many places around its rim, but nowhere as dramatic as Crookrise, where a long line of crags fall steeply to an un-natural green carpet. In between are a tumble of millstone-grit boulders, and this whole scene forms a splendid sight for travellers on the road between Skipton and Rylstone. The crags are substantial enough to be used by rock-climbers.

N

Tattersall Green

Embsay Reservoir

The reservoir has a fine setting under Embsay Crag and the moor behind. Its facilities are shared by the Craven Sailing Club and the Skipton Angling Association.

Embsay

car park

Inn

EASTBY

SKIPTON

Oddacres Farm

this attractive mill-pond is popular with ducks and swans. Note the house opposite with a 1665 date-stone.

WALK 22

PIKEDAW AND NAPPA CROSS

5½ miles

From Malham

A superb hill-walk, avoiding the crowds and giving fine views

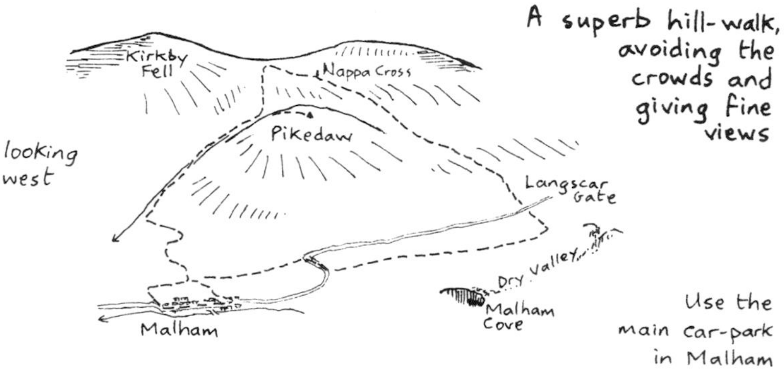
Kirkby Fell
Nappa Cross
Pikedaw
looking west
Langscar Gate
Dry valley
Malham Cove
Malham

Use the main car-park in Malham

THE WALK

From the car-park entrance do not join the road into the village, but turn up the walled track on the right, then right again almost immediately on a similar track. Ignore the first branch left (opposite a barn) and carry on to take the next track climbing to the left. On levelling out it forks, and our way lies to the left, with Kirkby Fell and Pikedaw Hill rising steeply ahead. At the fourth barn on the left leave the track by a stile on the right, and head across the field to a prominent barn. From the stile by it head up the field, keeping above the beck to reach a stile at the top. Above it continue on the same line, crossing the tiny beck where a broken wall comes in on the right. A sketchy path materialises and stays fairly close to the beck to arrive at a stile in the wall ahead.

From this point (or just a little earlier) the top of Pikedaw Hill can be gained by a short steep pull up to the right, the top being crowned by a substantial cairn. Steps must be retraced to the stile to resume the walk, which involves a loss of height to which there is no alternative. From the stile head straight up the hillside in front, passing by a marker-post confirming the way. At the top of a steep climb the gradient eases alongside an interesting-looking cave, and the path, now clearer, heads away in the same direction. Swinging round to the right, the path crosses a limestone pavement to meet a wider path at a signpost. Head to the left to climb gently to Nappa Gate, passing an old shaft on the way. The gate marks the high point of the walk.

After the gate leave the path and turn right on a lesser one, passing Nappa Cross and sloping across to a gate. Two further gates are encountered as the path makes its way down the fell, soon reaching a gate in a corner, and then descending a pasture to meet the lane out of the village at Langscar Gate. Cross straight over to another gate and head down the field: when a stile appears in front, turn sharp right to reach a prominent stile in the wall there. The path, though sketchy, is reasonably easy to follow as it runs roughly parallel with the road up to the right.

After crossing an intervening collapsed wall, two further ones are crossed by stiles, from where an improved path leads to two more in very quick succession. Malham Cove is now just across to the left, but our way continues, sketchily again, to two more neighbouring stiles, the latter returning us onto the lane. Turn uphill for a short distance to a sharp bend, and here take a gate on the left: a track heads down to a gate where it becomes enclosed by walls to lead in pleasant fashion back past an earlier junction and down to a T-junction. To include the village at the finish, turn left here and almost immediately right to land in the village opposite Beck Hall. A right turn will lead back to the car-park.

above: the cairn on Pikedaw, looking to Kirkby Fell

left: Nappa Cross, looking to Malham Tarn

Nappa Cross is one of several way-side crosses in the area, a guide-post for travellers since monastic times. Set into the wall, the restored shaft stands in its original base.

All three of the ways encountered on this west side of Malham are historic routes bound for the Settle district.

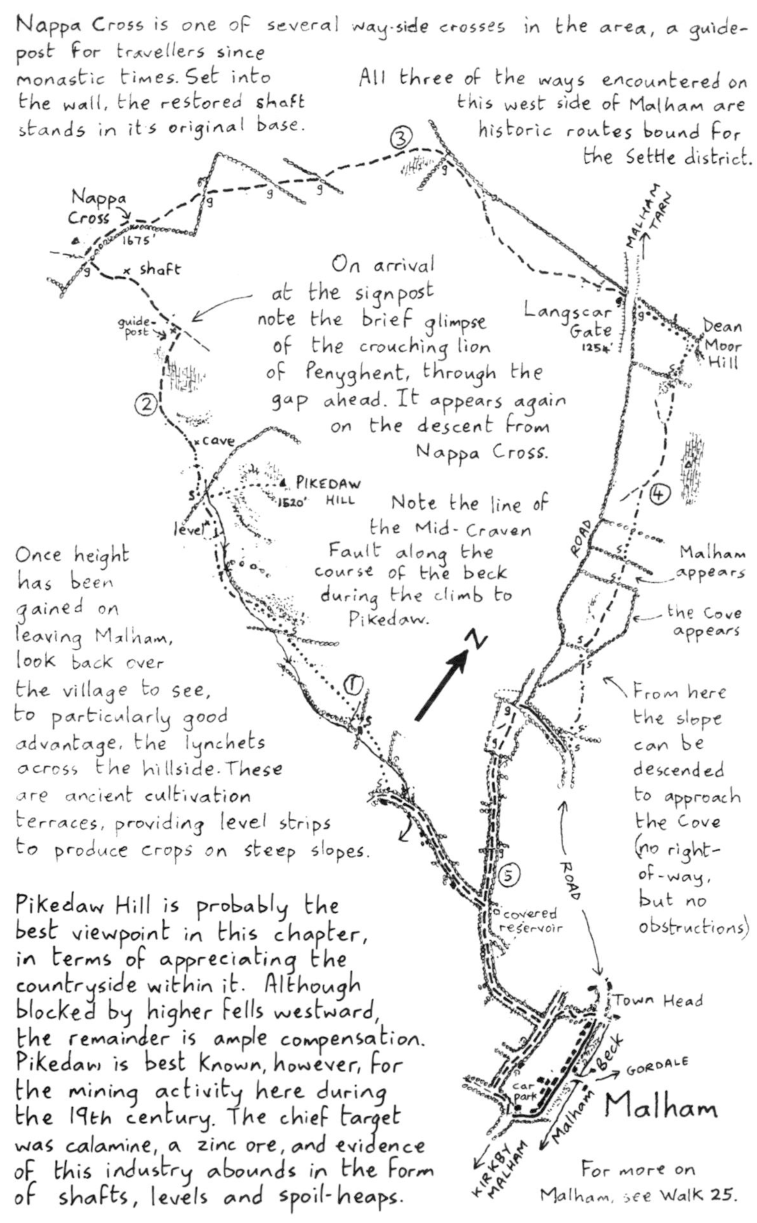
Nappa Cross
1675'
shaft
guide-post
cave
PIKEDAW HILL
1520'
level
Langscar Gate
1254'
MALHAM TARN
Dean Moor Hill
ROAD
Malham appears
the Cove appears
covered reservoir
Town Head
Beck
GORDALE
car park
Malham
KIRKBY MALHAM
Malham

On arrival at the signpost note the brief glimpse of the crouching lion of Penyghent, through the gap ahead. It appears again on the descent from Nappa Cross.

Note the line of the Mid-Craven Fault along the course of the beck during the climb to Pikedaw.

Once height has been gained on leaving Malham, look back over the village to see, to particularly good advantage, the lynchets across the hillside. These are ancient cultivation terraces, providing level strips to produce crops on steep slopes.

From here the slope can be descended to approach the Cove (no right-of-way, but no obstructions)

Pikedaw Hill is probably the best viewpoint in this chapter, in terms of appreciating the countryside within it. Although blocked by higher fells westward, the remainder is ample compensation. Pikedaw is best known, however, for the mining activity here during the 19th century. The chief target was calamine, a zinc ore, and evidence of this industry abounds in the form of shafts, levels and spoil-heaps.

For more on Malham, see Walk 25.

WALK 23 **OTTERBURN MOOR**

5½ miles from Otterburn

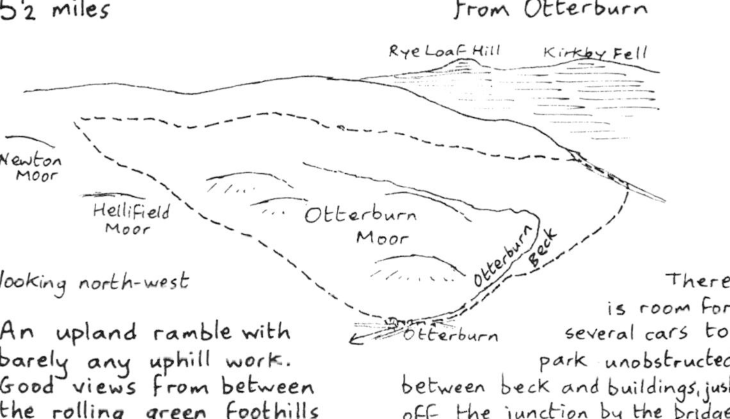
Rye Loaf Hill
Kirkby Fell
Newton Moor
Hellifield Moor
Otterburn Moor
Otterburn Beck
Otterburn
looking north-west

An upland ramble with barely any uphill work. Good views from between the rolling green foothills

There is room for several cars to park unobstructed between beck and buildings, just off the junction by the bridge

THE WALK

Leave the junction by the bridge along the unsignposted lane between Otterburn Beck and farm buildings. Almost immediately it becomes a wide track, and beyond a gate it runs free alongside the beck. On approaching another gate, leave the track by a gate on the right, and from it head half-left across the field to pick up a track rising towards a line of trees. From there head across to the top side of the wood in front, then accompany its upper boundary to a gate. Head straight across the field to a stile in the far corner, ignoring a neighbouring stile in the right-hand wall. Follow this wall away in the same direction as before, and when it parts company continue over the brow of the field: pick out a stile in the wall ahead, bearing left towards it to emerge onto Scosthrop Lane.

Turn left up this pleasant lane only as far as a walled farm-road striking off to the left. Head along its undulating course, which leads unerringly to Orms Gill Green, passing around the back of the farm buildings and continuing up the slope beyond. At the second cattle-grid after the farm the track becomes completely unenclosed, and after this grid leave it by heading half-left across the extensive open pasture. Aim for the bottom of the band of trees that appear ahead: as we near them Otterburn Beck appears down to the left, and where these two features meet, a stile will be found in the very corner. From it the beck is crossed

to an isolated signpost at a crossroads of footpaths: opt for the one climbing the slope behind. At the top it peters out, but continue on a sheep-trod past a wall-corner and then slope down to a stile in the wall ahead. This is one of the two walls enclosing the green road of Langber Lane.

Turn left along this wide by-way, all the way to its unfortunate demise when the right-hand wall parts company. Cross the stile and remain faithful to the left-hand wall, taking in another stile in a fence before arriving at a gate by a wall-junction. On the other side a track is picked up leading from the small building on the left, and it takes us down through the pasture to a gate. Here it disappears, but resumes its journey from the gate at the bottom of this field. Now entering a plantation the track continues without problem through the trees, emerging as a wide enclosed track known as Dacre Lane to descend very gently into Otterburn. On reaching the road turn left to round a corner to return to the junction by the bridge.

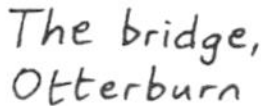

The bridge, Otterburn

The old kiln, Orms Gill Green

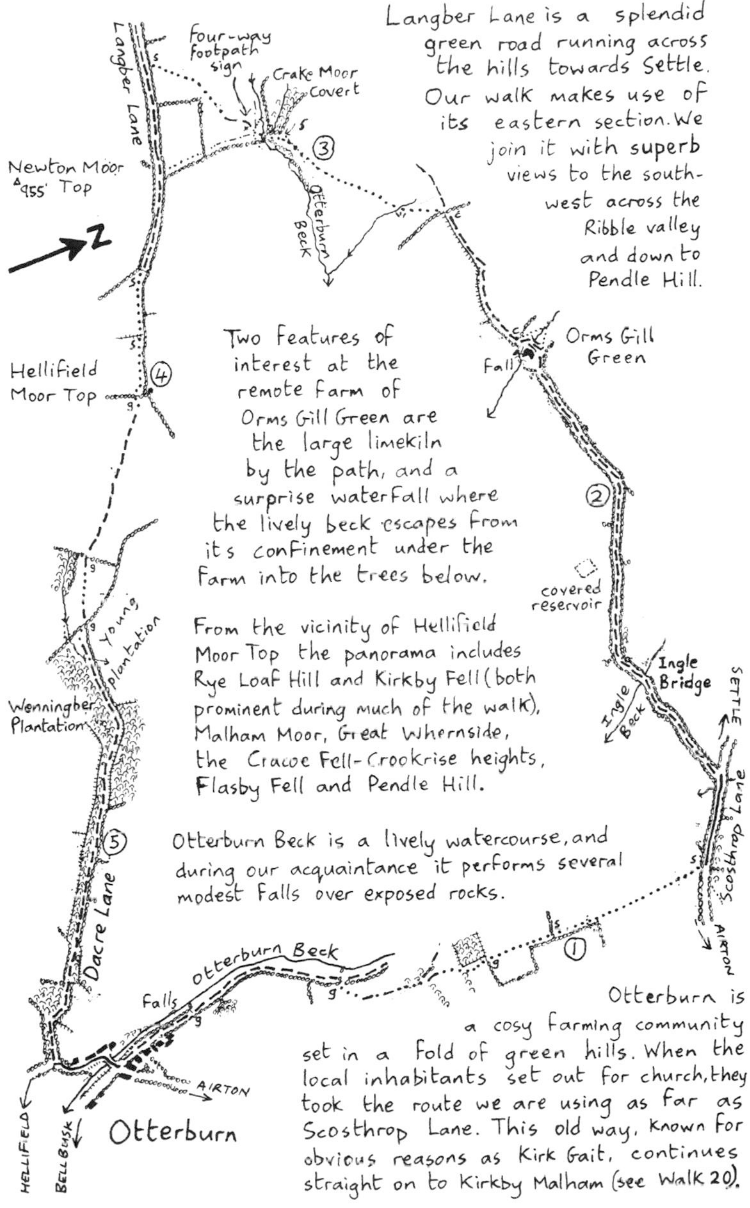
Langber Lane
Four-way footpath sign
Crake Moor Covert
3
Newton Moor Top
955'
N
Otterburn Beck
Orms Gill Green
Fall
Hellifield Moor Top
4
2
covered reservoir
Young plantation
Wenningber Plantation
Ingle Bridge
Ingle Beck
SETTLE
Scosthrop Lane
5
Dacre Lane
1
AIRTON
Otterburn Beck
Falls
AIRTON
HELLIFIELD
BELL BUSK
Otterburn

Langber Lane is a splendid green road running across the hills towards Settle. Our walk makes use of its eastern section. We join it with superb views to the south-west across the Ribble valley and down to Pendle Hill.

Two features of interest at the remote farm of Orms Gill Green are the large limekiln by the path, and a surprise waterfall where the lively beck escapes from its confinement under the farm into the trees below.

From the vicinity of Hellifield Moor Top the panorama includes Rye Loaf Hill and Kirkby Fell (both prominent during much of the walk), Malham Moor, Great Whernside, the Cracoe Fell-Crookrise heights, Flasby Fell and Pendle Hill.

Otterburn Beck is a lively watercourse, and during our acquaintance it performs several modest falls over exposed rocks.

Otterburn is a cosy farming community set in a fold of green hills. When the local inhabitants set out for church, they took the route we are using as far as Scosthrop Lane. This old way, known for obvious reasons as Kirk Gait, continues straight on to Kirkby Malham (see Walk 20).

24

WALK 24

EMBSAY CRAG

3½ miles

from Embsay

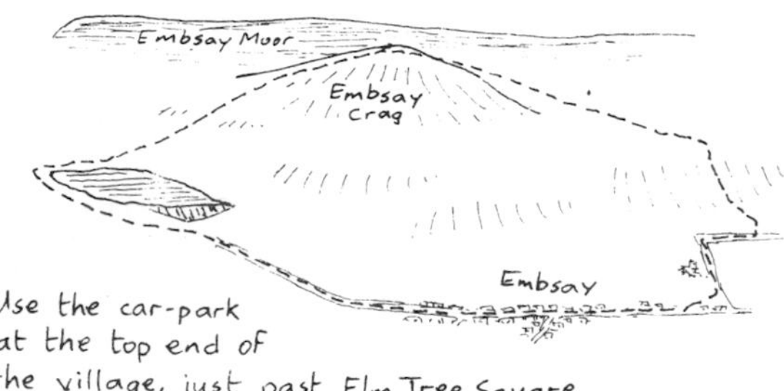
Embsay Moor
Embsay Crag
Embsay

looking north

A lively circuit, taking in a grand hill with a surprise view

Use the car-park at the top end of the village, just past Elm Tree Square.

THE WALK

Leave the car-park not by its entrance, but by a stile opposite it, and climb up the field half-right to another stile. An enclosed path leads away to a stile from where a large field is crossed, bearing a little left to emerge onto a lane via a small gate. Turn to the left up this lane, past the church to a sharp bend, and 50 yards beyond, leave it by a farm-road rising up between the houses. It rises to the farm-entrance, whereupon we go straight forward to a stile to maintain the uphill plod to a gate. Above it the path peters out, but continue up to a gate at the top-left corner to gain access to the open moor.

Take the path along to the left, which soon leaves the wall to rise towards the striking profile of Embsay Crag. As the ground steepens the path keeps above the increasing tumble of rocks to rise pleasantly to the highest point of the Crag, a location which is not in doubt. The main path can clearly be seen descending the steepest section directly below, and is well-blazed through the bracken beyond. A much nicer way down, however, is to follow a very sketchy path along the brink of the rocks across to the right: this descends in similar fashion to our route of ascent, and after exchanging the heather for bracken another path is met. Turn left along it to join up with the main path down from the Crag. This path leads unerringly down to a footbridge by the head of the reservoir, having earlier passed a left fork which takes in the old quarry (see map).

From the footbridge avoid boggy ground by bearing half-right to join a wide track, which followed to the left leads to a stile ushering us from the open moor. Turn left along the farm-track down the side of the reservoir and onto a lane which leads all the way down into Embsay, emerging into Elm Tree Square.

Embsay Crag is a notable landmark in the Skipton area of upper Airedale, jutting out as it does from the vast expanse of moorland. A rich cloak of bracken covers the lower slopes, while a delectable carpet of heather crowns the top. The 'Crag' is actually a tumble of modest crags and large boulders heaped together in wonderful chaos on the southern slopes of the hill.

This is gritstone country at its best, and the highest rocks are a perfect location for a long, lazy break on a hot summer's day, with the reservoir shimmering far below our airy vantage point.

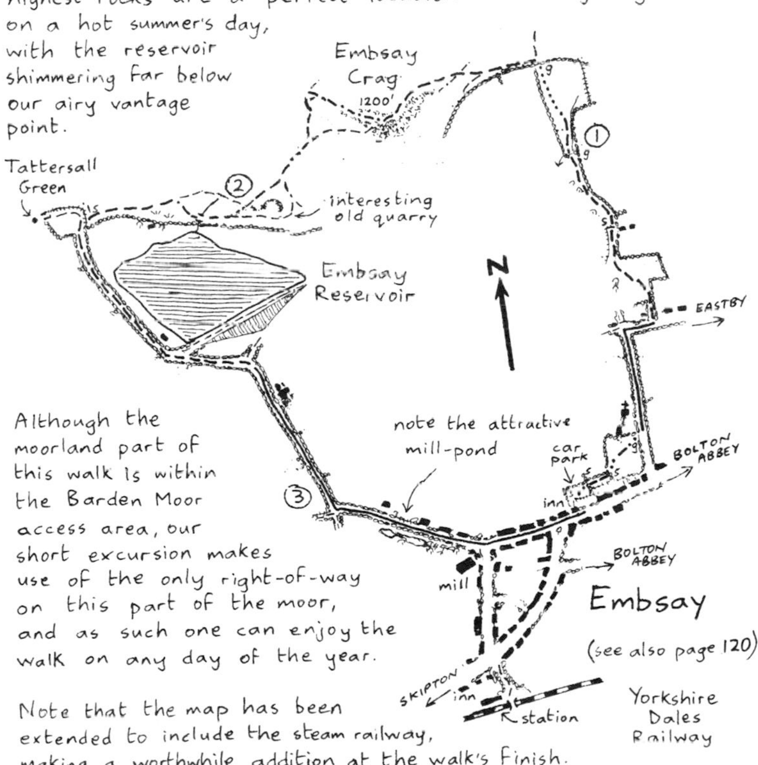
Embsay Crag
1200'
1
2
3
Tattersall Green
interesting old quarry
Embsay Reservoir
N
EASTBY
note the attractive mill-pond
car park
inn
BOLTON ABBEY
BOLTON ABBEY
mill
Embsay
(see also page 120)
SKIPTON
inn
station
Yorkshire Dales Railway

Although the moorland part of this walk is within the Barden Moor access area, our short excursion makes use of the only right-of-way on this part of the moor, and as such one can enjoy the walk on any day of the year.

Note that the map has been extended to include the steam railway, making a worthwhile addition at the walk's finish.

WALK 25 — ACRAPLATTS AND AIRE HEAD

3¾ miles — from Kirkby Malham

A perfect combination of upland views and valley features

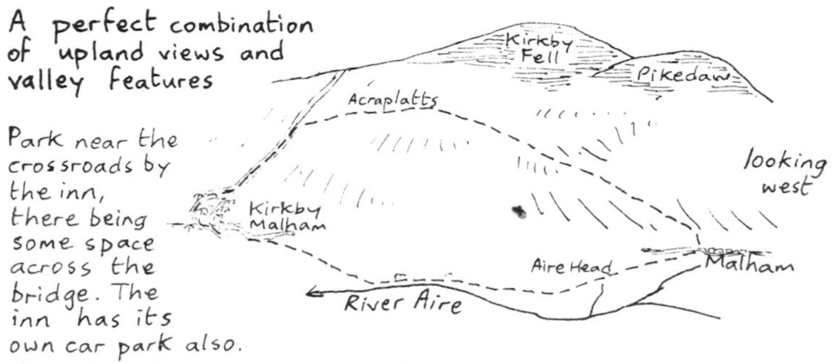
Kirkby Fell
Pikedaw
Acraplatts
looking west
Kirkby Malham
Aire Head
Malham
River Aire

Park near the crossroads by the inn, there being some space across the bridge. The inn has its own car park also.

An alternative would be to start the walk from Malham.

THE WALK

From the crossroads by the bridge head up the back lane past the inn and church and round to a T-junction. Turn up the lane to the left, gaining height rapidly and passing a farm-road to New Close before reaching the track forking right to Acraplatts. Follow it over a cattle-grid, and just past it take a stile on the right. Descend the field to another stile, then pass a ruined barn to a tiny footbridge over Tranlands Beck. From it head across the field without losing height, to be deflected left by a wall to a stile by another tiny beck. From it slope up gently across the field to another stile, then follow a wall on the right to drop down through two more stiles and through a larger field to a gate. Behind it is an enclosed track which leads all the way down into Malham village, emerging next to the car-park.

Turn left towards the village, but as the road meets the beck take a stile into a field on the right. With a wall separating us, follow the beck downstream, crossing a stile, then Tranlands Beck (again), and another stile. As the beck swings away to the left, continue straight ahead to arrive at the emerging waters of Aire Head Springs. From the stile just beyond continue alongside a wall: the next stile returns us nearer the river, by now having merged with the beck. An improving path now leads above a former mill-pond, whose leat leads to the former mill. Pass round the top side of it to its entrance gate. Instead of following the drive away, take the grass rake sloping to the right up to a stile, then head half-right to another and straight on to the next one. This stile is just next to the lane as it enters Kirkby Malham, and it takes us into a field to walk parallel with the lane to join it at a gate. Turn left along the lane to return to the village centre.

Aire Head Springs is the point of re-emergence of the beck that last saw the light of day at Water Sinks high on the moor (see Walk 18). It is not therefore the source of the Aire but it *is* certainly the first naming of the River Aire. Almost immediately after its resurgence (which after heavy rain becomes one mighty spring) the water joins with the newly-merged Malham and Gordale Becks to flow in unison as the Aire.

From the vicinity of Acraplatts the prospect of the rugged Pikedaw is particularly impressive.

Good view to the Cove

'In memory of William Wilkinson of Keighley, who loved the Dales'

The extensive mill-pond below Aire Head remains in good condition, as does the leat which we follow to the former manorial mill. This is now well-maintained as a dwelling.

This track gives an alternative return into Kirkby Malham via Hanlith Bridge.

Easily missed, this old milestone is inscribed thus: 'To Settle 5 miles'

Once height is gained on the climb out of Kirkby Malham, the view across to the vale of Malham provides an excellent insight into the topography of the area, with Kirkby Fell and Weets Top guarding each side of the valley, and Malham, the Cove and the heights of the Moor in between.

Kirkby Malham is, ecclesiastically at least, the main village of Malhamdale, although most visitors to the valley drive through almost without notice on their way to the tourist mecca of Malham. This tiny village is however worth a brief exploration, and not surprisingly the parish church is of most interest. Dedicated to St. Michael the Archangel, this highly attractive building dates from the 15th century and was restored a century ago, thanks mainly to Walter Morrison of Malham Tarn House: his memorial can be seen in the church. Also of note are a Norman font and a 16th century German window. Oliver Cromwell is reputed to have signed the register as witnessing a marriage during his stay in the district in the Civil War.

In the churchyard is an ancient preaching cross, and near the lych-gate are the former village stocks. The church is sandwiched by two other buildings of note, namely the inn at the bridge-end and the Old Hall just up the lane. Running alongside is Kirkby Beck, which joins the Aire a good quarter-mile from the village.

Monk Bridge, Malham

Malham is an attractive village whose appeal is very different to that of most other Dales villages, in that the *majority* of its visitors come to walk, even though for most it's simply a return trip to the Cove. The village itself does however have much of interest, both old and new. A good number of cottages date from the 17th and early 18th centuries, and form several attractive groups.

In monastic times the land hereabouts was shared between Bolton Priory and Fountains Abbey, and reminders of their granges here are found in the naming of two of the numerous bridges over Malham Beck which divides the village in two. Monk Bridge was once a packhorse bridge, now widened to form the road bridge, while Prior Moon's Bridge is the highest of the several clapper-bridges. Both the inns are centrally placed along with two modern purpose-built structures, namely the youth hostel and the National Park Information Centre.

WALK 26 BORDLEY AND THRESHFIELD MOOR

7½ miles

from Boss Moor

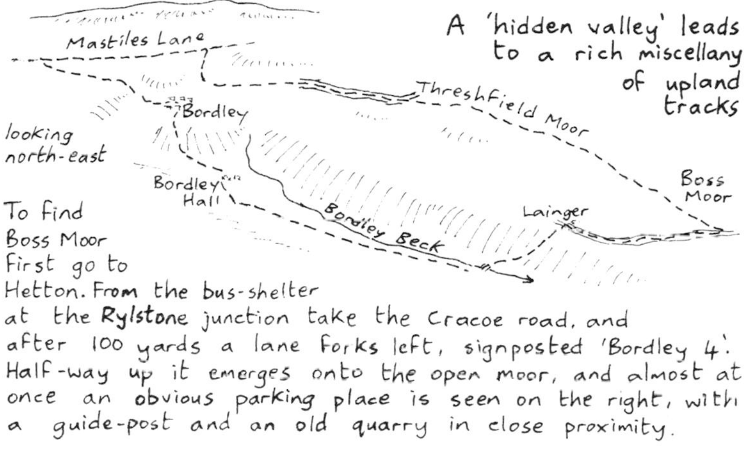
Mastiles Lane
Bordley
Threshfield Moor
looking north-east
Bordley Hall
Bordley Beck
Lainger
Boss Moor

A 'hidden valley' leads to a rich miscellany of upland tracks

To find Boss Moor first go to Hetton. From the bus-shelter at the **Rylstone** junction take the Cracoe road, and after 100 yards a lane forks left, signposted 'Bordley 4'. Half-way up it emerges onto the open moor, and almost at once an obvious parking place is seen on the right, with a guide-post and an old quarry in close proximity.

THE WALK

Before even starting, take a glance over the wall for a most complete view of Winterburn Reservoir, with Pendle Hill directly behind. The walk commences with a gentle stroll along the lane towards Bordley, as far as the phone box and farm at Lainger. Here leave the lane by the farm-track down to the left, accompanying a beck to cross the main beck in the valley bottom. Take a stile on the right to follow Bordley Beck upstream, over another stile and then across to a gate to the left of a small group of trees. From it head over the reedy brow of the field, now high above the beck. Keep straight on, dropping down to be deflected left by an inflowing side-stream. From the ladder-stile behind it, head away with the wall on the right. An incoming farm track is joined to lead unerringly along to approach Bordley Hall.

The track turns right to a gate to enter a field behind the farm. Advance the short way to a guidepost, leaving it to climb the path-less field to a gate. In the large field behind, a gate appears in the top wall. With the gradient easing, head half-right to locate a hidden stile in the corner. From it a farm-track is joined to

head through two gates to Bordley. Turn left in the hamlet on the track to the top corner, and a good track heads away from the gate. In a few yards take a lesser track right, rising gently and becoming less clear before it joins Mastiles Lane at a crumbling gateway. Follow it to the right: beyond a gate its less-clear course hugs the left wall to become enclosed again at Mastiles Gate. Here we sadly leave the lane by turning right on a faint track through a hollow, to arrive at a crossroads of ways marked by a guidepost. Turn left, through a gateway and up the tarmac arm.

As this lane levels out, branch across to the right to peer over the wall at the stone circle. The wall can then be followed left to rejoin the lane as it becomes enclosed. This quiet way is **trodden** for a long half-mile, to the point where guideposts indicate a junction with a bridle-path. From the gate on the right a string of posts guide us along a sketchy level track. At another gate we descend more clearly past a barn and along an enclosed way to a gate at the far end. From it a track heads right, crossing a small beck to head across the open moor, again with marker-posts assisting. On reaching a wall, a pleasant walled green track leads to the next section of moor, but here we remain with the right-hand wall as far as a gate. This leads onto Boss Moor, positively the last lap.

across ↗

↙ continued

A good track heads diagonally away from the gate, and with the Bordley lane soon in view, our track avoids it until reaching the old quarries and all being well, the car.

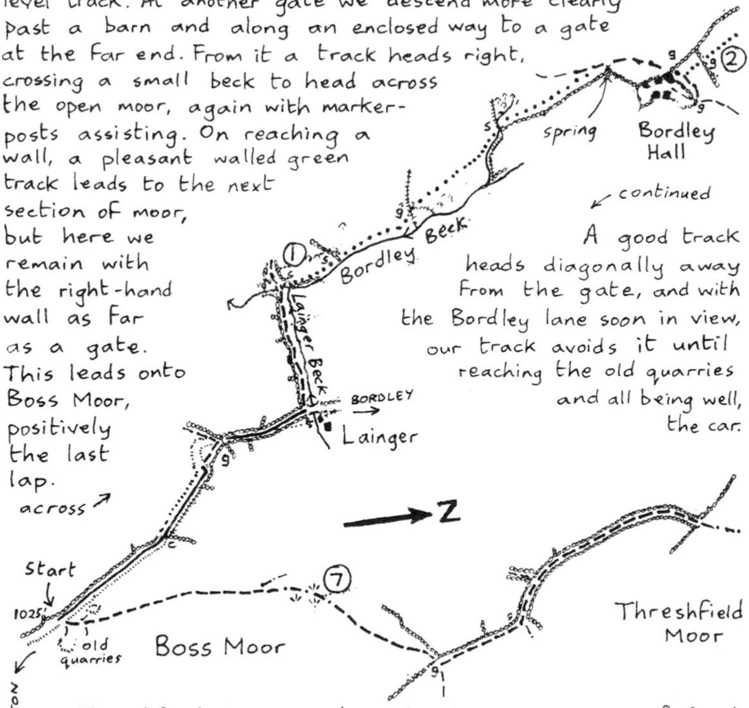

Threshfield Moor provides extensive views, notably of Great Whernside (north) and the Cracoe and Flasby fells (south).

Bordley is a tiny farming hamlet standing at a breezy 1100 feet above sea-level. Its remoteness is stressed by the fact that several lanes head towards it, but none actually reach it as public roads. The solid stone buildings are spread around a large green, which is workmanlike rather than picturesque. The hamlet is sheltered from the worst of the weather by virtue of its position in a hollow in the hills.

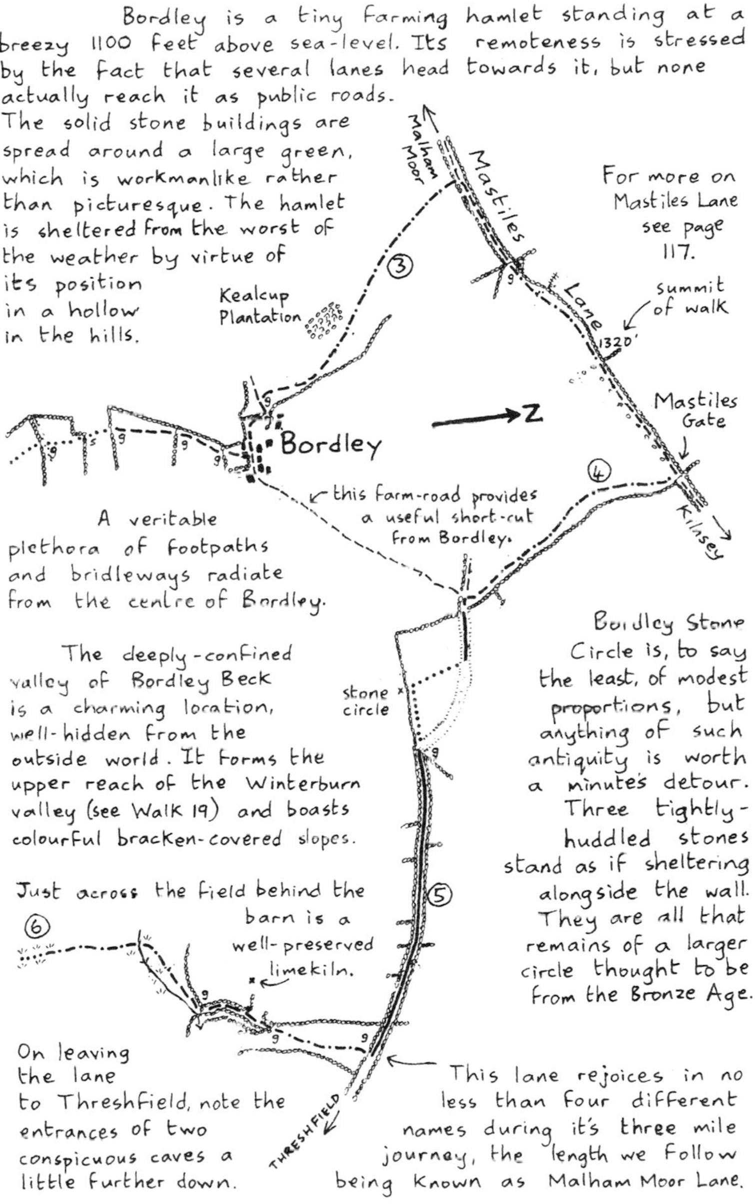
Malham Moor
Mastiles
Lane
For more on Mastiles Lane see page 117.
summit of walk
1320'
Kealcup Plantation
3
Mastiles Gate
Bordley
Z
4
Kilnsey
this farm-road provides a useful short-cut from Bordley.
stone circle
5
6
limekiln.
THRESHFIELD

A veritable plethora of footpaths and bridleways radiate from the centre of Bordley.

The deeply-confined valley of Bordley Beck is a charming location, well-hidden from the outside world. It forms the upper reach of the Winterburn valley (see Walk 19) and boasts colourful bracken-covered slopes.

Bordley Stone Circle is, to say the least, of modest proportions, but anything of such antiquity is worth a minute's detour. Three tightly-huddled stones stand as if sheltering alongside the wall. They are all that remains of a larger circle thought to be from the Bronze Age.

Just across the field behind the barn is a well-preserved limekiln.

On leaving the lane to Threshfield, note the entrances of two conspicuous caves a little further down.

This lane rejoices in no less than four different names during it's three mile journey, the length we follow being known as Malham Moor Lane.

WALK 27

ESHTON AND THE PENNINE WAY

5½ miles

from Gargrave

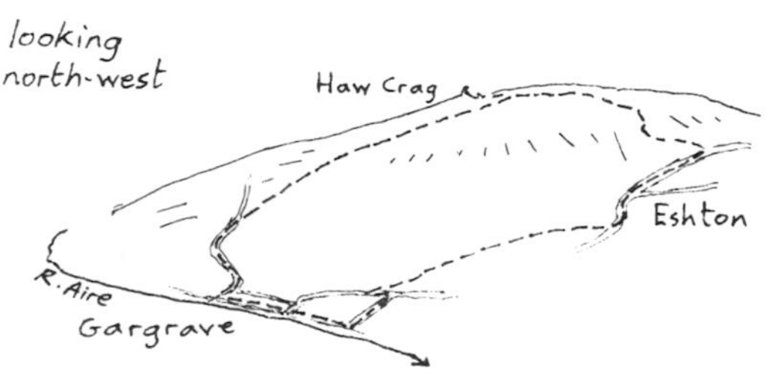
looking north-west
Haw Crag
Eshton
R. Aire
Gargrave

A rural stroll, calling for little effort

Gargrave has ample free car-parking

THE WALK

Leave the main street in Gargrave along West Street, almost opposite the bridge over the Aire, and at the second car-park continue straight ahead over the canal bridge. Ignore any turn-offs and remain on this leafy by-way for a gradual uphill march. Right after the demise of the trees on the right, take a stile into the field on the same side. Remain parallel with the lane for a short distance, then strike across the field, past an old tree stump to a stile. In the next field take the first opportunity to rise to a stile on the left, continuing the climb to the corner of the plantation on Harrows Hill.

A gate in the fence ahead is ignored in favour of a stile a little further to the left, from where one strikes diagonally across the field to another stile. Maintain this course to accompany the field boundary to a gate in the far corner. From it head off diagonally again to arrive at the crossroads marked by a post. For a while now, the white Ordnance column on Haw Crag has been in sight, and as a right-of-way runs through its field a 10-minute detour is worth the effort On returning to the guidepost, continue straight across the field until Throstle Nest Farm appears below. The recently diverted path now avoids it by bearing right, to a ladder-stile on the near side of a small plantation.

From the stile descend to the bottom-right corner, over a solid farm track and head away with the wall. From the stile at the end the farm drive is met, and accompanied out onto a road. Turn right to descend to the junction at Eshton, keeping right until after passing by Eshton Grange a stile is seen on the right. Take it and make for a stile in the fence ahead, then cross the field to another stile. Across the next narrow field a kissing-gate leads into the woods, and a good path heads through trees, passing a large remote dwelling before emerging from near-claustrophobic conditions into a large field. Descend straight down to an iron stile and maintain the same course to a stile to emerge onto the road just past a junction.

Double back to this junction and then turn right as far as the bridge over the canal. Here leave the road to join the towpath, following it along to the right and forsaking it at the next but one bridge encountered. This completes the full circle of the walk, and a left turn along the lane will return us to the car-parks on West Street.

The War Memorial and Main Street, Gargrave

Gargrave is an attractive village and is the best centre for the Craven Dales. Although Skipton is the main centre for the southern Dales, and is only 10 minutes distant by road, Gargrave has a far more intimate Dales atmosphere. The village is split by the busy A65 running through it, and the by-now sizeable Aire runs parallel. Lined by shops, the main street widens into a spacious area by the war memorial, and here a graceful bridge crosses the river to get to the Parish Church. Dedicated to Saint Andrew, it was restored in 1852: the tower, however, dates from the early 16th century.

The Pennine Way passes through the heart of the village, and the two central inns provide appropriately-placed lunchtime breaks for those midway between the youth hostels at Earby and Malham. The Leeds - Liverpool Canal also comes this way, reaching the northernmost point of its 127 miles as it meets, if only briefly, the National Park boundary. The waterway takes advantage of the Aire Gap to squeeze its way through the Pennines. Our mighty backbone also gives its name to the homespun bus firm based in the village, and their orange livery may well be seen threading the lanes hereabouts.

27

Haw Crag is the site of an old quarry, and the trig. point (S 5308) stands atop the steep drop.

Eshton is a scattered community with no defined centre. It has several fine buildings, including Eshton House, by the road junction and the Hall, now a residential home on the road towards Gargrave.

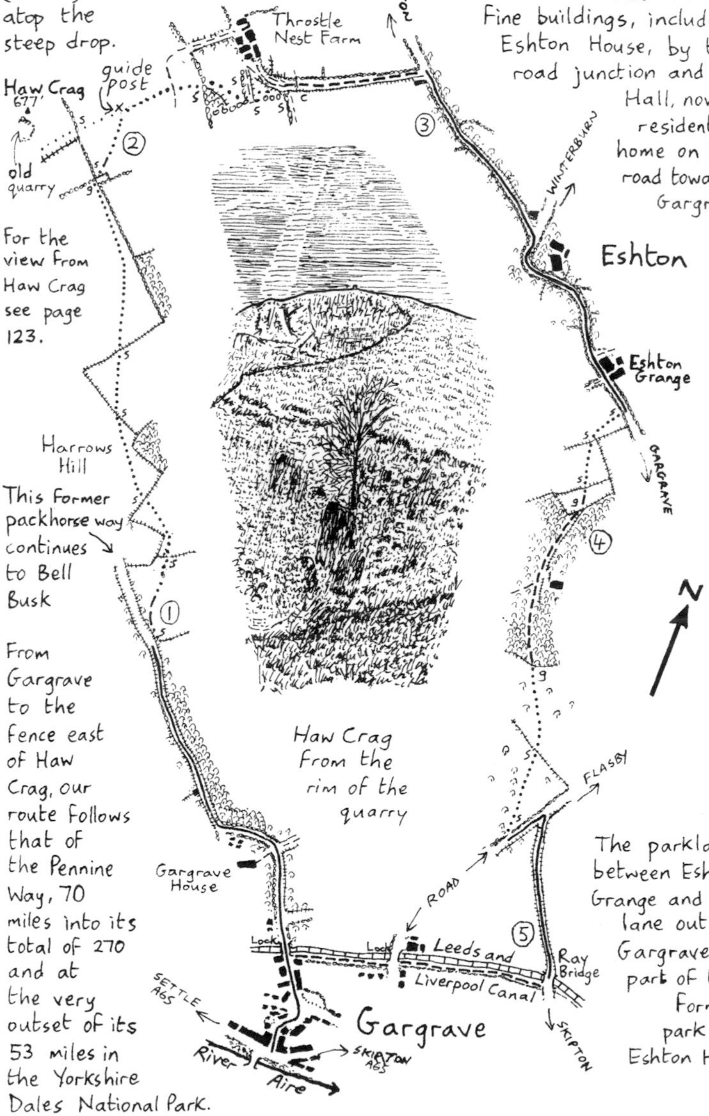

For the view from Haw Crag see page 123.

This former packhorse way continues to Bell Busk

From Gargrave to the fence east of Haw Crag, our route follows that of the Pennine Way, 70 miles into its total of 270 and at the very outset of its 53 miles in the Yorkshire Dales National Park.

Haw Crag from the rim of the quarry

The parkland between Eshton Grange and the lane out of Gargrave is part of the former park of Eshton Hall.

WALK 28

HETTON AND RYLSTONE

$4\frac{3}{4}$ miles

From Flasby

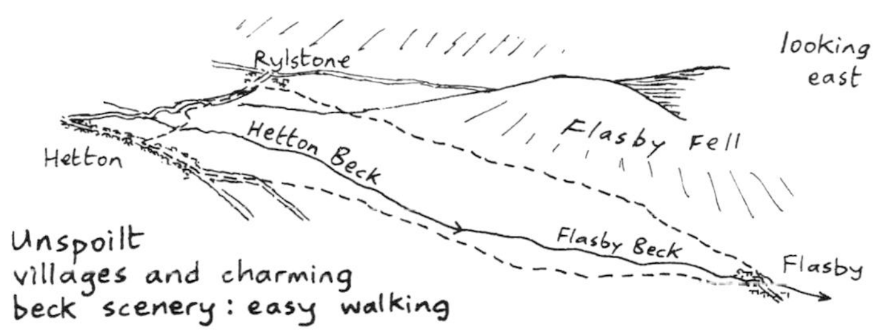
Rylstone
looking east
Hetton Beck
Flasby Fell
Hetton
Flasby Beck
Flasby

Unspoilt villages and charming beck scenery: easy walking

Park in one of the few roadside locations in the hamlet

THE WALK

Flasby stands just off the Gargrave - Hetton road, and a choice of two lanes wind down to it. Head down the dead-end road over the bridge and into the yard of Flasby Hall Farm. Take the track on the left after the last building, and follow it through a gate and around the edge of a field: at the other side keep going to a gate near the far corner. Head away from it alongside a fence on the left, and at the next gate a better track returns to lead straight to the farm of Flasby Moor Side.

Cross the farmyard to the diagonally-opposite corner, and after passing the last building turn right to climb the field to the plantation at the top. A path leads through the narrow strip of trees, and from the other side head away to descend a large field to the initially unseen Calton Gill Beck. From a stile and a footbridge head up the next field to the conspicuous bridge under the railway line. From the other side head half-left to locate a stile at the end of the plantation in front. Head across the bottom of the next field, and at the gate at the far end a track is joined: follow it left at the next gate and then right at a T-junction of enclosed tracks. At the farm buildings at the end, turn left along a lane which curves round to join the road on the edge of Rylstone, which is just up to the right and well worth a look.

Our way turns left, under the railway bridge and then along the track immediately to the left. It soon narrows into a delightful snicket, descending to a footbridge

(a stone slab) over the beck, and then rising between hedges to debouch onto the road through Hetton: the inn is but a few yards to the right. Once again however, our route turns left, and stays left as the road forks: within a minute a stile on the left is reached. Aim half-left across the field to a stile in the wall ahead, and do likewise in the next field, this stile being just above the beck. The beck is followed to the next stile, from where our sketchy path is deflected away by trees: do not return to the beck, but continue across to a stile in the wall ahead, with another shortly after.

Beyond this is a stile in a fence from where a broad 'ridge' descends parallel with the beck to arrive at another stile. Continue across the next field to a stile nearer the beck, beyond which the farm-road to Flasby Moor Side is crossed. From the stile just across it, take a gate almost immediately on the left, but instead of rejoining the beck follow the fence up the slope. When it breaks off to the right continue straight ahead, and a conspicuous mound is followed high above the beck to descend gradually to a barn. Just past it, take a gate almost next to the beck, which is now followed to the next gate. From it bear right across two small enclosures to emerge through a gate back onto the lane in Flasby.

Rylstone is the tiniest of villages, but there is much of interest here. Alongside the main road is the attractive pond, fringed in April by daffodils, and once the village green. Near the church was the home of the Norton family, who took part in 1536 in the Pilgrimage of Grace, and three years later the Rising of the North. Their unfortunate story is recounted by Wordsworth in his 'White Doe of Rylstone'.

The parish church of St. Peter stays prominent even though it hides up a back lane. Rebuilt in 1852, its position is an envious one, gazing across to Rylstone Fell with its cross clearly visible. Look also for the medieval gravestones with crosses.

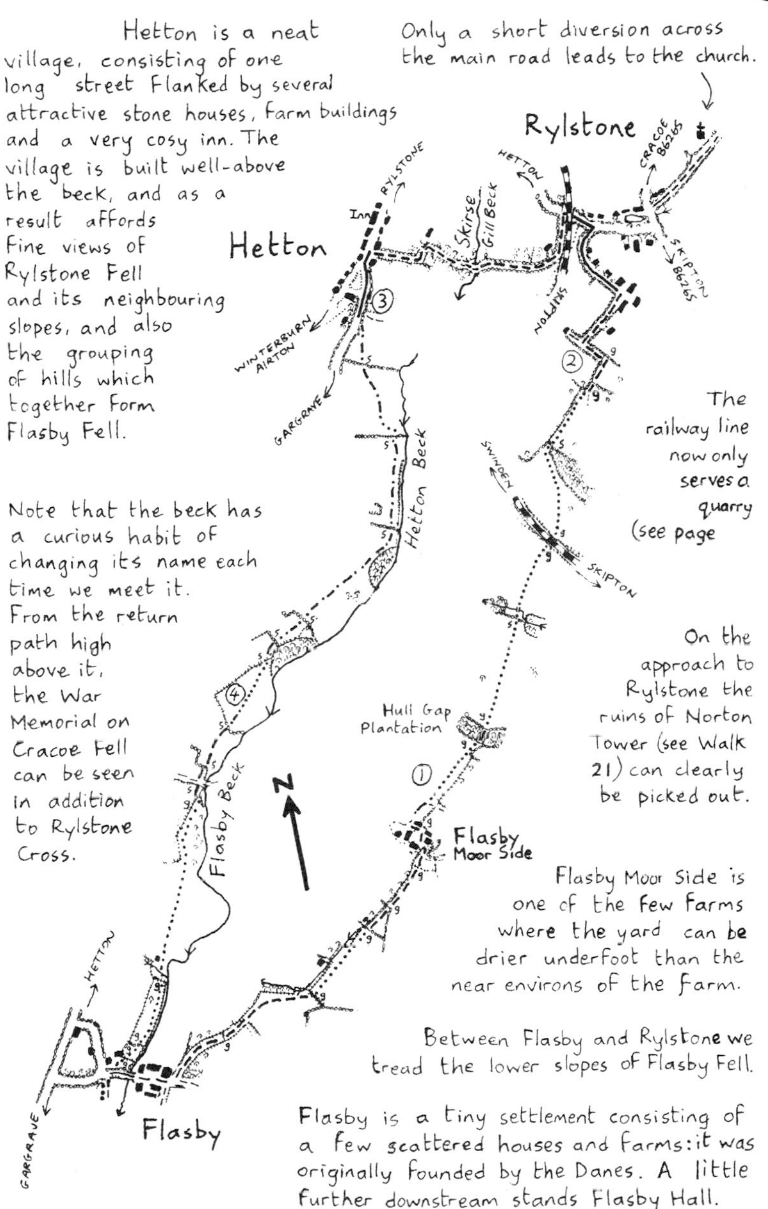
Rylstone
Hetton
Inn
RYLSTONE
HETTON
CRACOE B6265
SKIPTON B6265
SKIPTON
Skirse
Gill Beck
WINTERBURN AIRTON
GARGRAVE
Hetton Beck
SWINDEN
SKIPTON
Hull Gap Plantation
Flasby Moor Side
Flasby Beck
N
HETTON
GARGRAVE
Flasby
1
2
3
4

Hetton is a neat village, consisting of one long street flanked by several attractive stone houses, farm buildings and a very cosy inn. The village is built well-above the beck, and as a result affords fine views of Rylstone Fell and its neighbouring slopes, and also the grouping of hills which together form Flasby Fell.

Only a short diversion across the main road leads to the church.

The railway line now only serves a quarry (see page

Note that the beck has a curious habit of changing its name each time we meet it. From the return path high above it, the War Memorial on Cracoe Fell can be seen in addition to Rylstone Cross.

On the approach to Rylstone the ruins of Norton Tower (see Walk 21) can clearly be picked out.

Flasby Moor Side is one of the few farms where the yard can be drier underfoot than the near environs of the farm.

Between Flasby and Rylstone we tread the lower slopes of Flasby Fell.

Flasby is a tiny settlement consisting of a few scattered houses and farms: it was originally founded by the Danes. A little further downstream stands Flasby Hall.

WALK 29 — GORDALE, MASTILES LANE AND WEETS TOP

9½ miles

from Malham

looking north-east

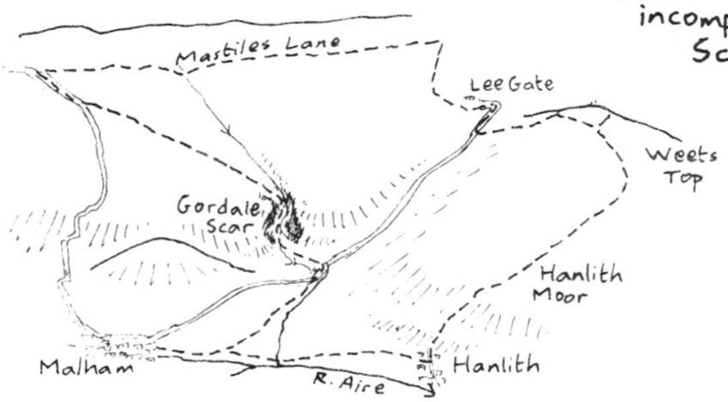

A splendid upland ramble, with the incomparable Gordale Scar only one of many fine features

Use the main car-park in Malham

THE WALK

From the car-park head into the village, crossing the beck by the road-bridge and doubling back to follow the beck downstream. The short lane ends at a stile, from where a good path heads across the fields. After two more stiles the path swings left to a barn, crosses to the left of the wall and continues in the same direction. One stile later Gordale Beck is joined and followed all the way upstream to enter the wooded environs of Janet's Foss. On reaching the waterfall the path breaks off left to emerge onto the road to Gordale. Turn right along it for a short distance, crossing the beck and arriving at a gate on the left just before Gordale House. A well-trodden path heads across the pasture to the unmistakeable cliffs of Gordale Scar, which converge on us as we enter the dark confines.

The way out is by negotiating the rock to the left of the lower falls: it is a straightforward short scramble with plentiful hand-holds, but nevertheless care is necessary (please don't fall on anyone). Having clambered up, the stony path clings to the left side of the gorge, passing the upper falls and breaking out onto green pastures once more. Beyond a stile the path becomes sketchy, but this matters little for the way appears fairly obvious as it passes through low outcrops. A long low line of the said outcrops deflect our path to the left, and a long trek ensues before arriving at a stile onto the moor-road to Malham Tarn. Follow this right, keeping by the wall when the road swings away, to arrive at a gate with an old sign pointing the way towards Grassington. This is Street Gate, and it signals the commencement of our march along Mastiles Lane. The walking is easy and pleasant as the track clings to the right-hand wall, even though in places it is not always clear on the ground. At a gate the way becomes confined, and shortly before the next gate in the lane we leave it by a gate on the right, where a good track doubles back alongside a fence.

This track becomes fully enclosed to drop down past the isolated Lee Gate Farm, with whose access road we merge to join the head of Smearbottoms Lane. Head along this undulating strip of tarmac to leave it by the second walled track on the left, which rises immediately to arrive at Weets Cross. Through the gate adjacent to it will be found, just up to the left, the Ordnance column marking Weets Top. Returning to the gate, a good path heads away from it beginning a gentle descent of the moor. Soon a guide-post on the right indicates a stile in the wall there, and from it a path heads across Hanlith Moor with a succession of marker-posts serving to confirm the route. Eventually a gate is reached, through which the rough track of Windy Pike Lane leads our steps unfailingly down into Hanlith.

Do not drop down all the way to the river, but at the second sharp bend in Hanlith (a left-hander) go straight on to the right, through the gate on the right of a farm. Contour across the field to be channelled into a stile alongside a gate, and continue along the top of a wood. In the next field a vague path contours the indentation of a tiny beck before descending another field to a footbridge over Gordale Beck. From the fence behind it head well to the left of the barn ahead, and at the economy-size stile our outward leg is rejoined. Retrace those first few steps back into the village, with a small stone clapper bridge providing an equally-small short-cut back to the car-park.

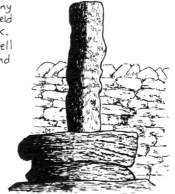

Weets Cross

From Hanlith back to Malham we follow the Pennine Way. On several occasions in the Malham area the popularity of that walk is emphasised by the provision of two adjacent stiles, but near Malham Beck we find ingenuity in the shape of a double-width stile.

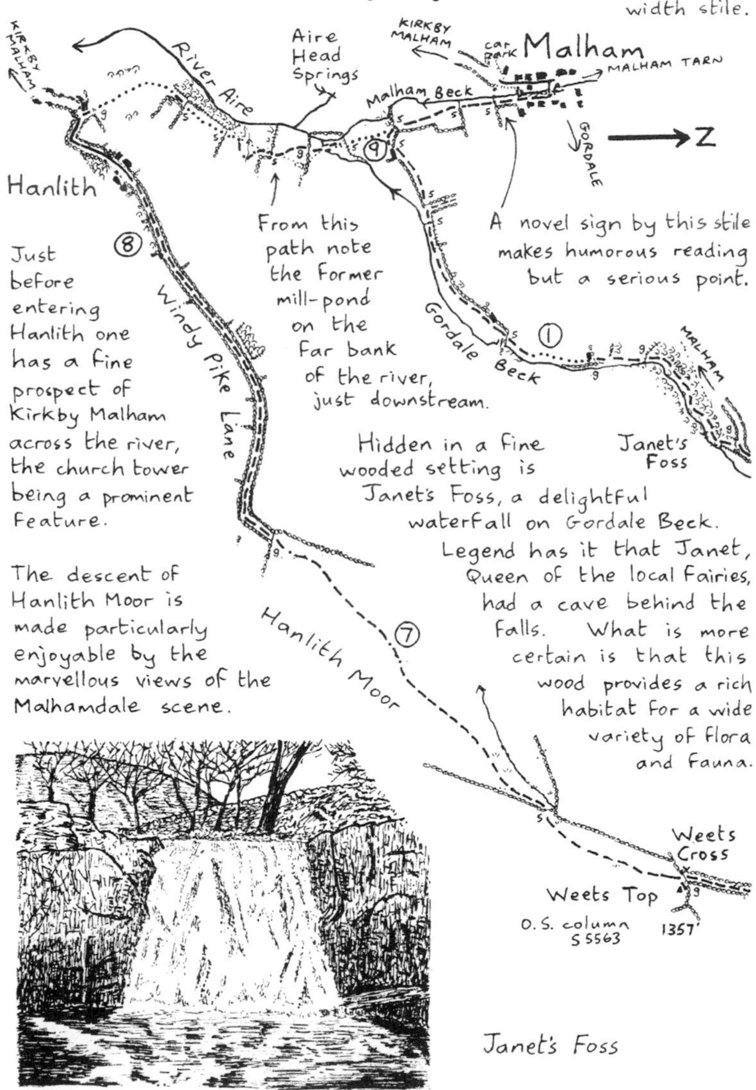

KIRKBY MALHAM
River Aire
Aire Head Springs
KIRKBY MALHAM
car park
Malham
MALHAM TARN
Malham Beck
GORDALE
Z
Hanlith
9
8
Windy Pike Lane
Gordale Beck
1
MALHAM
Janet's Foss
7
Hanlith Moor
Weets Cross
Weets Top
O.S. column S5563
1357'

From this path note the former mill-pond on the far bank of the river, just downstream.

A novel sign by this stile makes humorous reading but a serious point.

Just before entering Hanlith one has a fine prospect of Kirkby Malham across the river, the church tower being a prominent feature.

Hidden in a fine wooded setting is Janet's Foss, a delightful waterfall on Gordale Beck. Legend has it that Janet, Queen of the local fairies, had a cave behind the falls. What is more certain is that this wood provides a rich habitat for a wide variety of flora and fauna.

The descent of Hanlith Moor is made particularly enjoyable by the marvellous views of the Malhamdale scene.

Janet's Foss

It should be noted that at Gordale Scar one needs to partake of a short climb on rock – this is a fairly simple task with ample hand-holds, but may nevertheless be outside the scope of certain less-agile walkers. It is beyond all non-amphibious walkers after a good deal of rain. The best alternative is to return to Gordale Bridge from where a marked path crosses to the Malham Tarn road, for Street Gate, or straight across to return to Malham via the Cove.

※ This walk is particularly suitable for breaking down into two separate shorter rambles, by using the traffic-free Smearbottoms Lane (becoming Hawthorns Lane) as a link back to and out of Malham, for the two walks respectively.

Mastiles Lane is probably the most famous of old roads in the district. This classic green lane was used by the monks of Fountains Abbey to cross from Kilnsey to their valuable sheep-rearing pastures in the Malham area. Look out for the base of a wayside cross (see map). The lane is at its most inspiring when fully enclosed by walls. Note the large boulders incorporated into the lane's north wall – they are boundary stones separating Malham and Bordley.

Weets Top is one of the finest viewpoints in the area, with most of the features in the southern Dales in sight. Quite a number of parish boundaries meet here, and the restored Cross serves to mark this point.

Gordale Scar is probably the most awe-inspiring single feature of the Yorkshire Dales. Unlike the Cove at Malham, which bears all on first sighting it, the Scar has a far more intriguing nature, waiting for the visitor to turn the final corner before impressing him to the full.

Once in its dark confines the grandeur of the overhanging cliffs up above can initially be a little too daunting to fully appreciate the waterfalls: the upper fall spills in spectacular fashion through a circular hole in the rocks. The water is that of Gordale Beck, being funnelled from the lonely moors to the green valley.

above: the waterfalls

Gordale Scar

below: the approach

WALK 30

EMBSAY MOOR

7 miles

from Embsay

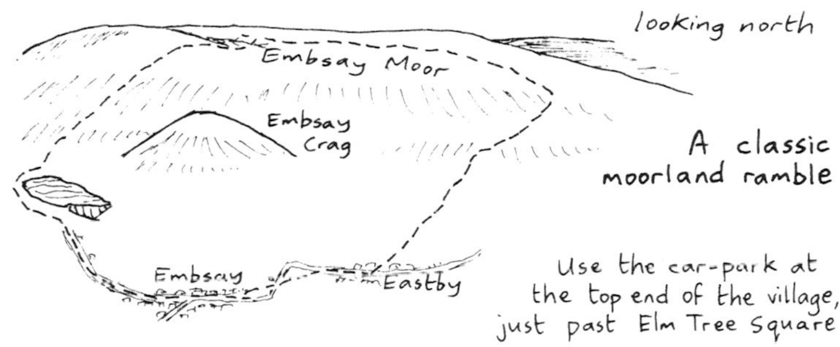
looking north
Embsay Moor
Embsay Crag
Embsay
Eastby

A classic moorland ramble

Use the car-park at the top end of the village, just past Elm Tree Square

THE WALK

From the car park return to Elm Tree Square and continue straight along the back lane (Pasture Road), which leaves the village on passing a mill, and rises to the foot of the dam of Embsay Reservoir. Follow the track up left, past the dam top and along the side of the reservoir. When the wall is replaced by a fence, take a stile in it to gain access to the open moor. Accompany the track away for only yards until crossing a tiny stream, then look for a vague path branching left. Though not easy to locate initially, an upper section can be more clearly seen, rising across the moor at a steady angle. Once joined this becomes an easy to follow shooting-track. The gradient soon eases and a most enjoyable trek across the moor ensues. After reaching the brow of East Harts Hill, a gradual descent is made to cross the upper reach of Waterfall Gill, from where the track climbs sharply to arrive at two attractive shooting-houses.

Just above these buildings the track merges into the Rylstone-Bolton Abbey bridle-track, which is sketchy to the west, but a pleasant wide track as we accompany it eastward thanks to its modern use as a shooting-track. This way is trodden for about two miles, and it is generally level throughout. A branch to Embsay is ignored long before we leave the track, our point of departure being where a footpath sign indicates a crossroads. An inviting green path heads off left, but ours is the pathless way to the right, aiming straight for two modern shooting-houses. Here a good track is met and followed up between the two buildings. With

a row of grouse-butts appearing to the left, the track soon peters out: head across and follow their line away. From the last one bear a little left to a stile which takes us off the moor.

A sketchy path bears right to descend the fields to a gate, another stile, and then drops down more directly and well-defined through several more stiles. The way becomes more confined in its lower section to emerge onto the lane in Eastby. Turn right, leaving the village and then leaving the road at a stile on the left. A clear path now heads diagonally across the fields, aiming directly for the church. On reaching the road, follow it for only a few yards down past the church, then opt for a small gate on the right. Aim half-left across the field to a stile, from where an enclosed path leads to another stile. Just below is Embsay's car-park, and a final stile leads back into it.

excellent view of Lower Barden Reservoir from here onwards.

The two shooting-huts above Waterfall Gill come as quite a surprise, being traditionally constructed of local stone with a delightful thatch-like topping. Even the shape is rather unique.

One of the greatest joys of walking is crossing heather moors on good paths, and in this vicinity we are indeed well-favoured. Note the crudely-paved section on this highest point.

Partly inside the National Park boundary, Embsay is a thriving and sizeable village, perfectly sandwiched between Skipton town and the open moors. It was here the Augustinians began work before opting for the Wharfe's banks to found Bolton Priory. Today Embsay is the home of a preserved railway, and a most enjoyable hour or two can be spent on a good honest steam train.

Much of this walk is within the Barden Moor access area (see page 76), and although our route incorporates two rights-of-way it cannot be done without the use of the splendid shooting-track over East Harts Hill.

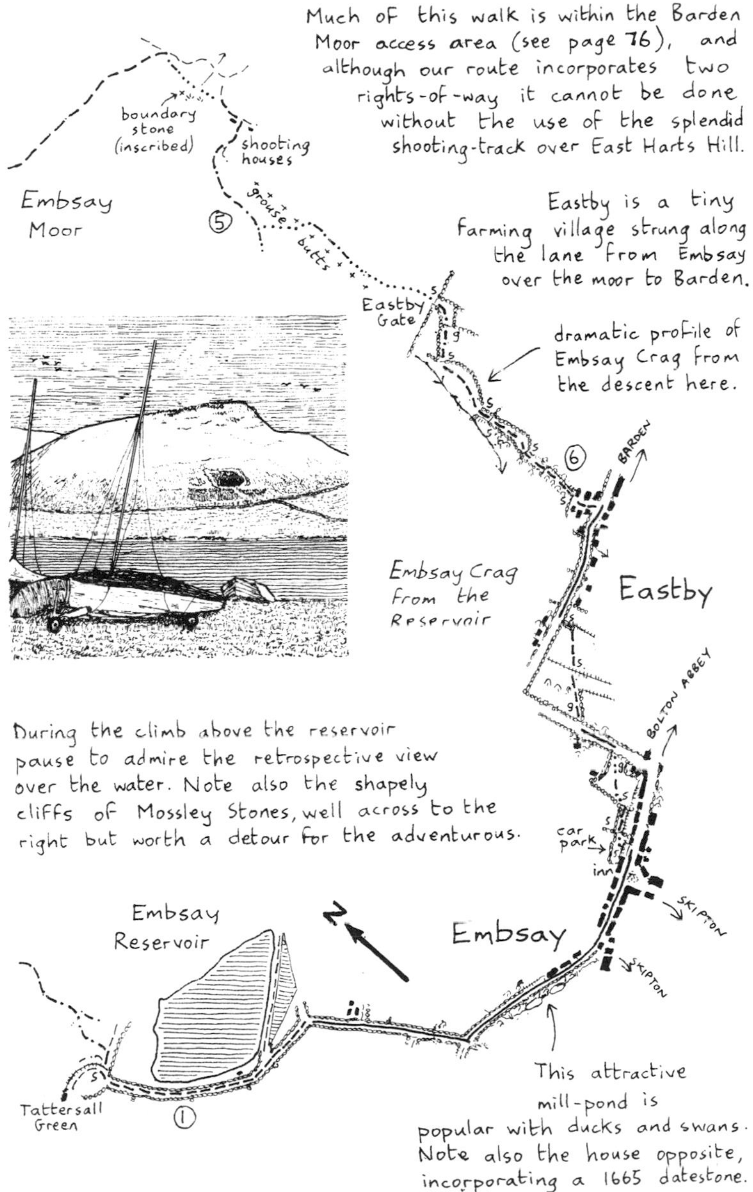
boundary stone (inscribed)
shooting houses
Embsay Moor
5
grouse butts
Eastby Gate
g
s
6
BARDEN
Eastby
BOLTON ABBEY
car park
inn
SKIPTON
Embsay
Embsay Reservoir
Tattersall Green
1

Eastby is a tiny farming village strung along the lane from Embsay over the moor to Barden.

dramatic profile of Embsay Crag from the descent here.

Embsay Crag from the Reservoir

During the climb above the reservoir pause to admire the retrospective view over the water. Note also the shapely cliffs of Mossley Stones, well across to the right but worth a detour for the adventurous.

This attractive mill-pond is popular with ducks and swans. Note also the house opposite, incorporating a 1665 datestone.

WALK 31

BELL BUSK AND THE AIRE

5 miles

from Airton

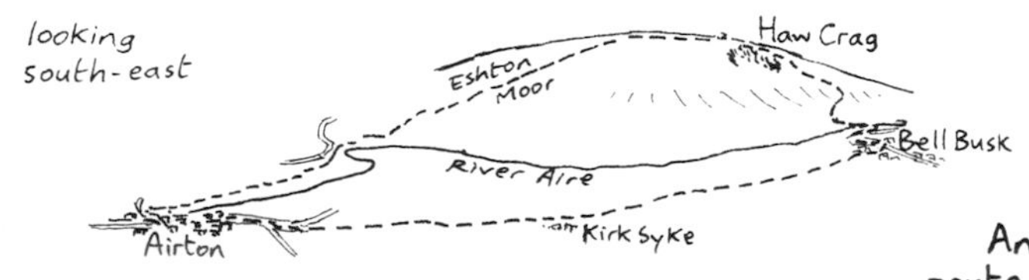
looking
south-east
Haw Crag
Eshton
Moor
Bell Busk
River Aire
Kirk Syke
Airton

An easy route over modest heights and along a lovely riverbank

Airton has reasonable roadside parking, notably by the green (but definitely NOT on it)

THE WALK

Leave the green by the telephone-box at the south-west corner, crossing straight over the main road and up the lane opposite (signposted Hellifield). Turn off it at the first opportunity along a lane to the left. This lane is also soon forsaken, this time along an enclosed track to the right. This farm-track is followed throughout its entire length, past the farm at Kirk Syke and then past a grouping of barns. A little past a gate, the track becomes sketchy as its left-hand boundary disappears. The way remains clear however, passing an old quarry, two ponds and a barn to emerge into a field. Head straight on with a fence on the right to a gate ahead, with the fence switching to the left to reach the next gate. A large field is entered: follow the fence down to the barn in front, behind which is a bridge over Otterburn Beck. From it a clear track leads past some barns onto the lane in Bell Busk.

Turn left along this lane, leaving it upon reaching a road-bridge over the beck. On crossing, fork right immediately along a lesser lane to cross a bridge over the Aire. It then heads uphill: on levelling out we pass an isolated dwelling, and the way becomes rougher, turning sharp left to climb again. Leave it at the next sharp bend right, taking the gate directly ahead to enter the pasture containing Haw Crag. Head straight up the slope to the edge of the old quarry, and then follow the rim around to the Ordnance column marking the highest point.

On leaving, re-trace steps along the rim and then swing left to rejoin the original line, arriving at a prominent gate in the wall ahead, with a less prominent stile alongside it. Again head directly across the field to arrive at an isolated four-way guidepost: here the Pennine Way is joined and now followed all the way back to Airton. Accompany the Pennine Way to the left, down to two stiles in the corner of the field, then follow the wall away as far as a gate in it. Do not use the gate, but instead bear gradually away from the wall to avoid a large dog-leg in it, descending the large field till walls converge alongside a road. This narrow, enclosed way takes us down to a stile on the left, and a small beck leads us left to a footbridge over the River Aire.

From the bridge follow the riverbank upstream, entering the wood on the left by a stile when there is no more room on the bank. Another stile leads back out of the trees, and the river again leads us upstream towards Newfield Bridge, a stile to its left emptying onto the road there. Cross the bridge and take a stile on the left to rejoin the river once more. From a stile by a gate follow the wall straight ahead, nearing the river again at two stiles in quick succession. From the second leave the river again for a stile in the next wall along, and then head across the large pasture, closing in on the river as Airton Bridge comes into view. From the stile to its right, cross the the bridge to climb the lane back onto the green at Airton.

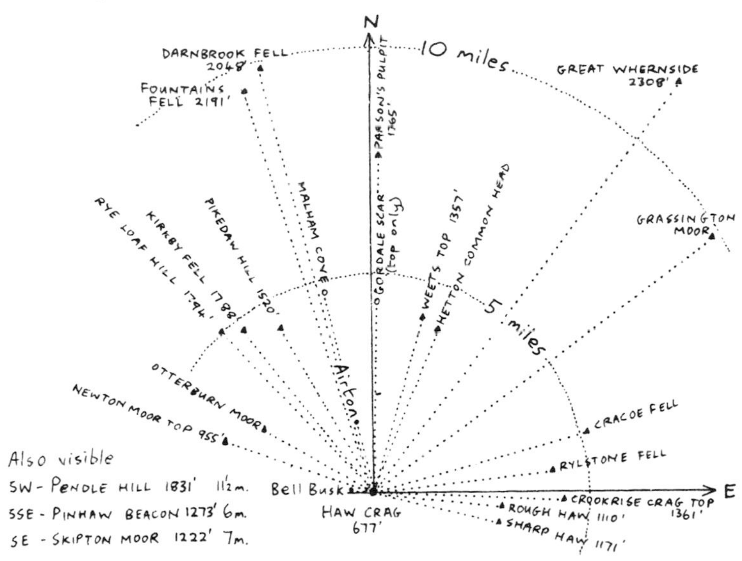
N
10 miles
DARNBROOK FELL 2048'
FOUNTAINS FELL 2191'
PARSON'S PULPIT 1765'
GREAT WHERNSIDE 2308'
GRASSINGTON MOOR
MALHAM COVE
PIKEDAW HILL 1520'
KIRKBY FELL 1788'
RYE LOAF HILL 1794'
GORDALE SCAR (top only)
WEETS TOP 1357'
HETTON COMMON HEAD
5 miles
Airton
OTTERBURN MOOR
NEWTON MOOR TOP 955'
CRACOE FELL
RYLSTONE FELL
Also visible
SW - PENDLE HILL 1831' 11½m.
SSE - PINHAW BEACON 1273' 6m.
SE - SKIPTON MOOR 1222' 7m.
Bell Busk
HAW CRAG 677'
CROOKRISE CRAG TOP 1361'
ROUGH HAW 1110'
SHARP HAW 1171'
E

The principle features of Craven from Haw Crag

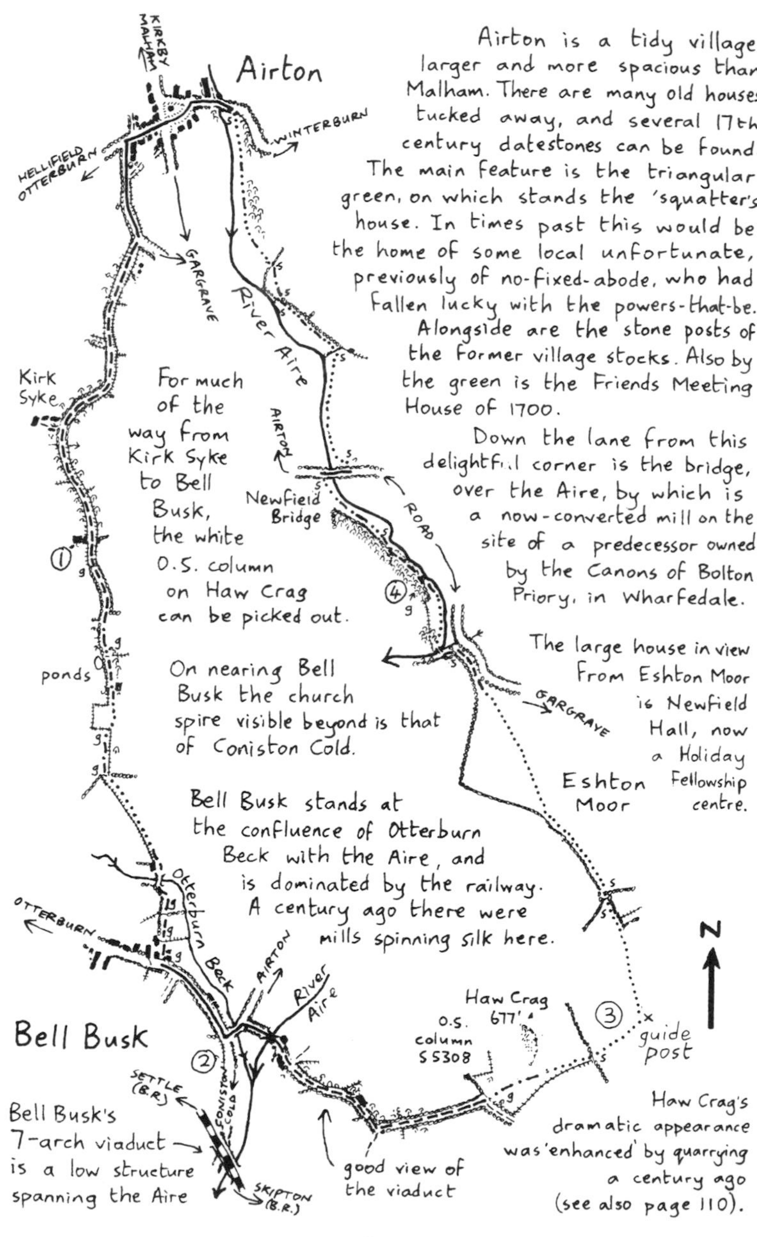
Airton
KIRKBY MALHAM
WINTERBURN
HELLIFIELD OTTERBURN
GARGRAVE
River Aire
Kirk Syke
AIRTON
Newfield Bridge
ROAD
ponds
GARGRAVE
Eshton Moor
OTTERBURN
Otterburn Beck
AIRTON
River Aire
Bell Busk
SETTLE (B.R.)
CONISTON COLD
SKIPTON (B.R.)
Haw Crag 677'
O.S. column S5308
guide post
N
good view of the viaduct
Airton is a tidy village, larger and more spacious than Malham. There are many old houses tucked away, and several 17th century datestones can be found. The main feature is the triangular green, on which stands the 'squatter's house. In times past this would be the home of some local unfortunate, previously of no-fixed-abode, who had fallen lucky with the powers-that-be. Alongside are the stone posts of the former village stocks. Also by the green is the Friends Meeting House of 1700.
Down the lane from this delightful corner is the bridge, over the Aire, by which is a now-converted mill on the site of a predecessor owned by the Canons of Bolton Priory, in Wharfedale.
The large house in view from Eshton Moor is Newfield Hall, now a Holiday Fellowship centre.
For much of the way from Kirk Syke to Bell Busk, the white O.S. column on Haw Crag can be picked out.
On nearing Bell Busk the church spire visible beyond is that of Coniston Cold.
Bell Busk stands at the confluence of Otterburn Beck with the Aire, and is dominated by the railway. A century ago there were mills spinning silk here.
Bell Busk's 7-arch viaduct is a low structure spanning the Aire
Haw Crag's dramatic appearance was 'enhanced' by quarrying a century ago (see also page 110).

WALK 32

AROUND MALHAM MOOR

8 miles

From Malham Tarn

A bracing ramble combining limestone uplands with the environs of Malham Tarn

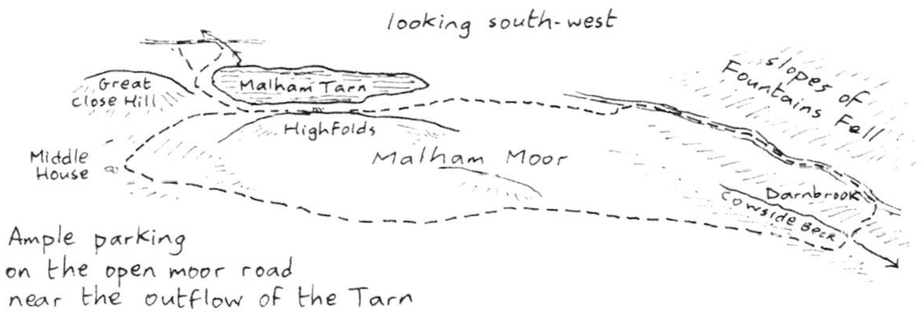
looking south-west
Great Close Hill
Malham Tarn
Highfolds
Middle House
Malham Moor
slopes of Fountains Fell
Darnbrook
Cowside Beck

Ample parking on the open moor road near the outflow of the Tarn

THE WALK

From the gate where the road crosses the beck follow the unenclosed road east for a couple of minutes, as far as the guide-post indicating the crossing of our old friend the Pennine Way. Turn left along the Way, on a green track which heads directly to a gate to merge with the main track to the Malham Tarn estate. Follow this track along the shore of the tarn until arriving at a cattle-grid at the entrance to a wood: do not enter, but instead climb the slope to the right. A green track materialises to swing right as the gradient eases, nearing a fence but not crossing it. As the fence bends left on the hill-top, the track soon fades: simply follow the fence down to a stile. From there follow the fence leading away to the isolated Middle House Farm, and on reaching another stile don't cross it but turn left to climb the field to a gate.

From this gate a good track heads across the limestone pasture, but within a minute or so take a fork right to join a wall there. Passing a cluster of barns embowered in trees, the path crosses a collapsed wall to a guide-post: here we leave the Arncliffe path and take the rather sketchier left fork. It contours round a hollow below some small outcrops to arrive at a stile, and beyond the wall heads away through more outcrops to fade completely as the ground slopes away. Follow the line of rocks downhill, with the farm at Darnbrook appearing ahead. As the wall below appears, look for a cairn just across to the right: it marks a fine viewpoint worth the

32

modest detour. Descending to the wall a gate is met: through it continue the descent through a long pasture to a stone-slab bridge over Cowside Beck. From the stile by the beck head for a gap by the barn in front, and continue across the fields by two more stiles and out by a footgate by a barn onto the road at Darnbrook.

Turn left along this narrow lane for 1¼ miles, a good deal of which can be trodden on the open verges. At a sharp left turn just after the track to Tennant Gill Farm on the right, leave the road along a sketchy path across the open pasture on the left to a stile. Climb beyond it to a wall-corner then turn to accompany the wall across undulating pastures. After a stile in a cross-wall continue alongside the wall to eventually reach another stile in a hollow. Just a little further a stile empties onto a wide track at Water Houses.

continued across

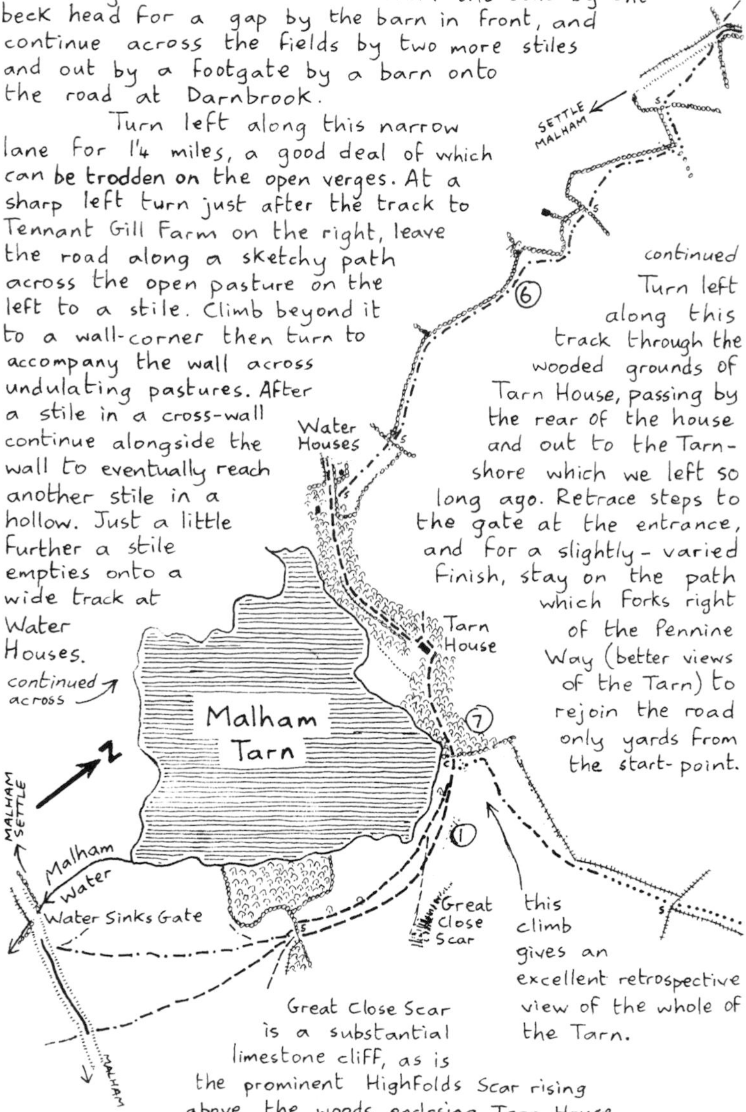

continued

Turn left along this track through the wooded grounds of Tarn House, passing by the rear of the house and out to the Tarn-shore which we left so long ago. Retrace steps to the gate at the entrance, and for a slightly-varied finish, stay on the path which forks right of the Pennine Way (better views of the Tarn) to rejoin the road only yards from the start-point.

SETTLE
MALHAM
6
Water Houses
Tarn House
7
Malham Tarn
N
MALHAM
SETTLE
1
Malham Water
Water Sinks Gate
Great Close Scar
MALHAM

this climb gives an excellent retrospective view of the whole of the Tarn.

Great Close Scar is a substantial limestone cliff, as is the prominent Highfolds Scar rising above the woods enclosing Tarn House.

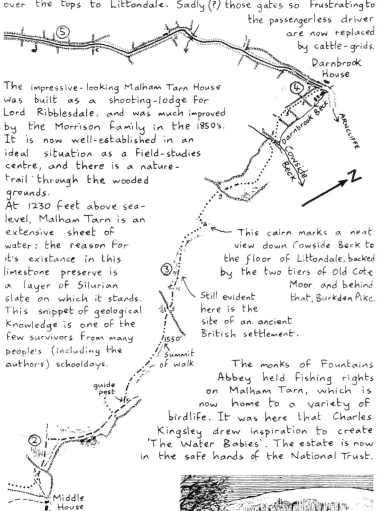

This partially unfenced road provides an exhilarating drive over the tops to Littondale. Sadly (?) those gates so frustrating to the passengerless driver are now replaced by cattle-grids.

The impressive-looking Malham Tarn House was built as a shooting-lodge for Lord Ribblesdale, and was much improved by the Morrison family in the 1850's. It is now well-established in an ideal situation as a field-studies centre, and there is a nature-trail through the wooded grounds.

At 1230 feet above sea-level, Malham Tarn is an extensive sheet of water: the reason for it's existance in this limestone preserve is a layer of Silurian slate on which it stands. This snippet of geological knowledge is one of the few survivors from many people's (including the author's) schooldays.

This cairn marks a neat view down Cowside Beck to the floor of Littondale, backed by the two tiers of Old Cote Moor and behind that, Buckden Pike.

Still evident here is the site of an ancient British settlement.

Summit of walk

The monks of Fountains Abbey held fishing rights on Malham Tarn, which is now home to a variety of birdlife. It was here that Charles Kingsley drew inspiration to create 'The Water Babies'. The estate is now in the safe hands of the National Trust.

Winter on Great Close Scar, from the path to Malham Tarn

CHAPTER THREE

RIBBLESDALE AND DENTDALE

Smearsett Scar　　　　opposite: Feizor and Pot Scar

RIBBLESDALE AND DENTDALE

The area of the western dales is based upon two major valleys, the Ribble and the Dee. These rivers rise on neighbouring moorland, yet finish at opposite ends of the National Park. The Ribble leaves at Settle, in the south, while the demise of the Dee is at Sedbergh, in the north. By way of a coincidence these two market towns make the best centres for the area, and they also serve to illustrate the substantial extent of the countryside involved. Although a much wider range of walks could be described, this is mountain territory, and major ascents of the high fells are not within the scope of this chapter.

Of the two well-defined areas dealt with, the southern half is the most visited, for not only is it closer to centres of population, but it also contains the famous Three Peaks. Ironically it is these summits that so many come so far to conquer - in this district it can therefore be quieter nearer the valleys! Besides the Ribble there are just two small dales, those of the Twiss and the Doe, which meet at Ingleton. This is limestone country at its most splendid, and these walks take in many of its fascinating features.

Across the heights of Whernside and Blea Moor is the northern half of the area, linked by the Ingleton-Dent and the Ribblehead-Dent Head roads. In striking contrast this is a region of deep-cut valleys. North of the Dee's Dentdale are Garsdale, the valley of the Clough, and Rawtheydale. All three meet rather tidily in the neighbourhood of Sedbergh. Here too are mountains, and none more attractive than the Howgill Fells, the finest massif in (and out of) the Dales Park. This chapter is even divided politically, with the northern dales having left Yorkshire for Cumbria.

Besides the winding roads, there is another method of linking the areas, a majestic, incomparable way known as the Settle-Carlisle railway. Having operated under the threat of closure for several years, its future was made more secure after the great campaigning victory of 1989. Though some long term doubts remain, it currently provides an unrivalled means of reaching and travelling within the western area of the Dales, running through the very heartland of the district from Settle to Garsdale Head.

The Skipton-Carnforth line also serves the very south of the area, departing from the above-mentioned line near Settle. Its future, too, is the subject of much concern.

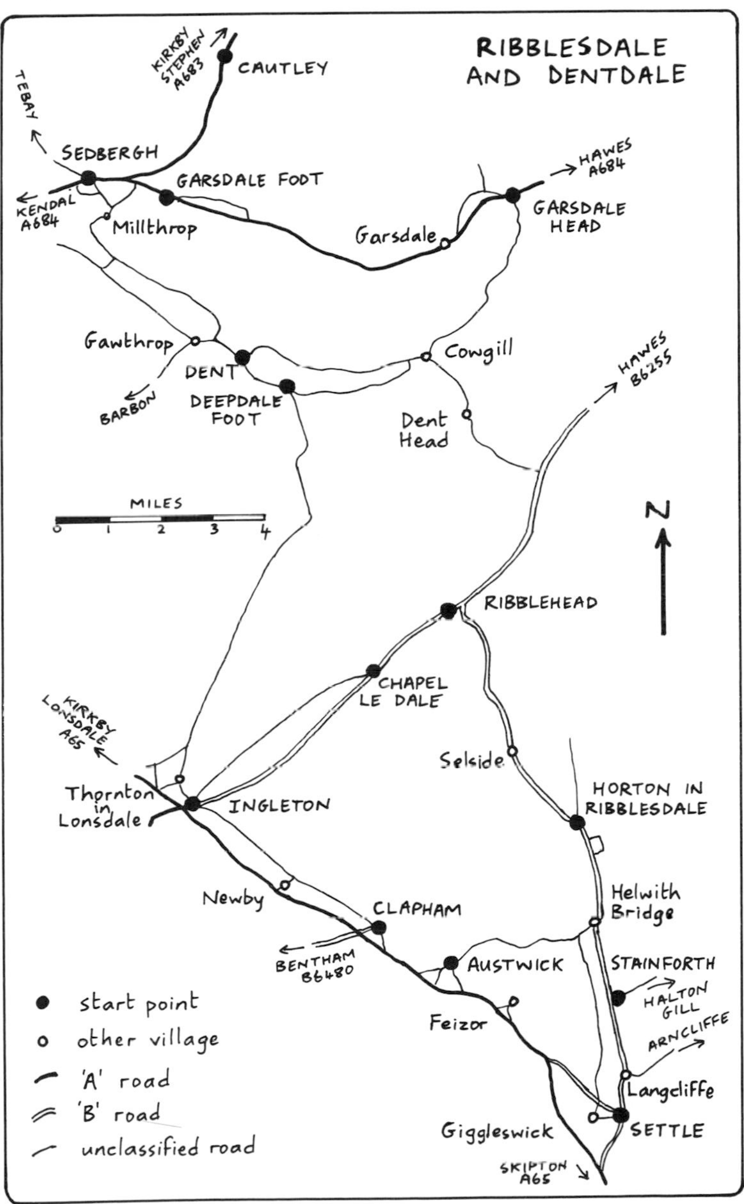
RIBBLESDALE AND DENTDALE
KIRKBY STEPHEN A683
CAUTLEY
TEBAY
SEDBERGH
GARSDALE FOOT
KENDAL A684
Millthrop
HAWES A684
GARSDALE HEAD
Garsdale
Gawthrop
DENT
Cowgill
BARBON
DEEPDALE FOOT
Dent Head
HAWES B6255
MILES
0 1 2 3 4
N
RIBBLEHEAD
CHAPEL LE DALE
KIRKBY LONSDALE A65
Selside
HORTON IN RIBBLESDALE
Thornton in Lonsdale
INGLETON
Newby
CLAPHAM
Helwith Bridge
BENTHAM B6480
AUSTWICK
STAINFORTH
HALTON GILL
Feizor
ARNCLIFFE
Langcliffe
Giggleswick
SETTLE
SKIPTON A65
start point
other village
'A' road
'B' road
unclassified road

WALK 33

THE HEART OF RIBBLESDALE

6½ miles

from Horton-in-Ribblesdale

An excellent way to appraise the varied features of the upper valley of the Ribble

slopes of Penyghent
looking north-east
Brants Gill Head
Horton
Brackenbottom
River Ribble
Helwith Bridge

Use the main car-park in the village centre

THE WALK

Leave the car-park by the footbridge at its northern end to by-pass the narrow road-bridges near the Crown Hotel. At once take a stile on the left to follow the Ribble downstream. We cling to its bank as far as Cragg Hill Farm, apart from a brief spell deflected by an enclosure containing the sewage works (preceded by a stile on the right as opposed to the obvious one straight ahead).

At the farm do not be tempted by a footbridge but remain with the river until the accompanying field boundary parts company, then head directly away from the Ribble to join a once-enclosed track which soon reverts to its original status. After passing another footbridge we go under the railway and out onto a lane. Turn left for a few minutes and with the inn at Helwith Bridge in sight take a stile to cross a field and emerge onto the road via the inn's car-park.

Cross the bridge to a junction and go left up the valley's main road a short distance before opting for a walled rough track up to the right. Follow this up to a fork and keep left to eventually emerge from confinement at a gate. From a gate at the next wall a crumbling wall reappears on the left, and within yards a level green fork takes us away from the main track. This new track leads down to a gate, but it is the stile in the bottom corner that takes us further. Descend to another stile to join a lane at Dub Cote Farm.

Turn right along this narrow byway to a

junction, then right again between the various buildings of Brackenbottom and circuitously around to Horton's little school. Though we are now back in the village, there is still another sight before finishing. Cross the footbridge and turn right, then fork left along a track which soon joins a similar walled track. Head right as far as a gate on the left 100 yards past a seat, and cross the field to another gate. Continue across to the prominent clump of trees marking the position of Brants Gill Head.

A stile in the wall right of the trees admits to the vicinity of the beck head, which is seen to better advantage by a scramble down the slope. Above and behind the beck is a stile in a wall: head directly away from it to a gate to join another walled track. This is Harber Scar Lane, which drops down into the village rather tidily by the front door of the Crown hotel.

Horton-in-Ribblesdale is the highest village in a valley which ends in the Irish Sea beyond Preston, and is the centre of the Three Peaks country. It is not particularly attractive, with a curious mixture of dwellings strung along the road. Horton's real attraction is its location, as the sight of countless boots being pulled on in its overfaced car park will testify. There is a true walkers atmosphere here, and the renowned cafe is the focal point: inside can be found the famous clocking-in machine where prospective Three Peakers start their day. Further up the road is the inn with two adjacent arched bridges, while at the southern end of the village is the church of St. Oswald. It displays Norman and 15th century work, and the solid-looking tower has leanings towards Pisa.

Horton church and Penyghent

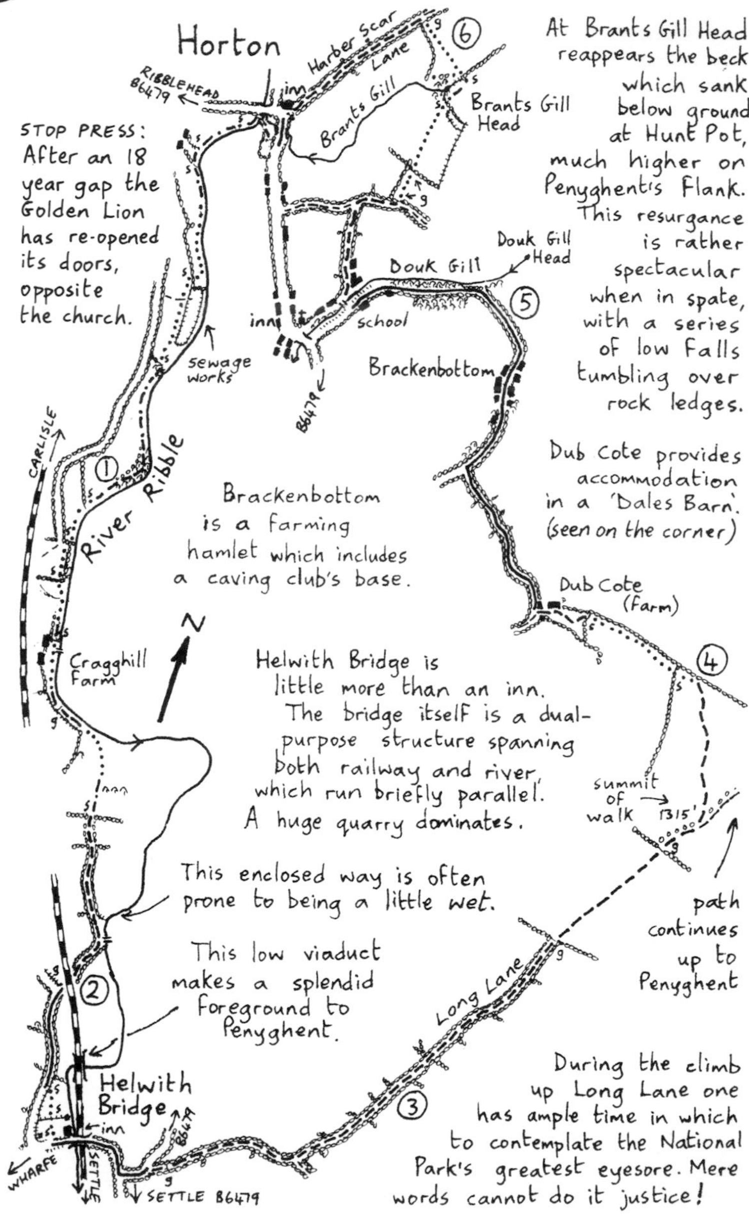

Horton
Harber Scar Lane
RIBBLEHEAD B6479
inn
Brants Gill
6
Brants Gill Head
At Brants Gill Head reappears the beck which sank below ground at Hunt Pot, much higher on Penyghent's Flank. This resurgance is rather spectacular when in spate, with a series of low falls tumbling over rock ledges.
STOP PRESS: After an 18 year gap the Golden Lion has re-opened its doors, opposite the church.
Douk Gill Head
Douk Gill
5
school
inn
sewage works
B6479
Brackenbottom
Dub Cote provides accommodation in a 'Dales Barn'. (seen on the corner)
CARLISLE
1
River Ribble
Brackenbottom is a farming hamlet which includes a caving club's base.
Dub Cote (Farm)
N
Cragghill Farm
Helwith Bridge is little more than an inn. The bridge itself is a dual-purpose structure spanning both railway and river, which run briefly parallel. A huge quarry dominates.
4
summit of walk 1315'
This enclosed way is often prone to being a little wet.
path continues up to Penyghent
This low viaduct makes a splendid foreground to Penyghent.
Long Lane
2
Helwith Bridge
inn
B6479
3
During the climb up Long Lane one has ample time in which to contemplate the National Park's greatest eyesore. Mere words cannot do it justice!
WHARFE
SETTLE
SETTLE B6479

WALK 34

FROSTROW FELLS AND MILLTHROP

$6\frac{3}{4}$ miles

from Sedbergh

Splendid mountain scenery from the feet of two valleys

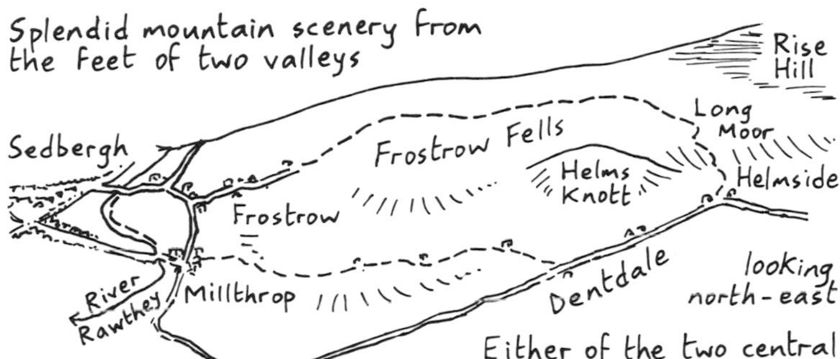
Rise Hill
Long Moor
Sedbergh
Frostrow Fells
Helms Knott
Helmside
Frostrow
Dentdale
looking north-east
River Rawthey
Millthrop

Either of the two central car parks are adequate, but a start from the lay-by at New Bridge (where the road to Hawes crosses the Rawthey) is more satisfactory.

THE WALK

New Bridge is reached by heading east along the main street and branching right on the Hawes road at the edge of town. After crossing the bridge remain on the main road only as far as the first junction, and heading along the narrow lane ignore branches left and then right to continue along the 'no through road' that is Frostrow Lane. It leads past several farms to an eventual demise alongside High Side Farm, and a stile directly ahead empties onto the Frostrow Fells.

Follow the track heading away along a minor ridge, with the dome of Rise Hill as a guide. Beyond a nearby wall-corner and barn, a wall-corner is reached above Holebeck Gill. The improved way rises as a sunken track above the beck, and as it peters out a slim trod takes up the running to slant up to the wall marking the watershed.

Head left with the wall as far as a stile, and take the green, wallside track bound for Dentdale. This is vacated, however, at the first stile in it, to now shadow another wall heading away. Through a gate the way steepens towards the valley bottom, a track forming to lead through a gate at the bottom left of this large enclosure. Continuing down to Helmside, use a gate on the right to pass by the farm and emerge onto the road alongside Dent Crafts Centre.

Turn right along the valley road for three-quarters of a mile, to leave it at the second cluster of buildings: Craggs Farm is readily identifiable as it is entirely on the left side of the road. Take the gate opposite and head up to a stile in the adjacent wall, then slant up to Leakses. Passing in front of the farmhouse go left to a gate by the farthest barn, then crossing several fields and rising slightly to Burton Hill Farm. Pass between the buildings and up to an ornate gate, then cross a field-bottom before aiming for Hewthwaite, the next farm. From a stile by the nearest barn, cross to a stile below a gate opposite, to cross two further fields to emerge onto the drive to Gap Farm by way of a near-hidden stile.

Pass along the front of the house, over a field and along the foot of Gap Wood. Enclosed for much of the way, a superb green track leaves the trees behind to round the ridge-end towards Sedbergh. At a distinct fork keep right to a stile, joining a wide track that winds down through an old golf course and becomes enclosed to enter Millthrop. Go right to a junction and left to Millthrop Bridge to re-enter Sedbergh. For New Bridge, simply take the riverside path instead: a grand finish.

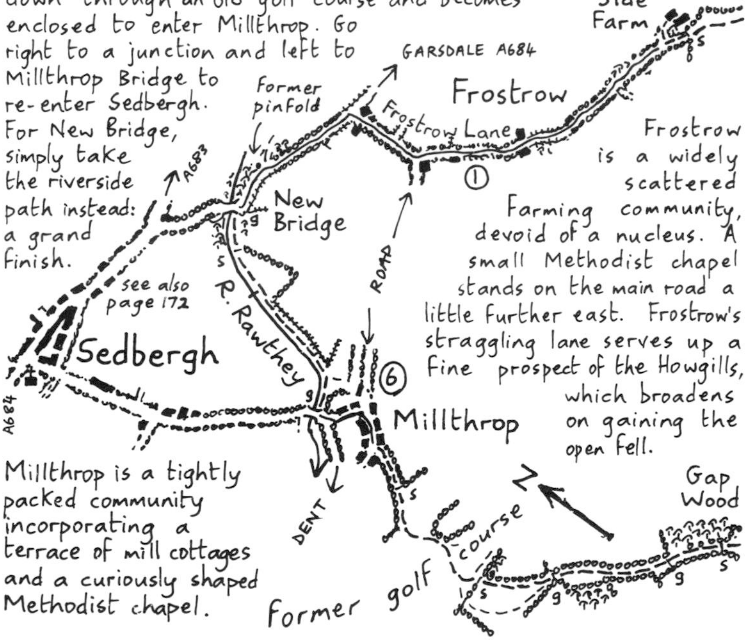

Frostrow is a widely scattered farming community, devoid of a nucleus. A small Methodist chapel stands on the main road a little further east. Frostrow's straggling lane serves up a fine prospect of the Howgills, which broadens on gaining the open fell.

Millthrop is a tightly packed community incorporating a terrace of mill cottages and a curiously shaped Methodist chapel.

Arrival above the old course is a breathtaking moment. In front are the Howgill Fells majestically dominating Sedbergh, with the Lune Valley to the west: perfect in evening sunlight.

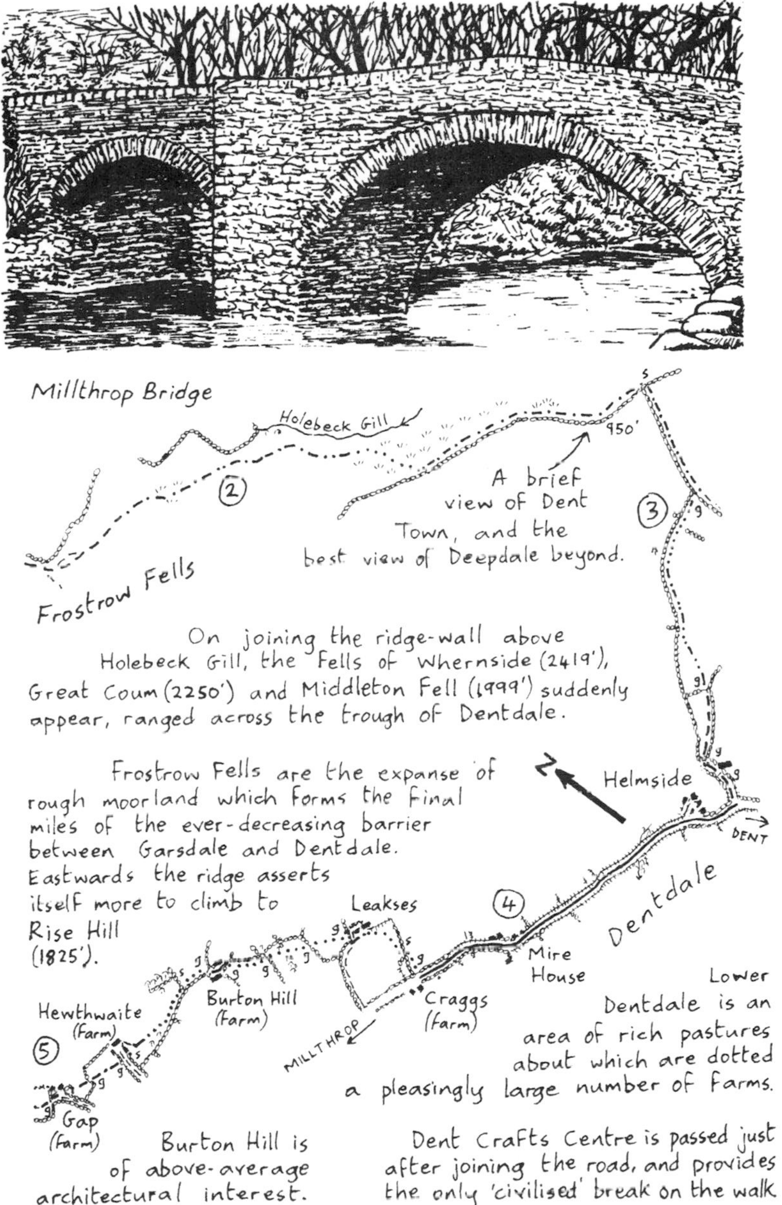
Holebeck Gill
950'
2
3
4
5
Frostrow Fells
Helmside
DENT
Dentdale
Leakses
Mire House
Craggs (farm)
Burton Hill (Farm)
Hewthwaite (Farm)
Gap (Farm)
MILLTHROP

Millthrop Bridge

A brief view of Dent Town, and the best view of Deepdale beyond.

On joining the ridge-wall above Holebeck Gill, the Fells of Whernside (2419'), Great Coum (2250') and Middleton Fell (1999') suddenly appear, ranged across the trough of Dentdale.

Frostrow Fells are the expanse of rough moorland which forms the final miles of the ever-decreasing barrier between Garsdale and Dentdale. Eastwards the ridge asserts itself more to climb to Rise Hill (1825').

Lower Dentdale is an area of rich pastures about which are dotted a pleasingly large number of farms.

Burton Hill is of above-average architectural interest.

Dent Crafts Centre is passed just after joining the road, and provides the only 'civilised' break on the walk

(35)

WALK 35

CATRIGG FORCE AND THE SETTLE CAVES

$6\frac{3}{4}$ miles

from Settle

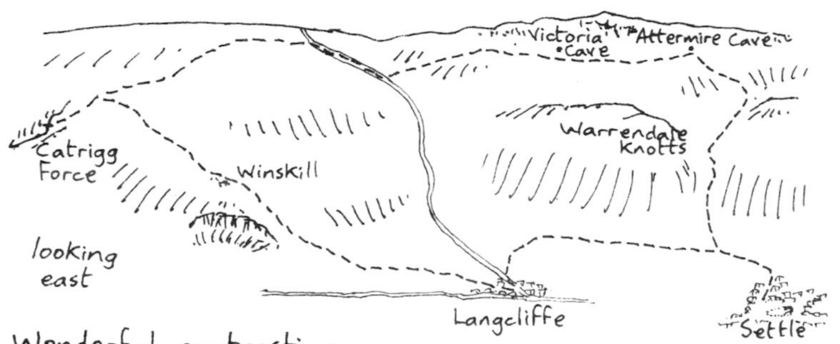
Victoria
Cave
Attermire Cave
Warrendale
Knotts
Catrigg
Force
Winskill
looking
east
Langcliffe
Settle

Wonderful contrasting natural scenery, from waterfall to cave.

There is ample parking in the centre of Settle

THE WALK

Leave the market-place by Constitution Hill, to the left of the Shambles. After a steep pull the lane turns left, and almost at once leave it along a rough track to the right. After a gate continue along the field bottom, using another gate to be briefly enclosed again before heading on to a stile on the left. Slope across to find another stile, then continue along with another left-hand wall, finally dropping left to a stile onto the lane just above Langcliffe.

Turn into the village and take the second lane on the right (opposite the green). Within a few yards is a little crossroads: head straight across and follow this enclosed track until its demise, there opting for the right-hand of two gates. Cross the field-top to a gate at the very end, then climb steeply above a former quarry to find a small gate in the top corner. Head up through a smaller pasture, and when a narrow track heads left, take a stile to its right, cutting a corner to another stile to rejoin the track. Turn right along it, and beyond a gate is the entrance to High Winskill.

Our way follows the track directly ahead, soon reaching a stile before petering out in the next field. Another stile soon appears ahead, and it is from here we make the detour to Catrigg Force. Its location is in no doubt, being enclosed in the trees at the bottom of the field. A pair of neighbouring stiles are the final obstacles, leading to the top of the waterfall, where with great care we are able to peer down to the bottom. The conventional view can be had by entering the trees on the left to descend a good path to the foot of the Force.

On returning to the stile at the top of the large field, go left along a farm-track which rises to join the road from Langcliffe to Malham Moor near a cattle-grid. Turn right along the verges of this unfenced strip of tarmac as far as the next cattle-grid, and from it strike left on a less-than clear track to rise to a stile in an intervening wall. After the outcrops beyond it turn left to another stile onto a wide track: up to the left are the conspicuous entrances of Jubilee Caves.

Follow the track right, leaving it at a gate and maintaining the same course on a path. After two stiles a path rises below a patch of scree to arrive at the enormous entrance to Victoria Cave. Another path returns us to the main one to resume the journey below a line of scars. After an open pasture Attermire Scar is reached, and the main path descends directly to a gateway. If wishing to explore Attermire Cave, do not descend but take a lesser path forking left and remaining level to arrive below the cave's modest entrance in the cliff just above. From it the gateway can be reached by descending a path across the scree.

Through the gateway follow the wall away, crossing a stile and rising to a gateway. An initially sketchy path bears right, passing a cave before arriving at a gap-stile by a gate. Descend to a wall-corner but then continue straight down a steep slope to rejoin the outward path: a left turn will lead in only a few minutes back into Settle's market-place.

Victoria Cave

35

Jubilee Cave, looking out

Catrigg Force

Settle is a bustling little town which acts as a focal point for an extensive rural area comprising largely of upper Ribblesdale. It is invariably busy, being a long-established resting place for those bound farther afield, and is also an ideal centre for the Three Peaks country. Market days present the liveliest scene when the small square is covered with stalls.

Settle boasts numerous old buildings, some hidden and others very much on display. Facing the market square is a historic row known as the Shambles, with its shops peeping from behind archways. Nearby is a striking 17th century structure known as The Folly, a large rambling place.

Also facing the square is the 'Naked Man', a cafe with an appropriate carved sign dated 1633 and the source of some humour. Two museums are worth visiting, namely the Museum of North Craven Life and the privately owned Pig Yard Museum, which displays finds of archaeological interest from Victoria Cave. Settle has now become even more pleasant with the 1988 completion of its by-pass.

Settle
CARLISLE
LANGCLIFFE
Banks Lane
INGLETON
SKIPTON
SKIPTON
KIRKBY MALHAM
N

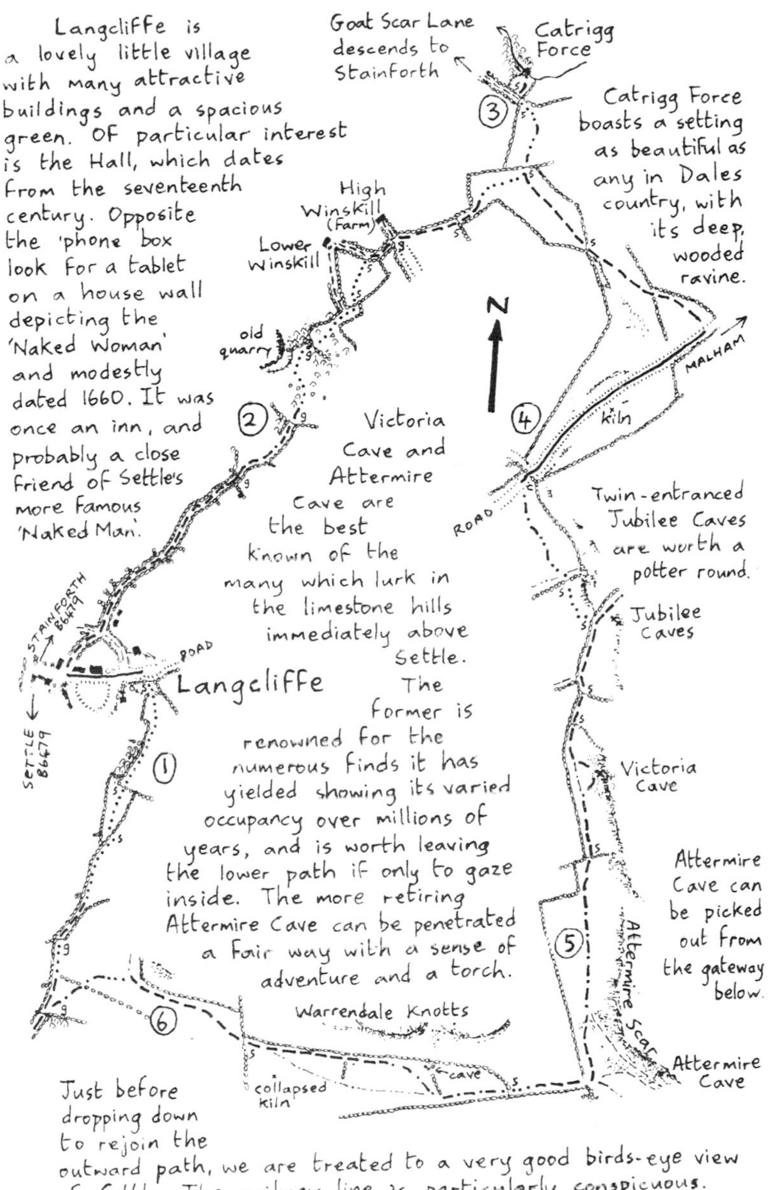

Goat Scar Lane descends to Stainforth
Catrigg Force
3
High Winskill (Farm)
Lower Winskill
old quarry
N
2
4
kiln
MALHAM
ROAD
STAINFORTH B6479
ROAD
Langcliffe
SETTLE B6479
1
Jubilee Caves
Victoria Cave
5
Attermire Scar
Attermire Cave
Warrendale Knotts
6
cave
collapsed kiln

Langcliffe is a lovely little village with many attractive buildings and a spacious green. Of particular interest is the Hall, which dates from the seventeenth century. Opposite the 'phone box look for a tablet on a house wall depicting the 'Naked Woman' and modestly dated 1660. It was once an inn, and probably a close friend of Settle's more famous 'Naked Man'.

Catrigg Force boasts a setting as beautiful as any in Dales country, with its deep, wooded ravine.

Victoria Cave and Attermire Cave are the best known of the many which lurk in the limestone hills immediately above Settle. The former is renowned for the numerous finds it has yielded showing its varied occupancy over millions of years, and is worth leaving the lower path if only to gaze inside. The more retiring Attermire Cave can be penetrated a fair way with a sense of adventure and a torch.

Twin-entranced Jubilee Caves are worth a potter round.

Attermire Cave can be picked out from the gateway below.

Just before dropping down to rejoin the outward path, we are treated to a very good birds-eye view of Settle. The railway line is particularly conspicuous.

WALK 36 — FLINTER GILL AND GAWTHROP

5½ miles

from Dent

Beckside and fellside walking combine to provide delightful close-hand and majestic distant views

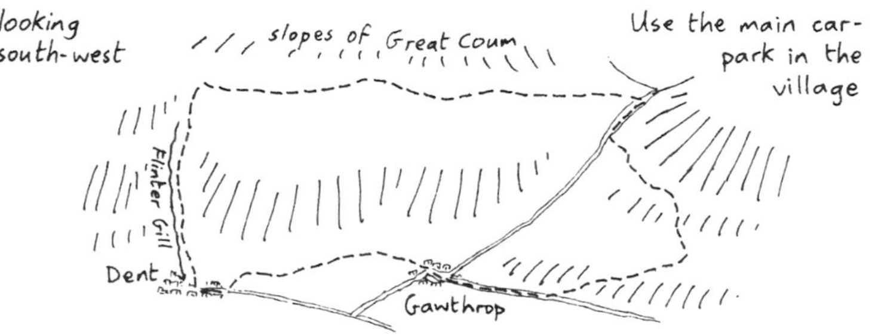
looking south-west
slopes of Great Coum
Use the main car-park in the village
Flinter Gill
Dent
Gawthrop

THE WALK

From the car-park cross the road and take the lane rising alongside the Memorial Hall. It soon takes the form of a stony track, climbing parallel with Flinter Gill. On opening out it becomes enclosed by walls and pleasanter underfoot to join a wide green lane. Follow this to the right to eventually descend onto the Dent-Barbon road.

Accompany it briefly to the right before a footpath sign points the way through a gate on the left. A sketchy track crosses to a stile at the far corner. From it head towards the steep slope to the left: as it is reached a path appears and heads along to the right as a superb green promenade. All too soon a gate is reached and the track fades at the sad ruins of an old farm. Pass round the back and follow a barely-discernable wall heading away.

Down the field a farm-track is joined to head left down through a gateway. Amidst many crumbling walls it continues down to another gateway to approach Tofts. Before crossing the tree-lined beck in front of it however, leave the track to search for a slab footbridge a few yards downstream. The opposite bank is surmounted to reach the farm buildings. Pass between them and out along the access track to drop down gradually onto a lane. Gawthrop is only minutes along to the right.

The hamlet is vacated by the third branch

right after the bridge (by the phone). The lane swings to the left between houses: after crossing another beck fork right, but within yards take an enclosed path left in front of a short row of cottages to rejoin the wider track by a barn. Take the gate to its right and head directly away through several fields to descend to a track to the farm complex at Mill Beck.

Remain on the track through the buildings, it becoming the drive to head away down to the road. Part-way, however, it passes a lone house, and here take two gates on the right to cross the bottoms of several fields to a large modern barn. Squeezing to its left, a field alloted to caravans is entered at High Laning Farm. Head right towards the yard, and then out along its drive to emerge onto the road in Dent adjacent to the Methodist chapel.

Dent Town

On passing through the gateway before the ruinous Combe House, the striking hollow of Combe Scar looms tantalisingly above. This colourful scene – unjustly bereft of a right of way – is chiselled out of the northern flank of Middleton Fell. It is a popular Dentdale landmark, and with its low crags there is more than a hint of Lakeland about it.

Gawthrop is a picturesque grouping of cottages and farms, well off the beaten track

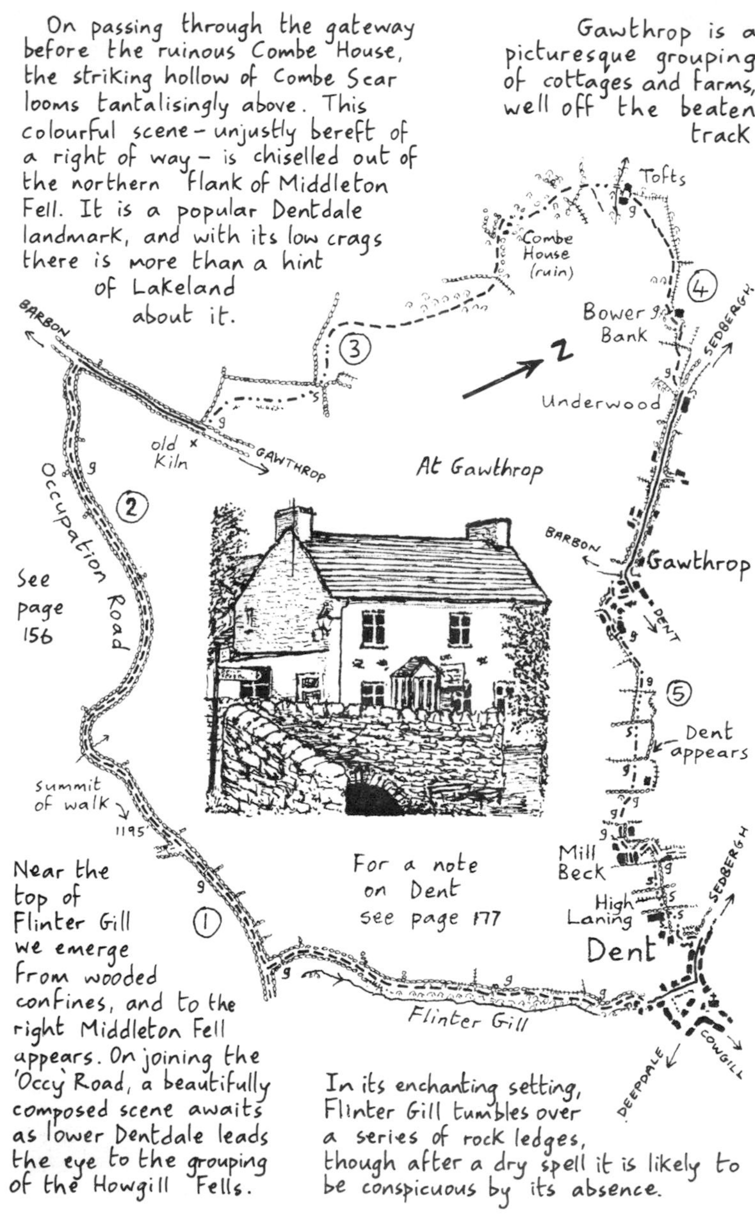

BARBON
Tofts
Combe House (ruin)
4
SEDBERGH
Bower Bank
3
N
Underwood
old Kiln
GAWTHROP
At Gawthrop
Occupation Road
2
BARBON
Gawthrop
DENT
5
Dent appears
summit of walk
1195'
Mill Beck
High Laning
1
Dent
SEDBERGH
Flinter Gill
DEEPDALE
COWGILL

See page 156

For a note on Dent see page 177

Near the top of Flinter Gill we emerge from wooded confines, and to the right Middleton Fell appears. On joining the 'Occy' Road, a beautifully composed scene awaits as lower Dentdale leads the eye to the grouping of the Howgill Fells.

In its enchanting setting, Flinter Gill tumbles over a series of rock ledges, though after a dry spell it is likely to be conspicuous by its absence.

WALK 37

LOWER GARSDALE

6¼ miles — from Garsdale Foot

A modest stroll through the pastures of the lower valley. Giant fells overshadow impressively.

slopes of Baugh Fell
looking north-east
Longstone Common
River Clough

There is a large parking area on Longstone Common, 2½ miles out of Sedbergh where the Hawes road (A684) becomes unfenced.

THE WALK

From the car-park take the minor road dropping to Danny Bridge over the River Clough, and follow this traffic-free byway updale for a good mile and a half. Several farms are passed and several gates encountered: after a long spell of being open to the left we become fully enclosed again to descend to a farm on a right-angle bend. A little further along is a short, steep pull, just past which is a gate labelled 'Bellow Hill'. Follow the track through the field, but at the first wall strike right to a stile. Head on by the wall to cross a tiny beck, to see the only gap in the next wall being a gate down to the right. Now aim for the farm across the field, using a stile in front of it to join its lane which drops down to the road.

Go left along the road for a quarter-mile or so, taking greater care as this is now the main road, not the back lane, and the verges offer little refuge. At the allotted distance - just beyond the first farm on the right - look for a half-hidden stile on a bend (left side of the road). Follow the wall away from it to a stile in the corner, and locate the next stile just left of the barn in front. Cross the next field to a gateway and then on to a stile back onto the road. Head left once again, this time in happily wider confines. After a long quarter-mile take a stile just past a barn to descend to the now close-at-hand River Clough.

The return leg now begins: at the end of the first pasture a gate and some trees deflect us briefly from the river, but then a long, pleasant and straightforward walk

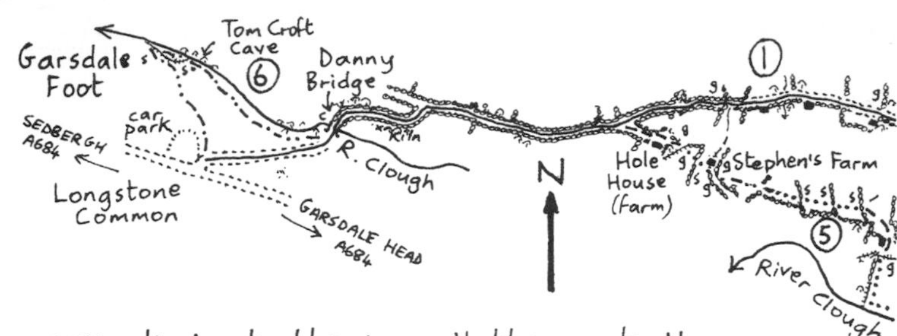
Garsdale Foot
Tom Croft Cave
Danny Bridge
6
1
car park
Kiln
R. Clough
SEDBERGH A684
Longstone Common
GARSDALE HEAD A684
N
Hole House (farm)
Stephen's Farm
5
River Clough

ensues, clinging to the river all the way to New Bridge, where the main road crosses to its south bank. Cross straight over the road and descend some steps to continue downstream as far as the first field boundary. Here a guidepost points us up to a barn. If its left-side is still defended by shoulder-high nettles then keep to the track, rising as far as the first bend above the barn. Now take a stile on the left, crossing several fields to arrive at the front of Stephen's Farm.

Continue across until Hole House farm appears just beyond it, and cross to a gate at the right side of a tiny plantation to enter its yard. Keep on past the buildings to emerge back onto our outward lane which then returns us to Danny Bridge. On crossing the bridge an enjoyable finish can be incorporated by following the riverbank downstream on the Sedgwick Geological trail. The trail ends beyond a short fenced section, and an initially sketchy path rises across the common and back to the car-park.

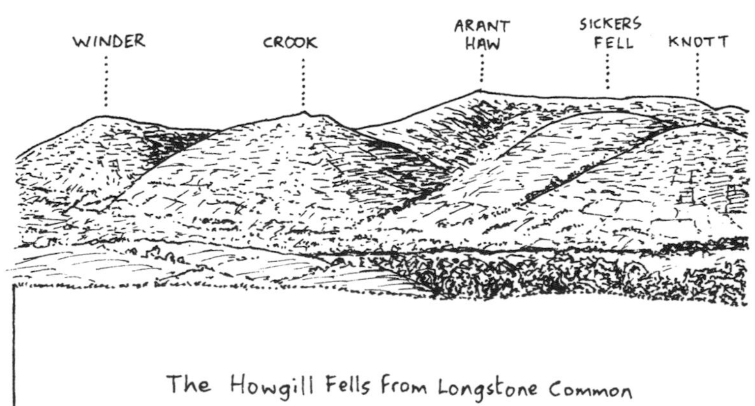
WINDER
CROOK
ARANT HAW
SICKERS FELL
KNOTT

The Howgill Fells from Longstone Common

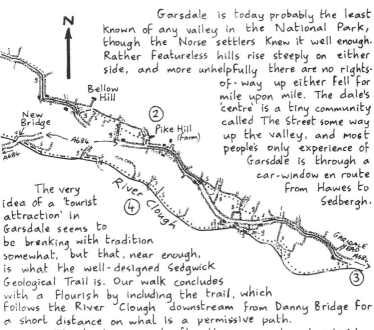

Garsdale is today probably the least known of any valley in the National Park, though the Norse settlers knew it well enough. Rather featureless hills rise steeply on either side, and more unhelpfully there are no rights-of-way up either fell for mile upon mile. The dale's 'centre' is a tiny community called The Street some way up the valley, and most people's only experience of Garsdale is through a car-window en route from Hawes to Sedbergh.

The very idea of a 'tourist attraction' in Garsdale seems to be breaking with tradition somewhat, but that, near enough, is what the well-designed Sedgwick Geological Trail is. Our walk concludes with a flourish by including the trail, which follows the River Clough downstream from Danny Bridge for a short distance on what is a permissive path.

The trail is named after the renowned geologist Adam Sedgwick (see page 177) and not after an imaginary nearby village as a new Dales guidebook would have us believe. A very detailed - beyond the author, to be honest - leaflet is available in Sedbergh or at the car-park explaining what to look for in this remarkable area, where the important Dent Fault is much in evidence.

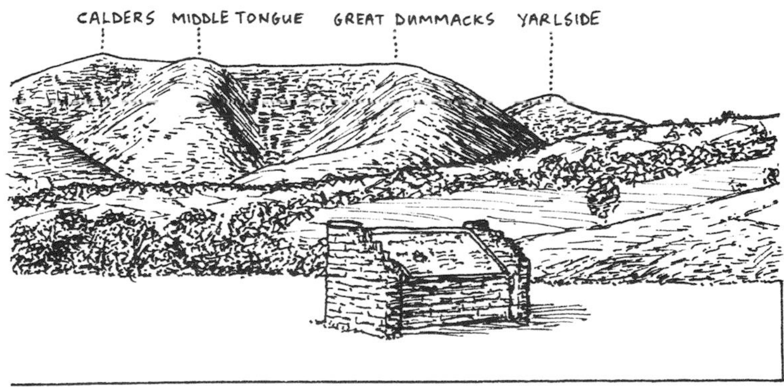
CALDERS
MIDDLE TONGUE
GREAT DUMMACKS
YARLSIDE

WALK 38 — BLEA MOOR AND DENT HEAD

9 miles — from Ribblehead

An invigorating march through the bleak country at the heads of two valleys

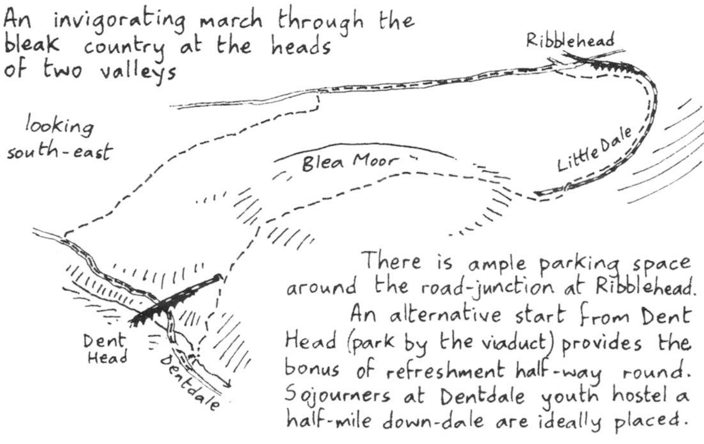
Ribblehead
looking south-east
Blea Moor
Little Dale
Dent Head
Dentdale

There is ample parking space around the road-junction at Ribblehead.

An alternative start from Dent Head (park by the viaduct) provides the bonus of refreshment half-way round. Sojourners at Dentdale youth hostel a half-mile down-dale are ideally placed.

THE WALK

From the inn walk a few yards in the Hawes direction then leave the road by the wide track heading for the viaduct. Fork right just before its arches on a reasonable path which runs parallel with the railway just over the wall. This situation continues for quite some time, though the path becomes damp underfoot and occasionally less clear as Blea Moor signal-box is passed. At the second bridge over the railway, just prior to Blea Moor tunnel, cross it and follow a crudely-paved path up to a gate. Here is a splendid view of the lower falls of Force Gill.

At this point the path is left and the fence is followed right to a stile. Our route now traces the course of the railway tunnel: descend to cross the trickle of Little Dale Beck, while making for the prominent spoil-heap just ahead. Here a good path is joined to rise up the hillside past two more heaps and attendant air-shafts, before levelling out to arrive at a stile in a boundary fence with Dentdale now in front.

The path descends past another air-shaft and through a plantation to meet the railway line again at the northern entrance to its tunnel. From a stile drop down by the left side of the line: the path soon moves away from it through a gateway to cross a footbridge. Just a little further downstream the farmyard of Dent Head is entered through a pair of gates. Cross the bridge to the right of the buildings and head half-right across a large field. From a stile in the far bottom corner, follow the right-hand fence down to an attractive farm-bridge onto the road through Dentdale. With the equally-attractive cottage of Bridge End opposite, this is the most distant part of the walk.

To begin the return, head right up the steep and narrow road, and under an arch of Dent Head viaduct. Continue climbing the road and as it levels out beyond a milestone, a stile and guidepost on the right indicate the way back. An undulating track is now followed, sometimes sketchy and more than occasionally wet. Two fences are met in quick succession and the way soon improves into a pleasanter green track.

At a guidepost just before the first farm (High Gayle) fork right off the main track to run along the top of the intake-wall above the farm. When the wall drops away follow it down to the dwellings at Winshaw, and then out along the access-road onto the Ingleton-Hawes road at Far Gearstones.

Turn right along it for a long mile's walking back to Ribblehead, passing the buildings at Gearstones on the way. This road-walking is not as tortuous as might be expected, as much of the tarmac can be avoided in favour of the grass verge.

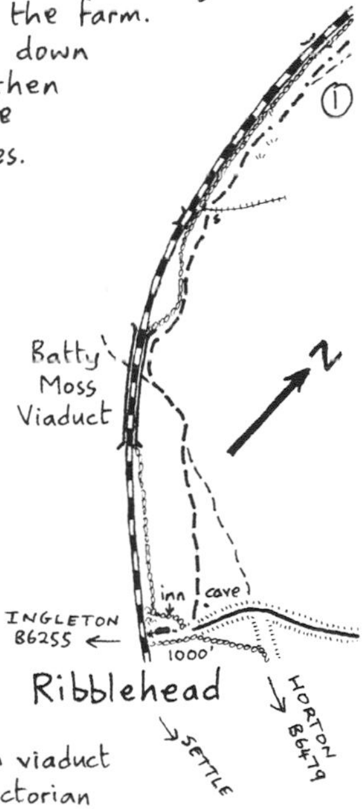

Ribblehead stands at the junction of two important Dales roads, where that from Ribblesdale meets the straight-as-a-die Ingleton to Hawes road. The only buildings here are the inn and some cottages by the railway. Ribblehead's nationally known feature, however, is its 24-arch viaduct which stands as a noble symbol of Victorian enthusiasm and engineering skills, but sadly also of the sheer folly and short-sightedness of our modern 'leaders'.

Had they but a fraction of their fore-fathers' vision!

Force Gill boasts two fine waterfalls, and it is the lower of these that we see from the gate. The short section of paved path after the aqueduct is a modern effort designed to protect a route rapidly becoming over-used through the diversion of the 'Three Peaks' ascent of Whernside.

The main track is an old packhorse route known as the Craven Way. It continues over the hill into Dentdale.

Force Gill
2
Blea Moor Tunnel (south entrance)
air shafts
Blea Moor
aqueduct
Little Dale Beck
Blea Moor Siding
Hare Gill

On reaching the air shafts the view improves as Baugh Fell's appearance signals the opening out to the north.

Blea Moor Tunnel is by far the longest tunnel on the Settle-Carlisle line. Constructed in the 1870's, it burrows under the moor for about 2630 feet. The central and deepest air shaft provides ventilation from more than 350 feet above the railway line.

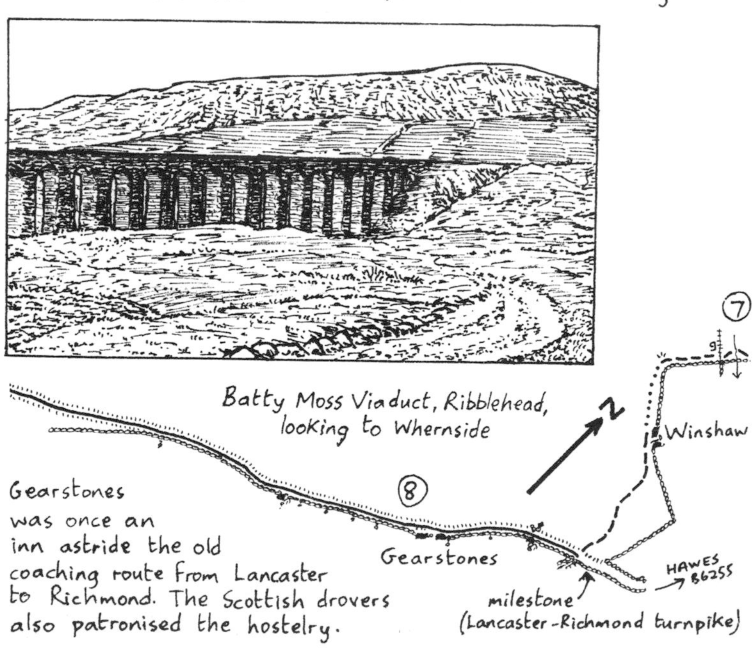
7
N
Winshaw
8
Gearstones
HAWES B6255
milestone
(Lancaster-Richmond turnpike)

Batty Moss Viaduct, Ribblehead, looking to Whernside

Gearstones was once an inn astride the old coaching route from Lancaster to Richmond. The Scottish drovers also patronised the hostelry.

On attaining the Dentdale side of Blea Moor's bleak top, the panorama over the valley is marvellous. Beyond the foot of the dale is a lengthy lakeland skyline, with the rounded Howgill Fells nearer to hand. Nearer still is Rise Hill backed by Baugh Fell, with Wild Boar Fell and High Seat filling the gap to the right before nearby Widdale Fell closes in. Artengill Viaduct and Dent Station can also be picked out at the dale head.

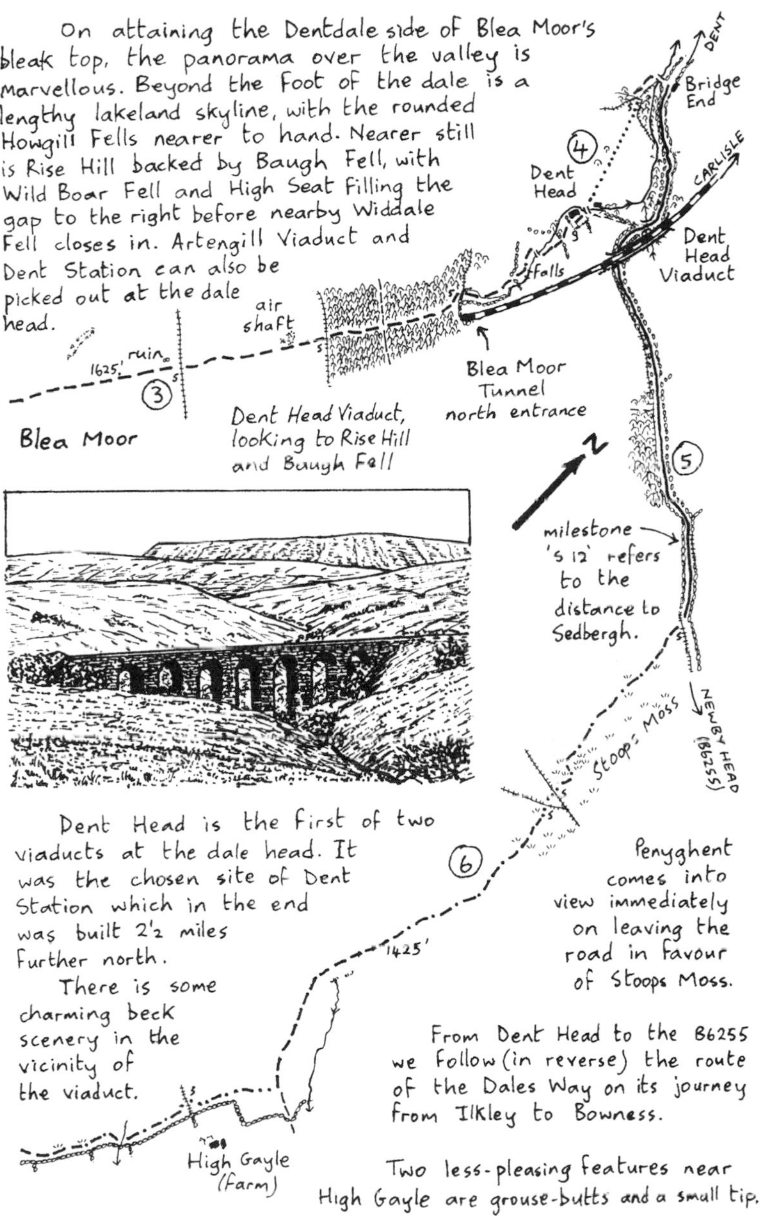
DENT
Bridge End
CARLISLE
4
Dent Head
Dent Head Viaduct
falls
air shaft
ruin
1625'
3
Blea Moor
Blea Moor Tunnel north entrance
N
5
milestone
NEWBY HEAD (B6255)
Stoops Moss
6
1425'
High Gayle (farm)

Dent Head Viaduct, looking to Rise Hill and Baugh Fell

'S 12' on the milestone refers to the distance to Sedbergh.

Dent Head is the first of two viaducts at the dale head. It was the chosen site of Dent Station which in the end was built 2½ miles further north.

There is some charming beck scenery in the vicinity of the viaduct.

Penyghent comes into view immediately on leaving the road in favour of Stoops Moss.

From Dent Head to the B6255 we follow (in reverse) the route of the Dales Way on its journey from Ilkley to Bowness.

Two less-pleasing features near High Gayle are grouse-butts and a small tip.

WALK 39 — GAPING GILL AND CLAPDALE

5¾ miles

from Clapham

A straightforward exploration of the many interesting limestone features that lurk in the fine valley above Clapham.

Gaping Gill
looking north-west
Trow Gill
Ingleborough Cave
Clapdale Farm
Clapdale
Clapham

Use the National Park car-park in the village centre

THE WALK

From the car-park cross the footbridge and take the lane up to the top of the village. Just after it turns left, a gate on the right leads to the cottage where modest dues must be paid for the worthy pleasure of experiencing the private grounds beyond. A wide track goes to the right of the cottage then zig-zags up to the foot of the Lake. This wide track is now followed unerringly past the numerous features of this fascinating valley. Beyond Ingleborough Cave a corner is rounded to climb through Trow Gill onto the open moor. A good path accompanies a wall, crossing it at the second stile reached. Just behind it is Bar Pot, and a few minutes further the path leads a little sketchily and damply to the unmistakeable hollow of Gaping Gill.

Having had a good - and cautious - potter about, steps can be retraced to the wall and back down through Trow Gill to Ingleborough Cave. A little further on, the return can be varied by taking a path rising up to the right just prior to entering Clapdale Wood. After a short climb Clapdale Farm is reached: take the stile on the left to enter its yard, then head directly away along its access track.

Good views across Clapdale to the plateau of Norber are enjoyed before the track descends (with views ahead of the Bowland moors) to the edge of Clapham again, emerging next to the ticket cottage. This varied finish can be concluded by crossing the first bridge to approach the church, then turning right to return to the car park.

Clapham is a beautiful village in a setting to match. Thankfully by-passed some years ago, it stands at the foot of Ingleborough from where the waters of Clapham Beck flow to form the centrepiece of the village. Several attractive bridges cross the tree-lined watercourse, and a splendid array of stone cottages line the parallel lane. On the east side of the beck are ranged all the individual features including the inn, the car park and National Park Centre - the old manor house -, the Cave Rescue Organisation HQ, and the church. Dedicated to St. James, its 15th century tower is the best feature.

Near the church is Ingleborough Hall, currently an outdoor centre, but formerly the home of the Farrer family. Best known of them was Reginald (1880 - 1920) who found fame as a botanist, collecting alpine plants on his journeys to far-flung parts and bringing many back to the grounds of the hall. The heavily-wooded grounds and the lake were created by the family earlier in the 19th century. The estate is still privately-owned, hence the small admission fee for enjoying the grounds.

Trow Gill

Gaping Gill

39

Gaping Gill is the great hole, the one that everyone has heard of and that a good number of non-cavers have descended. On the open moor in the lap of Ingleborough, this mighty chasm cannot fail to impress. The innoccuous stream of Fell Beck suddenly falls an unbroken 340 feet from the unfenced lip to the floor of the chamber, which is said to be of sufficient size to hold York Minster. This is no place for skylarking or unrestrained children.

At the two main bank holiday weekends one of two local caving clubs set up a chair and winch to lower the likes of you and me down. If not charged for the descent, you'll have to pay to return to the surface! Several miles of passages radiate from the main chamber, and the course of Fell Beck finally returns to daylight as Clapham Beck, at Beck Head alongside Ingleborough Cave. A connection by cavers was only established in the 1980's after many years efforts.

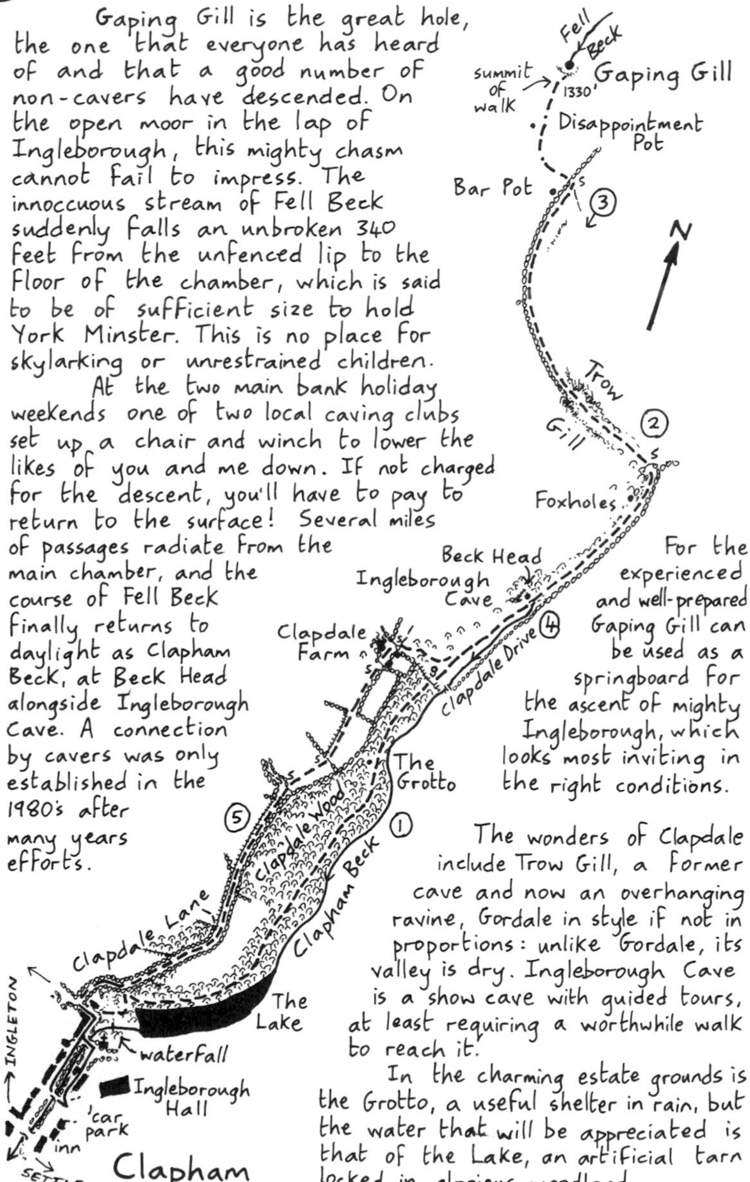

For the experienced and well-prepared Gaping Gill can be used as a springboard for the ascent of mighty Ingleborough, which looks most inviting in the right conditions.

The wonders of Clapdale include Trow Gill, a former cave and now an overhanging ravine, Gordale in style if not in proportions: unlike Gordale, its valley is dry. Ingleborough Cave is a show cave with guided tours, at least requiring a worthwhile walk to reach it.

In the charming estate grounds is the Grotto, a useful shelter in rain, but the water that will be appreciated is that of the Lake, an artificial tarn locked in glorious woodland.

Fell Beck
summit of walk
1330'
Gaping Gill
Disappointment Pot
Bar Pot
3
N
Trow Gill
2
Foxholes
Beck Head
Ingleborough Cave
4
Clapdale Drive
Clapdale Farm
The Grotto
5
Clapdale Wood
1
Clapham Beck
Clapdale Lane
The Lake
waterfall
Ingleborough Hall
car park
inn
INGLETON
SETTLE
Clapham

WALK 40 A CIRCUIT OF DEEPDALE

6½ miles from Deepdale Foot

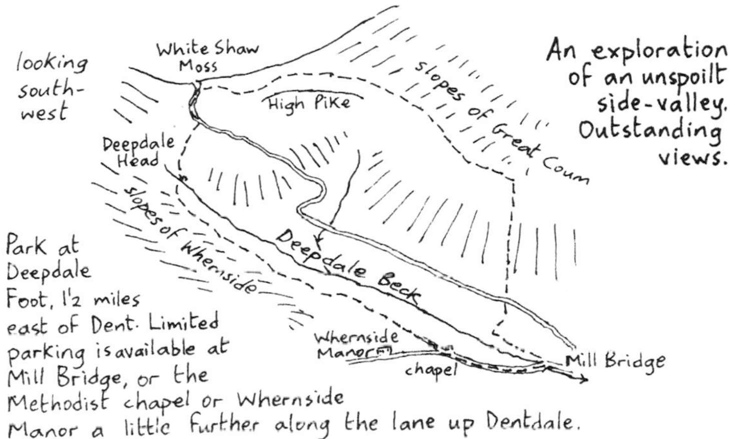
looking south-west
White Shaw Moss
High Pike
slopes of Great Coum
Deepdale Head
slopes of Whernside
Deepdale Beck
Whernside Manor
chapel
Mill Bridge

An exploration of an unspoilt side-valley. Outstanding views.

Park at Deepdale Foot, 1½ miles east of Dent. Limited parking is available at Mill Bridge, or the Methodist chapel or Whernside Manor a little further along the lane up Dentdale.

THE WALK

Take the farm lane rising alongside the Methodist chapel and remain on it until a sharp bend just beyond some barns. Here take the gate in front and continue the same course across the top of a field to an almost-hidden stile at the far end. Keep by a fence just above Deepdale Beck, and from the next stile several fields are crossed with stiles always there to confirm the way. Eventually a wall joins from the left to lead us to Mire Garth Farm.

Continue by the wall to a ruin, and from the stile to its right head past a barn to reach the gate to Deepdale Head farm. Instead of this gate take the smaller one a few yards beyond. A corner of the farmyard is crossed to another gate, from where a steep climb ensues alongside a tiny beck on the right. From a stile at the top a path runs to a guidepost, and from it head half-right, guided by posts up the open pasture. A small but conspicuous gully is the key to a stile just to its left, and here the Ingleton-Dent road is joined close to its summit.

Turn up the road a short distance and then leave it by a walled track to the right. Apart from one brief spell without walls, the way is completely foolproof

Whernside Manor was built about two hundred years ago when it was known as West House. It is now in the hands of the National Park Authority, and its proper title is the National Park Outdoor Recreation and Study Centre. Having initially specialised in caving, it now runs a range of courses in various outdoor activities.

Deepdale Methodist chapel stands in a typically isolated location, tucked hard by a lane junction embowered in trees.

COWGILL
Whernside Manor
Methodist chapel
Mill Bridge
Deepdale Beck
DENT
6
Peacock Hill (Farm)
INGLETON
DENT
Nun House Outrake
N
5
Occupation Road

The Occupation Road is a walled track which runs across the northern flank of Great Coum, linking the Dent-Ingleton road with that from Gawthrop to Barbon. An old packhorse way, it provides marvellous views from its strictly defined contour.

Nun House Outrake is a Jekyll and Hyde character, partly a delight, partly like a stony river bed.

THE WALK *continued*

as it winds its level course round the hillside under the shadow of the nearby summit of Great Coum. When another walled track presents an opportunity to leave, take it and follow it all the way down onto the Ingleton-Dent road once more.

Cross straight over and down a short track, crossing over a wider track and across a small field behind. From a gate at the far side descend by a hedge to a gate above some barns. Drop left to a stile by the nearest building and then commence a level course along to the left. At the end of the meadow is a stile near Deepdale Beck: continue on past a small limekiln, rising a little to the next field above a line of trees.

From the next stile head on below a short length of wall, then bear right to the trees shrouding the beck. A path descends to it to reach Mill Bridge only yards further downstream. Cross the bridge and the chapel will be found only a couple of minutes up to the right.

40

Gatty Pike and Great Coum from High Pike

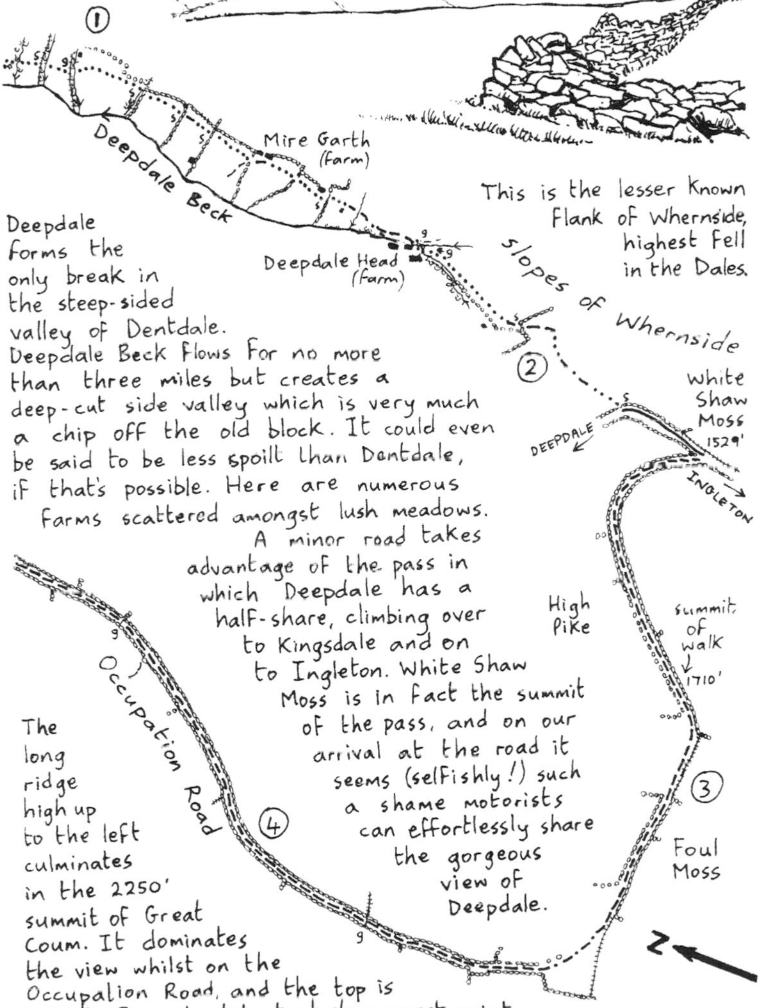

This is the lesser known flank of Whernside, highest fell in the Dales.

Deepdale forms the only break in the steep-sided valley of Dentdale. Deepdale Beck flows for no more than three miles but creates a deep-cut side valley which is very much a chip off the old block. It could even be said to be less spoilt than Dentdale, if that's possible. Here are numerous farms scattered amongst lush meadows.

A minor road takes advantage of the pass in which Deepdale has a half-share, climbing over to Kingsdale and on to Ingleton. White Shaw Moss is in fact the summit of the pass, and on our arrival at the road it seems (selfishly!) such a shame motorists can effortlessly share the gorgeous view of Deepdale.

The long ridge high up to the left culminates in the 2250' summit of Great Coum. It dominates the view whilst on the Occupation Road, and the top is only half a mile distant at its nearest point.

1
Deepdale Beck
Mire Garth (farm)
Deepdale Head (farm)
slopes of Whernside
2
White Shaw Moss 1529'
DEEPDALE
INGLETON
High Pike
summit of walk 1710'
3
Foul Moss
Occupation Road
4
N

WALK 41 — GRISEDALE AND TURNER HILL

3¾ miles — from Garsdale Head

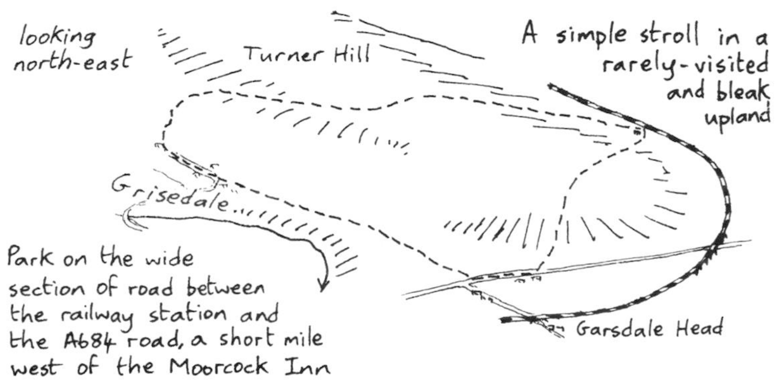

looking
north-east
Turner Hill
A simple stroll in a
rarely-visited
and bleak
upland
Grisedale
Park on the wide
section of road between
the railway station and
the A684 road, a short mile
west of the Moorcock Inn
Garsdale Head

THE WALK

Take the road down to the T-junction and cross straight over the main road to a stile. Head up the pasture to the next stile, from where the waterfall of Clough Force can be seen down to the left by a detour towards the beck. Back on the hillside continue in a near-straight line towards Grisedale. A prominent tree entices us towards a group of farm buildings, and from a stile to the right, several more lead us down into the valley. Without joining the road at Beck Side, take a stile just beyond some barns and continue parallel with the road, and use another stile near a barn to emerge onto the unenclosed road at Moor Rigg.

Turn right to the road's demise at East House, then continue up the track onto the open moor. Fork right by the intake wall, and when the track fades curve gently left on a level course to a gate in view well ahead. From it descend a rough pasture to a footbridge over the railway line. Do not cross it but take a stile between the line and the lone house, and head diagonally across to a collapsed wall. Rising behind it, use a depression between two gentle slopes to locate a stile in the next wall. Now a sketchy path continues across two pastures before beginning a direct descent to the main road, emerging at a stile opposite a farm.

The Garsdale Head road junction is now only a couple of minutes along to the right.

Swarth Fell from Blake Mire

Turner Hill is a brief levelling out of the ridge descending from Swarth Fell. The wall leads up to its broad top which provides an extension to the already distant views.

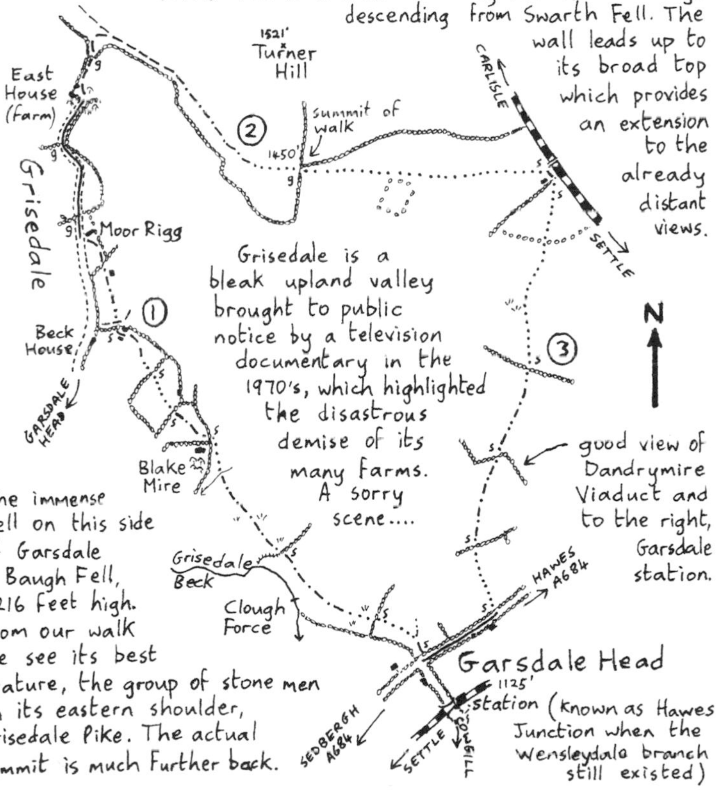

1521'
Turner Hill
East House (farm)
summit of walk
1450'
CARLISLE
SETTLE
Grisedale
Moor Rigg
Beck House
GARSDALE HEAD
Blake Mire
N

Grisedale is a bleak upland valley brought to public notice by a television documentary in the 1970's, which highlighted the disastrous demise of its many farms. A sorry scene....

good view of Dandrymire Viaduct and to the right, Garsdale station.

The immense fell on this side of Garsdale is Baugh Fell, 2216 feet high. From our walk we see its best feature, the group of stone men on its eastern shoulder, Grisedale Pike. The actual summit is much further back.

Grisedale Beck
Clough Force
HAWES A684
Garsdale Head
1125'
station (known as Hawes Junction when the Wensleydale branch still existed)
SEDBERGH A684
SETTLE
COWGILL

WALK 42

THE INGLETON GLENS

4¼ miles

from Ingleton

A classic, and rightly so. Don't go after a prolonged drought.

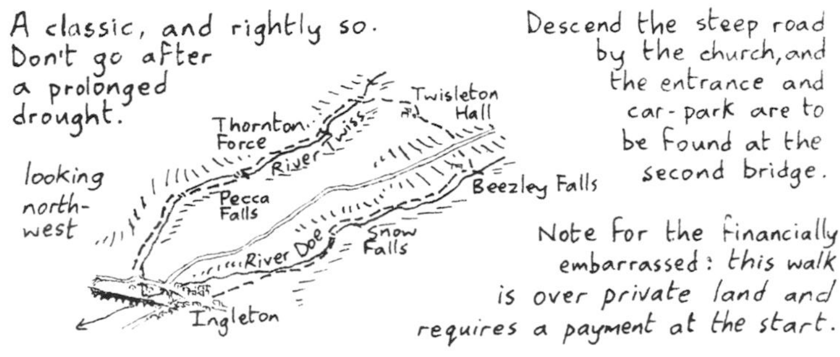
Twisleton Hall
Thornton Force
River Twiss
looking north-west
Pecca Falls
Beezley Falls
Snow Falls
River Doe
Ingleton

Descend the steep road by the church, and the entrance and car-park are to be found at the second bridge.

Note for the financially embarrassed: *this walk is over private land and requires a payment at the start.*

THE WALK

Few directions are needed for this walk, as the paths are very clear throughout, and the way obvious: from the car park the path heads up the valley of the Twiss, twice crossing the river to arrive at Pecca Falls. A little further is Thornton Force, beyond which the path soon crosses the beck to rise to an enclosed track. This is Twisleton Lane, which leads along to the right to the confines of Twisleton Hall Farm. Keep left of all the buildings, using two stiles and a track which descends a field to a lane. Cross straight over and down to Beezleys Farm, going between the buildings to a gate on the left.

A left fork leads to Beezley Falls, from where the River Doe is now accompanied downstream. Beyond Snow Falls a footbridge conveys us to the opposite bank, and our path rises through trees, emerging high above the river at Cat Leap Force. The path meets the head of a lane to enter the centre of Ingleton. Turn right, and beyond the church drop down to cross both rivers before reaching the car park.

Commonly referred to as the 'waterfalls walk', this is one of the two famous excursions available from Ingleton village, the other being the climb to the summit of Ingleborough. With much justification, the Falls walk has attracted visitors for over a century, and probably more so than any other walk in this book, it is worth savouring in one of the winter months when the jostling has ceased. The paths are everywhere well maintained - justifying the charge - but care is still needed when wet leaves carpet the ground. Be also aware that, for a low-level walk, there is a fair amount of 'up and down' work.

The two valleys explored on this walk are remarkably alike, each beautifully wooded and exposing interesting geological features, with the Craven Faults much in evidence. Even without the chief attractions, this would still be a fine walk. For some reason the names of the watercourses have caused confusion. The Twiss is known by some as the Greta, while more curiously Wainwright has transposed the Greta (Twiss) and the Doe. Maybe there's hope for the author yet! What is less in doubt is that at their meeting, if not any earlier, the Greta is born.

Above Thornton Force lies the flat valley floor of Kingsdale, at one time a glacial lake held back by Raven Ray, a good example of a moraine.

From the vicinity of Scar End, Ingleborough displays itself proudly

Ingleton is famed as the centre for Yorkshire's limestone country, and is certainly a good base for exploring the fells, scars, caves and valleys of the area. The roadside signs proclaiming 'Beauty Spot of the North' may raise the odd smile, but usually only from travellers on the busy A65 which avoids the village centre and its nearby attractions.

Note the striking tilted rock strata in the quarry opposite

The centre of Ingleton is dominated by a long-abandoned railway viaduct. Also prominent is the parish church, and there are numerous interesting little corners to the village. The youth hostel is centrally situated, as are several useful hostelries and shops.

The 'beauty' of Ingleton, however, must be its location.

42

Thornton Force

WALK 43 — CAUTLEY SPOUT AND THE RAWTHEY

6¼ miles

from Cautley

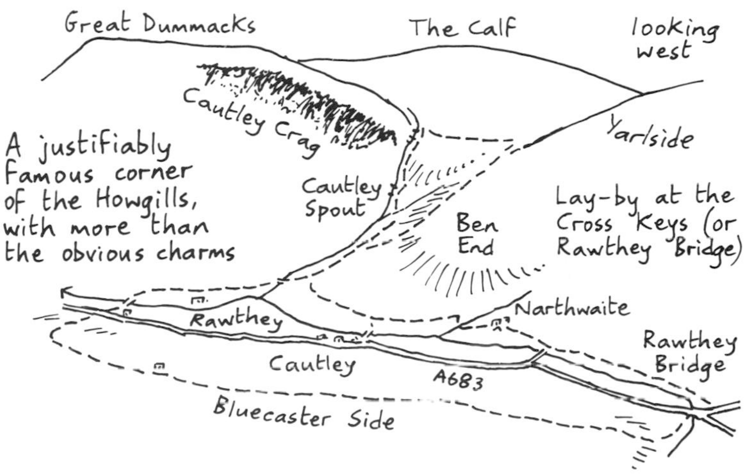
Great Dummacks
The Calf
looking west
Cautley Crag
Yarlside
A justifiably famous corner of the Howgills, with more than the obvious charms
Cautley Spout
Ben End
Lay-by at the Cross Keys (or Rawthey Bridge)
Narthwaite
Rawthey
Rawthey Bridge
Cautley
A683
Bluecaster Side

THE WALK

Cross the footbridge over the Rawthey just above the inn, and go straight ahead onto a wide track. Turn right along it, continuing as a pleasant green path to ford Backside Beck (a challenge after a wet spell) before a short pull to Narthwaite. Leave the farm buildings by the drive on the right, following it almost all the way down to the main road. A gate on a sharp bend points the way along a lesser track which ends at a wood. Through a gate, ford a stream to follow a path along the wood-bottom, and when the fence turns right it slants down to follow the Rawthey upstream. Emerging from the trees to cross a brace of fields, a tiny stream is crossed (by a bridge, at last!) to rise onto the road just above Rawthey Bridge.

Within a few yards of crossing the bridge take a gate on the left, from where a track heading away almost at once turns sketchily right in a distinctly 'moist' neighbourhood. Soon the track improves, and after a gentle rise it starts to run parallel with but high above the main road. Shortly after going past Bluecaster Cottage a gate is reached at a lane-head, and just after it take a gate on the right to descend a sunken track onto the road.

43

Cross the main road and down a farm road over the Rawthey and through the fields to Cautley Thwaite Farm. Keep straight on through two gates and to the right of a barn, then going a little left to a gate to emerge on a good path. Soon Cautley Holme Beck is crossed by a basic bridge, from where a path runs along to the foot of Cautley Spout. To enjoy a closer look, cross the side beck and tackle the steep path by the gill. Caution is urged when peering into the lower fall, which is partially obscured by hardy foliage.

Continuing up, the upper falls are free of obstruction and can be savoured more leisurely. At the top the path levels out, and here leave it after locating a trod along to the right. After a steady traverse it fades, leaving you to slant down to the incisive pass of Bowderdale Head. Turning right a good path forms to return with the side beck to the foot of the Spout. Omitting Cautley Holme Beck, head back round the base of Yarlside on the 'tourist' path, turning upstream with the Rawthey to quickly return to the footbridge at the start.

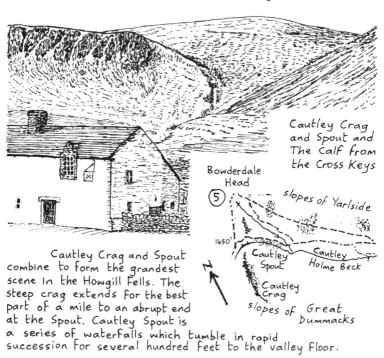

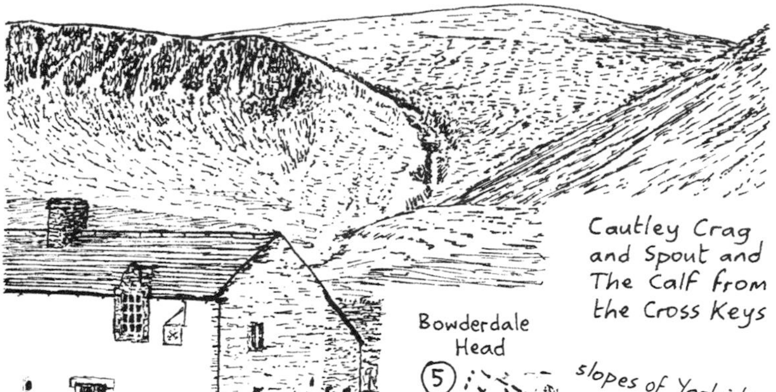

Cautley Crag and Spout and The Calf from the Cross Keys

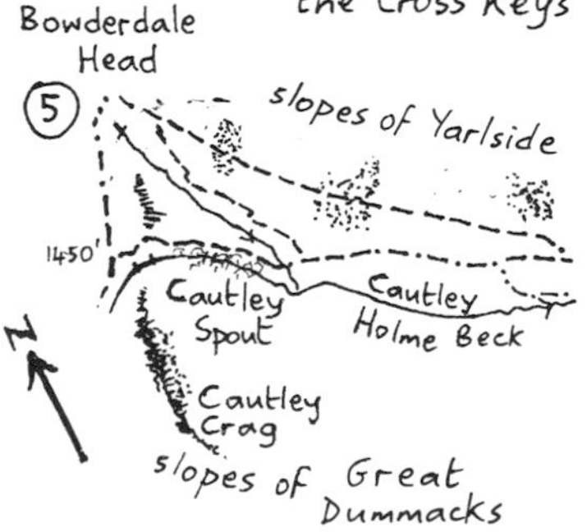

Bowderdale Head
5
slopes of Yarlside
1450'
Cautley Spout
Cautley Holme Beck
Cautley Crag
slopes of Great Dummacks

Cautley Crag and Spout combine to form the grandest scene in the Howgill Fells. The steep crag extends for the best part of a mile to an abrupt end at the Spout. Cautley Spout is a series of waterfalls which tumble in rapid succession for several hundred feet to the valley floor.

The river Rawthey flows for sixteen miles from near the lonely summit of Baugh Fell to its acceptance into the Lune beyond Sedbergh. On the journey there it absorbs the waters of the Clough and the Dee. All is preciously unspoilt hereabouts, and in the neighbourhood of this walk the river exudes all its charms, flowing along a green valley bottom with bare fells rising on each side.

Rawthey Bridge marks the old Yorkshire-Westmorland boundary and, as a result, the illogical National Park boundary also. Between the prosaicly titled Backside Beck and the bridge we therefore tread a mile of old Westmorland.

The Cross Keys is that rare creature the temperance inn. Though labelled Cautley there is no definable centre, just a scattering of farms, dwellings and a church along the Sedbergh road.

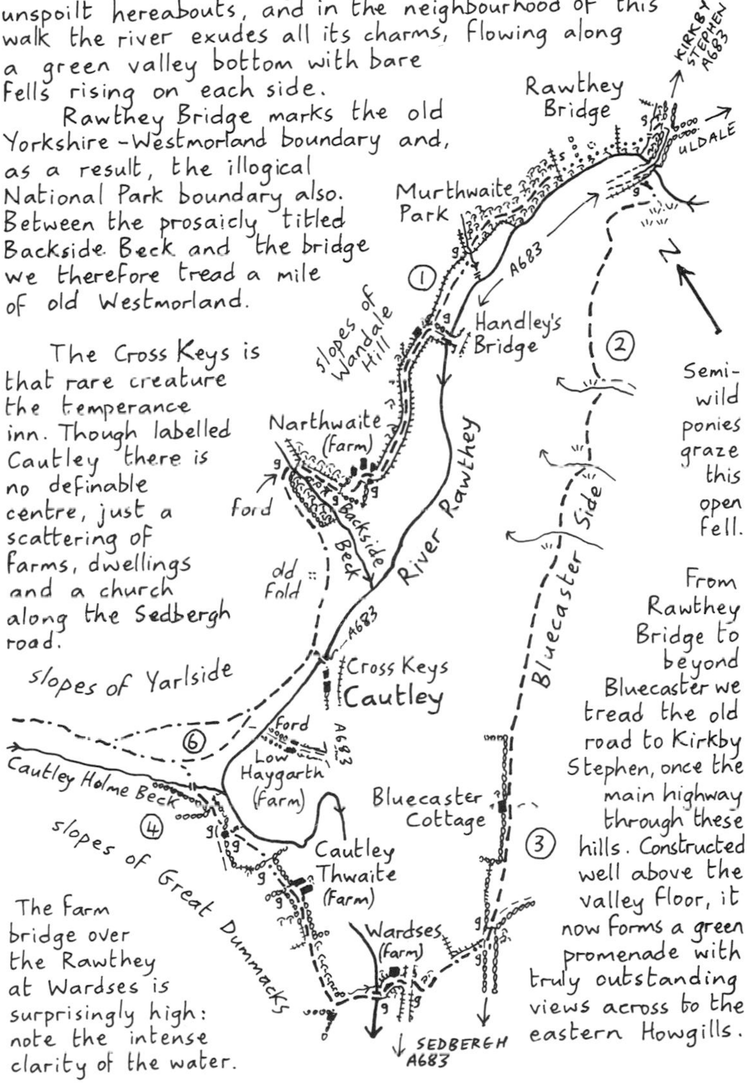

Semi-wild ponies graze this open fell.

From Rawthey Bridge to beyond Bluecaster we tread the old road to Kirkby Stephen, once the main highway through these hills. Constructed well above the valley floor, it now forms a green promenade with truly outstanding views across to the eastern Howgills.

The farm bridge over the Rawthey at Wardses is surprisingly high: note the intense clarity of the water.

WALK 44 SMEARSETT SCAR, FEIZOR AND THE RIBBLE

7½ miles

from Stainforth

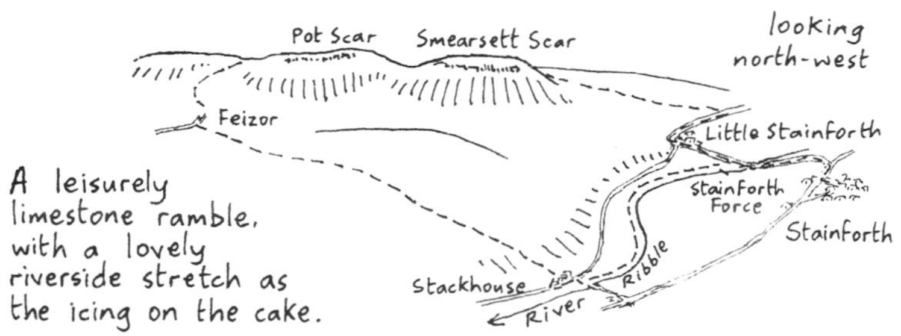
Pot Scar
Smearsett Scar
looking north-west
Feizor
Little Stainforth
Stainforth Force
Stainforth
Stackhouse
River Ribble

A leisurely limestone ramble, with a lovely riverside stretch as the icing on the cake.

Use the main car-park just off the main road

THE WALK

From the car-park join the main road alongside the village and turn right, leaving it almost immediately by a lane to the left. The railway line is bridged before descending to cross Stainforth Bridge then up to a junction at Little Stainforth. Head along the lane to the right, and at a bend take a track rising to a barn on the left. The right-of-way is officially the parallel enclosed way, joining the track above the barn. On rounding a wall-corner a stile is found, and when the track suddenly ends continue by the wall, the way being made clear by a string of four further stiles in the same direction. From the last one no more are visible: here continue straight across over the gentle brow, with the steep slope on the left rising towards the Ordnance column atop Smearsett Scar.

With no public right-of-way to the top, the route simply crosses the pasture to the next stile. Intermittently it heads half-right to another stile then remains by the wall to reach a stile onto the lane through Feizor Nick. Go left along it to descend into the heart of Feizor.

Follow the lane only to the cobbled watersplash, then take a rough track on the left between barns. Beyond a gate a wide track heads across a long pasture, continuing sketchily when the accompanying wall leaves us. Eventually a stile is reached, and the still-sketchy track maintains its direction through two gates. Just past the second take a gate on the right before resuming the trek. Beyond the next gate the track zig-zags down to a gate where it fades completely. Head straight across the field where a choice of neighbouring stiles precede a steeper drop to the outside of Stackhouse's private world. Go right, and a sketchy path through the trees leads to a stile onto a lane.

Turn left past two entrances to Stackhouse and take an enclosed track to the right to meet the Ribble at the Locks. Don't use the footbridge but follow the river upstream: at the end of a long pasture after Langcliffe paper mill we are briefly parted from the river, but other than that its bank leads unerringly to Stainforth Force. Just above the falls is the packhorse bridge, from where the first few steps of the walk can be retraced up into Stainforth village.

Knight Stainforth Hall

Feizor is an unspoilt settlement at the terminus for motor vehicles of a short cul-de-sac to this hollow in the hills. Footpaths, however, radiate in various directions.

Note the water pump and trough sited on the little green in front of the prettiest grouping of cottages.

Feizor Nick
N
2
Pot Scar
3
Feizor
TO A65
4

Smearsett Scar is the brother of Pot Scar, and boasts a shapely aspect when seen from the east (around Stainforth) or the west. Its south face falls away sharply with low crags giving way to scree slopes. Smearsett's character is rivalled admirably by its status as a viewpoint, and is probably the best vantage point for surveying Ribblesdale.

Pot Scar forms a striking backdrop to the cottages of Feizor, its gleaming scars apparently reaching for the sky.

Included are Horton and Helwith Bridge backed by Plover Hill, Penyghent and Fountains Fell. Then come Stainforth Scar and Settle's shapely hills. To the south are the Happy Valley and the Celtic Wall, both close at hand and contrasting with distant Pendle Hill. Moving westwards are the Bowland Fells, and closer again we have Norber, Moughton, Ingleborough and a tip of Whernside.

Penyghent from Feizor Nick

44

Stainforth is a sizeable village stood high above and back from the Ribble, and by-passed some years ago by the main road up the dale. In central locations are a pleasant inn and the mid-nineteenth century church of St. Peter. Stainforth's best-known features, however, are outside the village. The hand of man fashioned an eighteenth century mansion on the Horton road, which now serves as a youth hostel, and also Stainforth Bridge, a graceful structure which conveyed the packhorse trade over the Ribble on the old York-Lancaster route. It is now in the care of the National Trust. Only 100 yards downstream are the beautifully sparkling falls.

HELWITH BRIDGE
1191'
Smearsett Scar
HORTON
B6479
CARLISLE
Stainforth
Little Stainforth
Hall
SETTLE
car park
caravan site
Stainforth Force
SETTLE B6479
STACKHOUSE
River Ribble
N
paper mill
Stackhouse
weir
Locks
SETTLE

Little Stainforth, also known as Knight Stainforth, is a tiny hamlet, and a kid brother to Stainforth across the river. Very noteworthy is the rather austere hall, dating largely from the mid-seventeenth century, and on the site of an older hall.

An easy but harmless error is to continue along the north side of this wall, a short detour which, by mishap or design, is most fruitful for the view of Penyghent from the outcrops there.

Stackhouse is a cosy little grouping of rather superior dwellings, huddling beneath the hill and happy to remain half-hidden in its protective surround of greenery.

an attractive scene

WALK 45

CROOK AND WINDER

4 miles

from Sedbergh

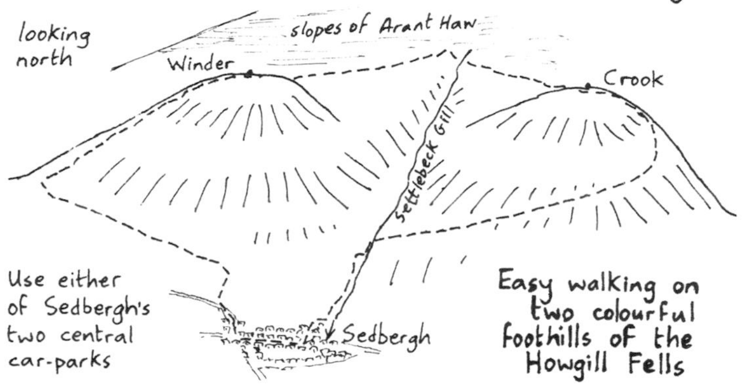
looking north
slopes of Arant Haw
Winder
Crook
Settlebeck Gill
Sedbergh
Use either of Sedbergh's two central car-parks
Easy walking on two colourful foothills of the Howgill Fells

THE WALK

Leave the main street by Joss Lane alongside the car-park. It rises past houses to a gate, there becoming a farm-track. Cross to the top corner of the field where a path climbs to run parallel with Settlebeck Gill, and a gate admits to the open fell. From a choice of paths take the least obvious one running down to the beck, which is forded just above the waterfall. The steep slope behind conceals a sunken track which rises sketchily to the high-point of the intake-wall. Take the good path sloping to the right across the face of Crook. It is well-graded throughout, and soon after swinging left above the valley of Ashbeck Gill a fork is met. Take the sunken way climbing left, and when it peters out the cairn atop Crook should be visible a little up to the left.

From Crook's top its brother Winder appears: as a bee-line is clearly out of the question, aim for the top of Settlebeck Gill, gaining a little height on the way. Cross the marshy beginnings of the beck and a parallel path before a gentle rise to the ridge running down to Winder from Arant Haw. A wide track is joined and despite a couple of forks the way to the Ordnance column on Winder is clear, only a modest ascent being required.

Leave the top by a path running west. It merges with another to descend to just above the intake-wall. Turn left above some trees to locate a narrow path through bracken. After Sedbergh appears the wall is joined: at a gate drop down through Lockbank farm onto Howgill Lane, turning left to re-enter Sedbergh.

The Howgill Fells are a compact, well-defined mountain group which must be suffering something of an identity crisis. Half the massif is in the Dales National Park, while half is not. Half was in the old county of Westmorland, half was in the West Riding of Yorkshire: since 1974 the entire group became part of Cumbria. To cap it all, these fells are alien to the Dales landscape and are more akin to Lakeland, whose National Park boundary is only 6 miles distant at one point. Wherever they are, or should be, there is no doubt that all the Howgills merit inclusion in a National Park.

Winder and Crook are two foothills of the group overlooking Sedbergh, with Winder in particular being a much trodden short climb. The Howgills rise to 2219 feet, are smooth, rounded and best of all free from walls and fences, leaving much freedom to roam.

Winder and Crook both claim excellent views of much of the Dales. At their feet is Sedbergh presiding over a complex meeting of valleys. The descent gives good views of the Lune Gorge and the western Howgills.

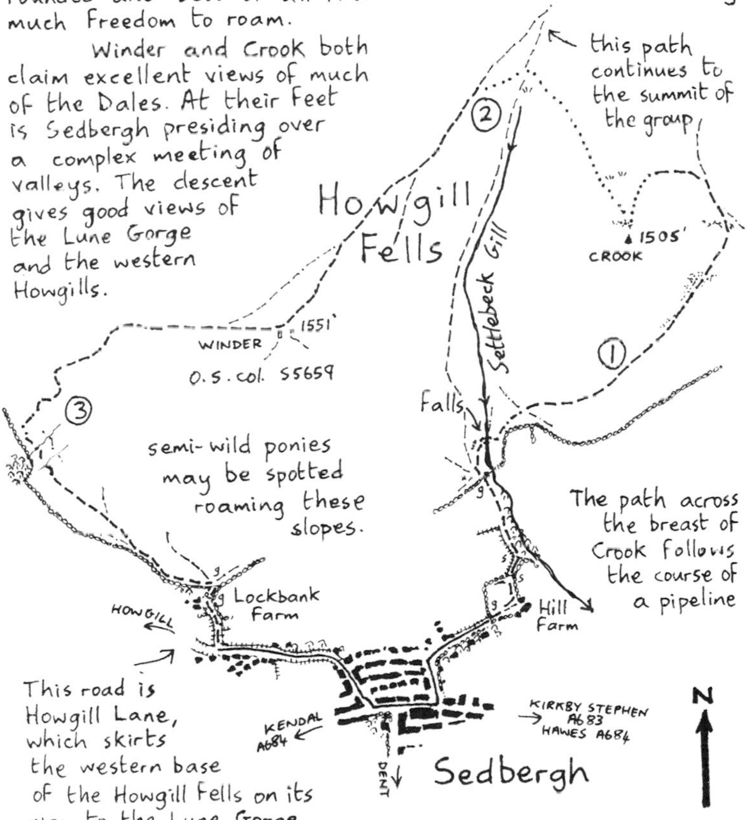

this path continues to the summit of the group

Howgill Fells

Settlebeck Gill

1505' CROOK

1551' WINDER

O.S. col. 55659

Falls

semi-wild ponies may be spotted roaming these slopes.

The path across the breast of Crook follows the course of a pipeline

Lockbank Farm

Hill Farm

HOWGILL

This road is Howgill Lane, which skirts the western base of the Howgill Fells on its way to the Lune Gorge.

KENDAL A684

KIRKBY STEPHEN A683
HAWES A684

DENT

Sedbergh

N

45

Sedbergh is the largest community in the Yorkshire Dales National Park, yet its isolation has helped it avoid the excesses of commercialism. Ceded to Cumbria in 1974, Sedbergh - omit the last two letters in pronunciation - was previously in the north-western extremity of the West Riding of Yorkshire, incredibly over 100 miles distant from its West Riding colleague Sheffield. Two simple facts prove that size is very much a relative thing.

This tiny market town boasts an unparalleled position on the lower slopes of its 'own' mountains the Howgill Fells, and the outlook on three sides is, in fact, of fells. This is the edge of the Dales, and to the west of the town runs the River Lune. In the neighbourhood of Sedbergh three lively rivers end their journeys, as the Dee, Clough and Rawthey join forces to swell the waters of the Lune.

Aside from the imposing Howgill Fells, Sedbergh itself is dominated by its public school. This famous establishment, which was founded in the early 16th century, includes Adam Sedgwick (see page 177) among its old boys. The oldest remaining part dates from 1716, and is now the library. Most other features of interest will be found on or near the lengthy main street, including a lovely parish church in an equally attractive wooded surround. Dedicated to St. Andrew it has a 15th century tower, with other parts dating back to Norman times as well as many other periods in between.

St. Andrew's Sedbergh

WALK 46 THE ENVIRONS OF CHAPEL-LE-DALE

5¼ miles from Chapel-le-Dale

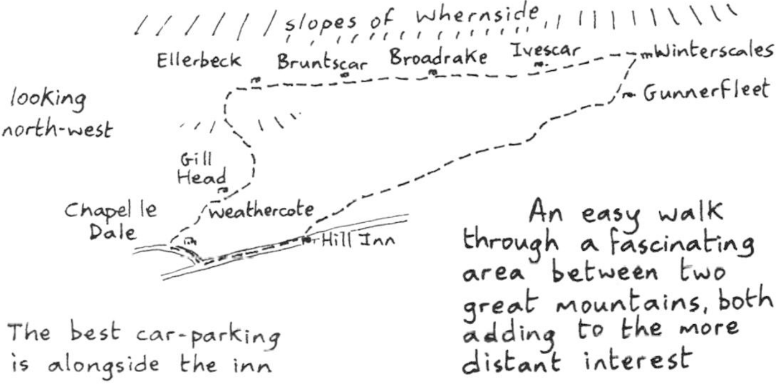
slopes of Whernside
Ellerbeck
Bruntscar
Broadrake
Ivescar
Winterscales
Gunnerfleet
looking north-west
Gill Head
Chapel le Dale
Weathercote
Hill Inn

An easy walk through a fascinating area between two great mountains, both adding to the more distant interest

The best car-parking is alongside the inn

THE WALK

From the Hill Inn head south along the Ingleton road, turning off to the right within minutes on a lane into the trees. At the church fork right again up an inviting lane: it is a farm road and is followed without deviation, passing along the front of Gill Head before crossing a large pasture to Ellerbeck. A rougher track passes in front of the buildings to a gate, crosses a field, and then runs through a long narrow pasture to Bruntscar.

Just beyond the buildings leave the farm road and go straight ahead to a gate. Across the next pasture Broadrake is reached. Once again pass along the front, and a less-clear path leads through several fields to join a track to Ivescar. Head straight on again - with the bulk of the buildings on the right - on another farm road until just short of Winterscales, where a branch right takes us across a pasture to Gunnerfleet.

Do not cross the beck to it, but remain on the farm road through more fields before it decides to cross the beck. Leave it after a cattle-grid soon after the bridge, a sketchy path following the wall to a gate. Head away from it with the left-hand wall, and when it departs continue on to descend to witness the disappearance of Winterscales Beck.

Cross to the stile opposite and follow the wall away. At a gate enter an enclosed track on the left which emerges onto another farm road. Follow it left past Philpin and out onto the main road only yards below the Hill Inn.

46

The Hill Inn, Chapelle Dale, and Ingleborough

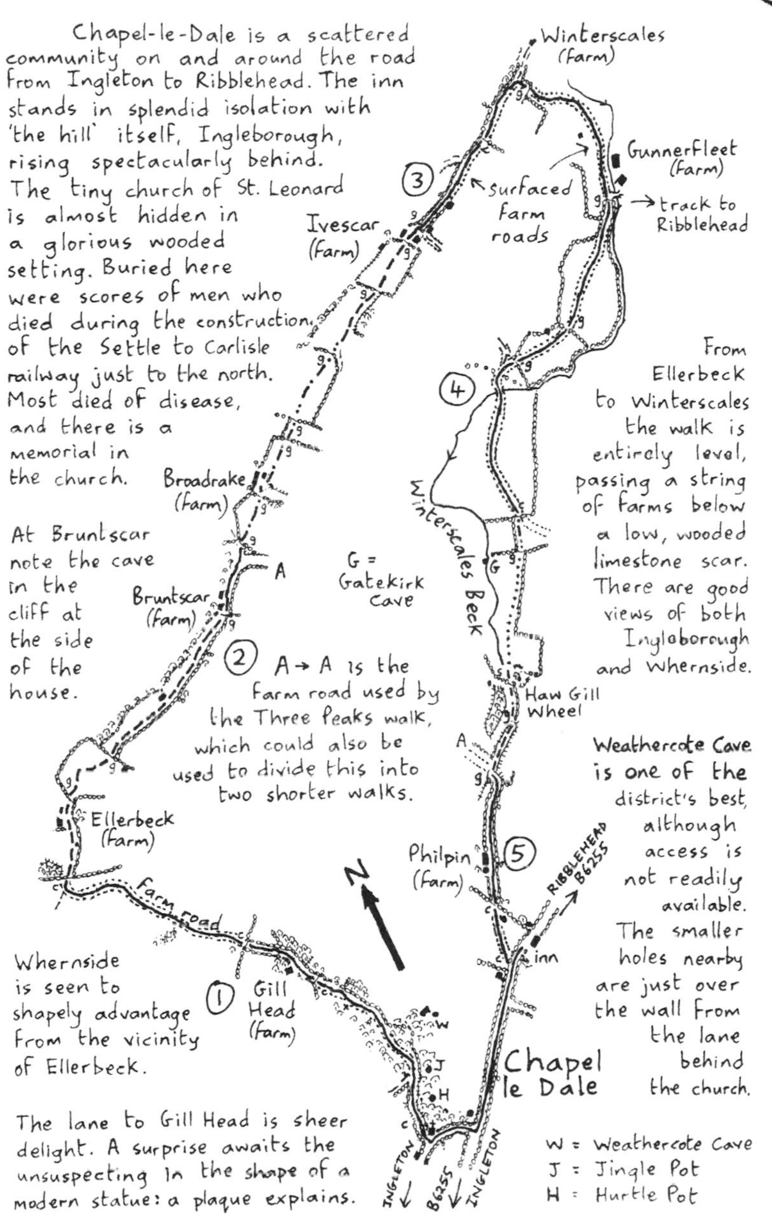
Chapel-le-Dale is a scattered community on and around the road from Ingleton to Ribblehead. The inn stands in splendid isolation with 'the hill' itself, Ingleborough, rising spectacularly behind. The tiny church of St. Leonard is almost hidden in a glorious wooded setting. Buried here were scores of men who died during the construction of the Settle to Carlisle railway just to the north. Most died of disease, and there is a memorial in the church.
At Bruntscar note the cave in the cliff at the side of the house.
Whernside is seen to shapely advantage from the vicinity of Ellerbeck.
The lane to Gill Head is sheer delight. A surprise awaits the unsuspecting in the shape of a modern statue: a plaque explains.
Winterscales (farm)
Gunnerfleet (farm)
track to Ribblehead
surfaced farm roads
Ivescar (farm)
3
4
From Ellerbeck to Winterscales the walk is entirely level, passing a string of farms below a low, wooded limestone scar. There are good views of both Ingleborough and Whernside.
Winterscales Beck
Broadrake (farm)
A
G = Gatekirk Cave
G
Bruntscar (farm)
2
A → A is the farm road used by the Three Peaks walk, which could also be used to divide this into two shorter walks.
Haw Gill Wheel
A
Weathercote Cave is one of the district's best, although access is not readily available. The smaller holes nearby are just over the wall from the lane behind the church.
Ellerbeck (farm)
Philpin (farm)
5
RIBBLEHEAD B6255
N
farm road
inn
1
Gill Head (farm)
W
J
H
Chapel le Dale
INGLETON
B6255
INGLETON
W = Weathercote Cave
J = Jingle Pot
H = Hurtle Pot

WALK 47 — THE BANKS OF THE DEE

4¾ miles

From Dent

looking south-west

A simple riverside stroll of peace and charm

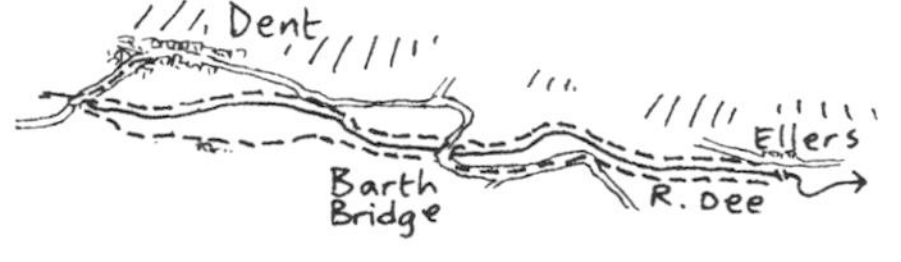
Dent
Ellers
Barth Bridge
R. Dee

Use the main car park in the village

THE WALK

From the car-park head along the cobbled street and out by the main up-dale road to Church Bridge across the Dee. Do not use it but take a stile to descend to the riverbank. The river is hugged almost all the way to the walk's turning-point, the footbridge at Ellers. The only breaks are firstly early on when the Dee nudges us onto the road for a few yards, and secondly approaching Barth Bridge, where stiles take a more direct course onto the road. The riverside path resumes straight across the road.

On reaching the wooden footbridge at Ellers, cross it and cling to the opposite bank until forced up to the road by the Elam monument. Turn right for a short stroll back to Barth Bridge, then take the enclosed byway heading straight on by the river. The Dee moves away, and forks to two farms are passed before a stile returns us to the river for the final yards back to Church Bridge. Now it can be crossed to re-enter Dent.

Church Bridge

The River Dee is a lively, sparkling watercourse, crystal clear and swift. It tumbles down the upper dale over endless limestone ledges, and in dry weather is liable to disappear for substantial lengths. Its grassy banks bear nothing larger than a hamlet.

Ellers

* Look for stile onto road before bridge

The roadside Elam monument is a small tablet erected by local people in honour of one Lucy Elam, who, in 1876, footed the bill for a re-routing of this very stretch of road

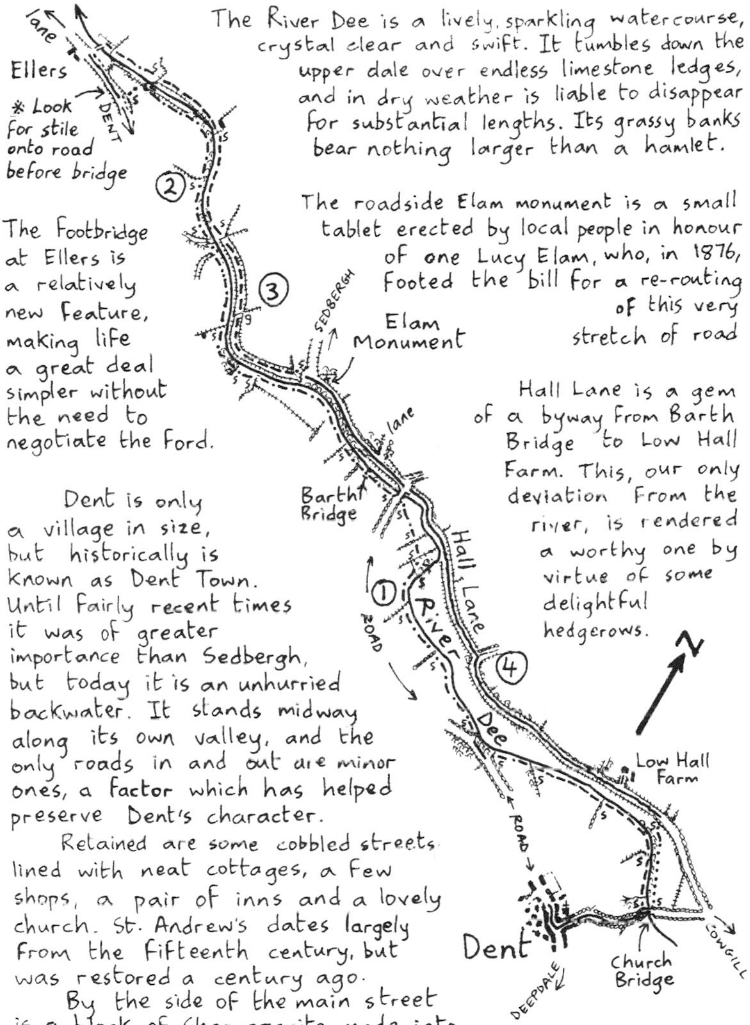

The Footbridge at Ellers is a relatively new feature, making life a great deal simpler without the need to negotiate the ford.

Hall Lane is a gem of a byway from Barth Bridge to Low Hall Farm. This, our only deviation from the river, is rendered a worthy one by virtue of some delightful hedgerows.

Dent is only a village in size, but historically is known as Dent Town. Until fairly recent times it was of greater importance than Sedbergh, but today it is an unhurried backwater. It stands midway along its own valley, and the only roads in and out are minor ones, a factor which has helped preserve Dent's character.

Retained are some cobbled streets lined with neat cottages, a few shops, a pair of inns and a lovely church. St. Andrew's dates largely from the fifteenth century, but was restored a century ago.

By the side of the main street is a block of Shap granite made into a drinking fountain carved with the name of Adam Sedgwick. Born here in 1785, he went off to Cambridge and spent over 50 years as Professor of Geology. He was one of the earliest and one of the best geologists, and did much research into the varied geology of his own back yard. The bicentenary of his birth was celebrated by the creation of a trail – see Walk 37.

WALK 48 — NORBER AND CRUMMACKDALE

8½ miles

from Austwick

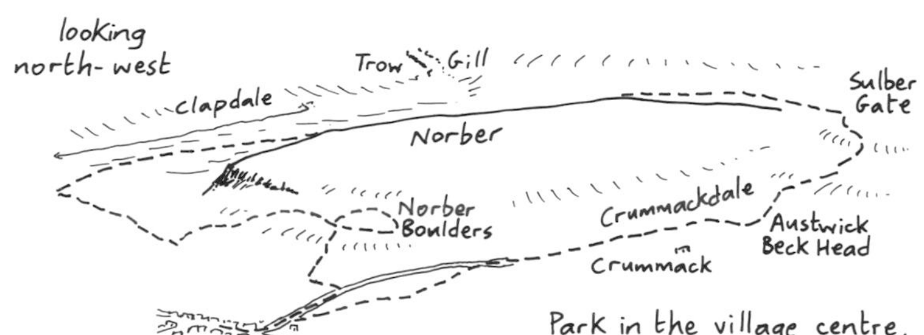
looking
north-west
Trow Gill
clapdale
Sulber
Gate
Norber
Norber
Boulders
Crummackdale
Austwick
Beck Head
Crummack
Austwick

A limestone classic, with the Norber Boulders a famous exception. Generally easy walking, much being along three unsurfaced green lanes.

Park in the village centre, with care as space is limited. ※ An alternative start-point is Clapham car-park. A glance at the Ordnance map will show how the walk can easily be joined by turning up by the church, under two tunnels to the junction of Thwaite Lane and Long Lane.

THE WALK

From the village centre head east past the inn and left up Townhead Lane. At a crossroads with a rough lane go left along it, but leave almost immediately over a stile on the right to follow a track to a gate. Do not use it, but accompany the wall up to a stile in the corner. Climb the slope behind to a guidepost, to which we shall soon return. For now though, continue up to where a path squeezes between limestone outcrops then fades on the Norber Boulders plateau.

After exploring the attractions return to the post and turn right on a sketchy path above a wall and below Robin Proctor's Scar. Beyond a stile the wall turns sharp left, while our path heads half-left across a large pasture to a stile back onto Thwaite Lane. Turn right along this walled track to a T-junction, then here turn right again along the similarly Roman-like Long Lane. Living up to its name, remain on it to its eventual demise into a green pasture.

Now turn up to the right on a track rising to a stile. Beyond it the track continues more clearly as it wends its way past Long Scar. Avoiding any lesser deviations, a wall-junction at Sulber Gate is eventually reached. Don't use the gate

The top of Norber, looking to Ingleborough

or even the adjacent stile, but opt for the smaller gate in the right-hand wall. A path descends to Thieves Moss: passing between moss and limestone it forks, the cairned right-hand path passing a variety of outcrops and running near the edge of a natural amphitheatre before dropping to Beggar's Stile.

Over the stile a path descends, soon becoming vague but maintaining its direction. An equally sketchy path diverts left to visit Austwick Beck Head, its location being fairly obvious. Back on the original path a stile is soon reached, with Crummack Farm just beyond. Here a gate in the wall in front avoids the farm, and its access road is joined to lead unerringly back to Austwick. ※

Long Lane runs parallel with Clapdale down to the left, and provides good views of Ingleborough Cave, Trow Gill, and Ingleborough's summit plateau.

※ A varied finish can be had by leaving Crummack Lane after it becomes surfaced, at a stile on the left. Drop to a stile by a barn then rise to join a rough lane. Cross straight over, head away with the wall to a stile onto a drive, then through small gates between houses onto Townhead Lane.

Unfortunately there is no public right-of-way onto the very top of Norber (1320'), though one does run to a stile to give access to it!

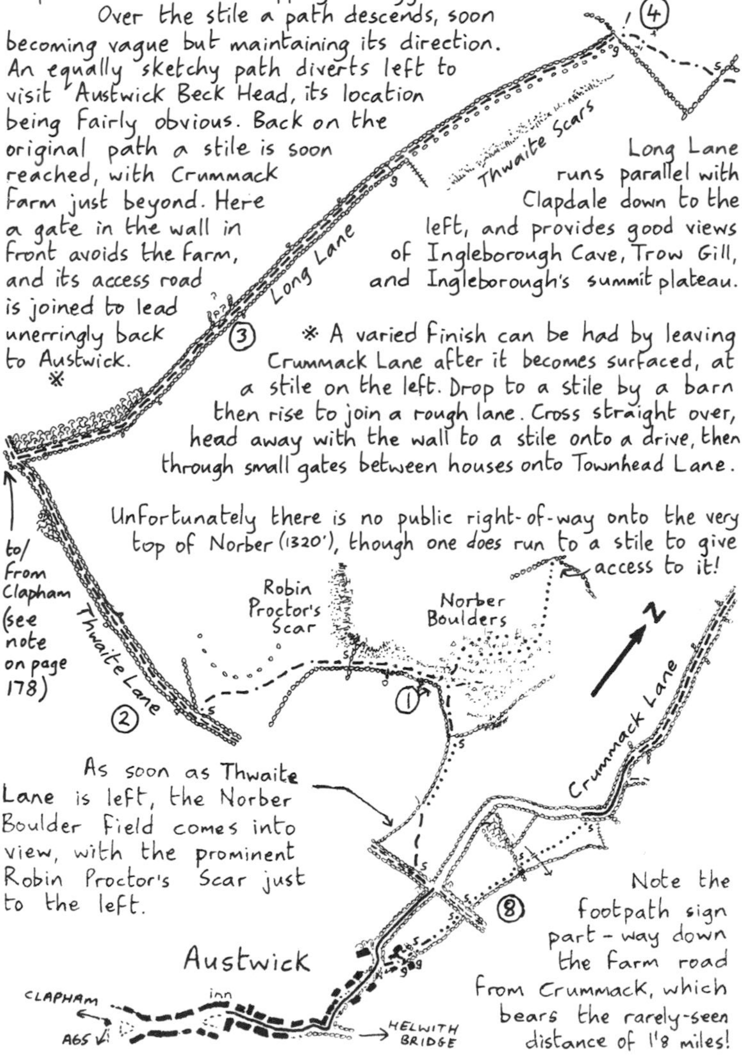

to/from Clapham (see note on page 178)

As soon as Thwaite Lane is left, the Norber Boulder Field comes into view, with the prominent Robin Proctor's Scar just to the left.

Note the footpath sign part-way down the farm road from Crummack, which bears the rarely-seen distance of 1'8 miles!

The Norber Boulders are geological freaks, famous specimens of something the Ice Age brought in. A retreating glacier carried rocks from further up Crummack Dale and deposited them in their present position. What is special is that they are dark Silurian rocks, now atop white Limestone pedestals which have worn more rapidly. They are termed 'erratic' and are also memorable.

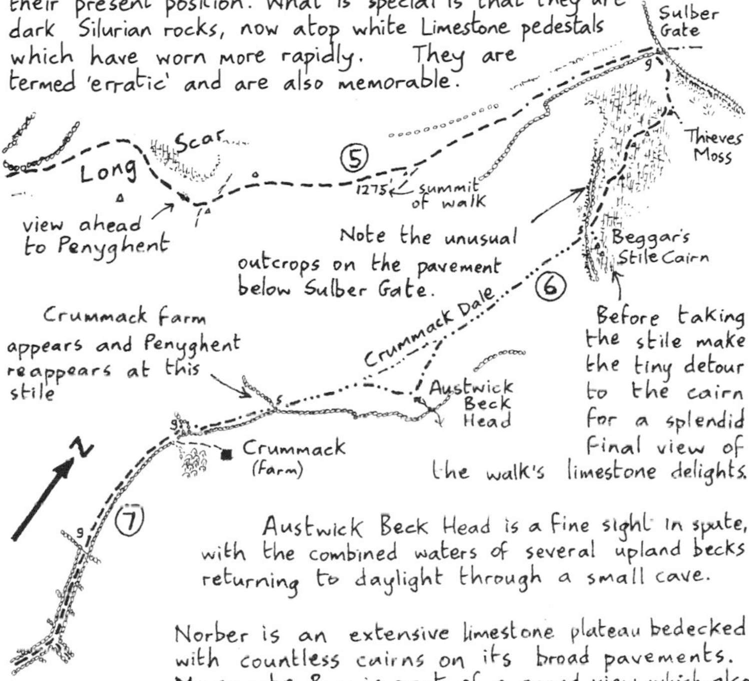

view ahead to Penyghent

Note the unusual outcrops on the pavement below Sulber Gate.

Crummack Farm appears and Penyghent reappears at this stile

Before taking the stile make the tiny detour to the cairn for a splendid final view of the walk's limestone delights.

Austwick Beck Head is a fine sight in spate, with the combined waters of several upland becks returning to daylight through a small cave.

Norber is an extensive limestone plateau bedecked with countless cairns on its broad pavements. Morecambe Bay is part of a grand view which also includes a wide panorama of the Bowland Fells.

Austwick is a hugely attractive village happily set well off the main A65 road. A small green, a cosy inn, a centuries-old hall and countless tidy cottages combine to create near-perfection.

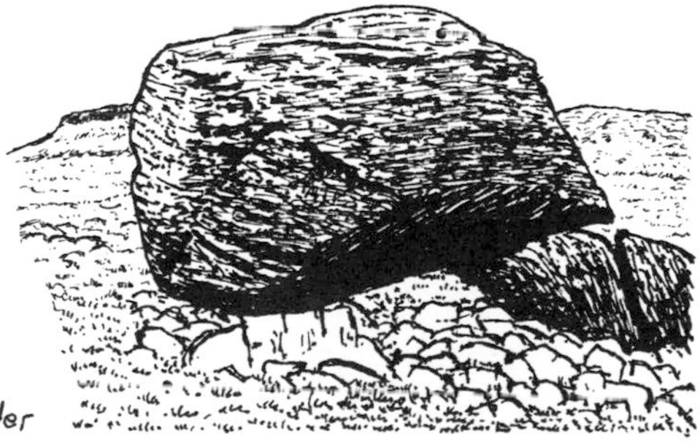

A Norber erratic boulder

CHAPTER FOUR

WENSLEYDALE

Penhill End

opposite : Aysgarth Falls

WENSLEYDALE

Wensleydale is a broad green valley with innumerable hidden features that more than make amends for its lack of instant grandeur. Here one must make an effort to seek out the attractions, and the ensuing pages lead the discerning walker to a host of splendid sights. An oft-made claim that this is Yorkshire's major dale is a point that Wharfedale would surely debate, unless the many side-valleys and the fertile pastures downstream of the National Park boundary are included. These lesser valleys are something unique to Wensleydale, for Coverdale, Walden, Bishopdale, Raydale and several more are all sizeable dales in their own right. Each contributes its share to the Wensleydale scene.

The individuality of the valley is also exhibited by its very name - this is the only major dale not to take its title from its river. The Ure - anciently the Yore, a name still applied in some quarters - lost out to the village of Wensley which lies just outside the Park on the road to Middleham. This the Dales' most fertile valley was once a great hunting forest, and other associations with history involve a Brigantes' hill-fort, Iron-age lake-dwellings, a Roman road, a Roman fort, a 13th century abbey, a 14th century castle, a 15th century fortified manor-house, a 16th century beacon-site, a 17th century hall, and traces of lead and coal-mining and of quarrying. Not bad for starters!

The natural attractions surely deserve a mention now. It will be noticed that not many walks take in the riverbank, for a good deal of its course is without rights-of-way: the river itself leads an uneventful life other than one or two famous moments which all who have visited the dale will already know. Neither are the high tops very inviting, indeed the bulk of Wensleydale's walking is to be had somewhere between the two extremities. The physical structure of the dale gives us a series of regular ledges on which some superb walking can be found. These mid-height terraces also generally provide the best views.

The crowning glory of Wensleydale however (despite the Ure's general lack of interest) are the waterfalls. Nowhere else can boast such a fine array of tumbling falls, for most of the side-valleys also proudly possess their own force. These are the gems that make Wensleydale special.

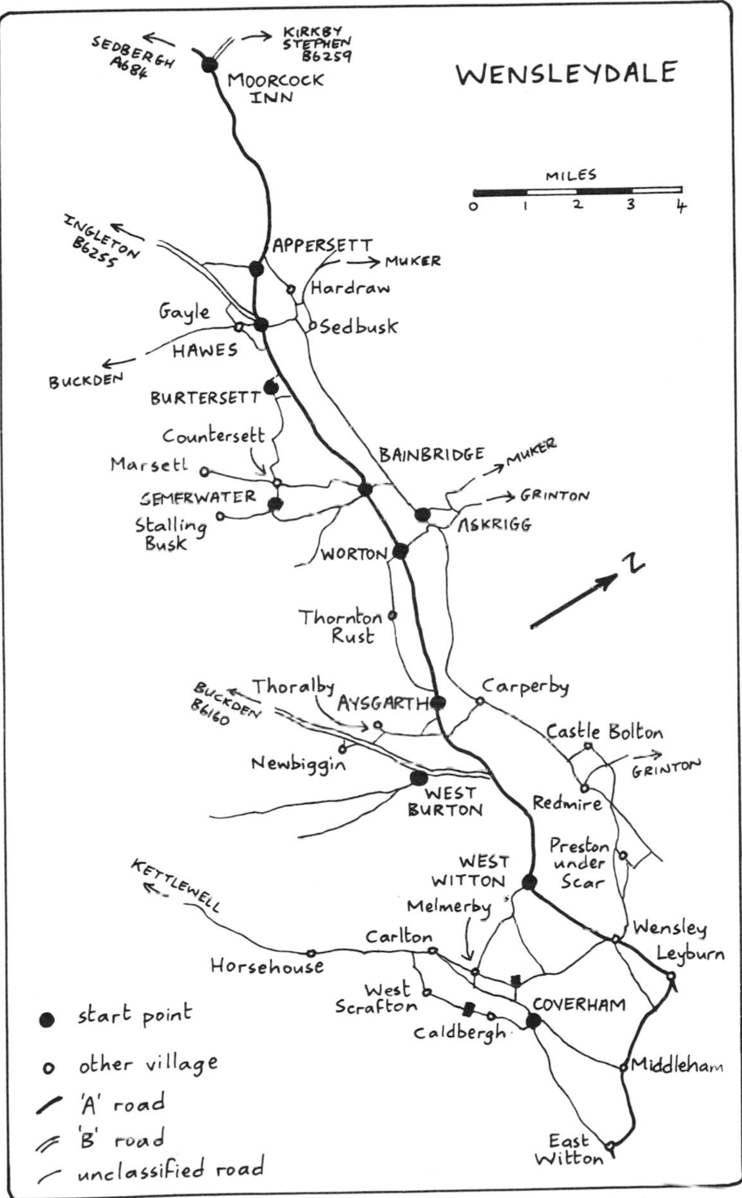
WENSLEYDALE
SEDBERGH A684
KIRKBY STEPHEN B6259
MOORCOCK INN
MILES
0
1
2
3
4
INGLETON B6255
APPERSETT
MUKER
Hardraw
Gayle
Sedbusk
HAWES
BUCKDEN
BURTERSETT
Countersett
BAINBRIDGE
MUKER
Marsett
GRINTON
SEMERWATER
ASKRIGG
Stalling Busk
WORTON
N
Thornton Rust
Thoralby
Carperby
BUCKDEN B6160
AYSGARTH
Castle Bolton
GRINTON
Newbiggin
WEST BURTON
Redmire
Preston under Scar
WEST WITTON
KETTLEWELL
Melmerby
Wensley
Carlton
Leyburn
Horsehouse
West Scrafton
COVERHAM
Caldbergh
Middleham
East Witton
start point
other village
'A' road
'B' road
unclassified road

WALK 49 CASTLE BOLTON AND AYSGARTH FALLS

7 miles

from Aysgarth

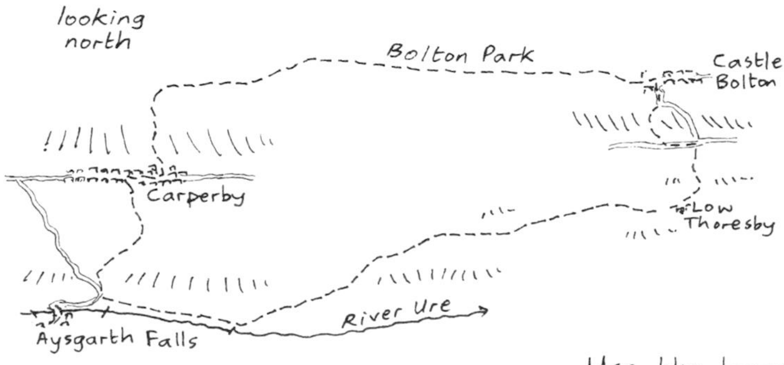

looking north
Bolton Park
Castle Bolton
Carperby
Low Thoresby
River Ure
Aysgarth Falls

Visits to two of the valley's most famous features, one natural, one the work of man

Use the large National Park car-park at Aysgarth Falls, east of the village.

THE WALK

From the car-park return to the road and turn left under the railway bridge. Within a few yards take a gate on the right, and a path rises through the wood, crossing a wide track to a stile just behind to leave the wood. Head straight up the field, and a string of five gap-stiles guide a sketchy path through the fields, turning left at the last one to emerge onto a farm-lane. Cross straight over and pass through a long narrow field, and after a gate at the end go on a little further to one on the right. Now go left again and a final gate between the houses empties into the centre of Carperby, just opposite the inn.

Turn right for a short distance, taking the first lane on the left. With a 'no through road' sign in evidence it rises out of the village to become a wide enclosed track. Beyond a couple of barns keep right at a fork to accompany the wall round to a gate barring the way. A large tract of rough pasture is entered, and with Bolton Castle in view down-dale our near-level approach to it can be well surveyed.

A generally clear track heads across the pasture to a gate in the opposite wall, then it crosses the bracken to arrive at a gate at the far end, then crosses Beldon Beck and runs a little less clearly along to a gate in the right-hand wall. From here the track becomes wide and clear to lead through half a dozen more fields towards the imposing bulk of Bolton Castle. Through a narrow wood the track leads to the very walls of the castle.

Between castle and church we emerge onto the village street alongside the green, and from the corner it is this road we descend to leave Castle Bolton village. Soon a track forks right between barns, descending to two houses and the defunct railway line. Across the old line a charming, leafy snicket drops down to join a road.

Go left along the road only as far as the Castle Bolton junction, then take a stile on the right. Cross to the far end of the field, and from the stile bear right down to another stile in the very bottom-left corner. It leads to a small footbridge onto Thoresby Lane. Along to the right the lane quickly ends at Low Thoresby.

At a gate to the right of the farm the lane is born again, now as a delectable green byway. Immensely rewarding throughout its entire hedgerowed length, it finally terminates just beyond an extremely wet junction. From a stile into a field follow the wall away to find a stile by a gate at the very far end. From one behind it follow a wall away to the next, then bear left over the brow to a stile near the far corner.

A farm track is joined to lead down to Hollin House, keeping right at the first building to a gateway before the barn complex. Take a gap-stile on the left to slant down to a gate from where a green track heads away: as it swings down the large field head straight across to a stile. Part-way along the fence-side drop down left to another stile.

At this point we meet up with the ever-popular Aysgarth Falls path at its terminus, and just below us are the Lower Falls. A distinct gap in the cliffs here permits a cul-de-sac descent to a water's-edge vantage point. A well trodden path heads up-river, passing by a short, circular detour to a more intimate viewpoint for the Lower Falls. Up above the path temporarily vacates the woodland before entering Freeholder's Wood to quickly reach the Middle Falls viewing platform. Only yards further we emerge onto the road just below the car park entrance.

To include the Upper Falls (best seen from Yore Bridge) turn down the road to gain the bridge, from where a path then leads directly back up to the car park.

Carperby is one of the most attractive and least spoilt villages in the dale. Its depth is virtually non-existant, for all its sturdy stone dwellings line the road running through the village. Standing well back from the valley bottom, it was once of greater importance as testified by the sizeable market cross. Dating from the seventeenth century it stands at one end of a narrow green. At the opposite end is a good grouping of chapels which have sadly been succumbing to modern trends. It is claimed that the Wensleydale breed of sheep was first named here.

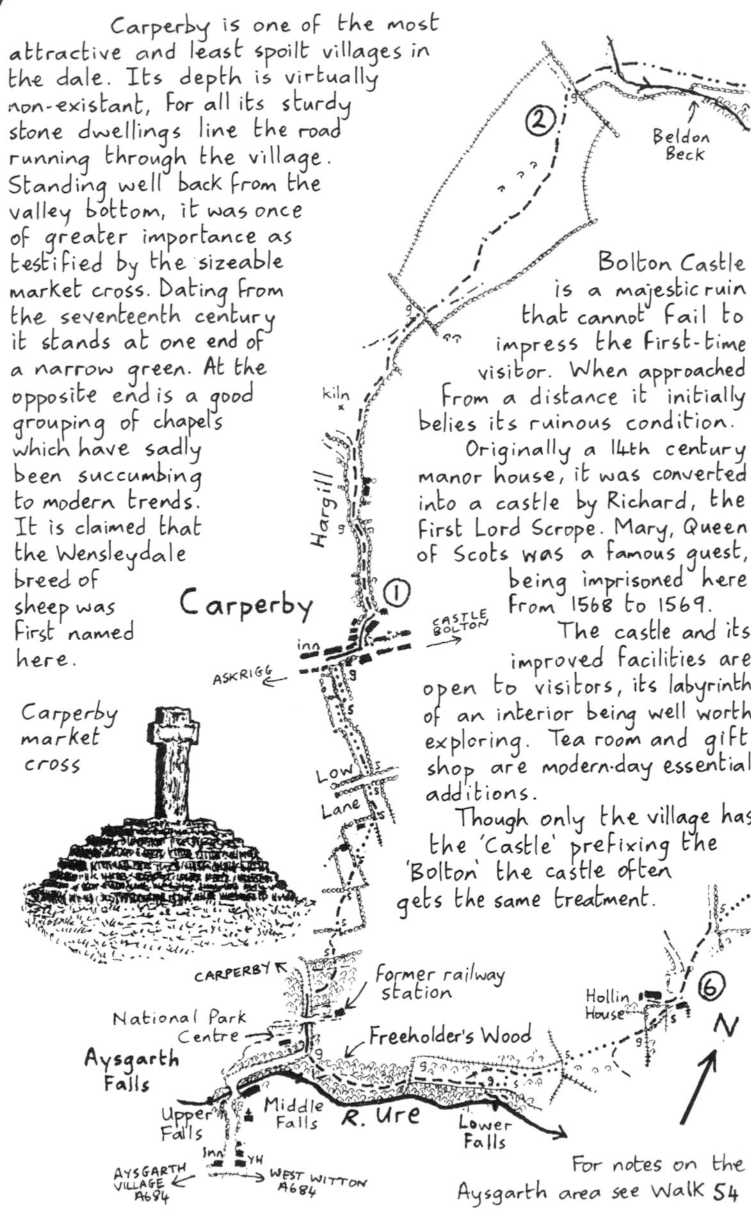

Beldon Beck
2
Kiln
Hargill
1
Carperby
inn
CASTLE BOLTON
ASKRIGG
Low Lane
CARPERBY
Former railway station
National Park Centre
Freeholder's Wood
Aysgarth Falls
Upper Falls
Middle Falls
R. Ure
Lower Falls
Inn
YH
AYSGARTH VILLAGE A684
WEST WITTON A684
Hollin House
6
N

Carperby market cross

Bolton Castle is a majestic ruin that cannot fail to impress the first-time visitor. When approached from a distance it initially belies its ruinous condition.

Originally a 14th century manor house, it was converted into a castle by Richard, the first Lord Scrope. Mary, Queen of Scots was a famous guest, being imprisoned here from 1568 to 1569.

The castle and its improved facilities are open to visitors, its labyrinth of an interior being well worth exploring. Tea room and gift shop are modern-day essential additions.

Though only the village has the 'Castle' prefixing the 'Bolton' the castle often gets the same treatment.

For notes on the Aysgarth area see Walk 54

Although comprehensively overshadowed by its castle, the village of Castle Bolton is highly appealing in its own right. A spacious green separates two intermittent rows of cottages, many of which housed the lead-miners of long ago. Today this is a peaceful place, which like Carperby is well up from the valley bottom. The church of St. Oswald stands almost at the castle wall. Dating back more than 600 years, this tiny place of worships reveals a surprisingly spacious interior.

Bolton Castle

Thoresby Lane is a centuries-old byway which feels to have changed little as we follow its enclosed section. At the junction* a fork descends to ford the Ure. Be grateful it's not our route.

The bulk of Penhill is a striking feature of many scenes in the lower dale, and on the descent to Low Thoresby it totally dominates the view directly ahead.

WALK 50

THE RIVER BAIN AND THE ROMAN ROAD

5¾ miles

from Bainbridge

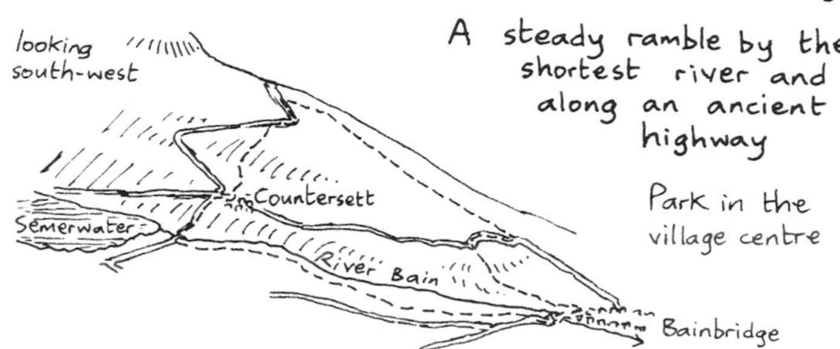
looking south-west
Countersett
Semerwater
River Bain
Bainbridge

A steady ramble by the shortest river and along an ancient highway

Park in the village centre

THE WALK

Leave Bainbridge by the main Aysgarth road at the corner of the green, crossing the bridge over the River Bain and climbing the steep hill. Leave the road by a stile on the right just before the junction and head across the pasture keeping well above the steep drop to the river. Pass to the left of an 'island' field and at the brow of the hill a sketchy path materialises to lead to a stile. Marker-posts show the way down the slope beyond, with Semerwater now fully in view ahead. Continue across several intervening walls by means of stiles, and on reaching a ladder-stile bear right to join the nearby riverbank. Its pleasant course is now followed upstream to shortly arrive at Semerwater Bridge. Before crossing it, have a potter along the foreshore of the lake itself: its foot is directly in front.

To resume the walk, cross the bridge and climb the steep road to the crossroads at Countersett. Turn right towards the hamlet, but just before the first house opt for an enclosed track to some cottages on the left. Take a gate by the first dwelling on the left to begin a steep climb to a barn, then up again to another barn. From it climb half-left to a stile and continue diagonally to the next top-corner. From the stile there follow a wall up to a gate to emerge onto the Countersett-Burtersett road at it's highest point. Follow it to the right for a couple of minutes to reach a stile on the right: beyond a collapsed wall head half-left down the rough pasture to a stile admitting onto the Roman road.

Turn right to follow the arrow-like course of the Roman road to eventually merge into a metalled road. Head up its gentle slope as far as the farm just ahead, going along its drive where a stile will be found on the left. Head down the field to a stile at the bottom and across two more fields with a sketchy path linking the stiles. From next to a barn a clearer path leads to the next stile, and our way continues to a stile and then a gate above the river before descending alongside the left-hand wall to a gate. From it a few cottages are passed to re-emerge onto Bainbridge's village green.

Bainbridge is a lovely village whose houses stand well back from an enormous green. Though the main road cuts across it, its effect seems insignificant. The most noticeable features are the stocks which still grace the green, and the whitewashed inn which is always in sight. It dates back several centuries and is possibly the oldest in the dale. The structure which gives the village its name is a shapely platform from which to see not only the best stretch of the river, but the only part before it sneaks quietly round the backs of the houses.

The village has notable historical connections, not least of all with the Romans. Brough Hill, peering over the houses at the east of the village, is the site of the Roman fort Braccium and a handy place to defend, which was no doubt just as well. Some centuries later the Norman lords based their foresters here, when the Forest of Wensleydale was a popular hunting-ground. At the inn can be seen a horn, and during the winter months it was blown at nine o'clock in the evening to guide benighted travellers to safety. Its origin goes back earlier still, as a warning sound in the days of the Forest. Happily this ancient event can still sometimes be seen, surviving purely as a quaint custom. Where our walk re-enters the village is a house that was once the 'Old Dame School', where over a century ago, pupils could learn the 'three R's' for 2d a week (that's 1p to you youngsters!)

Bainbridge: the inn from the green

Cam High Road is the Roman road running from Ribblehead to Bainbridge, and a note about it can be found on page 208. On this walk we tread the easternmost section which points itself unerringly at Bainbridge.

Even in this lower stretch, which is stony underfoot but not rough, the views are very good. An unrivalled length of Wensleydale can be seen, including Hawes, Askrigg, various individual features and most of the surrounding fells. Looking back up the road, Wether Fell and its outcrop Yorburgh are seen at their shapeliest.

Countersett is a small hamlet with an early Friends Meeting House and a lovely old hall also with strong Quaker connections. The steep slopes above command a superb panorama of Semerwater's side-valley. The best feature is Addlebrough across the valley.

Joining the Ure at Bainbridge, the River Bain is claimed to be the shortest in the country, a point which the Dibb, in Wharfedale would challenge. Our route explores it comprehensively, from the numerous falls over rock ledges above Bainbridge to its so tranquil meander from Semerwater Bridge.

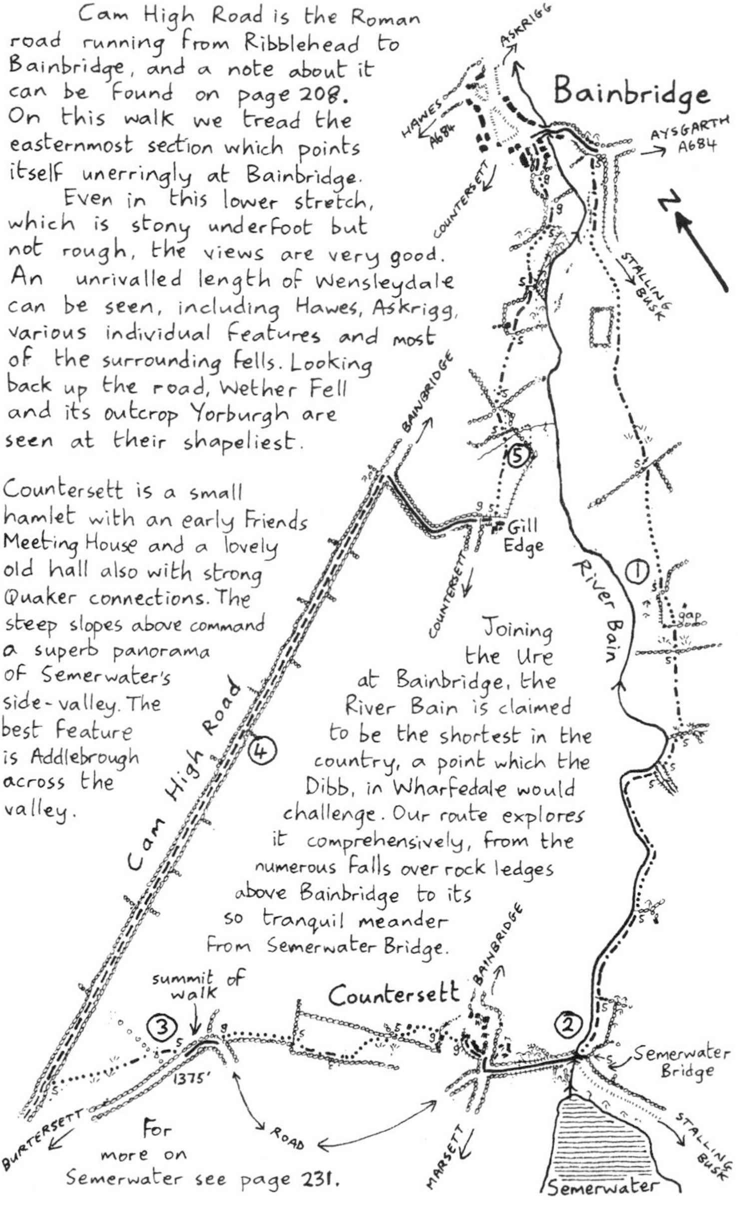

For more on Semerwater see page 231.

Askrigg
Bainbridge
Hawes A684
Aysgarth A684
Countersett
Stalling Busk
Bainbridge
5
Gill Edge
Countersett
1
River Bain
gap
Cam High Road
4
Bainbridge
summit of walk
3
Countersett
2
1375'
Semerwater Bridge
Burtersett
Road
Marsett
Stalling Busk
Semerwater

WALK 51 HARDRAW FORCE AND PIKE HILL BEACONS

7¼ miles

from Hawes

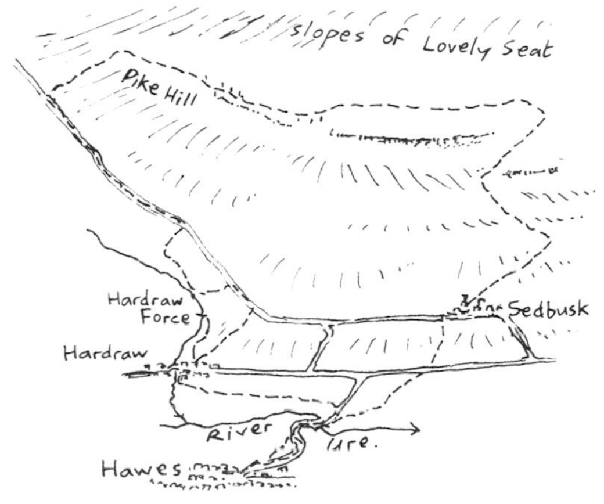
slopes of Lovely Seat
Pike Hill
Hardraw Force
Hardraw
Sedbusk
River Ure.
Hawes

looking north

A superbly varied walk with extensive views across Wensleydale

Use the main National Park car park in the old railway station yard

THE WALK

From the car-park take the path by the old railway bridge up onto the road, and turn right to follow it out of the village. Within a few yards a track heads off to the left, and with it a gate signals the route of the Pennine Way, whose flagged course we follow to rejoin the road a little further on. Continue on the road as it bridges the Ure, then take a stile which soon appears on the right. A sketchy path heads across to a small arched-bridge, then climbs half-right to another stile, beyond which a large field is crossed to a stile in the top corner. Cross over the lane to the stile opposite and resume the rise in the same direction. Two more stiles quickly ensue before a near-vertical climb to a stile in the top-right corner. Turn right along the lane to enter the hamlet of Sedbusk.

Take the lane up between the houses, and at the top end of the small green bear right as the lane deteriorates into a rough track. This climbs the hillside for a good while, and is left by a stile on the left just before arriving at a gate. A good track rises up the field, fades a little while passing a tiny plantation, then reverts to its original form to slope across to a gate. The track continues to another gate

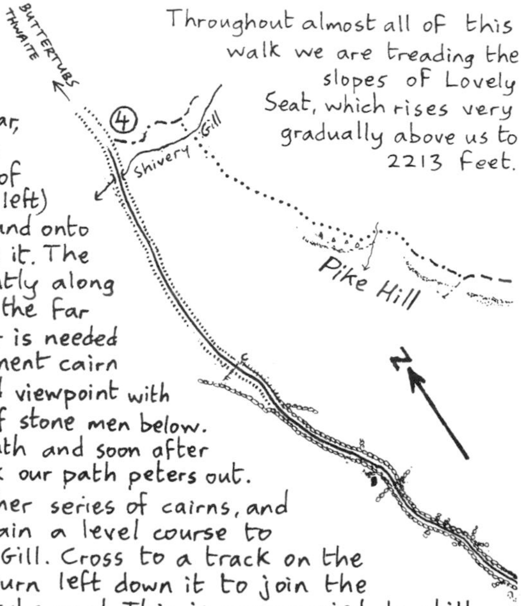

Throughout almost all of this walk we are treading the slopes of Lovely Seat, which rises very gradually above us to 2213 feet.

which gives access to the open fell. Head straight up, keeping left of the small scar, and the path then swings well clear of High Clint (on our left) before curving round onto the plateau above it. The path runs pleasantly along this plateau: at the far end a brief detour is needed to visit the prominent cairn which is a splendid viewpoint with two fine examples of stone men below.

Rejoin the path and soon after passing a left fork our path peters out. Keep on to another series of cairns, and from them maintain a level course to arrive at Shivery Gill. Cross to a track on the other side and turn left down it to join the unenclosed Buttertubs road. This is accompanied downhill for a good mile and a quarter to the first farm buildings.

Here, at High Shaw, take a lane signposted Fossdale, and within a few yards descend some steps to the heavily-wooded beck. After seeing the waterfall a few yards up, turn left to accompany the beck downstream. Almost immediately a footbridge gives a choice of which bank to follow. Two more small falls are passed before reaching another footbridge. We must leave the beck here to prepare itself for its big moment, which we shall soon be witnessing from below. A path leads up onto the road, but after only a minute to the right it is vacated again at a stile alongside a gate.

A good track heads away and down to West House Farm, and from a stile to its right a path descends two more fields to emerge via a back-yard into Hardraw. If not already aware, the Force is on private land, and access is through the inn where a modest charge is made. Through the inn, a 5-minute walk leads to the impressive amphitheatre of the Scaur. On returning to the inn, cross the road and take a track just left of the bridge. Behind the buildings go left to a small gate from where a good path crosses a number of fields to eventually join a road. Turn right to rejoin the outward route, over Haylands Bridge and back into Hawes.

From Sedbusk to Hardraw we enjoy extensive panoramas of Wensleydale. Rising above Hawes are those ubiquitous 2000-footers Wether Fell, Dodd Fell and Widdale Fell. The road to Wharfedale over Fleet Moss (1934') is clearly in sight.

Sedbusk is an unspoilt hamlet of farms and cottages, looking across the dale to Hawes and beyond from an altitude little under 1000 feet. It is so laid back it has even avoided the back-road from Hardraw to Askrigg, being reached only by a narrow lane.

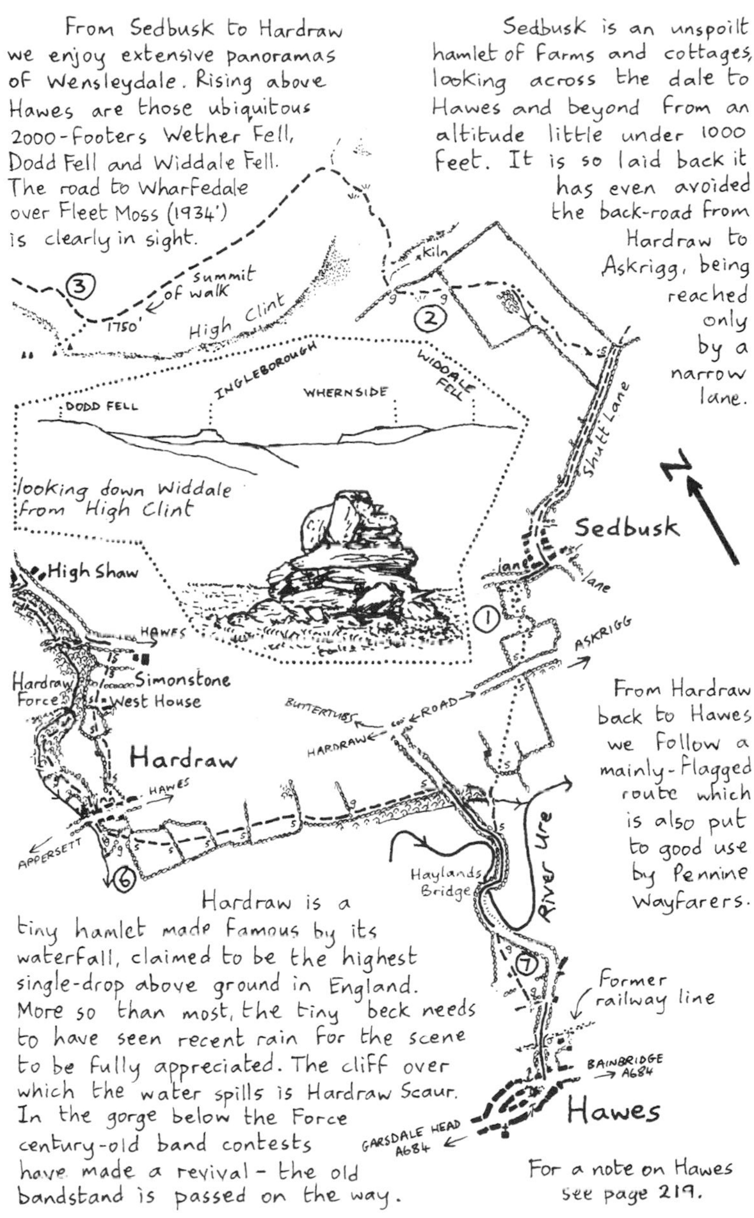
3
summit of walk
1750'
High Clint
kiln
2
DODD FELL
INGLEBOROUGH
WHERNSIDE
WIDDALE FELL
looking down Widdale from High Clint
Shutt Lane
Sedbusk
lane
lane
High Shaw
HAWES
Simonstone
Hardraw Force
West House
Hardraw
BUTTERTUBS
ROAD
HARDRAW
ASKRIGG
1
HAWES
APPERSETT
6
River Ure
Haylands Bridge
7
Former railway line
BAINBRIDGE A684
Hawes
GARSDALE HEAD A684

From Hardraw back to Hawes we follow a mainly-flagged route which is also put to good use by Pennine Wayfarers.

Hardraw is a tiny hamlet made famous by its waterfall, claimed to be the highest single-drop above ground in England. More so than most, the tiny beck needs to have seen recent rain for the scene to be fully appreciated. The cliff over which the water spills is Hardraw Scaur. In the gorge below the Force century-old band contests have made a revival - the old bandstand is passed on the way.

For a note on Hawes see page 219.

WALK 52 CALDBERGH AND MIDDLEHAM LOW MOOR

6½ miles

from Coverham

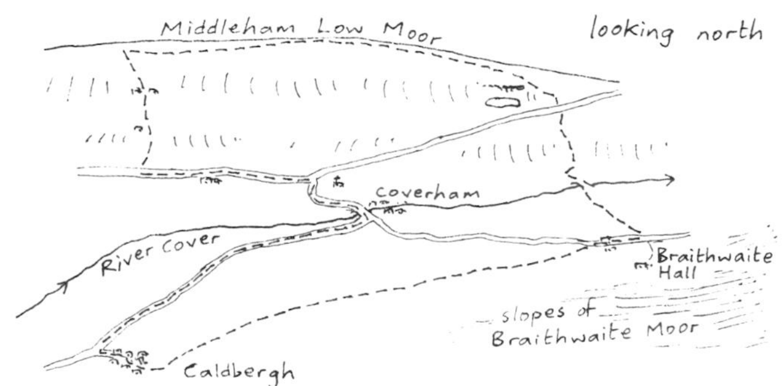

Middleham Low Moor
looking north
Coverham
River Cover
Braithwaite Hall
slopes of Braithwaite Moor
Caldbergh

This leisurely ramble takes in several of lower Coverdale's interesting features

Parking can be found at the junction in front of the church, or down the lane just before the bridge

THE WALK

Leave Coverham by crossing the bridge and taking the quiet lane to Caldbergh, turning up into the tiny village on a lane which terminates at the last house. At a gate a farm-track takes over, and is followed along to the left over several cattle-grids to arrive at Ashes Farm. A track then continues across the fields to cease at the second gate reached. From it carry on with a wall on the left: at the next gate the accompanying wall calls it a day. Continue straight across to a gate in a fence, then cross an extensive pasture by passing a plantation before gradually dropping to the very far corner, where a gate empties onto a lane.

Turn right along it, past a farm and on to the drive to Braithwaite Hall with the familiar National Trust sign in evidence. Opposite is a gate from where a track heads away down to the river, interrupted by another gate on the gradual descent. The River Cover is crossed by the stone-arched Hullo Bridge. From it a track heads left up a steep slope, then fades as it rises more gently over a large pasture. At the top a gate precedes the unfenced Coverham-Middleham road over Middleham Low Moor.

Head straight up the slope opposite to join a wide track which can be followed left to a wall-corner. It is worth venturing a little left off this way for a birds-eye view of the whole of Pinker's Pond. At the wall the track begins to fade, and here it can be left by striking a little to the right across the pathless moor. This couldn't be much less like the moors we are used to, and the short-cropped turf is a joy to tread. While keeping an eye open for racehorses the trig. point ahead soon appears, and is attained equally soon.

From it continue along the broad moor-top a good while yet: the boundary wall on the left remains in view for the most part, and on seeing the first set of buildings behind it head in that direction. Do not leave the moor here but follow a track alongside the wall, and within a couple of minutes a solid farm-road is met. This heads through a gate and down to the left, passing between the buildings of Ashgill Stables and alongside those of Tupgill to drop down onto a lane.

Turn left, passing a creamery to return to the junction at Coverham church. The branch right leads straight down to the bridge, but a visit to the attractive church can be included by the lych-gate just in front. A path also leads from its right (south) side down onto the lane to Coverham Abbey, which also merits a look to conclude the journey in style.

Coverham boasts a sylvan setting at the lower end of its dale, and is well and truly off the beaten track. Though barely even a hamlet, it has several features of interest. The Abbey was founded by Premonstratensian Canons, and the scant remains include some 14th century arches, now by a private house. Also ancient is the bridge over the Cover, while up above is the church of the Holy Trinity, now no longer in use.

The gatehouse arch, Coverham

52

Middleham is rightly renowned for its horse-racing connections and the Low Moor is a favourite venue for putting the horses through their paces. On our crossing of it, note the fine view of two valleys (Cover left and Ure right) divided by Penhill.

Though outside the scope of this guide, Middleham is only a mile distant, and combines with this walk to create a full day.

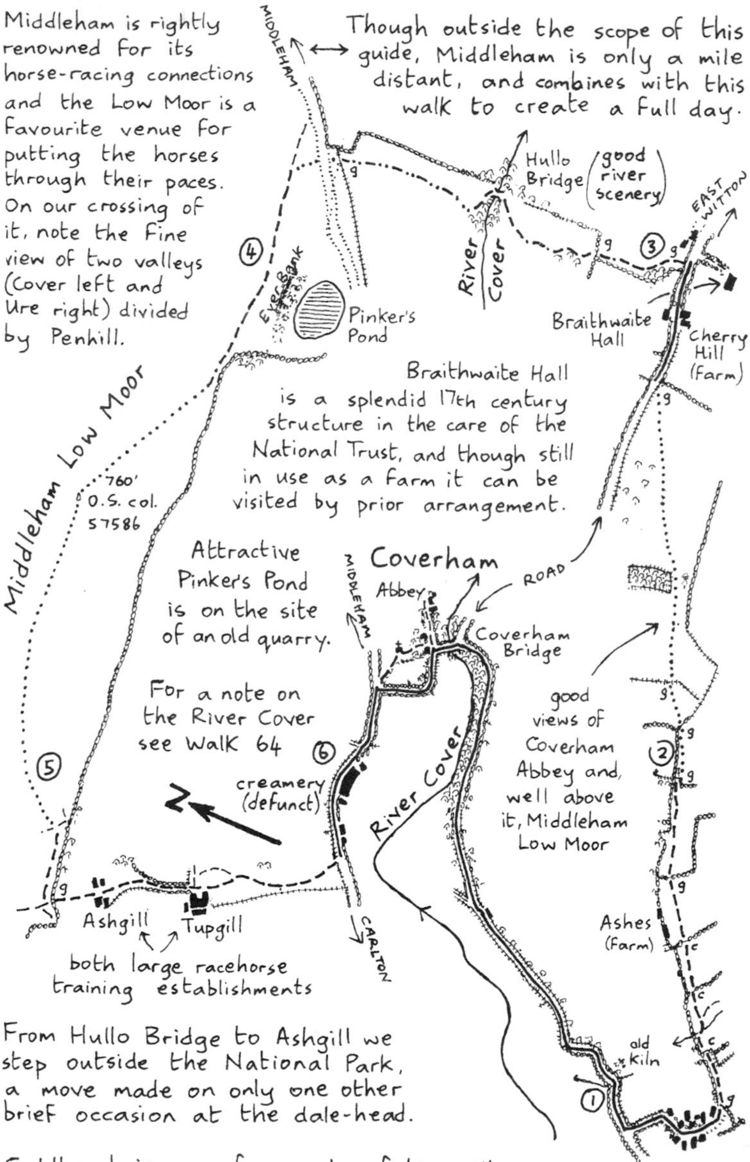

MIDDLEHAM

Hullo Bridge (good river scenery)

EAST WITTON

River Cover

④

Eyer Bank

Pinker's Pond

③

Braithwaite Hall

Cherry Hill (Farm)

Middleham Low Moor

760' O.S. col. 57586

Braithwaite Hall is a splendid 17th century structure in the care of the National Trust, and though still in use as a farm it can be visited by prior arrangement.

Attractive Pinker's Pond is on the site of an old quarry.

MIDDLEHAM

Coverham

Abbey

ROAD

Coverham Bridge

For a note on the River Cover see Walk 64

⑥

good views of Coverham Abbey and, well above it, Middleham Low Moor

②

⑤

creamery (defunct)

N

River Cover

Ashgill

Tupgill

CARLTON

both large racehorse training establishments

Ashes (Farm)

old kiln

①

From Hullo Bridge to Ashgill we step outside the National Park, a move made on only one other brief occasion at the dale-head.

Caldbergh is one of a number of tiny villages in the area which remain pleasantly unspoilt.

Caldbergh

WALK 53 AROUND ADDLEBROUGH

6½ miles from Worton

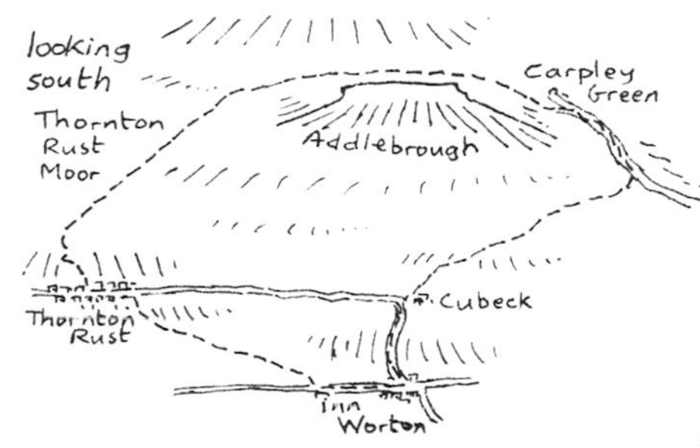
looking south
Thornton Rust Moor
Addlebrough
Carpley Green
Cubeck
Thornton Rust
Inn
Worton

A straightforward circuit of this shapely fell, with outstanding views of the district

Park in the spacious lay-by opposite the inn, on the Aysgarth road out of the village.

THE WALK

Head back into the village and turn left at the first junction up the steep lane to Cubeck. Turn right into the farming hamlet and then immediately left up a steep track enclosed by walls. At a gate the track runs more freely, sloping across a field and then steeply up to a gate at the top corner. Beyond it the track fades away: head across to a gate over to the right, after which the path sketchily re-appears to continue its now-level course. The path heads across to a gate, then accompanies a wall away to emerge onto the cul-de-sac lane to Carpley Green: turn left.

Just prior to reaching the first barn, take a gate on the left to follow a wall away to another gate. A large pasture is entered and with no visible path simply contour across it, keeping roughly parallel with the wall down to the right. On rounding to a gate a sketchy path materialises to reach another gate and continues on to a gate in the right-hand wall. The path now surmounts a vague ridge to head towards a stile. Across it, the expanse of Thornton Rust Moor is entered and our reasonable path strikes out half-left across the undulating terrain. On reaching a gate the track descends to enter walled confines which channel our steps unerringly down into Thornton Rust village.

Turn left along the lane as far as the edge of the village, then take a small gate on the right labelled Nipe End. From a stile just below, a path leads through the trees to emerge via a stile into a field. Here the

Final leg begins, a pathless trek through pleasant fields taking in no less than a dozen gap-stiles in rapid succession. The only potentially confusing one is the first, found in the crumbling wall half-left of our emergence from the trees. This is the general direction taken to eventually reach the main road: the inn at Worton is now only minutes along to the left.

Addlebrough is a classic table-topped fell that seems to crop up in almost every Wensleydale view. Modest crags line its northern side, and help to accentuate the abrupt edge of the plateau. The Brigantes are thought to have occupied a hill-fort here - no doubt in stark contrast to the Roman fort in the valley bottom.

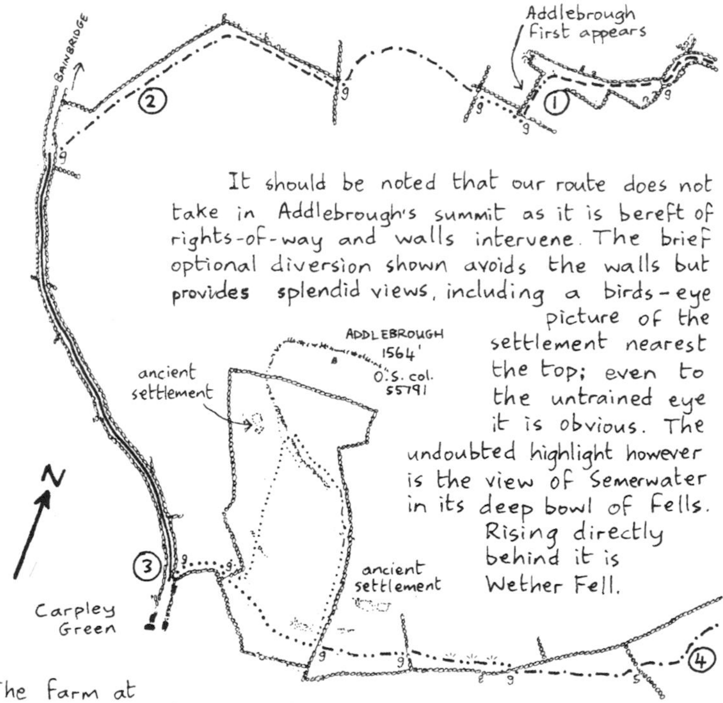

BAINBRIDGE
Addlebrough first appears
ADDLEBROUGH 1564'
O.S. col. 55791
ancient settlement
ancient settlement
Carpley Green
N

It should be noted that our route does not take in Addlebrough's summit as it is bereft of rights-of-way and walls intervene. The brief optional diversion shown avoids the walls but provides splendid views, including a birds-eye picture of the settlement nearest the top; even to the untrained eye it is obvious. The undoubted highlight however is the view of Semerwater in its deep bowl of fells. Rising directly behind it is Wether Fell.

The farm at Carpley Green stands at the end of the road as far as motor traffic is concerned, but an old packhorse way continues over the Stake to the Kidstones Pass and Wharfedale, a splendid route for walkers.

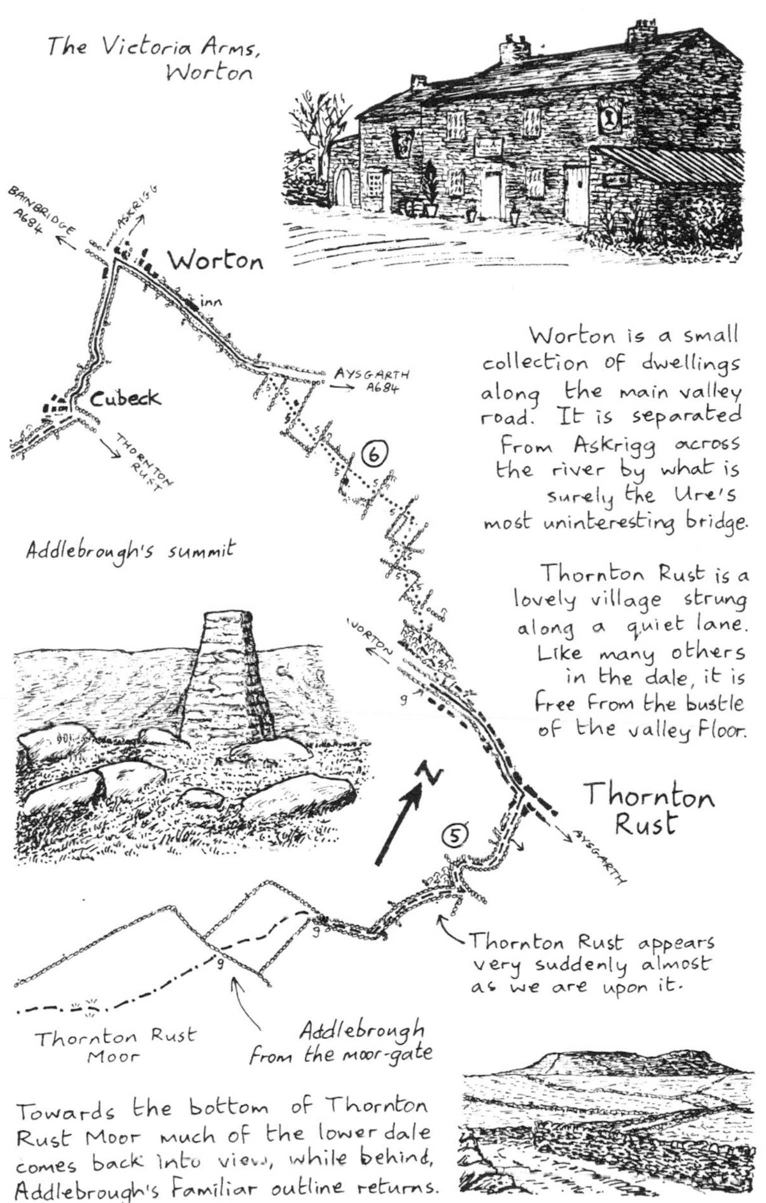
The Victoria Arms, Worton
BAINBRIDGE A684
ASKRIGG
Worton
inn
AYSGARTH A684
Cubeck
THORNTON RUST
6
Addlebrough's summit
WORTON
Thornton Rust
5
AYSGARTH
Thornton Rust Moor
Addlebrough from the moor-gate

Worton is a small collection of dwellings along the main valley road. It is separated from Askrigg across the river by what is surely the Ure's most uninteresting bridge.

Thornton Rust is a lovely village strung along a quiet lane. Like many others in the dale, it is free from the bustle of the valley floor.

Thornton Rust appears very suddenly almost as we are upon it.

Towards the bottom of Thornton Rust Moor much of the lower dale comes back into view, while behind, Addlebrough's familiar outline returns.

WALK 54 — IVY SCAR, CARPERBY AND THE URE

6¼ miles — from Aysgarth

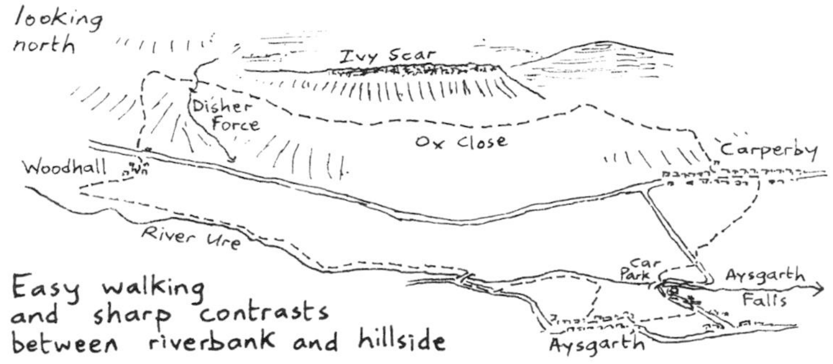

looking north
Ivy Scar
Disher Force
Ox Close
Carperby
Woodhall
River Ure
Car Park
Aysgarth Falls
Aysgarth

Easy walking and sharp contrasts between riverbank and hillside

Use the information-centre car-park over the bridge at the Falls

THE WALK

Leave the car-park at the opposite end to the entrance to find a footpath leading down to the bridge by the upper Falls. Cross it and climb the steep road as far as a stile on the right. An intermittent path goes across the fields, keeping generally level and squeezing through a multitude of identical gap-stiles. On the edge of Aysgarth village the path drops to a gate to join a back lane which is accompanied up to the Methodist church on the edge of the green.

This is also the point where the village is left, through a narrow gap between houses on the right. A path descends through two stiles and down alongside a wall, using a stile in it to cross half-right to another stile to reach an old mill. Stiles on its left lead onto an enclosed track which is followed left until it swings up the hill: here leave it by a stile on the right. Beyond a barn a stile gives access to a pleasant path through trees by the river, emerging to continue to a stile where river and road converge. Continue along the road for a very short distance to arrive at a long, narrow footbridge which we use to cross the Ure.

A stile on the left marks the commencement of a long, easy stretch along the riverbank. This pathless trek clings to the river to become confined in a rough

A stile on the left marks the commencement of a long, easy stretch along the quiet riverbank. This pathless trek clings to the river to become temporarily confined in a rough section between an old railway embankment and the Ure. On emerging remain with the wall, crossing a small beck as the wall parts company before reaching a stile. Continue on to the next stile to join an enclosed farm track, and turn up beneath a former railway bridge. The improved lane rises up through the hamlet of Woodhall and out onto the Carperby - Askrigg road.

Cross straight over and pass between house and barns opposite to take a farm track up the steep field. Towards the top of the steep section opt for the right branch to the gate just ahead. The day's climbing is now complete, and a good, level track runs along to the right, through a gate to a ford at the top of Disher Force. While there is no right of way, a brief detour through the gate just before the ford provides a first-class view of this fine waterfall.

From a gate behind the ford, our track heads across Ox Close Pasture to the old lead mines under the shadow of Ivy Scar. Weaving through spoil heaps the track emerges at the far end to continue on it's way a little sketchily. Eventually arriving at a gate, swing right to a gate - the second on the right - in the far corner, descending similarly a farm track through another field

Passing the remains of an old quarry the track falls to a gate on the right, continuing down through two fields. Half-way down the second locate a stile on the left, and cross a field-bottom to another stile. Descend the narrow enclosure to gates by farm buildings to emerge onto the road in Carperby.

Turn left along the main street as far as the inn, and take a gate opposite to enter a slender field in between houses. Keep on as far as a stile on the right, then continue on through a similar field to emerge via a stile onto a farm road, Low Lane. Cross straight over and follow a wall away to a stile on the right. From it an intermittent path strikes half-right through several fields, with a string of traditional gap-stiles serving to confirm the way.

Before long the path enters an attractive pocket of woodland: cross straight over the main track through it, and a path leads half-right down onto a road. Turn left, under the old railway bridge, and the Falls car park is immediately on the right. To round off the walk in style, a gate just across the road gives speedy access to the Middle Falls.

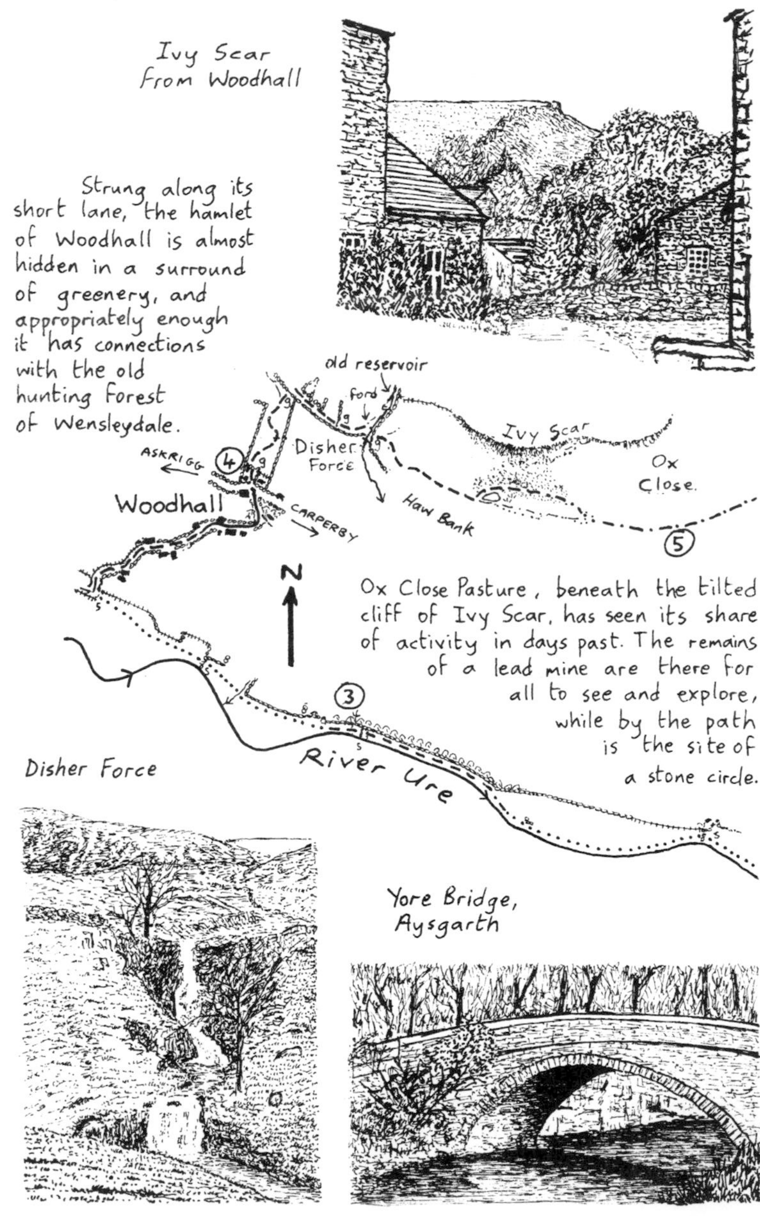
old reservoir
ford
g
g
g
g
Disher Force
Ivy Scar
Ox Close
ASKRIGG
4
Woodhall
CARPERBY
Haw Bank
5
N
3
s
s
s
s
River Ure

Ivy Scar from Woodhall

Strung along its short lane, the hamlet of Woodhall is almost hidden in a surround of greenery, and appropriately enough it has connections with the old hunting forest of Wensleydale.

Ox Close Pasture, beneath the tilted cliff of Ivy Scar, has seen its share of activity in days past. The remains of a lead mine are there for all to see and explore, while by the path is the site of a stone circle.

Disher Force

Yore Bridge, Aysgarth

The village of Aysgarth stands high above the river, and has a spacious air about it. A small green flanks the main road which divides the village. Aysgarth however stands quite aloof from the attraction that brings visitors in their tens of thousands to this corner of the dale, its famous waterfalls. Half a mile east of the village is the series of Upper, Middle and Lower Falls which make Aysgarth famous. Here the Yoredale series of rocks make their greatest showing to create a water-wonderland. It is the grand scale of things rather than their height that provides the spectacle. What makes all this truly *beautiful* is the setting – thickly-wooded with rich plant-life. The best viewpoint for the Upper Falls is Yore Bridge, a gracefully tall single-span structure. Originally from the 16th century, it has since been much-widened.

Yore, of course, is the older name for the river Ure.

For a note on Carperby see page 188

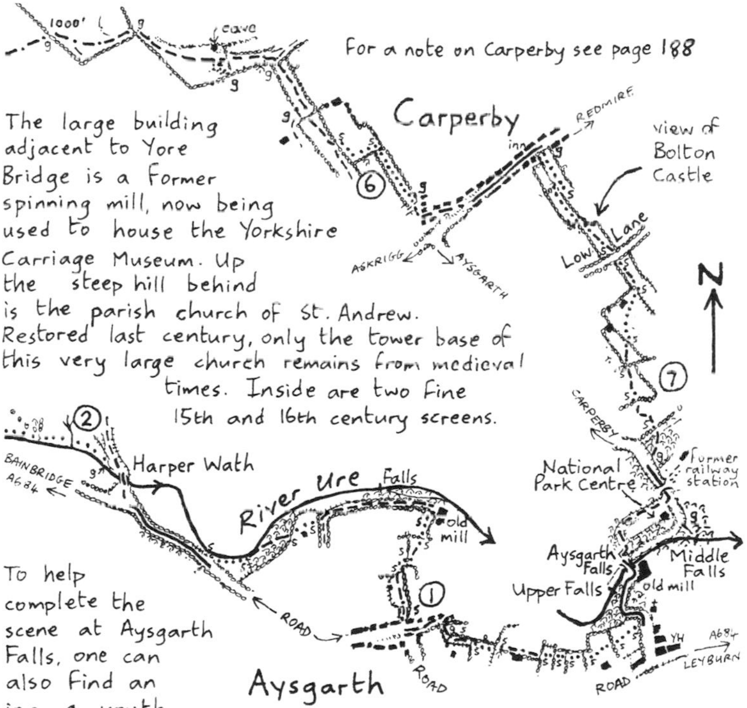

The large building adjacent to Yore Bridge is a former spinning mill, now being used to house the Yorkshire Carriage Museum. Up the steep hill behind is the parish church of St. Andrew. Restored last century, only the tower base of this very large church remains from medieval times. Inside are two fine 15th and 16th century screens.

To help complete the scene at Aysgarth Falls, one can also find an inn, a youth hostel, a gift-shop, a cafe and a National Park Centre at the car-park on the north bank

WALK 55 THE ASCENT OF WETHER FELL

5¼ miles from Burtersett

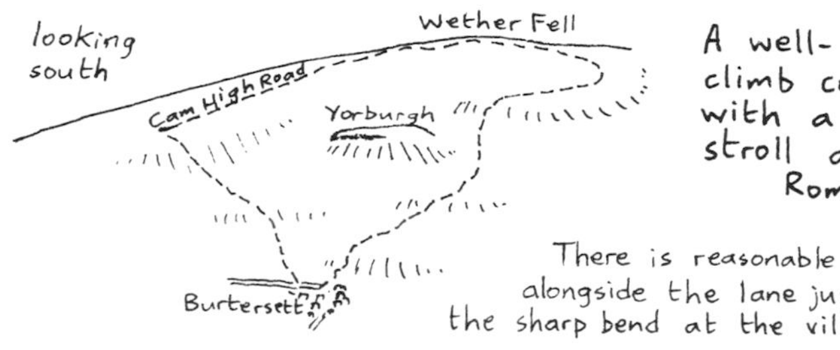
looking south
Wether Fell
Cam High Road
Yorburgh
Burtersett

A well-defined climb combined with a bracing stroll along a Roman road

There is reasonable parking alongside the lane just above the sharp bend at the village head

THE WALK

From the sharp bend at the top end of the village (by the tiny green), take the 'no through road' branching to the right at the very corner, alongside a chapel. Almost at once it forks, and our track climbs to the left leaving the last cottage behind and heading up a steep slope. This wide track is still used by the farmer and is therefore easy to follow, climbing the hillside and always sloping to the right. On gaining equal height with the prominent upthrust of Yorburgh just to the left, ignore a fork right to a gate and continue straight up: shortly the nearby wall at last leaves us for good, and the track, briefly a little less clear, crosses level ground to a gateway.

Beyond it the track improves again and a sunken green way climbs across the fellside. Ignoring lesser branches left and then right, the track arrives at the last gate of the climb. Ahead is the summit of Wether Fell, but the inviting track heading towards it should be treated with contempt: within five minutes it will lead the unfortunate walker into dark, deep peat groughs, definitely not recommended. Instead then, accompany the wall along to the right, passing the old quarry on Flint Hill and being greeted by new views across to the west. This rather more circuitous course should not be hastily abandoned: our sketchy path heads ever nearer the top and the temptation to strike out to the left is best avoided until the slope there becomes invitingly steep. At the same time as this our wall-side way becomes much wetter, path-less and generally less appealing. Climbing the grass to the left some peat groughs are encountered at the top, and now the summit cairn appears only a couple of minutes beyond. A level grassy stroll completes a relatively dry ascent.

To begin the return journey head down the only significant drop from the summit to join the wide track of the Roman road just to the south. This well-trodden route is now followed for quite a distance on it's gentle descent towards Bainbridge, soon becoming fully enclosed at a gate. The location of our departure from it is about a mile beyond the gate, where a footpath sign at a stile indicates the way to Burtersett. A sketchy path slopes down to a stile from where the sketchy path is left in favour of an invisible one straight ahead. A stile is reached just left of a wall-corner. A few yards further and Burtersett appears: the way is now obvious, passing through a broken wall down to the bottom corner of a plantation and through three more stiles to emerge onto the lane where we began.

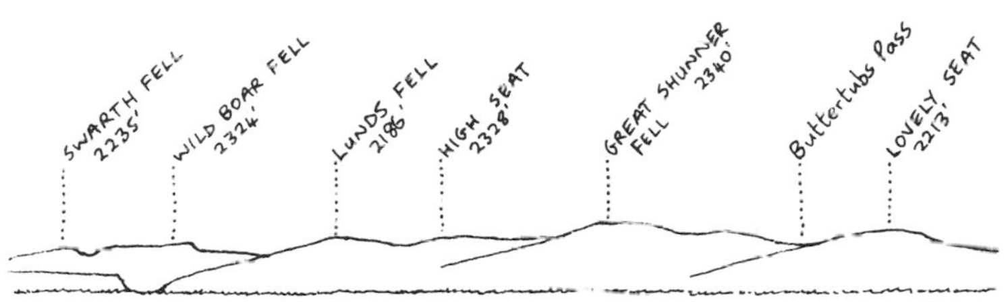
SWARTH FELL 2235'
WILD BOAR FELL 2324'
LUNDS FELL 2186'
HIGH SEAT 2328'
GREAT SHUNNER FELL 2340'
Buttertubs Pass
LOVELY SEAT 2213'

looking north-west from the summit

Wether Fell is a rare venture for us, a climb to 2000 feet. This 'rush of blood' is due to the ease by which this fell can be conquered: Wensleydale's other mountains are set much further back from the valley and constitute a far greater challenge.

The summit is known as Drumaldrace, and is probably as good a viewpoint for the Dales mountains as anywhere.

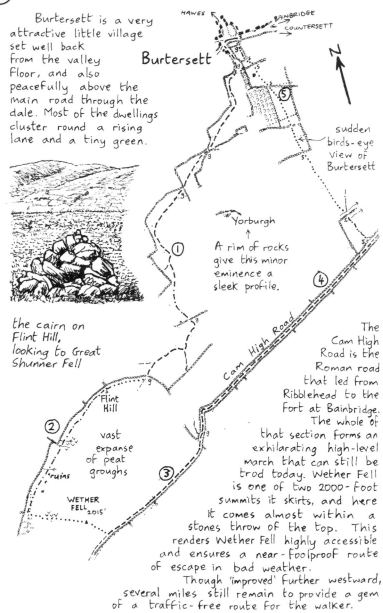

Burtersett is a very attractive little village set well back from the valley floor, and also peacefully above the main road through the dale. Most of the dwellings cluster round a rising lane and a tiny green.

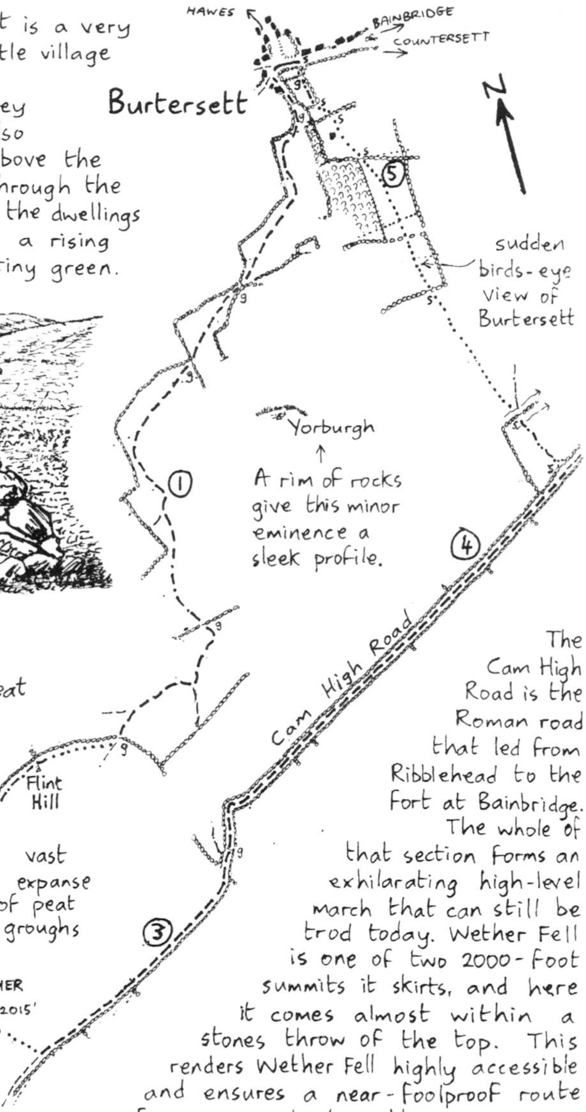

HAWES
BAINBRIDGE
COUNTERSETT
Burtersett
N
5
sudden birds-eye view of Burtersett
Yorburgh
A rim of rocks give this minor eminence a sleek profile.
1
4
Cam High Road
Flint Hill
2
vast expanse of peat groughs
ruins
3
WETHER FELL 2015'

the cairn on Flint Hill, looking to Great Shunner Fell

The Cam High Road is the Roman road that led from Ribblehead to the fort at Bainbridge. The whole of that section forms an exhilarating high-level march that can still be trod today. Wether Fell is one of two 2000-foot summits it skirts, and here it comes almost within a stones throw of the top. This renders Wether Fell highly accessible and ensures a near-foolproof route of escape in bad weather.

Though 'improved' further westward, several miles still remain to provide a gem of a traffic-free route for the walker.

WALK 56 MOSSDALE AND COTTERDALE

7¼ miles

from Appersett

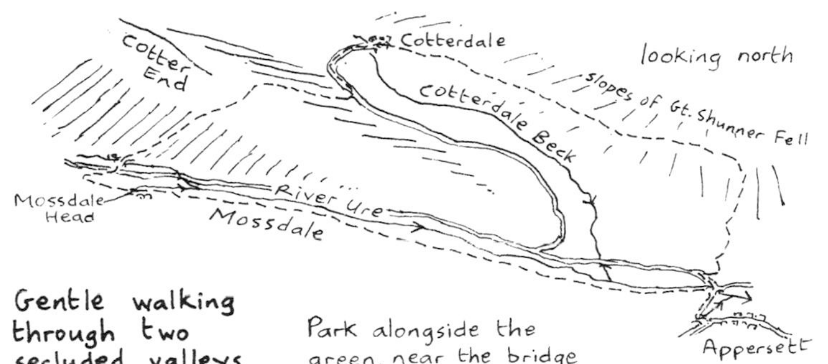
Cotterdale
looking north
Cotter End
Cotterdale Beck
slopes of Gt. Shunner Fell
Mossdale Head
River Ure
Mossdale
Appersett

Gentle walking through two secluded valleys

Park alongside the green, near the bridge

THE WALK

From the green cross the adjacent road-bridge over Widdale Beck and just beyond a barn take a stile on the left. Walk parallel with the road as far as the next bridge (this time over the Ure) but stay in the field and cross a stile to follow the Ure up-dale. On emerging from trees forsake the riverbank and slope up the field: pass along the top of the trees, over a stile and across a large hollow to eventually reach a stile into the woods. Descend to cross a tiny beck as it enters the river, then head left to a barn. From the gate there carry on to a farm track, which bends left to a gate by another barn.

This track is followed only to the next gate, where instead of continuing up to Birk Rigg Farm, fork left on another track through the gate in front. The track is now followed through four further gates. When it swings to the left to climb through low outcrops to Mid Mossdale Farm, leave it and head on to the far end of the field. Now simply follow the river upstream, past a farm-bridge to a wedge of trees deflecting us from the water. At a gate in the next substantial wall a sketchy farm-track strikes left to the now-prominent Mossdale Head Farm.

Pass to the right of the main building to use the bridge over Mossdale Beck. From it ignore the various tracks left and right, and instead climb the field with a wall on the right. Through a gateway head right to a gate in the fence on the right: Follow the fence striking right, and when it swings away continue on to a steep slope

down to the A684 at Thwaite Bridge. Cross straight over road and bridge and up a path through the trees. From a stile at the top climb diagonally up the steep pasture to a stile at the top-right corner, then continue across a gentler slope to locate a stile in a long wall climbing the fell. From it make similarly for the next one, from where a steady descent can be made to the unfenced road in Cotterdale. Turn left along this quiet lane into the hamlet of Cotterdale.

On nearing the last buildings leave the road by a footbridge, crossing two fields to obvious gap-stiles. Then accompany a tiny watercourse to the next stile and continue along a field-bottom. At a collapsed intervening wall strike left up a pronounced grassy rake to a stile in the top wall.

continued across

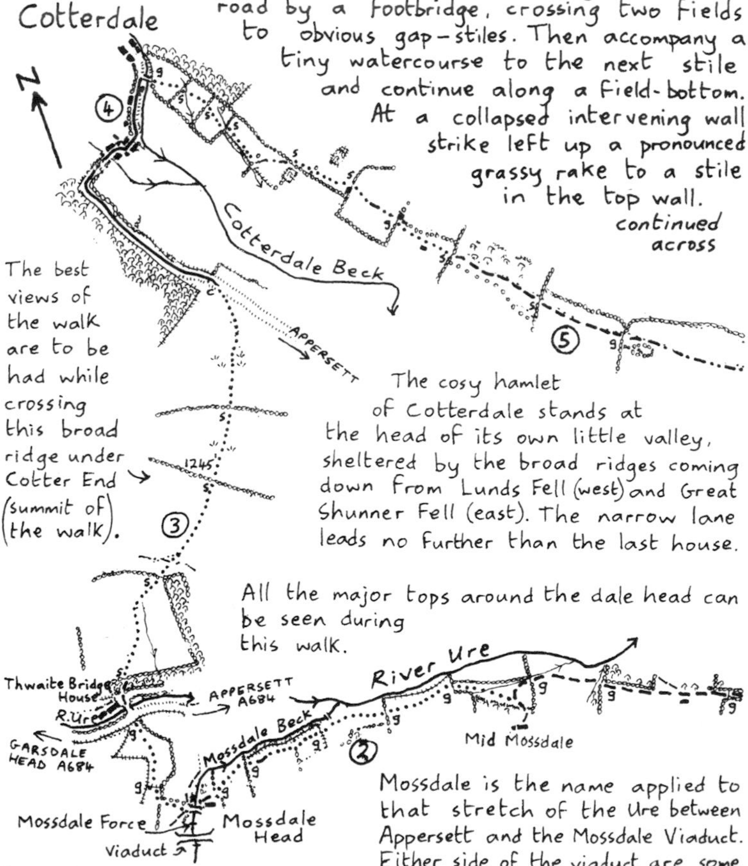

The best views of the walk are to be had while crossing this broad ridge under Cotter End (summit of the walk).

The cosy hamlet of Cotterdale stands at the head of its own little valley, sheltered by the broad ridges coming down from Lunds Fell (west) and Great Shunner Fell (east). The narrow lane leads no further than the last house.

All the major tops around the dale head can be seen during this walk.

Mossdale is the name applied to that stretch of the Ure between Appersett and the Mossdale Viaduct. Either side of the viaduct are some lovely falls. The 4-arch structure once carried the branch line from Hawes to Garsdale Head (then Hawes Junction) on the Settle-Carlisle line.

Turn to follow the wall to a stile by a barn and a gateway below the next barn. Our way now continues on a level course through some varied pastures. Having given us a brief clear spell the path becomes indistinct beyond the crumbling walls of an extensive fold: at the very end of the pasture rise to a gap-stile, then keep right of a short length of wall on a sheep-trod contouring round towards a stile. From it contour yet again to join a wide track descending to a gate. From the stile by it head down the now-enclosed track only as far as the first gate on the right.

Descend by a wall to a stile, then head down across a large field to the wall at the very far end. Find a gate a few yards up to the left then drop down to a more conspicuous gate in the next wall. Aim now for a stile in front of roadsigns which indicate arrival at the Hardraw junction of the A684.

Turn left along the main road, almost immediately crossing Ure Bridge and soon re-entering Appersett via the bridge over Widdale Beck.

From Cotterdale back to the Ure we tread the extensive slopes of Great Shunner Fell.

On the track over Bluebell Hill our walk makes a brief acquaintance with the Pennine Way

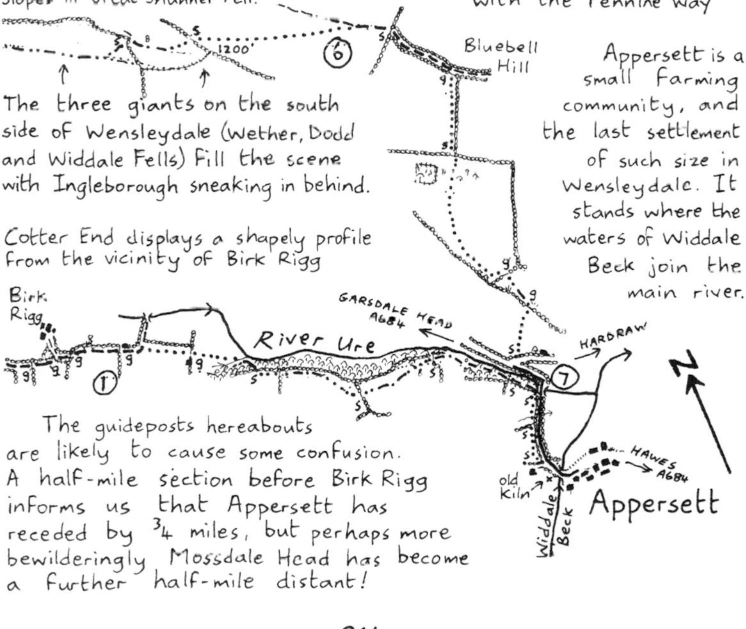

Appersett is a small farming community, and the last settlement of such size in Wensleydale. It stands where the waters of Widdale Beck join the main river.

The three giants on the south side of Wensleydale (Wether, Dodd and Widdale Fells) fill the scene with Ingleborough sneaking in behind.

Cotter End displays a shapely profile from the vicinity of Birk Rigg

The guideposts hereabouts are likely to cause some confusion. A half-mile section before Birk Rigg informs us that Appersett has receded by ¾ miles, but perhaps more bewilderingly Mossdale Head has become a further half-mile distant!

WALK 57

6 miles

PENHILL BEACON

from West Witton

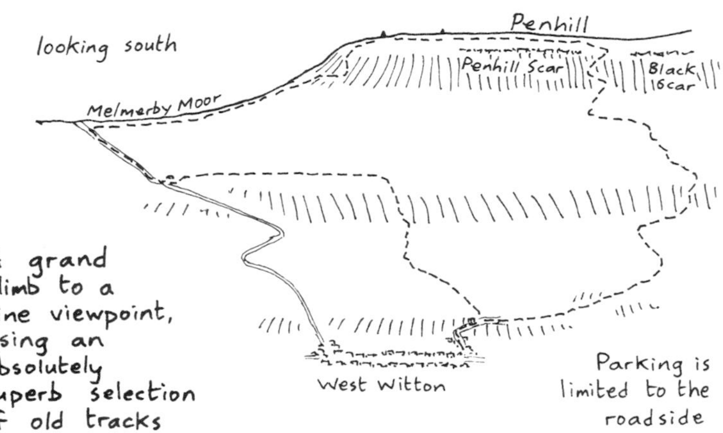

looking south
Penhill
Penhill Scar
Black Scar
Melmerby Moor
West Witton

A grand climb to a fine viewpoint, using an absolutely superb selection of old tracks

Parking is limited to the roadside

THE WALK

Leave West Witton by a lane at the west (Aysgarth) end of the village, by a small grass triangle opposite the former school. Leaving the last dwellings behind, it climbs to a crossroads of tracks : go straight ahead and the lane becomes an enclosed track to rise past an old quarry before arriving at a junction with a splendid green road (High Lane). Take the gate in front and resume the rise on a sketchy green track, passing through two more gates before emerging onto the broad plateau directly under the cliffs of Penhill.

Our green path heads left before we fork away from the wall to cross to the most distant of the four spoil-heaps. From there double back along the tops of the three other prominent spoils, exploring as you go. At the last one a path (only one of many hereabouts) rises just behind it, and gently climbs an expertly-engineered sunken way to the edge of Penhill's summit plateau.

Turn left alongside the wall to a stile, and continue on a sketchy path along the edge, passing the trig. point over the wall before arriving at a small cairn. Only a little further on is the big cairn overlooking the eastern slopes. From it our descent over Melmerby

Moor is well laid-out, as is the alternative bridleway through the fields to the left. A path drops immediately away from the beacon to a stile in the wall-corner below, but the steepness can easily be by-passed by the various paths in the vicinity. From the stile a good path stays fairly close to the wall to cross the moor to join the Melmerby-West Witton road at its highest point.

Go left over the cattle-grid and down to Penhill Farm, after which leave the road by a track along to the left known as Flint Lane. Its level course is trod as far as a stile a short distance beyond a prominent clump of trees, from where a steep field is descended to a stile onto a similar green lane. From the stile opposite drop through two more fields onto a third and final green lane.

Turn left to a barn then bear right across the field behind to a stile. Be sure to peer over the fence ahead to see the waterfall in the wood, then take a wicket-gate to the left. A path crosses the caravan-site to leave by a similar gate, then descends steeply through the trees onto the very lane by which we departed the village. Turn right, therefore, to re-enter West Witton.

Penhill is Wensleydale's best-known fell, its ability to stand out in views from afar outpointing its popularity as a climb. When its top is gained, it is usually by a quick stroll from a car at the top of Melmerby Moor. Its abrupt northern/north-eastern edge however renders Penhill as easily identifiable from most parts of Wensleydale, and it is a regular feature of views westward from the North York Moors.

Penhill's own virtues as a viewpoint are assisted by the dramatic plunge of the Scar, the top of which provides near-birds-eye pictures of the lower dale. It is the aforementioned advantages which have given the hill historical significance. It was the site of a beacon, one of a chain throughout the land which when lit could rapidly spread the message of some impending danger. The coming of the Spanish Armada was of course top of the list. Something which is less certain is that this was also the location of an Iron Age chieftain's last resting-place.

Strictly speaking, the true summit of Penhill is a mile to the south-west of the Ordnance column, but an hour-long return plod is not recommended. To clarify what exactly is what on the summit plateau, the true top is over 1800', the O.S. column is at 1727', and the small cairn on the mound (the beacon site) is 1685'. To the east, and a little lower still is the big cairn on Penhill End.

(57)

West Witton is a pleasant village sadly split almost in two by the incessant traffic racing through. On the slopes of Penhill, it looks out across the valley from high above the river. The village is perhaps best known for an annual event here, the burning of Owd Bartle. An effigy, presumably of Saint Bartholomew to whom the church is dedicated, is joyfully burnt in Guy Fawkes fashion. The meaning of this seems to have gone up in the smoke of the years.

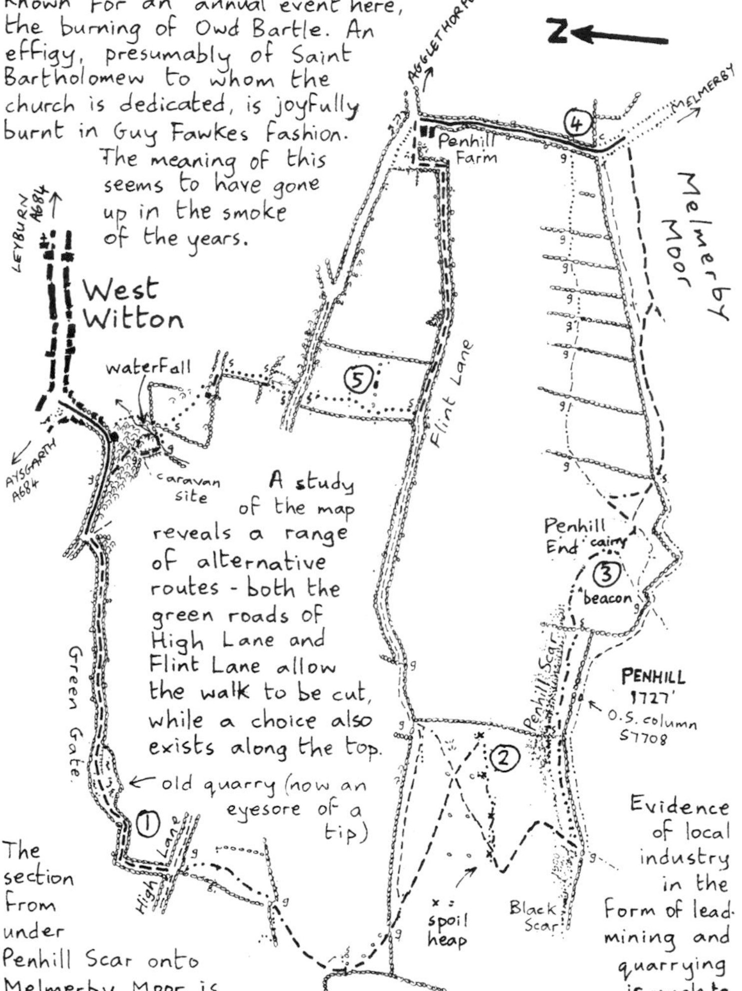

A study of the map reveals a range of alternative routes - both the green roads of High Lane and Flint Lane allow the walk to be cut, while a choice also exists along the top.

← old quarry (now an eyesore of a tip)

Evidence of local industry in the form of lead-mining and quarrying is much to be found hereabouts.

The section from under Penhill Scar onto Melmerby Moor is not an official right-of-way, but stiles are provided at the only two obstacles, and as long as we behave we should have no problem.

N ←
AGGLETHORPE
MELMERBY
Penhill Farm
Melmerby Moor
LEYBURN A684
West Witton
waterfall
AYSGARTH A684
caravan site
Flint Lane
Penhill End
cairn
beacon
Green Gate
Penhill Scar
PENHILL 1727'
O.S. column S7708
High Lane
spoil heap
Black Scar

WALK 58 — HELL GILL AND THE HIGH WAY

7¼ miles — from the Moorcock Inn

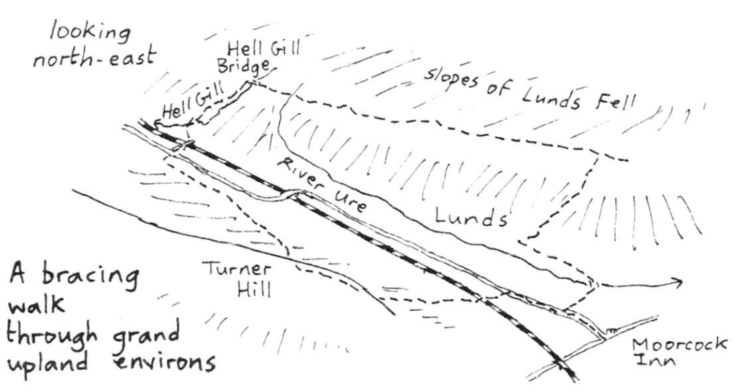
looking north-east
Hell Gill Bridge
Hell Gill
slopes of Lunds Fell
River Ure
Lunds
Turner Hill
Moorcock Inn

A bracing walk through grand upland environs

There is ample parking in the vicinity of the inn at the junction of the Kirkby Stephen road with the Hawes – Sedbergh road

THE WALK

From the inn head down the Kirkby Stephen road and leave it by a farm-track on the right towards Yore House. After crossing the Ure (choice of two bridges) turn left on a sketchy track upstream. This soon fades, but continue to a farm-bridge from where a track leads to Blades Farm. Pass between the buildings and at the end take a gate to the right. A track crosses the field to another gate, and a detour through two more leads to the steep pasture behind. When the track fades climb straight up to a gate, and maintain this course through three more fields up to the derelict farm of High Dyke. Use gates to its right to get onto the open fell.

Running alongside the intake-wall is a track: this is the High Way and it leads us on a generally-level course all the way to Hell Gill Bridge. For the most part the wall stays with us. When it eventually parts company the track continues on to the top of a line of trees above a gorge. Sketchily the way continues by small outcrops to join a wide green track just before getting to Hell Gill Bridge.

On crossing the bridge take the track on the left to descend past farm buildings and down through the fields. A little before crossing the railway bridge onto

58

the road, be sure to deviate right a few yards for a splendid view of Hell Gill Force. On joining the road at Aisgill Moor Cottages cross straight over to a gate and from it follow the fence left to a wall. Though pathless the way is straightforward, remaining fairly level with a wall as company again for the most part. Beyond the barns at High Shaw Paddock the last gate is encountered before entering a large tract of rough pasture

While crossing this pasture gain height gently to arrive at a small beck, ideally just at the top of its steepest section. Further across is a wall which is followed uphill to gain the south ridge of Swarth Fell at a gate. Turn left with the wall over the gentle rise of Turner Hill and then down as far as a gate in the wall.

From the gate descend a rather rough pasture to a highly prominent footbridge over the railway line. A track heads away from it to rejoin the road, and the Moorcock Inn is only a few minutes along to the right.

Turner Hill is an excellent viewpoint, chiefly for the fine surround of fells. Besides a good length of railway, the best single feature is the entire length of Wensleydale stretching away.

Blades is the only farm we encounter which is still operating. The prominent white building on the hillside above-left is the former youth hostel.

High Dyke was once an inn catering for travellers on the old road.

The Moorcock's strategic position places it in that small band of well-known (from the outside at least) outpost-hostelries.

58

This walk is a real treat for railway enthusiasts, the famous line being visible much of the time. Just south of the cottages is Aisgill Summit, at 1169 feet the highest point on a main line in Britain.

This splendid waterfall makes a vertical drop over a cliff, and youngsters should be kept on a tight rein.

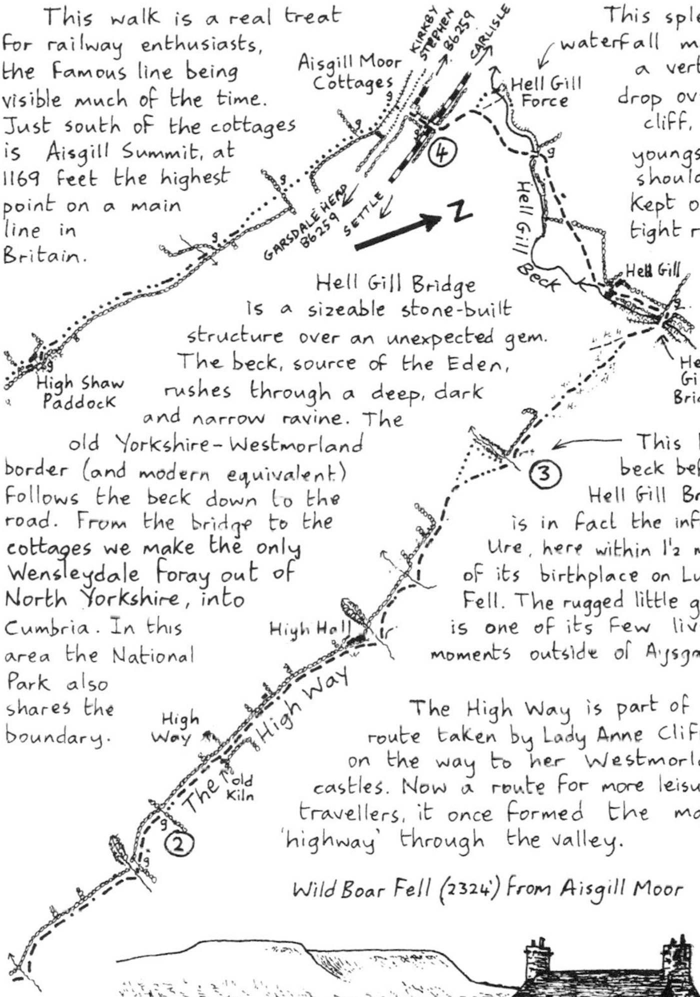

Hell Gill Bridge is a sizeable stone-built structure over an unexpected gem. The beck, source of the Eden, rushes through a deep, dark and narrow ravine. The old Yorkshire-Westmorland border (and modern equivalent) follows the beck down to the road. From the bridge to the cottages we make the only Wensleydale foray out of North Yorkshire, into Cumbria. In this area the National Park also shares the boundary.

This last beck before Hell Gill Bridge is in fact the infant Ure, here within 1½ miles of its birthplace on Lunds Fell. The rugged little gorge is one of its few lively moments outside of Aysgarth.

The High Way is part of the route taken by Lady Anne Clifford on the way to her Westmorland castles. Now a route for more leisurely travellers, it once formed the major 'highway' through the valley.

Aisgill Moor Cottages
KIRKBY STEPHEN B6259
CARLISLE
Hell Gill Force
GARSDALE HEAD B6259
SETTLE
N
Hell Gill Beck
Hell Gill
Hell Gill Bridge
High Shaw Paddock
High Hall
High Way
The High Way
old Kiln

Wild Boar Fell (2324') from Aisgill Moor

WALK 59

3½ miles

AYSGILL FORCE AND GAYLE

from Hawes

looking south-west

A simple stroll in the valley of Gayle Beck

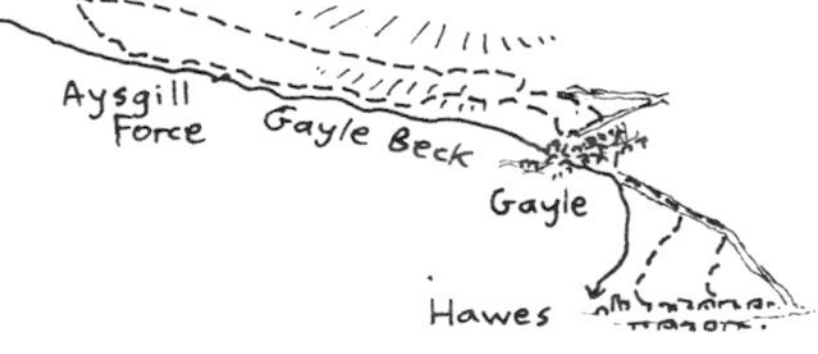
Aysgill Force
Gayle Beck
Gayle
Hawes

Use the main National Park car-park in the old station yard

THE WALK

Leave Hawes through the small car-park on the main street almost opposite the Board Inn. From a stile in its left corner a sketchy path rises half-right across two fields to join the Gayle road adjacent to the large creamery. Turn left up into the heart of Gayle, and after leaning on the bridge to survey the falls on Gayle Beck take the short cobbled way to the right, continuing along a lane to an old kissing-gate after the last house on the left. Climb half-right past a wall corner and on to a stile with Pennine Way signs in residence. Continue at the same angle as before to a stile above the beck, then descend to its bank.

The way is now straightforward, with Gayle Beck being followed upstream to Aysgill Force. Beyond the waterfall remain with the beck past two footbridges, the second by a barn. At the end of the next field we leave the beck by rising right to join a farm-track at a gate. This green track is followed to the right, soon becoming enclosed and eventually becoming a lane after a gate by a barn on a bend. A few yards further is a stile from where the Pennine Way is traced back to Hawes.

Firstly two fields are crossed, and from the stile we used earlier turn left to accompany a wall down onto a lane. Almost immediately then use the lane joining it to drop down onto the edge of Gayle. The Way then avoids the village centre by branching left across two fields, passing between modern housing to emerge onto the lane to Hawes. Turn briefly left

Hawes is the 'capital' of upper Wensleydale, the lively colourful market town to which all visitors are drawn. The place gains even more character on its market-day when there are, happily, as many local people to be seen as tourists. Once the last stop on the Wensleydale branch line, the station has now been put to good use as a National Park Centre. Alongside it in the old station yard is the Upper Dales Folk Museum, where one can learn of the old local industries, including probably the best-known, that of cheese-making. Hawes has retained an unconventional layout, including some cobbled road, and a leisurely exploration really is needed. Other buildings include the parish church of St. Margaret, and a modern youth hostel at this major staging-post on the Pennine Way.

<u>THE WALK</u> *continued* and then leave by a barn on the right. A flagged footpath leads through two fields to arrive at the parish church. Take the path to its left, through its yard and out onto Hawes main street.

Note the profusion of field-barns above Gayle

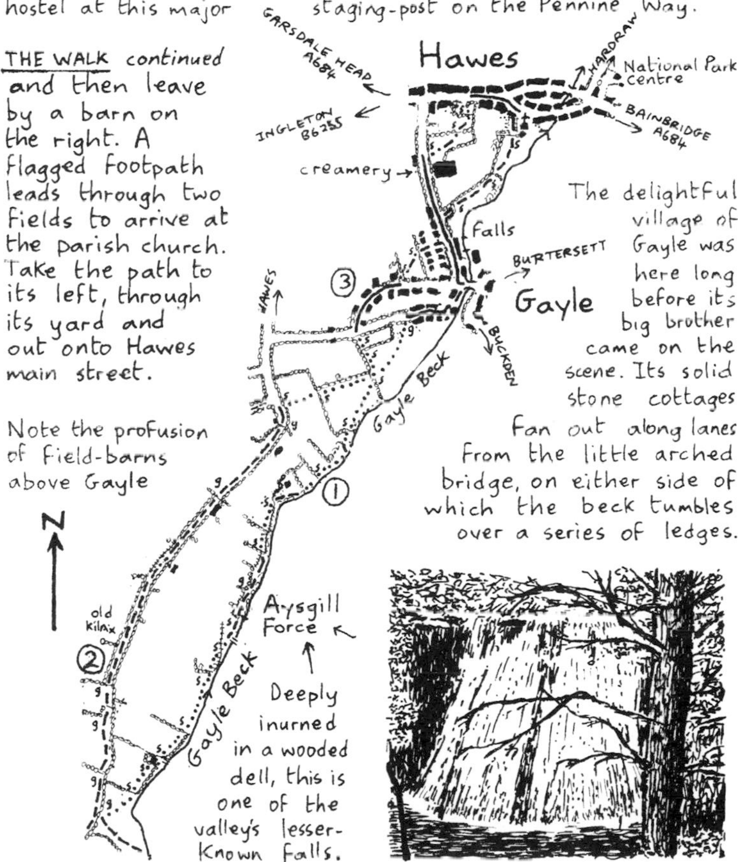
Hawes
GARSDALE HEAD A684
HARDRAW
National Park centre
INGLETON B6255
BAINBRIDGE A684
creamery
falls
BURTERSETT
Gayle
HAWES
BUCKDEN
3
Gayle Beck
1
old kiln
2
Aysgill Force
Gayle Beck
N

The delightful village of Gayle was here long before its big brother came on the scene. Its solid stone cottages fan out along lanes from the little arched bridge, on either side of which the beck tumbles over a series of ledges.

Deeply inurned in a wooded dell, this is one of the valley's lesser-known falls.

WALK 60 — **NAPPA HALL AND ASKRIGG'S FALLS**

7 miles — from Askrigg

Park in the centre of Askrigg

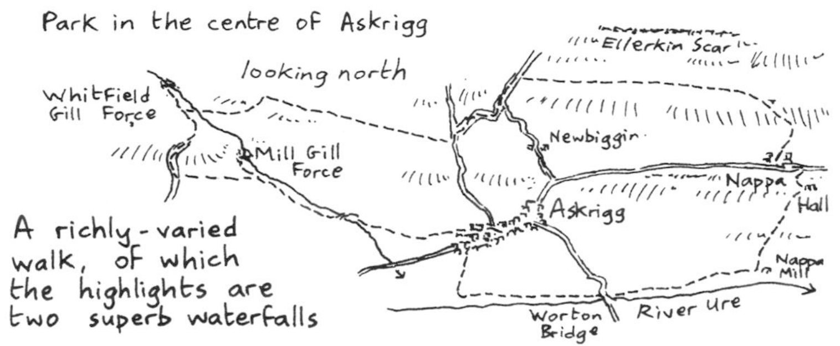

looking north
Whitfield Gill Force
Mill Gill Force
Ellerkin Scar
Newbiggin
Askrigg
Nappa Hall
Nappa Mill
Worton Bridge
River Ure

A richly-varied walk, of which the highlights are two superb waterfalls

THE WALK

From the village centre follow the Hawes road out of the bottom end of the village, and after the last house on the left take a track down past an animal feeds works. From the gate at the bottom pass between the ramparts of a former railway bridge and continue in the same direction through a series of five stiles. From the last a sketchy path heads straight for the river, but instead of following it to the bank turn left on a low embankment to arrive at a stile in a wall-corner. Follow the fence away from it (parallel with the river) to a gate from where the riverbank is at last joined. Accompany the Ure downstream to soon emerge onto a road adjacent to the characterless Worton Bridge.

At a stile opposite continue down the river. A footbridge, gate and second footbridge lead to a gate behind which is Nappa Mill Farm: take the farm-drive up to the left, but leave it by a stile on the right just before crossing the beck. Climb diagonally away to the right-hand gate of two, and continue in the same direction to another gate admitting to the environs of Nappa Hall. Take the enclosed track up past the Hall and out onto the road.

Turn left along the road only as far as the first branch right (signposted 'no through road) and head through the hamlet of Nappa Scar. Stay on this lane which at the top of the hill becomes an unmade track: it now swings left for a long and pleasant level march to debouch onto a lane rising out of Askrigg. Turn down towards the valley, ignoring a lane left, a track right and another lane right (to Muker). Just below is another walled track, and this we follow along to the right. Remain on it throughout its entire length, and just before it escapes into a field take a stile on the left. Whitfield Gill Force immediately appears through the trees directly below. Our route must take a circuitous course in order to stand at its foot, for the steep slopes prevent a direct descent. Instead, the path heads downstream high above the wooded beck before dropping down to a footbridge, then rises to meet the path to the waterfall. Turn upstream to arrive at the fall, care being needed as this can be a slippery path.

To resume the walk retrace steps to the path junction and then continue straight on to a stile. This recently created route has replaced a path which previously had to deviate from the beck, but now we can accompany the numerous yellow blobs downstream. A side beck and then a stile are encountered before the way skirts above the walled, wooded beckside, only to then enter the trees at a stile which soon appears. Very quickly we are to be deposited back into a field to continue down, meeting another stile before one returns us to the trees.

The path runs along the top of the trees to a junction, and here the second detour to our second waterfall is made, the wooded confines being almost a replica of the situation already experienced further up the beck. This time however it is but a very brief stroll along a much better path upstream to witness the delights of the equally impressive waterfall of Mill Gill Force.

After admiring the cascades return to the path junction and continue downstream on an excellent path along the top side of the wood, with the bonus of a distant view across the main valley in addition to peering into the gill itself. At the bottom end of the wood two neighbouring stiles lead to a footbridge across the beck, and within a few yards our track forsakes the beck to pass to the left of an old mill, under a modest aqueduct to a stile. A flagged path then leads to a lane which in turn takes us back into the centre of Askrigg.

60

Askrigg is a wonderfully different village, seeming of another age to the 'typical' Dales village. Formerly a market town and a famous clockmaking centre, Askrigg gradually gave way to Hawes as centre for the upper dale.

The village centre still clearly recalls those days: the market cross, the three-storeyed houses along the main street and the 15th century St. Oswald's church with its splendid old beams. Flat-topped Addlebrough is prominent in the Askrigg scene.

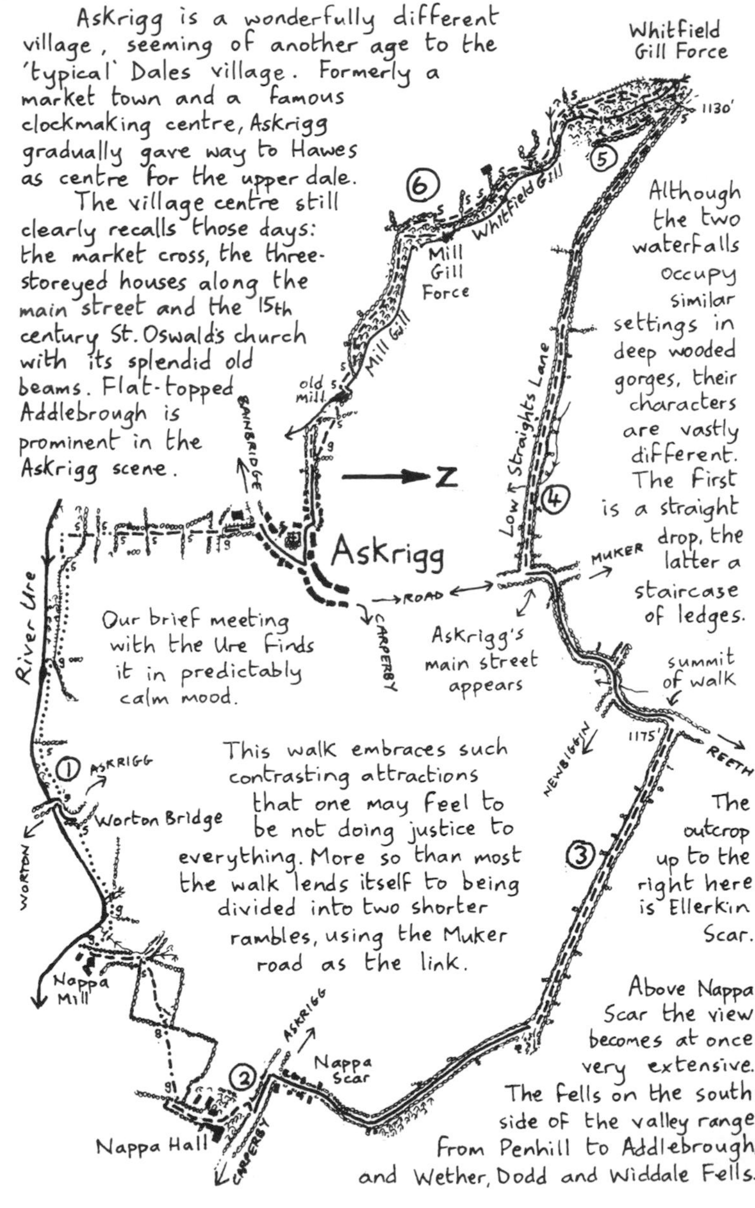

Whitfield Gill Force
1130'
5
6
Whitfield Gill
Mill Gill Force
Mill Gill
old mill
BAINBRIDGE
Z
Low Straights Lane
4
Askrigg
MUKER
ROAD
CARPERBY
Askrigg's main street appears
River Ure
summit of walk
1175'
NEWBIGGIN
REETH
1
ASKRIGG
Worton Bridge
WORTON
3
Nappa Mill
ASKRIGG
Nappa Scar
2
Nappa Hall
CARPERBY

Although the two waterfalls occupy similar settings in deep wooded gorges, their characters are vastly different. The first is a straight drop, the latter a staircase of ledges.

Our brief meeting with the Ure finds it in predictably calm mood.

This walk embraces such contrasting attractions that one may feel to be not doing justice to everything. More so than most the walk lends itself to being divided into two shorter rambles, using the Muker road as the link.

The outcrop up to the right here is Ellerkin Scar.

Above Nappa Scar the view becomes at once very extensive. The fells on the south side of the valley range from Penhill to Addlebrough, and Wether, Dodd and Widdale Fells.

Whitfield Gill Force

Mill Gill Force

Nappa Hall dates from the mid-fifteenth century, and was a fortified manor house of the influential Metcalfe family. It is now a farm, and a peep through the entrance arch reveals the scene below. Note the stunning carpet of snowdrops in the adjacent wood (*in the season!*)

WALK 61

THE WALDEN VALLEY

6½ miles

from West Burton

An intimate exploration of an unfrequented side-valley. Almost gradient-free

looking south-east

Walden Beck
Cote Bridge
Falls
West Burton

Park alongside the village green but *not* on the grass

THE WALK

Leave the village-green by a narrow lane signposted to 'Walden only'. When it forks take the left arm towards Walden South, and after passing a barn take a stile on the right. Here a long pathless trek begins across the sloping fields above Walden Beck. Follow the wall away from the road to a stile in it, then commence a level walk which calls for little description: every intervening wall is graced with a stile.

The first deviation from this occurs after a good mile, when a wall deflects us half-right across a field with a beck in it. From the stile there the rise continues over a fenced pasture, beyond which a small gate precedes a footbridge over Cowstone Gill. Pass to the right of the house, over a stile and head across the field to a gate opposite. Through it join a farm-track to enter the confines of Hargill Farm. From the right-hand building cross the tiny beck to a footgate, and then resume the level hike across the fields. This is maintained through several more stiles before descending to the next farm, Bridge End. At this most distant point of the journey, take a stile to the right of the buildings to round them to a small farm-bridge over Walden Beck.

On the opposite bank take a stile found immediately on the left, and continue downstream to a stile in a fence. Now the beck is left by climbing half-right to a gate at the top-corner. From it turn left to commence a long, level march to complement that on the outward leg. Again virtually pathless, the way this time is broken up mostly by gates, and before long the farm of Whiterow appears ahead. Pass along the front of the buildings and the access-road takes over to guide us out onto a lane. Turn left to accompany this ultra-quiet lane for a long mile until arriving at Cote Bridge over Walden Beck.

Without crossing it take the gate on the right, and follow the beck down as far as a footbridge across it. Once again forego the crossing, and this time head half-right away from it to a stile. Rise up the side of the next field to a stile half-way, then break across a field to an easily-located gapstile. Now head straight across three more fields in a direct line: beyond that a track descends left, but we branch off it to a stile just before it reaches a gate. Follow the left-hand wall around to a final stile and descend the edge of a field to a small gate on the left. Steps lead down to a footbridge below West Burton Falls, which can be enjoyed at a closer range before turning right to re-appear back on the village green.

The Walden valley is one of the least-known and least-changed in the Dales, and the reason certainly for the former, is that it is a dead-end for motor vehicles. Not only that, the quiet lanes that set off up each side of the valley fail to connect again, thereby denying any circular tour. The individual farms are the only settlements up-dale of West Burton. The beck flows a good 7 miles to reach the village, being born under the summit of Buckden Pike.

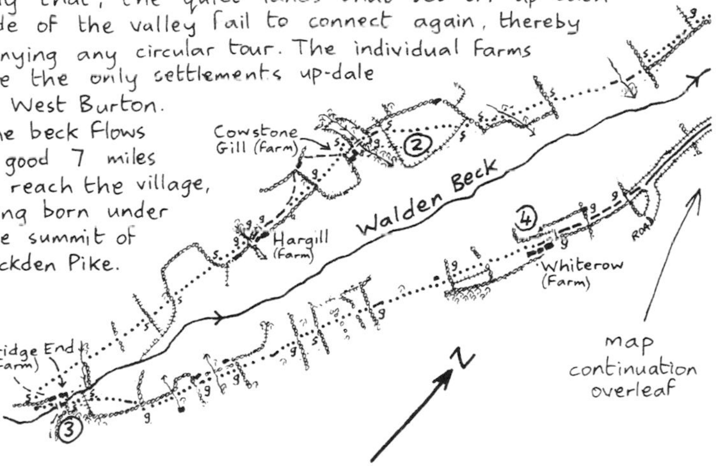

Cowstone Gill (Farm)
2
Walden Beck
4
Hargill (Farm)
Whiterow (Farm)
ROAD
Bridge End (Farm)
3
N
map continuation overleaf

(61)

West Burton is an absolute gem of a village, not only well away from the main road through Wensleydale but also hidden from the lesser road that runs through Bishopdale to join it. Strictly speaking the village is in the Walden valley, and jealously guards the only entrance to it. Outstanding is the extensive green, with cottages stood back in appreciation. An obelisk of 1820 stands on market-cross steps, with village stocks nearby: 'round the back' are the delightful falls in a wooded dell. This is surely Wensleydale's best!

Where a track joins the lane just before Cote Farm note the remains of a chimney and flue of a smelting mill of a former lead-mine.

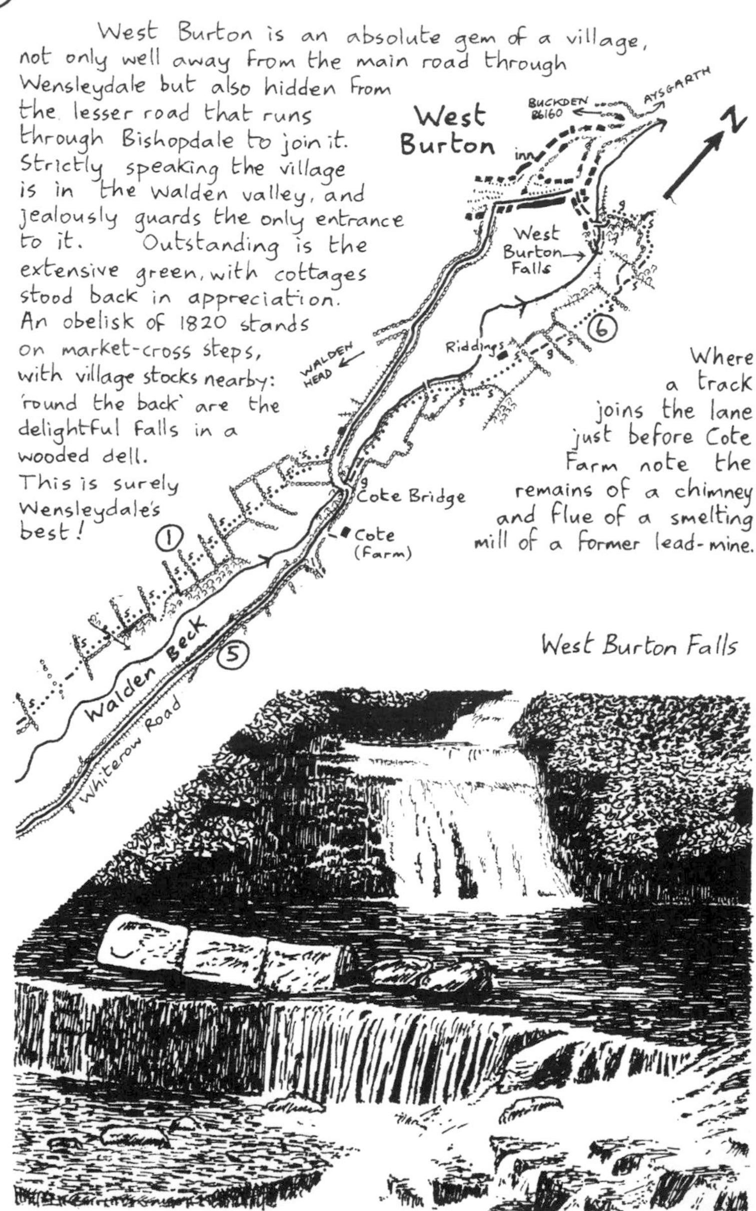
West Burton
BUCKDEN B6160
AYSGARTH
N
inn
West Burton Falls
6
Riddings
WALDEN HEAD
Cote Bridge
Cote (Farm)
1
Walden Beck
5
Whiterow Road

West Burton Falls

WALK 62 REDMIRE FORCE AND THE TEMPLARS' CHAPEL

$6\frac{3}{4}$ miles

from West Witton

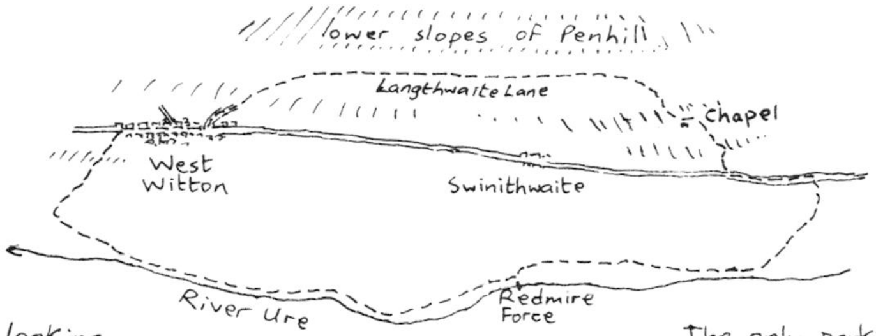

lower slopes of Penhill
Langthwaite Lane
Chapel
West Witton
Swinithwaite
River Ure
Redmire Force
looking south

Easy walking and easy route-finding. Included is the best long section of riverbank in the valley

The only parking is along the main street, with the best place being found at the eastern end of the village. Here there is a wide verge just after the last houses on the left. This is also where the walk begins.

THE WALK

From the east (Leyburn) end of the village take a walled track just after the last house on the left. Almost at once it forks: take the right-hand option. Twisting and turning, this way leads steadily downhill towards the river, becoming narrower in its latter stages. At the very end do not take the obvious gate directly in front, but opt for the one just to the right. In the field cling to the left-hand boundary wall, until its many indentations lead down to a gate with the river now in close proximity. Cross the stream behind the gate and drop to another gate in the fence to the right.

The riverbank is now joined, and plain-sailing ensues as the Ure is followed up-dale through a succession of gates in pleasant pastures. Eventually, beyond a large wooded island and a lively bend, a wall commences to separate us from the river. Stay with the wall, crossing an intervening stile and continuing on to a stile hidden in the very corner of the next field. From it a good path heads through the trees, and almost immediately the grandeur of Redmire Force greets the eye.

Almost as soon as it reaches the Falls,

62

the path climbs a stairway away from the river to a stile out of the woods. A field is crossed to another stile and then the right-hand wall leads through several more fields. High above the river the route follows a fence to two neighbouring stiles from where the fence heads across an extensive pasture. When it bends away continue straight ahead to a stile in the far corner.

A good path drops through the trees to briefly rejoin the river, but on emerging into a large riverside pasture we finally leave the river with the wall curving up to the left. A partially-enclosed track materialises to lead up onto the main road. Turn left along it almost to the first farm, then take a stile on the right to follow a farm-track to the top end of the field. From a gate it climbs through trees, and a stile on the left at the top gives access to the remains of the Knights Templars' Chapel.

From here follow a now sketchy track to a gate at the top of the field, going on to join a concrete farm-road.

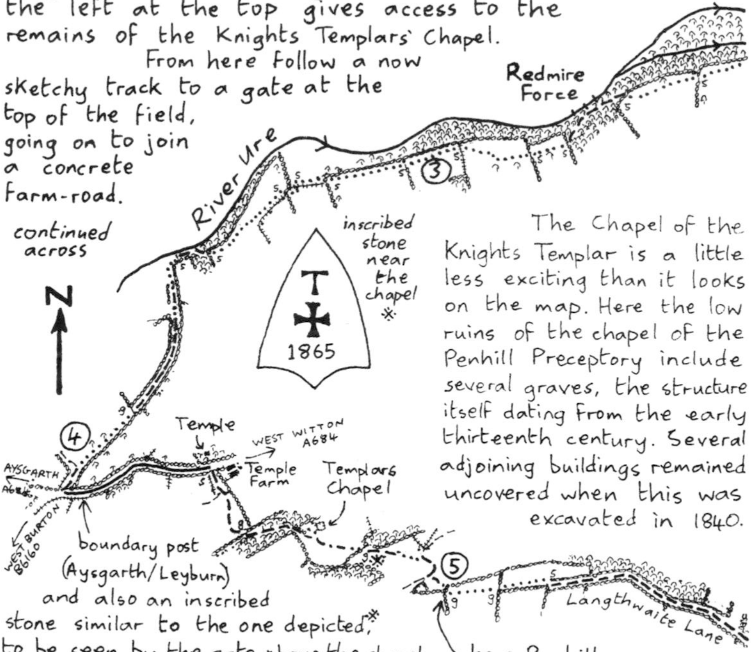

continued across

The Chapel of the Knights Templar is a little less exciting than it looks on the map. Here the low ruins of the chapel of the Penhill Preceptory include several graves, the structure itself dating from the early thirteenth century. Several adjoining buildings remained uncovered when this was excavated in 1840.

inscribed stone near the chapel ⁜

T ✠ 1865

boundary post (Aysgarth/Leyburn) and also an inscribed stone similar to the one depicted, ⁜ to be seen by the gate above the chapel.

here Penhill appears directly above, looking moody and menacing in the right conditions.

The roadside Temple (all very confusing this) was built in 1792 as a belvedere by the owners of nearby Swinithwaite Hall.

Follow the farm-road uphill only as far as a pronounced bend right, then head up a vague track to the top of the field. From a gate in an angle of the wall head across the now-level pasture to another gate. Now with a wall on the right, accompany it as far as a stile which gives access to the terminus of a green lane.

This is Langthwaite Lane, and all is plain sailing as this superb way is trod all the way back to West Witton. Towards the end it becomes a little rougher and finally joins a narrow tarmac lane to descend into the village.

Despite being a major valley of the Dales, Wensleydale only attracts large numbers to its river at a very short stretch at Aysgarth. This much less-known section however provides outstanding company for several beautifully-wooded miles.

On descending Back Lane note the stately Bolton Hall on the opposite bank. Set in graceful parkland, this home of the Lords Bolton dates back three centuries.

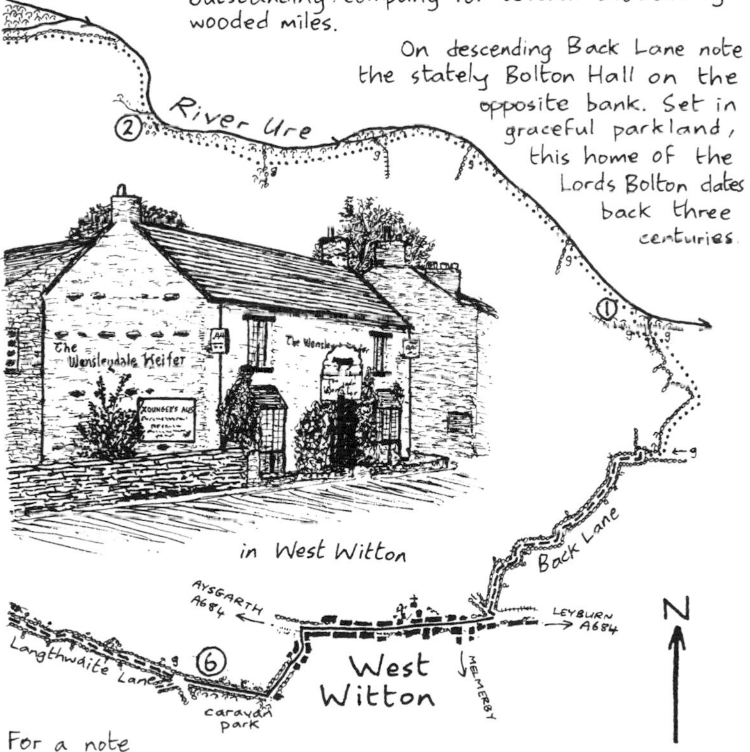
River Ure
2
1
The Wensleydale Heifer
Younger's Ales
Back Lane
AYSGARTH A684
LEYBURN A684
MELMERBY
West Witton
Langthwaite Lane
6
caravan park
N

in West Witton

For a note on West Witton see page 214.

WALK 63

SEMERWATER AND RAYDALE

4 miles

from Semerwater

A very easy circuit of Semerwater.

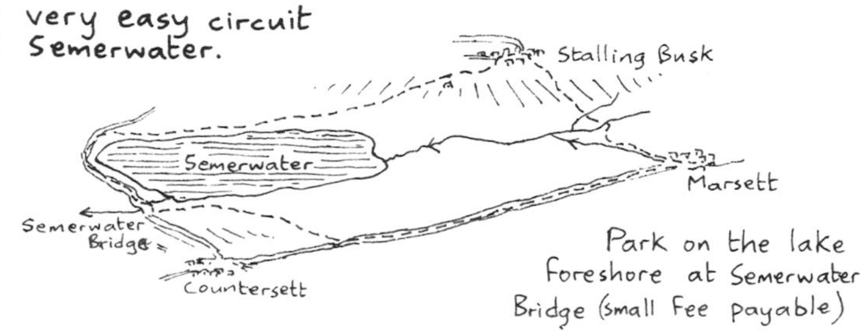

Stalling Busk
Semerwater
Marsett
Semerwater Bridge
Countersett

Park on the lake foreshore at Semerwater Bridge (small fee payable)

THE WALK

From the foreshore of the lake head along the lane away from the bridge (not over it) and at the foot of a hill take a stile on the right, just opposite a farm. Maintain a level course across the fields, taking in several stiles to emerge very close to the lake-shore. By now a good path has materialised and it heads gradually upwards across rough pastures alongside the head of Semerwater. More stiles ensue to arrive at the ruined chapel of Stalling Busk. A stile is provided to enable a look-round. Only yards beyond it the barely-evident path forks: head up to the left on an improving path alongside a small beck. It leads unerringly up onto the cul-de-sac road in the hamlet of Stalling Busk.

Walk only a few yards to the right, and before a sharp bend take a rough track down to the right. This enclosed way takes us down to a ford over Cragdale Water, then heads away, forsaking it at a bend (by a footbridge) to cross two lesser becks directly ahead. Beyond, the track becomes enclosed to enter Marsett alongside Marsett Beck. Cross the green to the road-bridge, and follow this quiet, level lane for about one and a third miles. Shortly after a brief climb, journey's end beckons at the lake-foot, and as the lane descends a stile on the right admits to a field. Follow the tiny beck down to a gate: once through it the beck is crossed, and a short muddy section through the trees leads to a gate adjacent to Semerwater Bridge which is crossed to complete the walk.

Semerwater was the largest lake in the old North Riding of Yorkshire, and in a district not over-endowed with sheets of water it has become a popular venue for a variety of water-sports. An Association exists to control the activities and help protect bird-life. Near the lakefoot is the Carlow Stone, once dropped by a giant.

The best-known legend of the district relates how a visitor, inhospitably treated, caused a whole 'city' to disappear under the waters. What seems a little more certain is that Iron Age lake-dwellings existed here.

If one's boots should still be clean on leaving Marsett, a potentially squelchy finish can be avoided by remaining on the lane to the Countersett road-junction, and there turning right.

The old church at Stalling Busk stands in strange isolation some 200 feet below the hamlet. The ruins romantically overlook the lake, and exude an atmosphere not felt at the replacement St. Matthews up by the houses.

COUNTERSETT
River Bain
Semerwater Bridge
Carlow Stone
Low Blean
STALLING BUSK
Semerwater
Carr End
3
1
N
ruined church
BAINBRIDGE
Marsett Beck
Marsett
Raydale Beck
2
Cragdale Water
Busk Lane
Stalling Busk

Both Marsett and Stalling Busk are peaceful farming hamlets, Marsett in the valley bottom and Stalling Busk perched on the hillside with good views of the lake.

A cul-de-sac for motorists, but the start of a good walkers track over to Wharfedale.

The side-valley containing Semerwater has no satisfactory name, though Semerdale has sometimes been offered as a makeshift title. Above the lake it is generally referred to as Raydale, this being the central, the largest and the only level one of the three valleys which merge between Marsett and Stalling Busk. Bardale and Cragdale are the lesser two.

WALK 64 **OVER THE MOORS TO COVERDALE**

11 miles from West Burton

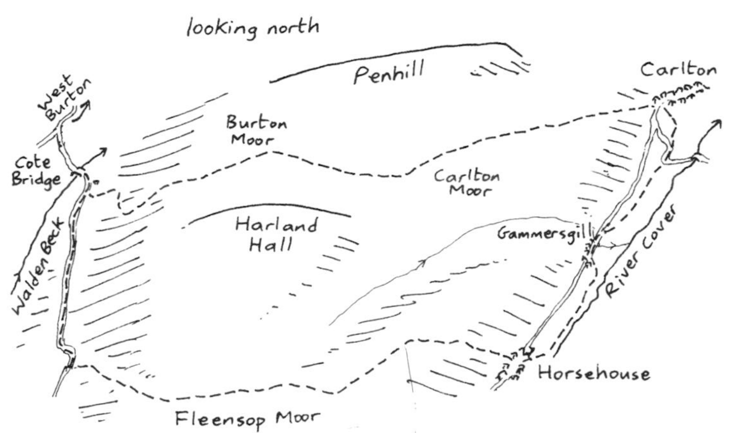
looking north
Penhill
Carlton
West Burton
Burton Moor
Cote Bridge
Carlton Moor
Harland Hall
Gammersgill
Walden Beck
River Cover
Horsehouse
Fleensop Moor

An invigorating if mildly strenuous walk, using two fine inter-valley paths on high moorland to visit two Coverdale villages. Not surprisingly the views are extensive.

Take your sandwiches and make a day of this one!

There is reasonable parking just beyond Cote Bridge, which is reached from West Burton by the lane to 'Walden only'. Fork left at the first junction and the lane descends to the bridge. If walking from West Burton, use the map in Walk 61 to reach and return from Cote Bridge. This adds an extra 1½ miles.

THE WALK

Leave Cote Bridge by the lane heading up the valley, and remain on its traffic-free course for about 1¼ miles. Above a steep rise a guide-post indicates the departure of a bridle-road to Horsehouse. Take this track to the left, passing through a gate and rising across the slope to swing left to a gate onto the moor-top. Now virtually level a good path heads away, but after a short distance be sure to opt for the

less-clear left path at a fork. It crosses the undulating moor to a gate, there becoming clear again to reach the headwaters of the Fleensop valley.

At another junction fork right to a gate, and after fording Fleemis Gill the track rises past grouse butts to a gate on the left. The last section of moor is crossed more sketchily to arrive at and follow a wall along to the left. Use the first gate in it to begin the drop into Coverdale. Head down the pasture finally veering left to a stile in the bottom corner, then make use of the walled confines of a wooded beck to descend into Horsehouse.

Turn right only as far as the inn then take the lane running behind it for a few yards, to leave it by a gate down to the right. Descend to another gate, left to yet another and then cross to a small gate right of a barn. The River Cover is joined and accompanied downstream for some distance. Several intervening fences are crossed and beyond a wooded bend the path squeezes between fence and river, but the gates at either end of the field by-passed provide an easier passage.

In the next pasture we leave the river behind by taking a gate at the far end and heading up the field to the next gate. Continue up to a stile well to the right of the farm buildings, and a wooded enclosure leads onto the road through Gammersgill. Turn right as far as the second field after the beck, then take a gate on the right and bear left to a stile. A green lane is entered and this delightful narrow byway is followed to its terminus.

WEST BURTON
Cote Bridge
Cote
Walden Beck
N
Whiterow Road
1
ROAD
Dove Scar
2
continued overleaf

On emerging into a field continue across to a wall-corner then across again to the top far end of the next pasture. A beck is crossed to a well-hidden stile

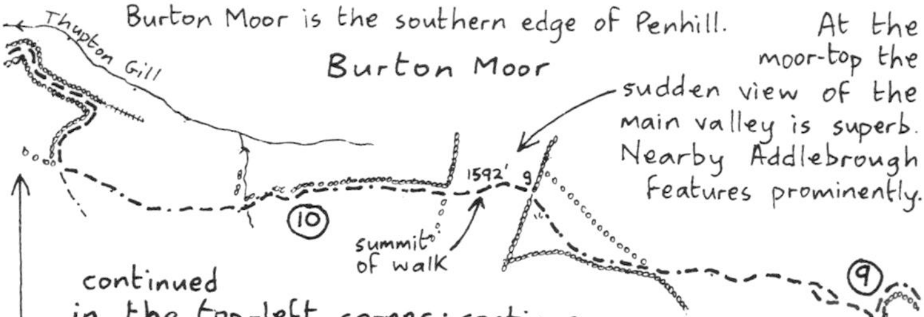

Burton Moor is the southern edge of Penhill. At the moor-top the sudden view of the main valley is superb. Nearby Addlebrough features prominently.

Thupton Gill

Burton Moor

1592'

summit of walk

(10)

(9)

Howden Lodge

Carlton Moor

continued from overleaf

continued in the top-left corner: continue across to accompany a fence, using a stile in it to reach a stile onto a lane. Head left only as far as the next bend, then take a stile along a field-bottom. From the next stile head to one in the top corner, then climb the steep field to a gate to emerge onto a lane. Turn right to enter Carlton.

If not wishing to potter around the place (or look for the inn) take the lane climbing left at the first junction at the edge of the village. At once it starts to climb: at a fork take the rough track going up to the right. It climbs steeply before rising across the moor always with at least one wall for company. With the tree-shrouded Howden Lodge in view, the track by-passes a short walled section before crossing an open pasture to join a wall leading to the lodge's entrance.

Do not enter, but take the track climbing to the right. The gradient soon eases again and the way continues, at times a little sketchily through a collapsed wall before going right to a gate in the wall along the moor-top. The track continues to the brow of the hill, then throws itself into a rapid descent. In its final section it becomes enclosed to emerge onto the road in the Walden valley. Cote Bridge is just along to the right.

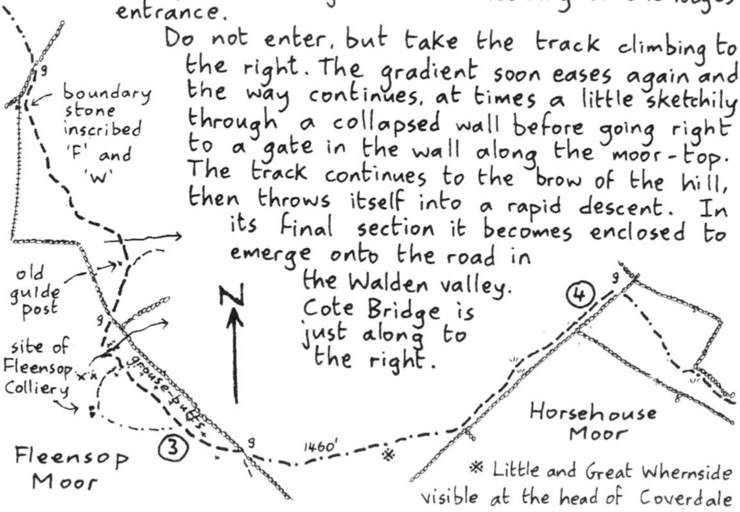

boundary stone inscribed 'F' and 'W'

old guide post

site of Fleensop Colliery

grouse butts

N

Fleensop Moor

(3)

1460'

(4)

Horsehouse Moor

* Little and Great Whernside visible at the head of Coverdale

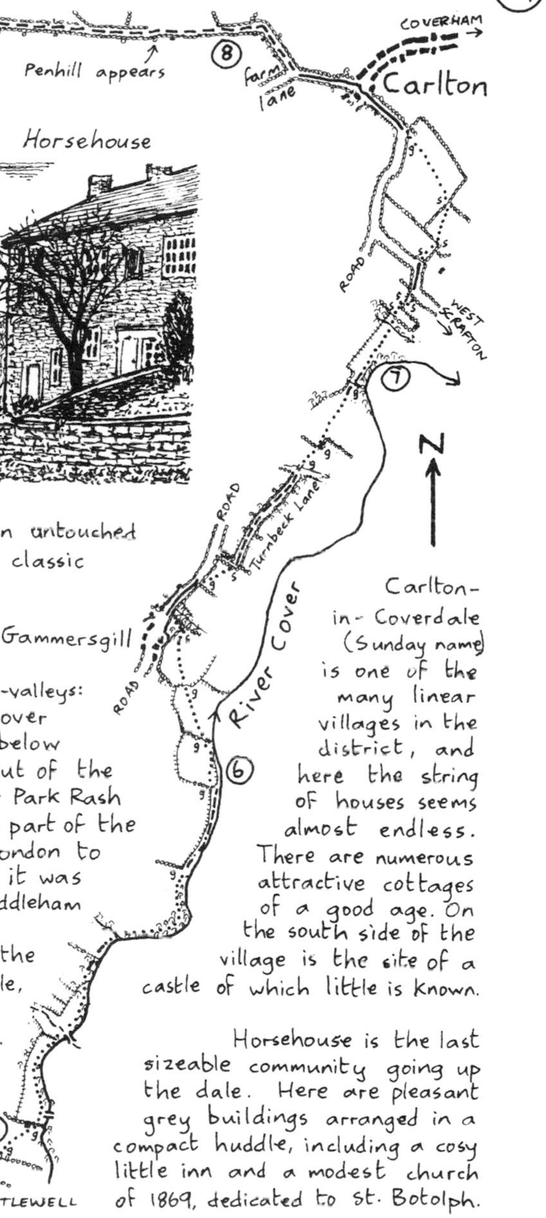

COVERHAM
Penhill appears
farm lane
Carlton
Carlton Moor

Horsehouse

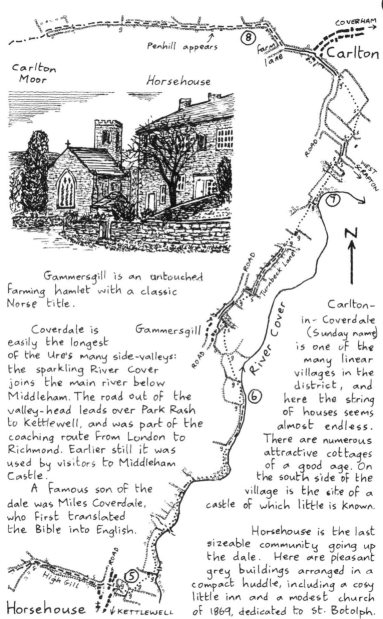

ROAD
WEST SCRAFTON
N
ROAD
Turnbeck Lane
River Cover
Gammersgill
ROAD
High Gill
ROAD
Horsehouse
KETTLEWELL

Gammersgill is an untouched farming hamlet with a classic Norse title.

Coverdale is easily the longest of the Ure's many side-valleys: the sparkling River Cover joins the main river below Middleham. The road out of the valley-head leads over Park Rash to Kettlewell, and was part of the coaching route from London to Richmond. Earlier still it was used by visitors to Middleham Castle.

A famous son of the dale was Miles Coverdale, who first translated the Bible into English.

Carlton-in-Coverdale (Sunday name) is one of the many linear villages in the district, and here the string of houses seems almost endless. There are numerous attractive cottages of a good age. On the south side of the village is the site of a castle of which little is known.

Horsehouse is the last sizeable community going up the dale. Here are pleasant grey buildings arranged in a compact huddle, including a cosy little inn and a modest church of 1869, dedicated to St. Botolph.

CHAPTER FIVE

SWALEDALE

Ivelet Bridge

opposite: Calver Hill from Booze Moor

SWALEDALE

The area explored in the pages of this chapter is a very well defined one, being the valley of the river Swale from its beginnings in the tumbling becks of the wild Pennines to its departure from the Yorkshire Dales National Park near Richmond. Swaledale is the most northerly of Yorkshire's Dales and its remoteness from major centres of population has helped it remain relatively quiet and unchanged. Without insulting all of the other beautiful Dales valleys, it must be said that Swaledale is a little bit special.

Throughout its entire length the dale loses none of its grandeur, remaining steep-sided virtually all the way to Richmond. There is only one side-valley of any size, this being Arkengarthdale, the valley of Arkle Beck. It shares all the characteristics of the main dale. With its colourful, sweeping fellsides, there is a strong hint of lakeland in Swaledale.

This is walkers territory *par excellence*, the dale's attractions being largely of the natural variety from heather moors to the waterfalls of Keld, and inevitably back to the swift-flowing and often tree-lined river. The Pennine Way crosses the valley head and the Coast to Coast Walk treats its followers to the entire length of the dale. There are two distinct types of walking in Swaledale, the lush meadows and the mining-ravaged hillsides. These two aspects of the dale are its very trademark. No other dale in the park has a riverbank which can be followed so closely for such a distance, and no other has such an intense concentration of remains of the lead mining industry. Every corner of the dale displays the evidence, from the mines on the moors down through the gills with their smelt mills to the villages with their miners cottages. Many of the paths we follow lead up to the sites of former workings, which are slowly blending back into their hillsides. There is an impressiveness and even a certain beauty about these places which stem partly from an image of those hardy souls who, not that long ago, would walk several miles every day to slave away in these dark, damp holes.

The magnificent gateway to this glorious valley is Richmond, one of the finest little towns in the land. Its medieval charm and unrivalled character are a perfect match for the dale it guards. For those with transport it would make a reasonable base, but Reeth, the largest village, is far more satisfactorily situated in walking terms, with ample accommodation and several shops and inns.

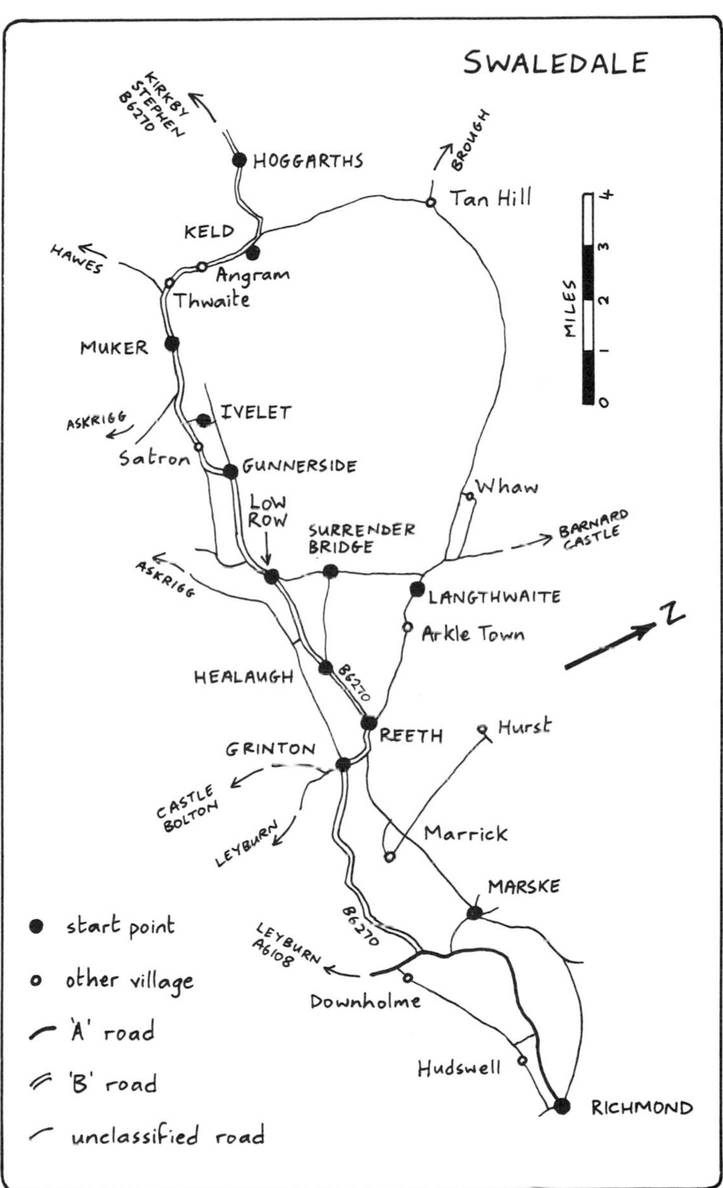
SWALEDALE
KIRKBY STEPHEN B6270
HOGGARTHS
BROUGH
Tan Hill
KELD
HAWES
Angram
Thwaite
MUKER
IVELET
ASKRIGG
Satron
GUNNERSIDE
Whaw
LOW ROW
SURRENDER BRIDGE
BARNARD CASTLE
ASKRIGG
LANGTHWAITE
Arkle Town
N
HEALAUGH
B6270
REETH
Hurst
GRINTON
CASTLE BOLTON
LEYBURN
Marrick
MARSKE
B6270
LEYBURN A6108
Downholme
Hudswell
RICHMOND
MILES
0
1
2
3
4
start point
other village
'A' road
'B' road
unclassified road

65

WALK 65 THE CORPSE ROAD AND THE SWALE GORGE

6 miles

from Keld

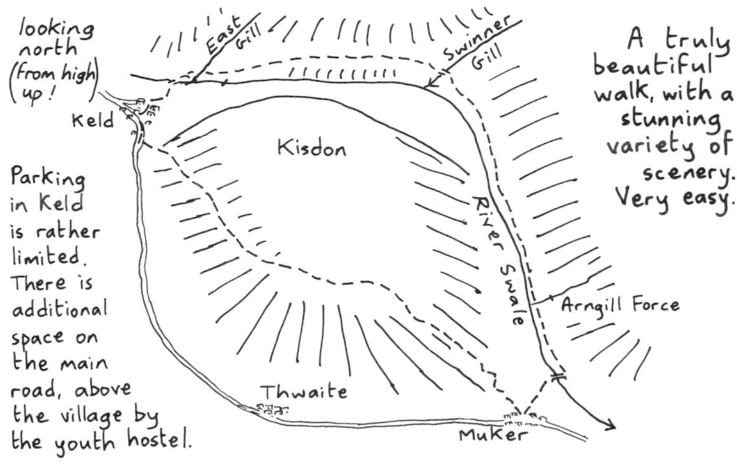
looking north (from high up!)
East Gill
Swinner Gill
A truly beautiful walk, with a stunning variety of scenery. Very easy.
Keld
Kisdon
Parking in Keld is rather limited. There is additional space on the main road, above the village by the youth hostel.
River Swale
Arngill Force
Thwaite
Muker

THE WALK

Leave Keld by the lane up to the main road, and turn left along it for a couple of minutes until a rough track drops down to the left. This is the old corpse road, which will lead unerringly over the hill to Muker. On crossing a tiny beck it begins to climb, soon easing out and passing through several gates as it goes. Just beyond a short, walled section by some mining debris the summit of the track is reached, and a little down the other side the route of the Pennine Way is crossed as Kisdon Farm is seen across to the right. Continue down, briefly enclosed before joining the farm's access road. This well surfaced way takes us steeply down through the final two pastures to enter Muker along a short lane. Note the point of exit just to the left (signposted) on entering the village.

On leaving Muker take the stile by a gate at the 'rear' of the village - as mentioned above - and a well-defined path crosses seven fields linked by solid stiles to arrive at the riverbank. Turn right to another stile to follow the Swale the few yards down to Rampsholme Bridge. On the opposite bank drop down left to the river and soon a wide track is joined: it is accompanied almost all the way back to Keld. On crossing the first inflowing beck, be sure to stroll a short distance up its course to appreciate a charming waterfall.

65

Continuing by the river the track crosses a bridge below the ravine of Swinner Gill, then rises steeply before easing out above an increasingly impressive wooded, rocky gorge. This same track eventually descends to a farm bridge over East Gill - note the shared 'Pennine Way' and 'Coast to Coast' signpost - straight after which we take a left fork by East Gill Force to a footbridge over the Swale. From it take the path climbing right to a gate, and within minutes Keld is re-entered.

Lovely Seat from Hooker Mill Scar on the Corpse road

Muker

65

Swinner Gill, above our crossing, was once a thriving lead-mining scene.

The route over the shoulder of Kisdon to Muker is the first and most impressive section of the former corpse road which leads all the way down the valley to Grinton. For the deceased of the Keld area, it was only the start of a long trip to the burial ground.

The youth hostel is a former shooting lodge.

On the climb from Keld there are good views of the mountains around the head of the dale, all 2000-footers, from Lovely Seat to Great Shunner Fell, High Seat and Nine Standards Rigg.

The steep descent to Muker reveals views far down the dale, as well as Rampsholme Bridge and Muker at our feet.

Keld is the last outpost of any size in Swaledale, for beyond here are only isolated dwellings beneath the moors. Most of the buildings of this Norse settlement group around a tiny square just below the main road and high above the Swale. Keld is best known for its waterfalls, one seen here and another on Walk 74. It also marks the junction of Pennine Way and Coast-Coast.

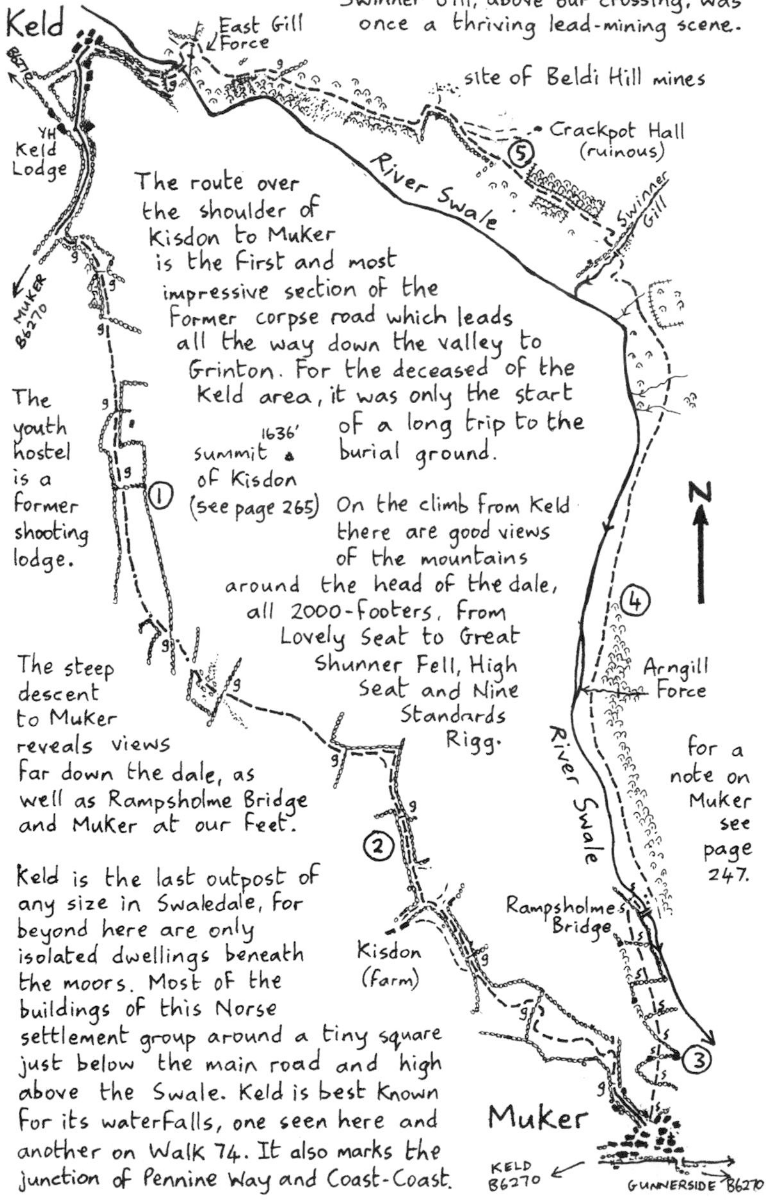

for a note on Muker see page 247.

Keld
B6270
East Gill Force
site of Beldi Hill mines
Crackpot Hall (ruinous)
YH Keld Lodge
River Swale
Swinner Gill
MUKER B6270
1636' summit of Kisdon (see page 265)
N
Arngill Force
Rampsholmes Bridge
Kisdon (farm)
Muker
KELD B6270
GUNNERSIDE B6270

WALK 66 — FREMINGTON EDGE AND ARKLE BECK

7¾ miles — from Reeth

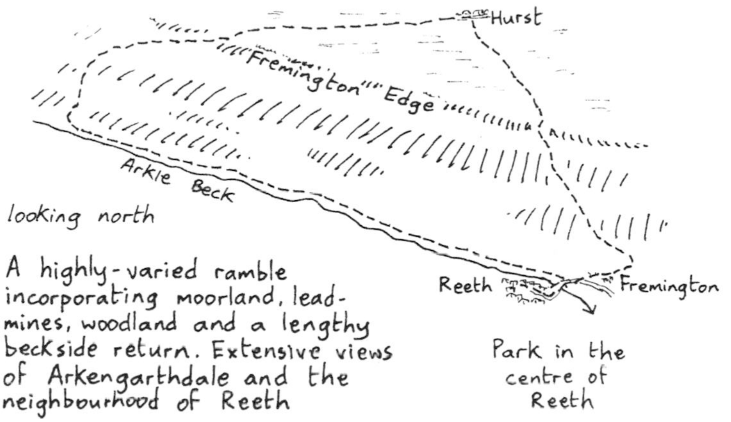
Hurst
Fremington Edge
Arkle Beck
looking north
Reeth
Fremington

A highly-varied ramble incorporating moorland, lead-mines, woodland and a lengthy beckside return. Extensive views of Arkengarthdale and the neighbourhood of Reeth

Park in the centre of Reeth

THE WALK

Leave Reeth by the Richmond road, and immediately after crossing the bridge over Arkle Beck take a stile on the left. From the one just across to the right head ½-left across the next field to another stile, then follow the right-hand wall to a stile to empty onto a narrow lane in Fremington. Turn almost at once up the walled track to the left to join another narrow lane. Head left along this, ignoring a bridleway branching off and begin the long climb to Fremington Edge.

We remain on this lane throughout its course: at a gate it begins to deteriorate into a rough track, passing the aptly-named White House and continuing up to another gate. Only a little more climbing and the top is reached. From the gate in the wall along the top a wide track heads away, and leads unerringly across the moor towards Hurst, which comes into sight only on nearing it. Through a gate a prominent old chimney is passed before reaching the hamlet of Hurst.

Turn left along its lane which ends before two gates back onto the moor. Yet another wide track heads over it, taking us gradually up through a vast expanse of mining debris back towards Fremington Edge. After passing through a row of grouse butts the wall along the top appears. Here leave the track in favour of a gateway in a tiny angle of the wall.

66

With no path to follow now, head across to the scars of mining just ahead, keeping to the bottom side of them as far as possible. Continue on a generally level course with North Rake Hush prominent directly ahead across the side-valley of Slei Gill. As the gradient steepens bear round to the left, and a path should be located descending the slope to a gate. From it drop down by the wall to emerge onto a farm-lane by Strothwaite Hall. Turn left along it until it ends at the next farm, then head across two fields to near Arkle Beck at a footbridge.

Do not use the bridge but take the gate in front, beyond which our footpath breaks off the bridleway to remain nearer the beck. This it does for a good while before being deflected away from a bend in the beck by yellow blobs of paint on numerous trees. From here on the way avoids the beck for some time, crossing the fields by means of stiles in a near-straight line to arrive at a group of farm buildings.

Our route heads away in the same direction, with as many collapsed walls as intact ones. Beyond a long-since abandoned farm the beck is rejoined, but within yards the path forks and our choice is the good track branching left. This soon passes through a gateway and alongside a wall on the right. After two more intervening stiles, take one on the right, descending past a barn to two stiles in line. Follow a wall to another stile and continue on through two more fields. The latter and lengthier of these returns us to the road at Reeth Bridge, where we left the village.

For a note on Reeth see page 280.

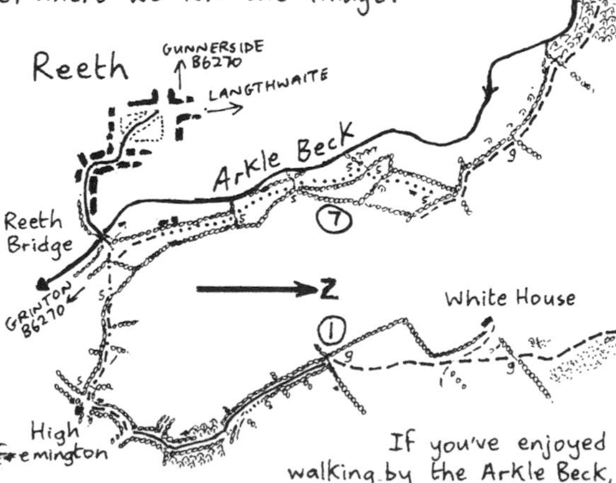
Reeth
GUNNERSIDE B6270
LANGTHWAITE
Arkle Beck
Reeth Bridge
GRINTON B6270
7
N
1
White House
High Fremington

Reeth Bridge is the graceful gateway to the village for those travelling up-dale.

If you've enjoyed walking by the Arkle Beck, Walk 80 takes in a good deal more of it.

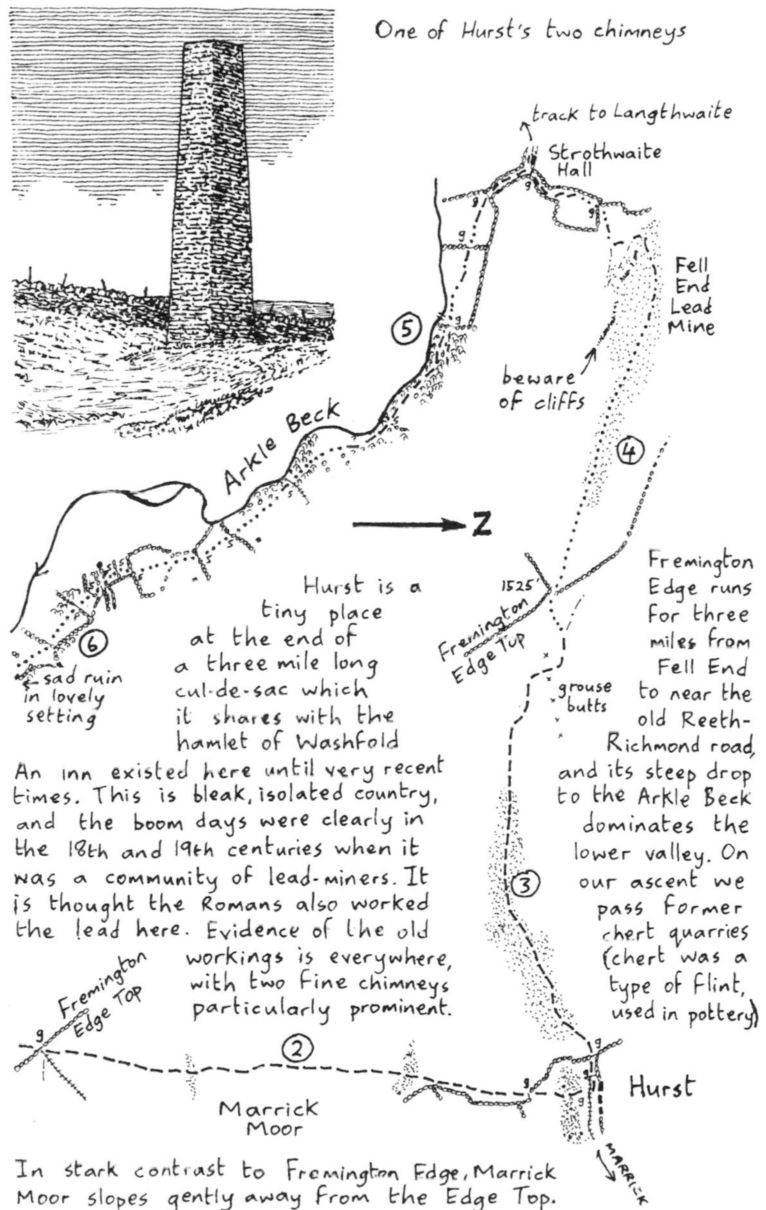
One of Hurst's two chimneys
track to Langthwaite
Strothwaite Hall
Fell End Lead Mine
beware of cliffs
Arkle Beck
5
4
Z
1525'
Fremington Edge Top
grouse butts
6
sad ruin in lovely setting
3
Fremington Edge Top
2
Marrick Moor
Hurst
MARRICK

Hurst is a tiny place at the end of a three mile long cul-de-sac which it shares with the hamlet of Washfold. An inn existed here until very recent times. This is bleak, isolated country, and the boom days were clearly in the 18th and 19th centuries when it was a community of lead-miners. It is thought the Romans also worked the lead here. Evidence of the old workings is everywhere, with two fine chimneys particularly prominent.

Fremington Edge runs for three miles from Fell End to near the old Reeth-Richmond road, and its steep drop to the Arkle Beck dominates the lower valley. On our ascent we pass former chert quarries (chert was a type of flint, used in pottery)

In stark contrast to Fremington Edge, Marrick Moor slopes gently away from the Edge Top.

67

WALK 67

THE SWALE BELOW MUKER

$4\frac{3}{4}$ miles

from Muker

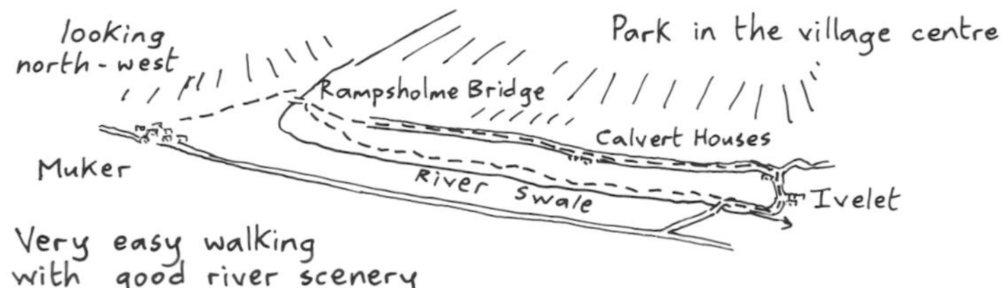
looking north-west
Park in the village centre
Rampsholme Bridge
Calvert Houses
Muker
River Swale
Ivelet

Very easy walking
with good river scenery
and good views both up and down the dale

THE WALK

Leave Muker by a well-signposted stile by a gate between buildings at the 'rear' of the village, at the top of a short lane leading up to and behind the right of the post office. A well-defined path crosses seven fields linked by solid stiles to arrive at the riverbank. Turn right to another stile to follow the Swale downstream a few yards to Rampsholme Bridge. Just upstream on the opposite bank a wide track is joined and then followed to the right. It climbs a little and soon receives a tarred surface, but remains unenclosed and traffic-free to run parallel with the river all the way to a junction at Gunnerside Lodge. Turn right to descend to Ivelet.

Continue down the lane from Ivelet to the river, and just along to the right is Ivelet Bridge. Do not cross it, however, but take a gate on the right to accompany the Swale upstream. The way is straightforward, with an intermittent path staying close to the river after an early detour from its bank. After a long mile the path cuts out a bend in the river by means of a line of obvious gap-stiles in parallel walls, then rejoins the Swale for the last five minutes to Rampsholme Bridge. Re-cross it and retrace steps through the fields back to Muker.

Rampsholme Bridge

Rampsholme Bridge is a tall modern footbridge, and is the only crossing of the Swale between Keld and Ivelet Bridge. It is an excellent viewpoint for the lonely Swale gorge, as far upstream as the cleft of Swinner Gill.

The Farmers Arms, Muker

The path alongside the Swale witnesses some good river scenery as it flows over a wide, stony bed.

Muker is a good centre for the head of the dale, with accommodation, shops and an inn. The latter is the farthest up the valley, begging the pardon of Tan Hill, which at 1732 feet can in no way be said to be in a valley! Muker is also probably the most picturesque village in the dale, with a fine grouping of buildings rising above the beck. The river Swale rejoins the main road just below the village, after their enforced split by Kisdon.

Prominent in most views is St. Mary's church, which was first built in 1580 to relieve Grinton's load, taking off its hands the upper dale which then made Muker an extensive parish, in areal extent at least. The present structure dates largely from 1890. Other interesting buildings are the Literary Institute of 1868, and the school, with tablets proclaiming that the famous Kearton brothers of Thwaite were former pupils. Muker is also the venue for the Swaledale Agricultural Show in September.

WALK 68 GREAT PINSEAT AND HARD LEVEL GILL

$5\frac{3}{4}$ miles from Surrender Bridge

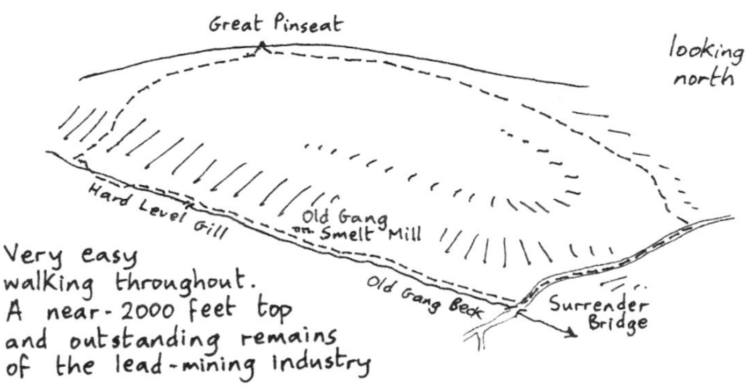
Great Pinseat
looking north
Hard Level Gill
Old Gang Smelt Mill
Old Gang Beck
Surrender Bridge

Very easy walking throughout. A near-2000 feet top and outstanding remains of the lead-mining industry

Surrender Bridge stands at the junction of two unfenced moor-roads, a mile north of Low Row, 2½ miles south of Langthwaite, and two miles west of Healaugh. It is named on O.S. 2½" maps but not on smaller scale maps. There are various parking spots.

THE WALK

From the bridge take the steeply-climbing road towards Langthwaite in Arkengarthdale. After the climb has subsided a wide track heads off to the left, and it leads unerringly and uneventfully up the moor. On levelling out Great Pinseat appears unspectacularly ahead, with a large sheepfold in front. Passing the fold, the track rises left to a cairn amidst mining spoil.

Only a couple of minutes across to the right is the wall running along the top of Great Pinseat, and a brief detour can be made to the highest point. The Ordnance column only appears as the wall is reached, for it is located just on the other side. Don't cross the wall to it - this gains nothing but involves a double-risk of damaging the wall.

Return to the track at the next area of spoil (again cairned), and the track now descends through a band of mining debris to reach a gate. From it the track accompanies Flincher Gill downstream, twice crossing it before passing Level House Bridge. Hard Level Gill leads down through the Old Gang smelt mill, and our track remains above the beck to return eventually to Surrender Bridge.

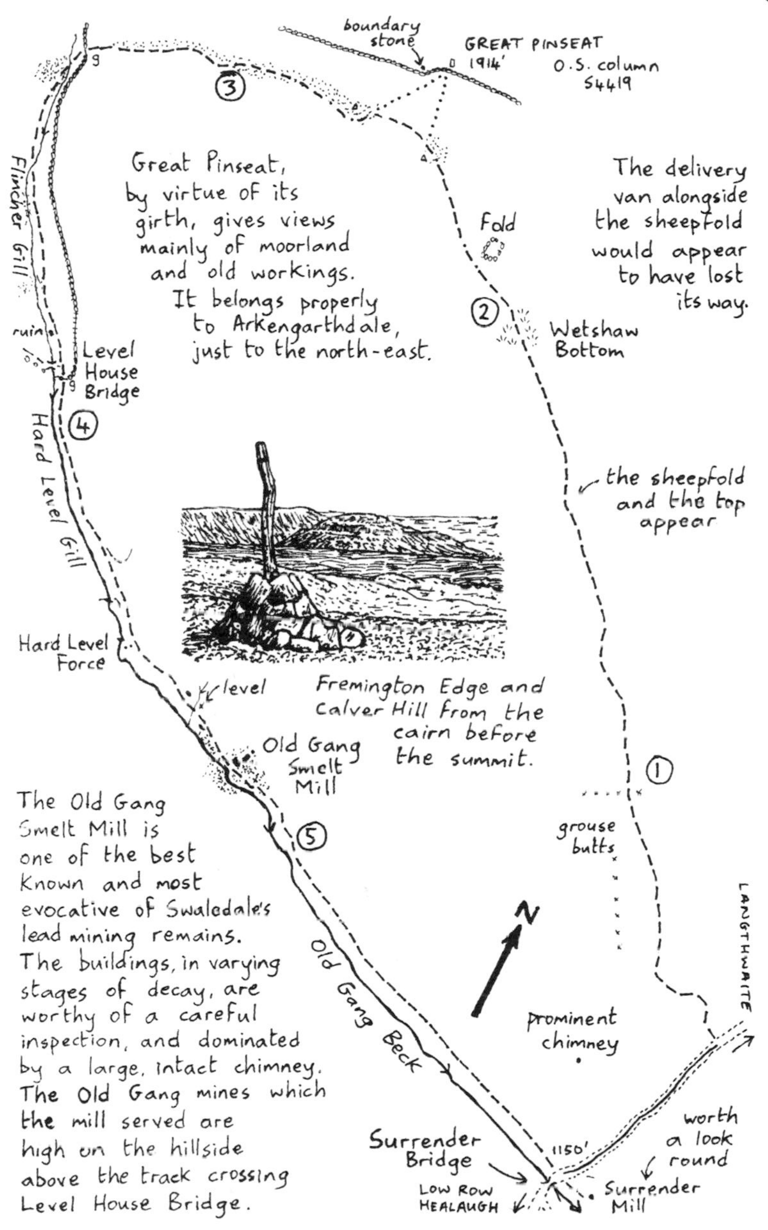
boundary stone
GREAT PINSEAT 1914'
O.S. column S4419
3
Great Pinseat, by virtue of its girth, gives views mainly of moorland and old workings. It belongs properly to Arkengarthdale, just to the north-east.
The delivery van alongside the sheepfold would appear to have lost its way.
Fold
2
Wetshaw Bottom
Fincher Gill
ruin
Level House Bridge
4
Hard Level Gill
the sheepfold and the top appear
Hard Level Force
level
Fremington Edge and Calver Hill from the cairn before the summit.
Old Gang Smelt Mill
1
grouse butts
5
The Old Gang Smelt Mill is one of the best known and most evocative of Swaledale's lead mining remains. The buildings, in varying stages of decay, are worthy of a careful inspection, and dominated by a large, intact chimney. The Old Gang mines which the mill served are high on the hillside above the track crossing Level House Bridge.
Old Gang Beck
N
LANGTHWAITE
prominent chimney
worth a look round
Surrender Bridge
1150'
LOW ROW HEALAUGH
Surrender Mill

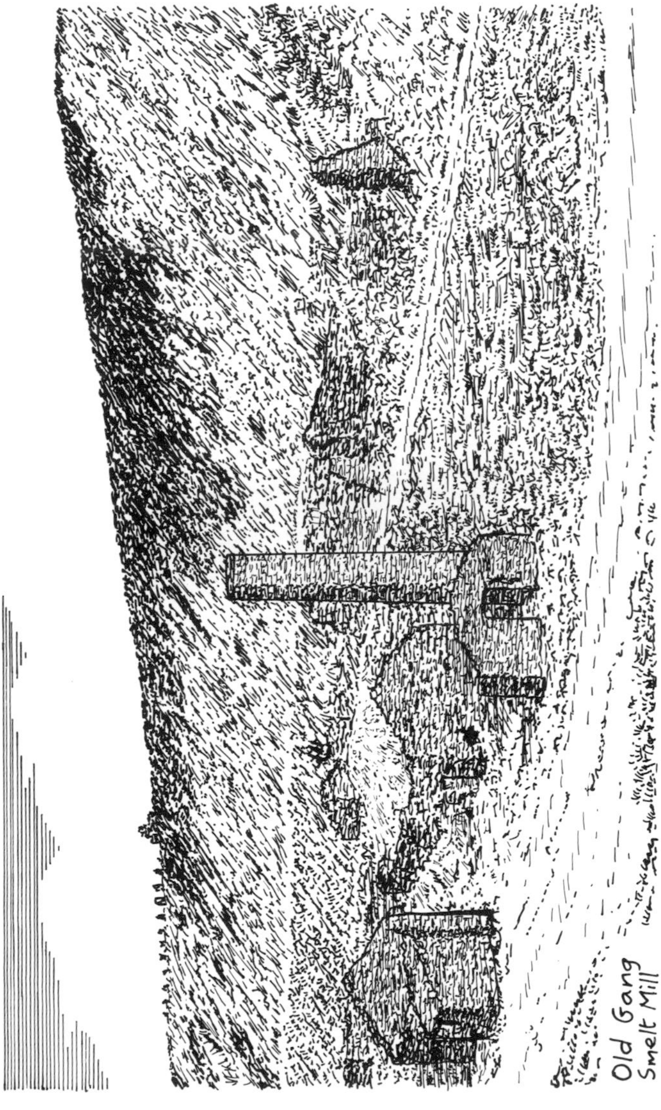

Old Gang Smelt Mill

WALK 69

THE BANKS OF THE SWALE

5 miles

from Gunnerside

A simple, intimate riverside stroll

looking north

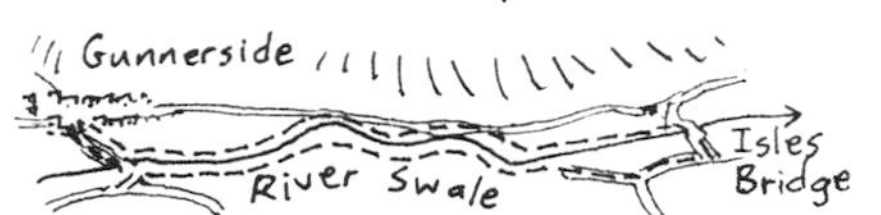
Gunnerside
Isles Bridge
River Swale

Parking area by bridge in village centre

THE WALK

Take the up-dale road out of the village to cross the bridge over the Swale, then leave it on the turn-off to Crackpot. This side road is quickly vacated after a cattle-grid in favour of a track to the left. This is Dubbing Garth Lane, which leads unfailingly down-river, generally sandwiched between a wall and the Swale itself. Eventually it becomes surfaced at a farm before reaching a T-junction. Turn left and soon left again to Isles Bridge.

Cross the bridge and use a stile on the left to commence the return, sticking with the river only until the first bend.

continued across

For a note on Gunnerside see page 259

As the river turns away an intermittent path strikes a direct course through the fields, a large pasture preceding two fences before arriving at a stile just before a crumbling barn. From it join the road as it approaches the returning Swale. As the road rises away rejoin the river's wooded bank, a path now clinging to it until forced back up onto the road at a steep, wooded bank.

This time the road is left at once, by a gate into a field. Drop steeply to regain the Swale's bank, which is followed pleasurably back to New Bridge. Just before Gunnerside Beck and the bridge, take a gate by a barn for a delightful finish by way of stiles and small fields back into the village.

WALK 70 — AROUND CALVER HILL

6¼ miles

from Healaugh

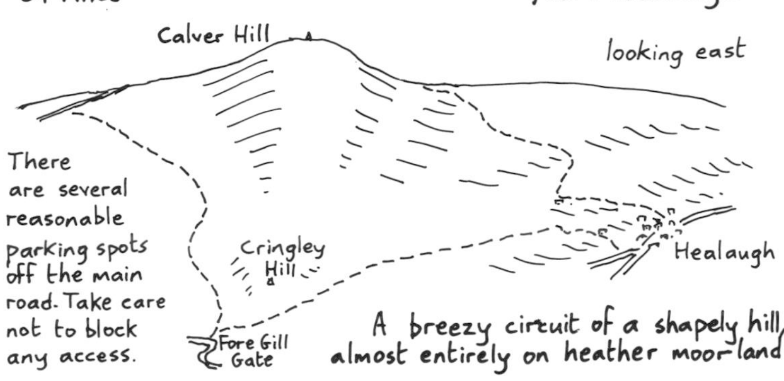
Calver Hill
looking east
Cringley Hill
Healaugh
Fore Gill Gate

There are several reasonable parking spots off the main road. Take care not to block any access.

A breezy circuit of a shapely hill, almost entirely on heather moor-land

THE WALK

Leave the village by the up-dale Gunnerside road, and almost immediately turn right up a lesser road towards Kearton. This too is left at the first opportunity, up a drive to Thiernswood Hall. The track keeps left of the house to enter trees: at the end ignore the stile in front and take a gate on the right. In the wall-corner behind is a stile from where a track resumes to climb by the left-hand wall. Generally clear, it rises past the house at Nova Scotia to run below a walled enclosure to merge with another track. Now head up to the bottom side of another walled enclosure, and virtually pathless, head away from its far corner to pass above a fenced enclosure. Directly ahead the track reasserts itself while breasting the slope of Cringley Hill, and then remains clear to run undulatingly to arrive at the roadside at Fore Gill Gate.

Just before the gate, however, is a merging of tracks, and it is this other wide way we follow, now doubling back over the northern side of Cringley Hill. This infallible track eventually descends to join the road through Arkengarthdale. Turn right along its unfenced course for a good half-mile, then opposite a farm track a footpath sign points us back onto the moor. A path rises to a prominent sheepfold: here turn left along a very short-lived path, from whence a spot of heather-bashing takes over. All that is needed is to maintain a level course just beneath the markedly steeper slopes of Calver Hill.

Beyond a fenced fold a gentle rise leads to a fair length of wall on the brow of Riddings Rigg. Head away in the same direction as before, a track materialising to lead down to near a wall-corner. Just to the right a better track is joined at an acute bend to lead down to Thirns farm. Here turn left, our route becoming surfaced to drop steeply into Healaugh.

Healaugh was once the important manor hereabouts, and even included neighbouring Reeth. Today however it is a sleepy backwater of tidy stone cottages left alone by the passing tourists.

The watersplash at Fore Gill Gate is a charming little place, given a degree of fame by the opening shots of a popular TV series. Between here and the Tan Hill road are fine views into Arkengarthdale.

Although we pass just beneath, there is no actual right-of-way to Calver Hill's summit, which is a classic Swaledale viewpoint.

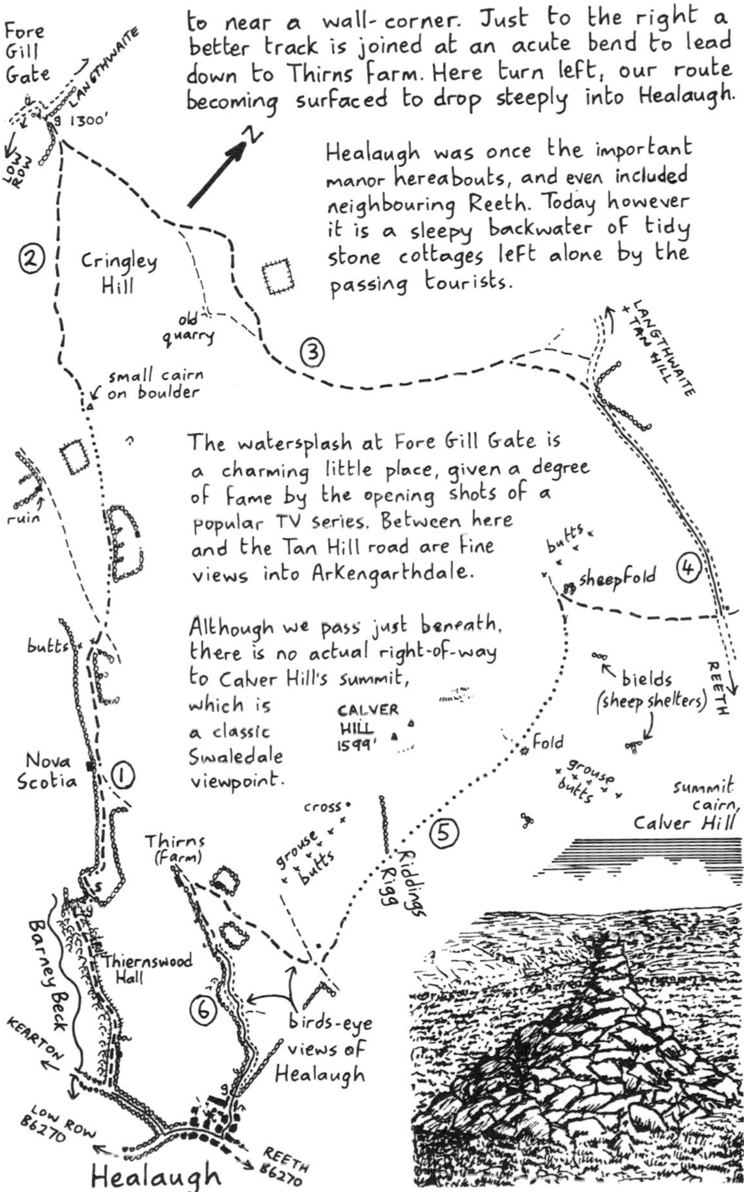
Fore Gill Gate
LANGTHWAITE
1300'
LOW ROW
N
2
Cringley Hill
old quarry
3
LANGTHWAITE + TAN HILL
small cairn on boulder
ruin
butts
sheepfold
4
butts
REETH
bields (sheep shelters)
CALVER HILL 1599'
Fold
Nova Scotia
1
grouse butts
summit cairn, Calver Hill
cross
grouse butts
5
Thirns (Farm)
Riddings Rigg
Barney Beck
Thiernswood Hall
6
birds-eye views of Healaugh
KEARTON
LOW ROW B6270
REETH B6270
Healaugh

71

WALK 71

MARSKE BECK AND SKELTON MOOR

6¼ miles

from Marske

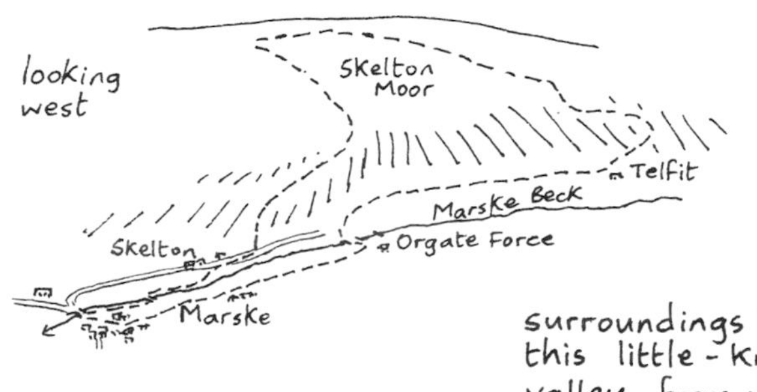
looking west
Skelton Moor
Telfit
Marske Beck
Orgate Force
Skelton
Marske

A splendid variety of surroundings is found in this little - known side valley, from woodland to moorland, and both of high quality

The best parking is just across the bridge from the village centre

THE WALK

From the spacious road junction above the church in the village centre, take the road branching off the 'through' road, and when it turns uphill continue on the level. Past a few cottages our way becomes a broad drive, and a charming woodland walk ensues. On eventual arrival at a fork, bear left on a woodland footpath where the main track keeps right to a gate. Continue on, emerging into the open to approach Orgate Farm. Just before the buildings turn down the concrete farm road to Marske Beck. A footbridge is provided next to the ford, and Orgate Force tumbles a little upstream.

Leave the beck by climbing the lane to a junction by a large barn, and turn right along the long farm drive to Telfit. Keep above the farm on a still-broad track scaling the hillside and doubling back to a gate. Rising by a wallside to a second gate, Skelton Moor is now gained. Go forward a few yards to a T-junction, and take the one straight ahead. It passes an old fold and then an Ordnance column atop the moor.

The track runs along to a gate into a lanehead, but instead of using it, turn sharp left on another track which links up with a wall to head back over the moor. Remain with the wall through a gate in an intervening wall, now joining a broader track with the valley and our outward route appearing far below. A splendid march to the next gate, and our way is enclosed to drop down onto a lane.

Turn briefly to the right before taking a stile on the left after a small barn. Head diagonally across the field to a stile in a fence, then follow another fence away from it. When it turns left go straight on to drop to a stone bridge just past an old waterwheel. Cross it and follow the beck downstream using a gate into a short, wooded section before emerging at Marske Bridge.

Orgate Force

Marske Hall

71

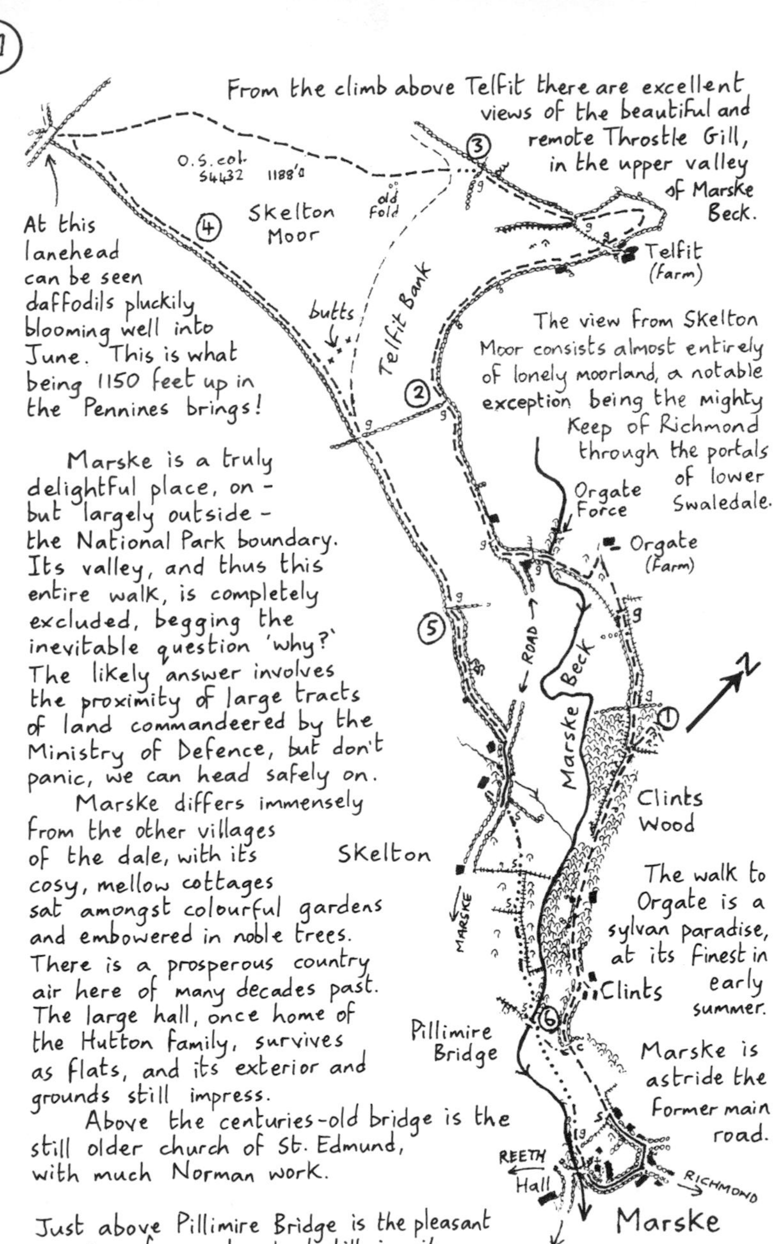

O.S. col.
54432 1188'
old Fold
Skelton Moor
Telfit Bank
butts
Telfit (Farm)
Orgate Force
Orgate (Farm)
ROAD
Marske Beck
Clints Wood
Clints
Skelton
MARSKE
Pillimire Bridge
REETH
Hall
RICHMOND
Marske
TO A6108
N

From the climb above Telfit there are excellent views of the beautiful and remote Throstle Gill, in the upper valley of Marske Beck.

At this lanehead can be seen daffodils pluckily blooming well into June. This is what being 1150 feet up in the Pennines brings!

The view from Skelton Moor consists almost entirely of lonely moorland, a notable exception being the mighty Keep of Richmond through the portals of lower Swaledale.

Marske is a truly delightful place, on - but largely outside - the National Park boundary. Its valley, and thus this entire walk, is completely excluded, begging the inevitable question 'why?' The likely answer involves the proximity of large tracts of land commandeered by the Ministry of Defence, but don't panic, we can head safely on.

Marske differs immensely from the other villages of the dale, with its cosy, mellow cottages sat amongst colourful gardens and embowered in noble trees. There is a prosperous country air here of many decades past. The large hall, once home of the Hutton family, survives as flats, and its exterior and grounds still impress.

Above the centuries-old bridge is the still older church of St. Edmund, with much Norman work.

The walk to Orgate is a sylvan paradise, at its finest in early summer.

Marske is astride the former main road.

Just above Pillimire Bridge is the pleasant surprise of a waterwheel still in situ.

WALK 72

GUNNERSIDE GILL

6 miles

from Gunnerside

A fascinating exploration of this deeply-confined valley. The extensive remains of the lead-mines will stir the imagination. Overall, an absolute feast of colour.

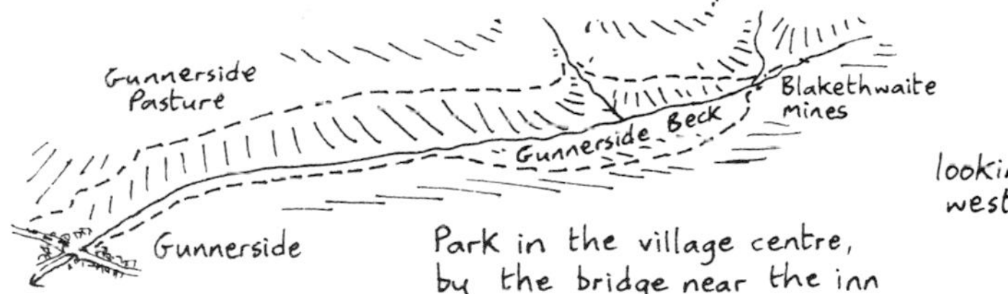
Gunnerside Pasture
Blakethwaite mines
Gunnerside Beck
looking west
Gunnerside

Park in the village centre, by the bridge near the inn

THE WALK

From the bridge by the inn in the village centre, take the wide track which follows the beck upstream. After being deflected round Gunnarside Hall the beck is rejoined and soon a path becomes clear to remain with it for a good while. On entering thicker trees a stile leads into a long sliver of woodland from where we rise high above the beck. The wood is vacated in dramatic fashion as we near the beck again, and after two close stiles a left-hand wall leads up-dale, taking in two more stiles to reach the beckside location of a former crushing mill.

Keep left of the ruins to arrive at a stile, from where the path rises to another before continuing above the beck to reach - already - the last stile of the walk. From it a wide green track rises across the pasture before levelling out to run parallel with the beck, now far below. Soon an amazing scene of devastation greets the eye as an extensive lead-mining area is reached. Just beyond the last ruin in the immediate workings the path forks: take the left one down to the beck, which is followed up to Blakethwaite Smelt Mill.

Amidst these ruins a large slab takes us over the beck, and after an exploration the inflowing Blind Gill is crossed with ease. This is the turning point of the walk, but a worthwhile detour is to follow the path up the west bank of Gunnerside Beck for a couple of hundred yards for a closer view of Blakethwaite Force.

Back at the confluence a superb green way rises gently away from the beck, and this is the way to go.

Avoid any deviations and continue to rise to the last mining remains of the walk, where the track becomes level before it contours round Botcher Gill. Here we merge with a wide shooting-track, which beyond a gate commences a very gradual descent high above Gunnerside Gill.

When the track eventually curves sharply to the right, leave it and bear left across the open pasture on a broad spur. Soon the rooftops of Gunnerside appear below. Now descend a little more steeply to the right to join an unfenced road as it meets a cattle-grid to enter the village.

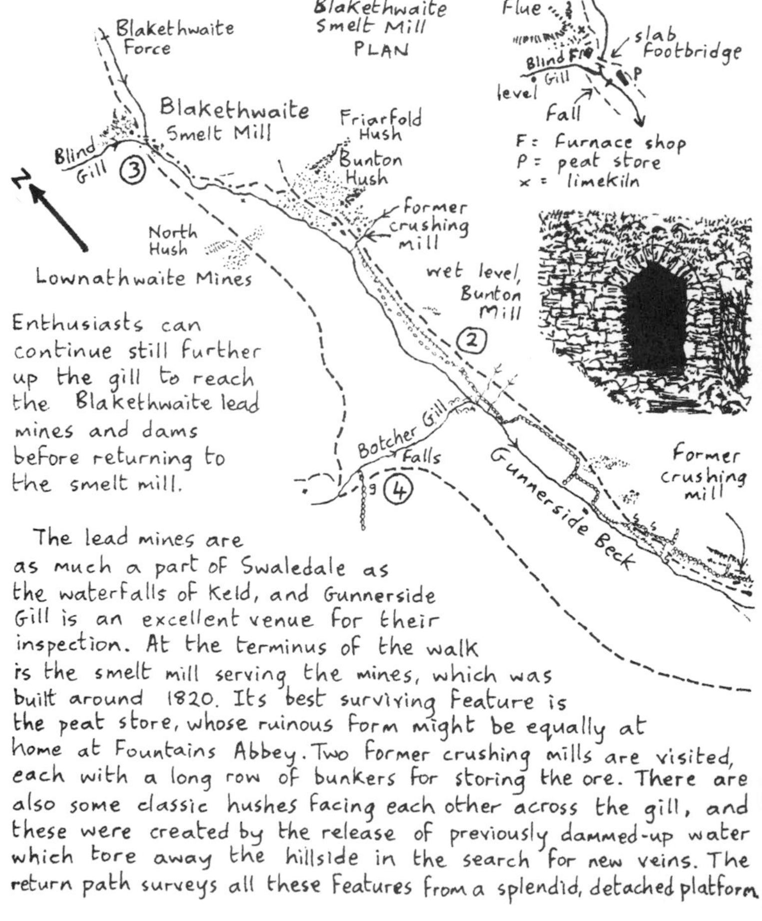
Blakethwaite Smelt Mill PLAN
Flue
slab footbridge
Blind Gill
F
P
level
Fall
F = furnace shop
P = peat store
x = limekiln
Blakethwaite Force
Blakethwaite Smelt Mill
Blind Gill
3
N
Friarfold Hush
Bunton Hush
former crushing mill
North Hush
Lownathwaite Mines
wet level, Bunton Mill
2
Botcher Gill
Falls
4
Gunnerside Beck
Former crushing mill

Enthusiasts can continue still further up the gill to reach the Blakethwaite lead mines and dams before returning to the smelt mill.

The lead mines are as much a part of Swaledale as the waterfalls of Keld, and Gunnerside Gill is an excellent venue for their inspection. At the terminus of the walk is the smelt mill serving the mines, which was built around 1820. Its best surviving feature is the peat store, whose ruinous form might be equally at home at Fountains Abbey. Two former crushing mills are visited, each with a long row of bunkers for storing the ore. There are also some classic hushes facing each other across the gill, and these were created by the release of previously dammed-up water which tore away the hillside in the search for new veins. The return path surveys all these features from a splendid, detached platform

Blakethwaite Smelt Mill

Gunnerside, like most of its neighbours, had its heyday in lead mining times, when it was a busy centre for the once-thriving industry. Again in common with neighbouring villages it is now a sleepy place. It was founded by the Norsemen, and it would appear that Gunnar was a Viking chieftain: until recently the inn sported a superb pictorial sign depicting the said invader.

The village stands astride its own beck, which apart from a level quarter-mile from here to the Swale, spends all of its time tumbling down the deep gill immediately above the village. Gunnerside Gill, even without its open air lead mining 'museum', is arguably the most impressive in the Dales. For virtually four miles its steep sides sweep uninterruptedly down to the beck, with scale and colour of lakeland proportions.

The mines, however, do add an extra element, and a gloomy day should be no deterrent to this walk. If anything, lingering cloud adds an almost tangible eeriness to the scene, assisted by the spirits of old miners, perhaps?

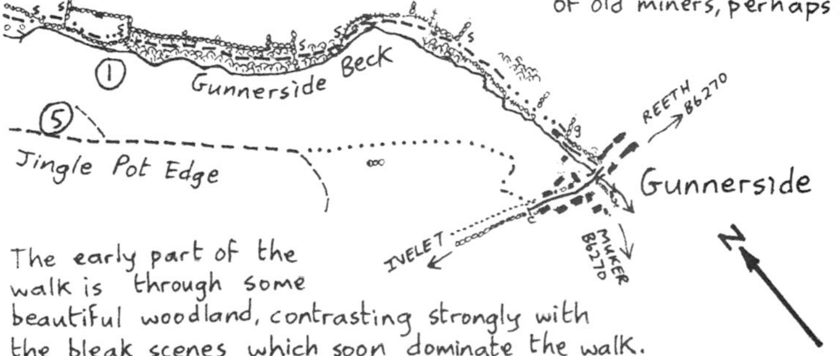
1
Gunnerside Beck
5
Jingle Pot Edge
REETH B6270
Gunnerside
IVELET
MUKER B6270
N

The early part of the walk is through some beautiful woodland, contrasting strongly with the bleak scenes which soon dominate the walk.

WALK 73 — COGDEN GILL AND GRINTON MOOR

4 miles — from Grinton

Some steep gradients, but easy route-finding and worthy objectives

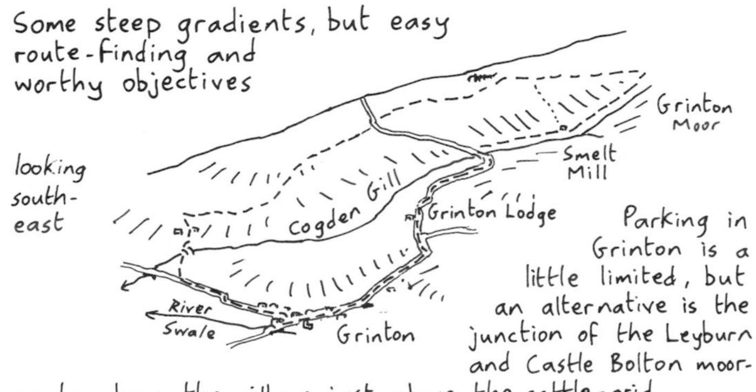
looking south-east
Grinton Moor
Smelt Mill
Cogden Gill
Grinton Lodge
River Swale
Grinton

Parking in Grinton is a little limited, but an alternative is the junction of the Leyburn and Castle Bolton moor-roads above the village, just above the cattle-grid.

THE WALK

Leave Grinton by the lane climbing steeply from the angle of the main road by the inn. After emerging onto the open moor keep left at a fork, and the gradient finally fades as the youth hostel is passed. Within a further half-mile the road bends sharply to cross Cogden Gill. Take the track up the left bank to soon arrive at the remains of Grinton Smelt Mill.

After an inspection there is a choice of routes to the top of the highly conspicuous flue on the left. From the buildings there are tracks up either side of the beck. When the one on the opposite bank rejoins the main one, continue a little further to a minor brow roughly level with the top of the flue. Now turn sharp left to contour across the slope, possibly locating a very sketchy trod through the heather. The site of the former chimney at the flue top is soon reached. Anyone in a hurry could reach it even sooner by simply following the flue up from the mill to its very abrupt terminus.

From the flue top descend a few yards then swing round to the right below the crags of Sharrow Hill. A green track is joined which runs below the rocks then continues on to meet the moor-road to Leyburn. Cross straight over to a gate from where another pleasant track heads through two pastures before descending to Cogden Hall. Keeping to the left of most of the farm buildings and the hall, the access track is joined to debouch onto the Richmond road. Turn left for the final ten minutes back into Grinton.

Grinton, today a tiny village, was once the major centre for the dale above Richmond. A more curious feature is that it is the only settlement of any size on the south bank of the Swale. This no doubt stems from the south-facing slopes opposite seeing more of the sun. Grouped alongside the graceful bridge are the aptly-named inn and the church, which is known as the 'Cathedral of the Dales' because of its size. Until a chapel was established at Muker, Grinton parish was one of the largest in the land, extending westward through the entire valley as far as the Westmorland border.

As this was the only consecrated ground, the deceased of the upper dale had to be carried a long and arduous journey which we know today as the 'corpse road' (see Walk 65). The church itself is of Norman origin, but what we see is largely from the fifteenth century, being restored in the late nineteenth century.

Grinton is a good, honest Anglo-Saxon name, and nearby can be seen some of their strip lynchets, or cultivation terraces.

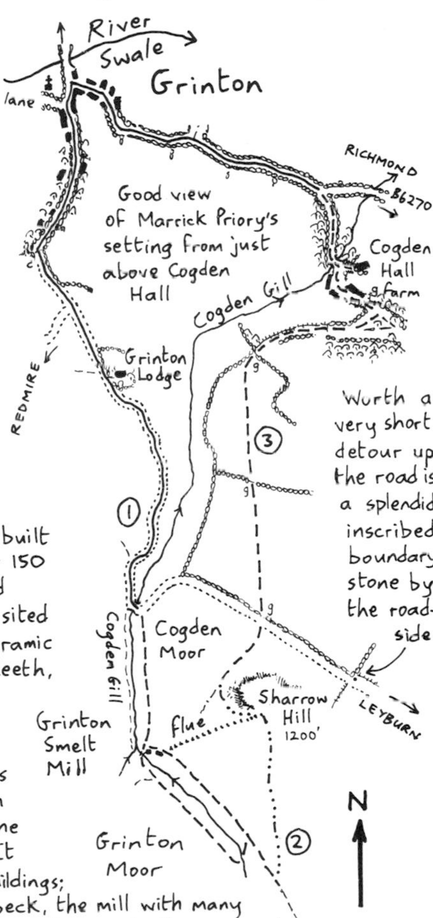
River Swale
Grinton
lane
RICHMOND
B6270
Good view of Marrick Priory's setting from just above Cogden Hall
Cogden Hall
farm
Cogden Gill
Grinton Lodge
REDMIRE
3
Worth a very short detour up the road is a splendid inscribed boundary stone by the road-side.
1
Cogden Gill
Cogden Moor
Sharrow Hill
1200'
LEYBURN
flue
Grinton Smelt Mill
Grinton Moor
2
N

Grinton Lodge was built as a shooting lodge about 150 years ago. This castellated building is now a superbly-sited youth hostel with a panoramic view across the dale to Reeth, Calver Hill, Arkengarthdale and Fremington Edge.

Grinton Smelt Mill was built early in the nineteenth century, and operated for the best part of that century. It boasts two well-preserved buildings; the peat store and, by the beck, the mill with many interesting features. The flue is also excellently preserved.

Grinton Lodge youth hostel

The old Flue, Grinton Smelt Mill

WALK 74 AROUND KISDON AND THWAITE

5½ miles from Keld

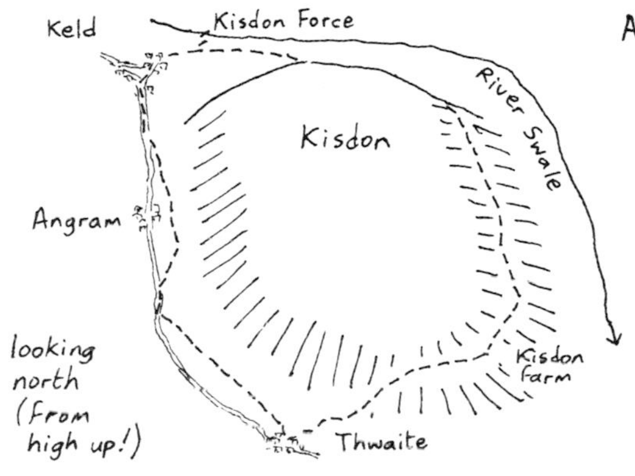
Keld
Kisdon Force
River Swale
Kisdon
Angram
Kisdon farm
Thwaite
looking north (from high up!)

A circumnavigation of a colourful little fell with excellent views on the return from Thwaite to Keld

Park in the centre of Keld (if possible) or on the road at the top of the village

THE WALK

From the youth hostel head along the main road down the valley, and a little beyond a bridleway on the left a stile will be found. Here begins an invisible path through pleasant pastures, rendered easy to follow by punctuation by stiles at regular intervals. A good dozen are encountered, most being visible well in advance.

The road is rejoined after skirting the hamlet of Angram, and within a couple of minutes is vacated again at a stile on the left. Once more the path is but dots on the map, but the stiles again make life easy as we slope down to join a tiny beck. Thwaite is entered at the point where the Pennine Way departs it: after a look around and possibly a cuppa, return to this point. From here we trace the big daddy of the long distance paths back to Keld, and as a result the route-finding is made easy.

After two stiles our path strikes left through two fields to a bridge, then clings to the right of a field to climb to a stile at the top. A pleasant rise across a heathery slope ensues, continuing past a wall-corner to swing left up to another stile. Now with a wall on the left, go round to a gate, and then right alongside a wall to Kisdon farm.

Keep left of the farm to a gate, then take a walled track up to the left. When the wall parts company go straight ahead to join a track rising to the left. At a stile the way joins a near-level terrace which continues through many gateways and stiles and an occasional rash of stones. With trees now on the right and the path following the hillside round to the left, a gap in the accompanying wall is reached. Make use of it to descend to a junction of paths. Keld is but a few minutes along to the left, but for a short detour to see Kisdon Force, go to the right. Just down a slope is a gateway in the wall on the left, and from it a path goes down through the trees to a viewpoint for the waterfall. The descent to the very riverbank is somewhat steep.

To return to Keld rejoin the top path and go back along to the right, passing beneath tall cliffs before the way becomes enclosed to enter the village.

Kisdon Force

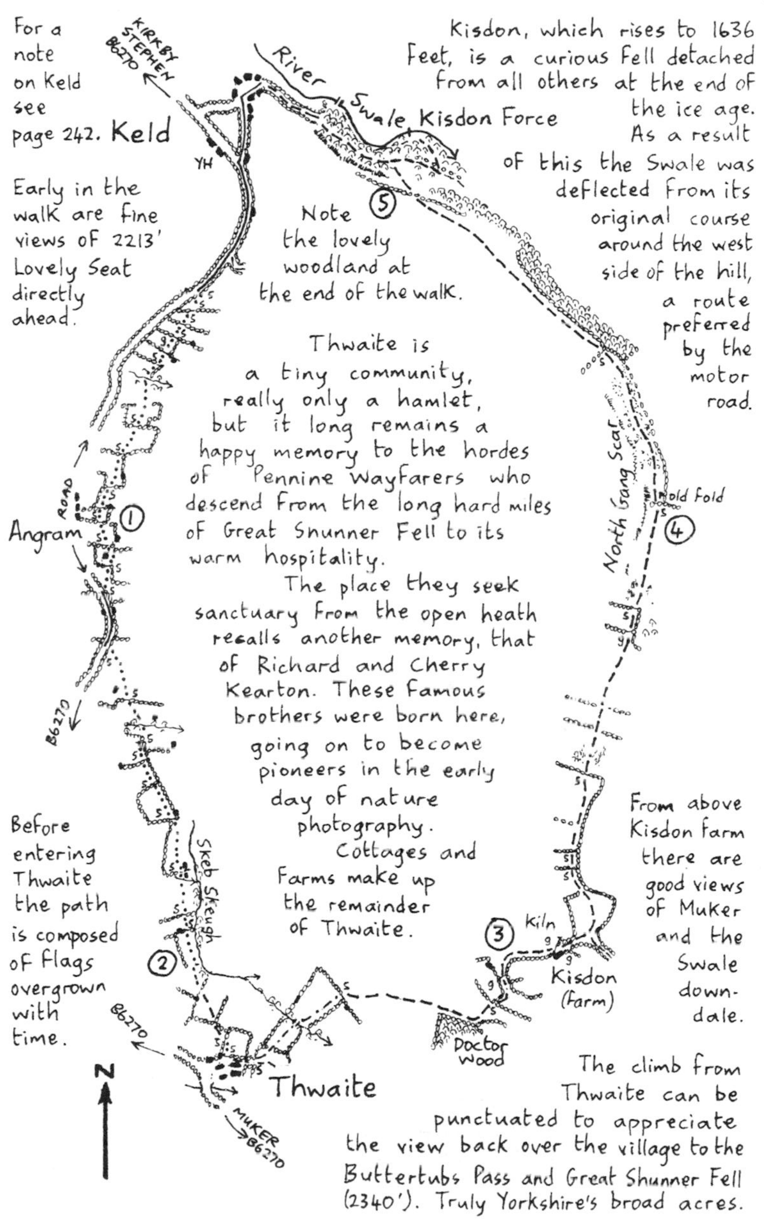
For a note on Keld see page 242.
Keld
KIRKBY STEPHEN B6270
River Swale
Kisdon Force
YH
Kisdon, which rises to 1636 feet, is a curious fell detached from all others at the end of the ice age. As a result of this the Swale was deflected from its original course around the west side of the hill, a route preferred by the motor road.
Early in the walk are fine views of 2213' Lovely Seat directly ahead.
Note the lovely woodland at the end of the walk.
5
ROAD
Angram
1
Thwaite is a tiny community, really only a hamlet, but it long remains a happy memory to the hordes of Pennine Wayfarers who descend from the long hard miles of Great Shunner Fell to its warm hospitality.
The place they seek sanctuary from the open heath recalls another memory, that of Richard and Cherry Kearton. These famous brothers were born here, going on to become pioneers in the early day of nature photography.
Cottages and farms make up the remainder of Thwaite.
North Gang Scar
Old Fold
4
B6270
Skeb Skeugh
Before entering Thwaite the path is composed of flags overgrown with time.
2
B6270
Thwaite
MUKER B6270
N
Doctor Wood
3
Kiln
Kisdon (Farm)
From above Kisdon farm there are good views of Muker and the Swale down-dale.
The climb from Thwaite can be punctuated to appreciate the view back over the village to the Buttertubs Pass and Great Shunner Fell (2340'). Truly Yorkshire's broad acres.

WALK 75 — SLEI GILL AND BOOZE MOOR

$5\frac{3}{4}$ miles — from Langthwaite

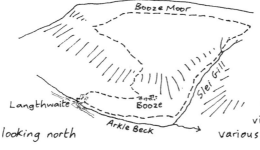

Booze Moor
Slei Gill
Langthwaite
Booze
Arkle Beck
looking north

A fine combination of beck and moorland surrounds

Parking can be found in the tiny village centre or various locations on the road just above

THE WALK

Cross the bridge into the heart of the village and turn right immediately behind the first house. A wide track accompanies the beck downstream before striking away from it into a wood. At a fork keep left, rising out of the wood and crossing a field to a gate. Here leave the main track by taking the grassy path continuing straight on. It crosses several fields to reach the environs of the old lead mines of Slei Gill, and continues to rise as a superb green trod above the beck.

After a spell near the beck, a stone arch amidst more spoil is reached. Keep left of it to cross the by-now tiny beck just above it. Here it suddenly peters out: head directly away from the beck to cross an even smaller beck, continuing on to run parallel with a beck on the right (the right arm from the fork by the arch). At about the third grouse-butt leave the beck's environs and rise left to a prominent track. At a T-junction continue up to the left, rising a little before swinging left to drop past a wooden shooting box. At a fork beyond more butts, the left hand option is to be preferred: it rejoins the main track to arrive at a cairn overlooking the valley. Continue down to a sharp bend above a wall, and here leave it for the inviting track branching left. When it forks just before a wall, keep left to near another wall with a barn behind: a stile in the wall-corner takes us off the moor.

Descend to a gate at the field-bottom and turn left on a track down between crumbling walls. Continue through a gate, past a ruin and out onto the lane in Booze. Turn left for a glimpse into its privacy, and then back to the right to return unfailingly - and finally steeply - down into Langthwaite.

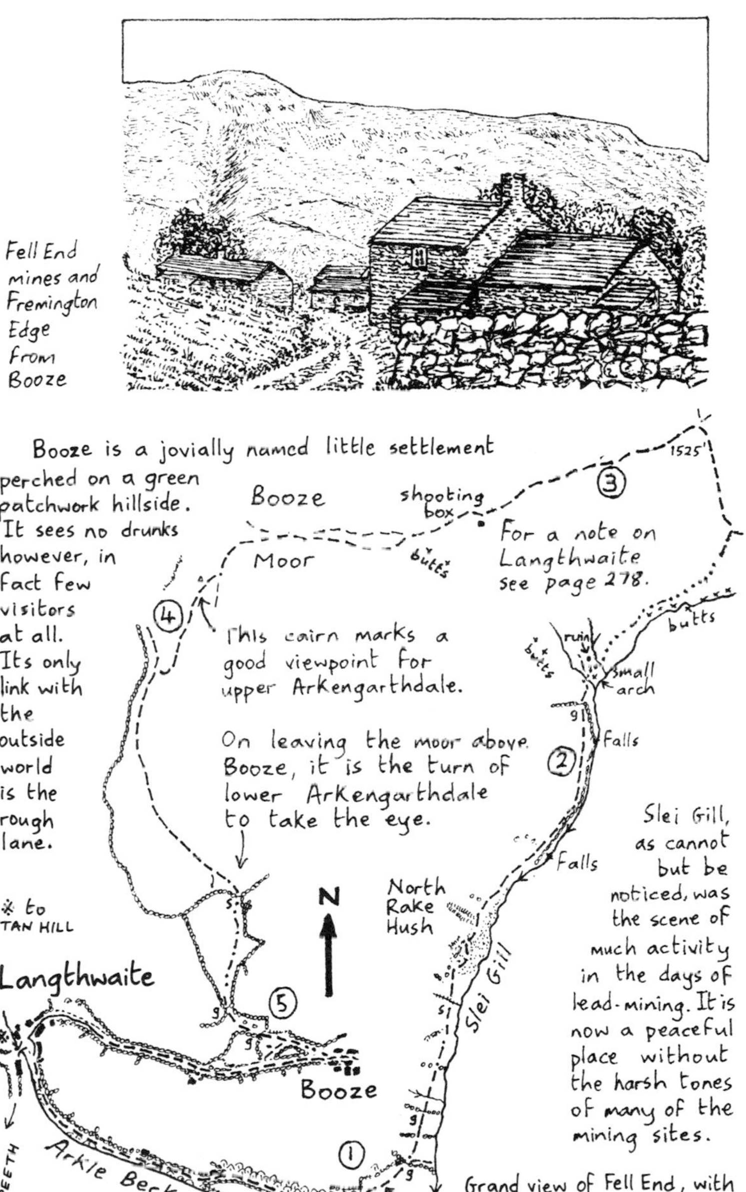
Booze Moor
shooting box
butts
1525'
3
4
2
1
5
ruin
small arch
Falls
Falls
North Rake Hush
Slei Gill
Langthwaite
Booze
Arkle Beck
REETH
※ to TAN HILL
g
s

Fell End mines and Fremington Edge from Booze

Booze is a jovially named little settlement perched on a green patchwork hillside. It sees no drunks however, in fact few visitors at all. Its only link with the outside world is the rough lane.

For a note on Langthwaite see page 278.

This cairn marks a good viewpoint for upper Arkengarthdale.

On leaving the moor above Booze, it is the turn of lower Arkengarthdale to take the eye.

Slei Gill, as cannot but be noticed, was the scene of much activity in the days of lead-mining. It is now a peaceful place without the harsh tones of many of the mining sites.

Grand view of Fell End, with Storthwaite Hall in the foreground.

WALK 76 — A CIRCUIT OF OXNOP GILL

6½ miles — **from Ivelet**

Substantial gradients
Splendid views
Simple navigation

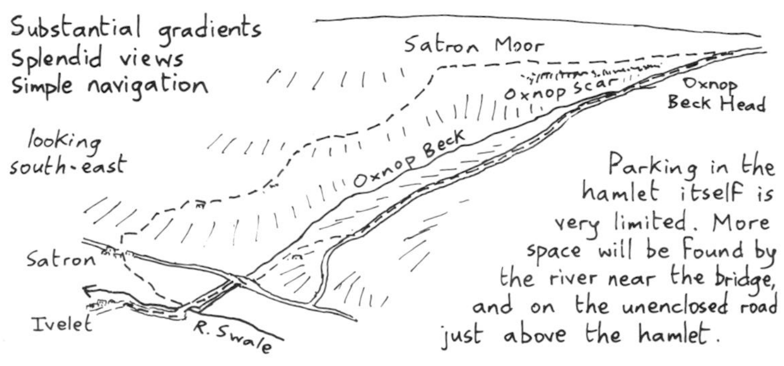
Satron Moor
Oxnop Scar
Oxnop Beck Head
Oxnop Beck
looking south-east
Satron
Ivelet
R. Swale

Parking in the hamlet itself is very limited. More space will be found by the river near the bridge, and on the unenclosed road just above the hamlet.

THE WALK

From the houses at Ivelet descend the lane to the river and cross Ivelet Bridge, then take a stile on the left to accompany the Swale downstream. On nearing a wall bear right to a stile, from where a short, steep path leads up to another stile. The next stile is just left of the barn in front, then cross the field to one just right of a barn. One more field takes us to the hamlet of Satron, with a short snicket leading onto the road just to the right.

Cross straight over to a narrow byway which begins its steep pull immediately. This well-surfaced way is beneath our feet all the way to Oxnop Beck Head. At the several forks avoid the lesser branches right to farms: fortunately the steeper parts are out of the way fairly soon. Eventually it completely levels out to run above the rim of Oxnop Scar before merging into the Muker to Askrigg moorland road just short of its highest point.

Double back to the right along the road to commence the long descent. As far as the cattle grid a good deal of the walking can be enjoyed on the grassy verges. When the road becomes enclosed remain on it for a further three-quarters of a mile before taking a gate on the right marked by a footpath sign. Descend the field to a stile left of a wood, then round the next field-bottom keeping above the trees. When a farm comes into sight below, drop steeply right to a stile right of a barn. Two fields are now crossed to a stile alongside Oxnop Bridge. Cross the road bridge then turn down a narrow lane to return to Ivelet Bridge.

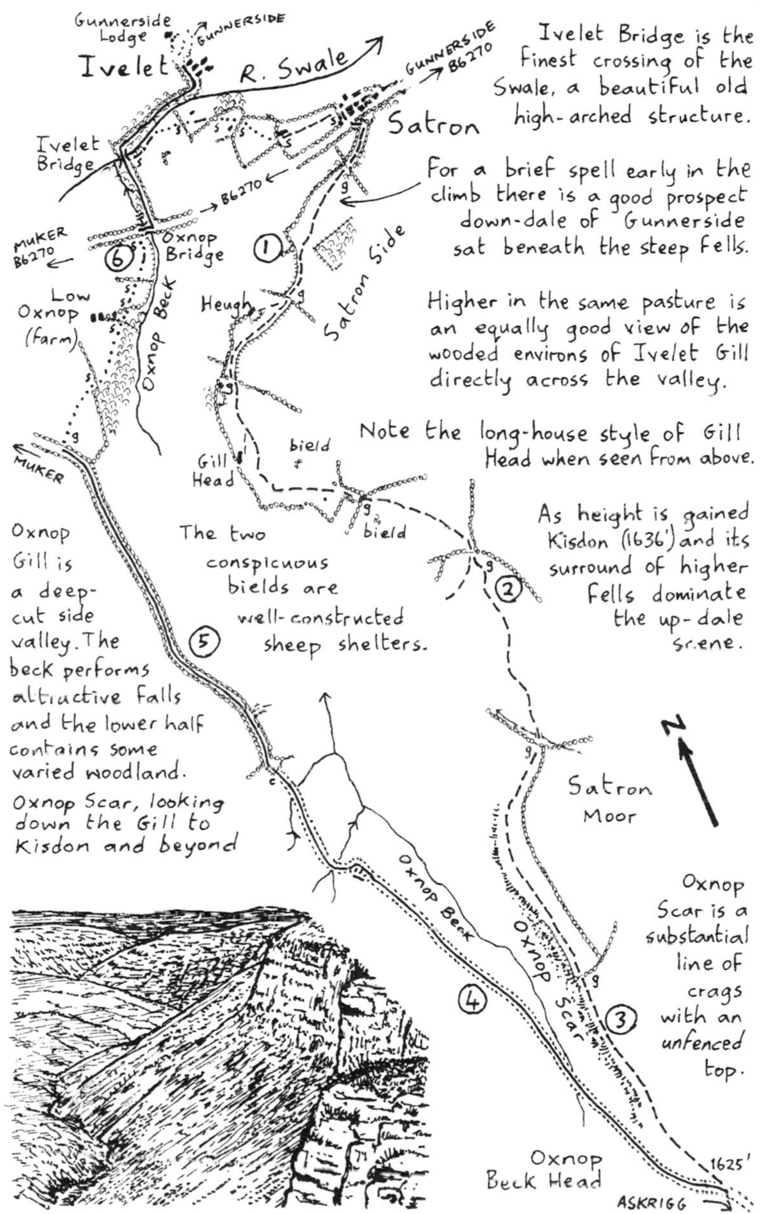
Gunnerside Lodge
GUNNERSIDE
Ivelet
R. Swale
GUNNERSIDE B6270
Satron
Ivelet Bridge
B6270
MUKER B6270
6
Oxnop Bridge
1
Satron Side
Low Oxnop (farm)
Oxnop Beck
Heugh
Gill Head
bield
bield
MUKER
2
5
Satron Moor
N
Oxnop Beck
Oxnop Scar
4
3
1625'
Oxnop Beck Head
ASKRIGG

Ivelet Bridge is the finest crossing of the Swale, a beautiful old high-arched structure.

For a brief spell early in the climb there is a good prospect down-dale of Gunnerside sat beneath the steep fells.

Higher in the same pasture is an equally good view of the wooded environs of Ivelet Gill directly across the valley.

Note the long-house style of Gill Head when seen from above.

As height is gained Kisdon (1636') and its surround of higher fells dominate the up-dale scene.

Oxnop Gill is a deep-cut side valley. The beck performs attractive falls and the lower half contains some varied woodland.

The two conspicuous bields are well-constructed sheep shelters.

Oxnop Scar is a substantial line of crags with an unfenced top.

Oxnop Scar, looking down the Gill to Kisdon and beyond

77

WALK 77 — HARKERSIDE MOOR AND APEDALE

11 miles — From Grinton

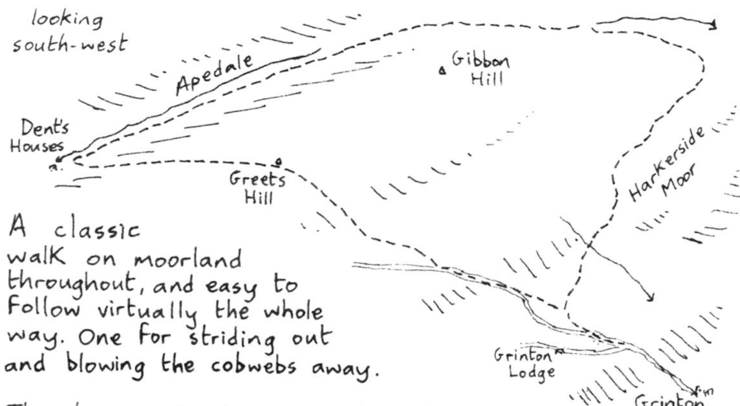
looking south-west
Apedale
Gibbon Hill
Dent's Houses
Harkerside Moor
Greets Hill
Grinton Lodge
Grinton

A classic walk on moorland throughout, and easy to follow virtually the whole way. One for striding out and blowing the cobwebs away.

Though mapped and measured from the centre of Grinton village, the best starting point is the junction of roads from Castle Bolton and Leyburn on the moor-edge south of the village. There is parking for several cars here.
This walk is also ideal for sojourners at the superbly sited Grinton Lodge youth hostel.

THE WALK

From the junction opt for the right-hand fork (to Castle Bolton) and after a few minutes climbing, a wide bridlepath takes us off to the right. Beyond a fence a beck is crossed and the track rises slowly towards Harker Hill. The track becomes briefly vague in a grassy patch, but it continues straight on, crossing another wide track and rising to become clear again and clearer still on merging with another track. As a green strip it rises up through highly conspicuous earthworks on the hill-top: from a guidepost there we have a few faint yards to a cairn, then the track heads off again on a level course across the moor.

At an area of old lead workings cross to the far side of them and then follow the track's sketchy green downhill course alongside the remains. As the track winds down it soon becomes clear again, swinging left to join a wider track before arriving at a large shooting-hut. Go through the gateway by it and maintain a level course on what is now a narrower footpath. At a fork of thin green strips take the right one to the foot of a magnificent limekiln just beyond. Climb the slope after it to join the higher path and resume a level course past a cairn.

The path now begins its only real sketchy spell with the most imperceptible of rises, passing above a prominent large cairn and bending round to the left. On welcome return to more heathery surroundings the path becomes clear with a conspicuous shapely cairn a little ahead. From it the path continues to Birks Gill, rising past two grouse-butts before crossing above a tiny waterfall. Here the butts also cross the beck, but keep right of them and their peaty environs to rise to a cairn in front of a large spoil-heap.

A cairned track is followed left along a devastated strip to the moor-top. At the last cairn before the fence, bear right to a gateway with a large crater behind. From it a green track commences, first going left to another cairn then heading directly away from the fence. This is the head of Apedale, and the track is followed all the way down the valley to a crossroads of moorland tracks at Dent's Houses. Take the left arm which rises to Greets Hill, passing through an old fence on the top to commence what is positively the last leg of the journey.

The track descends away from the angle of fences, and on reaching lead mining remains it becomes unclear. Keep on the right side of the debris to join an unfenced moor-road. With its green verges it can be followed most pleasantly back down to the junction above Grinton, but a little alternative does exist: at the first bend go straight on down an almost hidden grass strip, crossing straight over a wide track and continuing down a path alongside grouse-butts to join another wide track. This is the one on which the walk began, and it soon rejoins the road just above the junction.

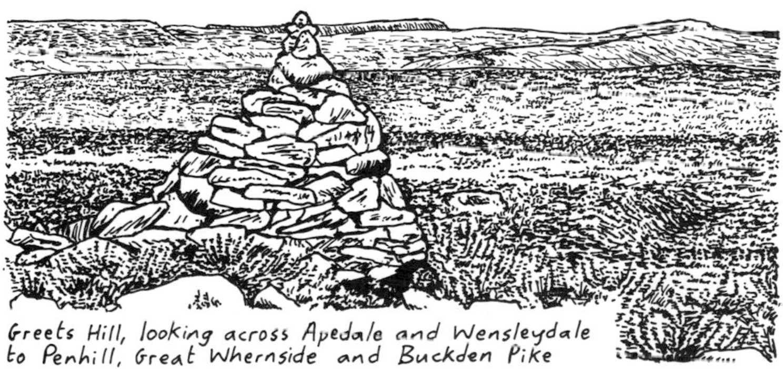

Greets Hill, looking across Apedale and Wensleydale to Penhill, Great Whernside and Buckden Pike

77

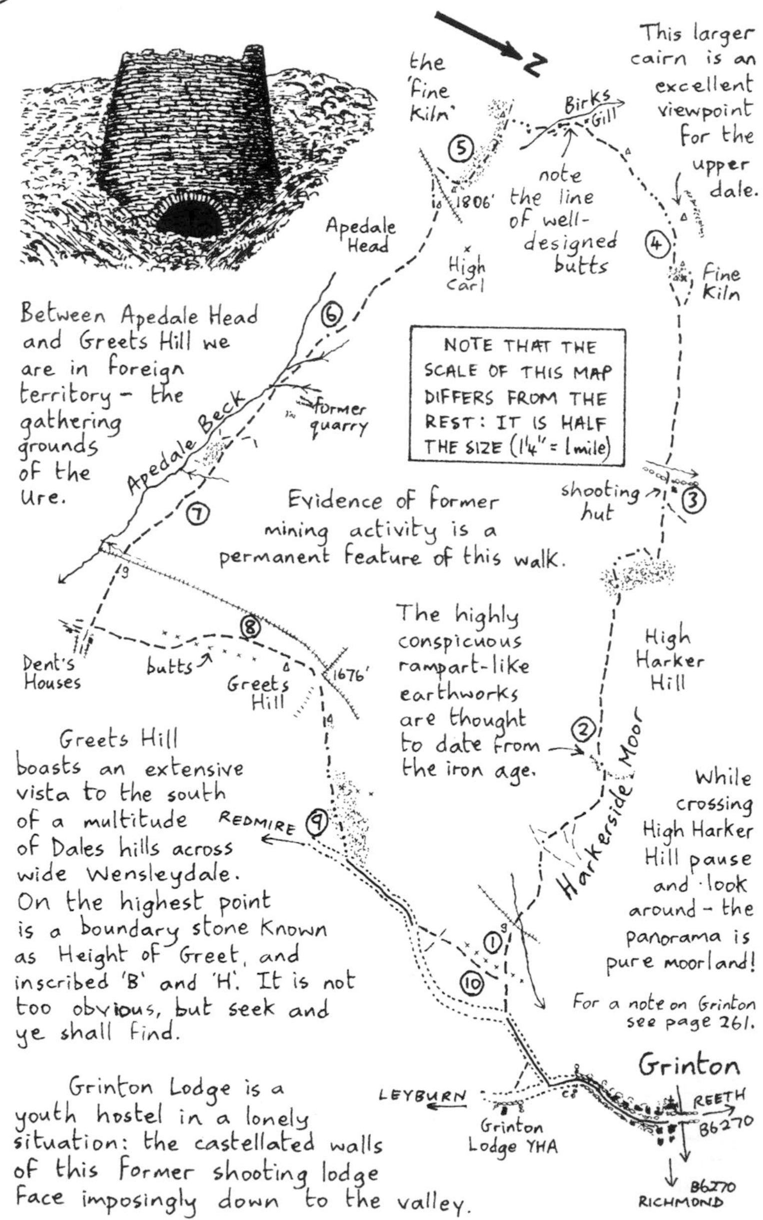

N
the 'Fine Kiln'
Birks Gill
This larger cairn is an excellent viewpoint for the upper dale.
5
1806'
note the line of well-designed butts
Apedale Head
High Carl
4
Fine Kiln
Between Apedale Head and Greets Hill we are in foreign territory - the gathering grounds of the Ure.
6
NOTE THAT THE SCALE OF THIS MAP DIFFERS FROM THE REST: IT IS HALF THE SIZE (1¼" = 1 mile)
former quarry
Apedale Beck
shooting hut
3
7
Evidence of former mining activity is a permanent feature of this walk.
The highly conspicuous rampart-like earthworks are thought to date from the iron age.
High Harker Hill
8
Dent's Houses
butts
Greets Hill
1676'
2
Harkerside Moor
Greets Hill boasts an extensive vista to the south of a multitude of Dales hills across wide Wensleydale. On the highest point is a boundary stone known as Height of Greet, and inscribed 'B' and 'H'. It is not too obvious, but seek and ye shall find.
REDMIRE
9
While crossing High Harker Hill pause and look around - the panorama is pure moorland!
1
10
For a note on Grinton see page 261.
Grinton
LEYBURN
REETH B6270
Grinton Lodge YHA
Grinton Lodge is a youth hostel in a lonely situation: the castellated walls of this former shooting lodge face imposingly down to the valley.
B6270 RICHMOND

WALK 78 — THE ENVIRONS OF LOW ROW

3½ miles

From Low Row!

The attractive surroundings of Low Row include a superb riverside ramble

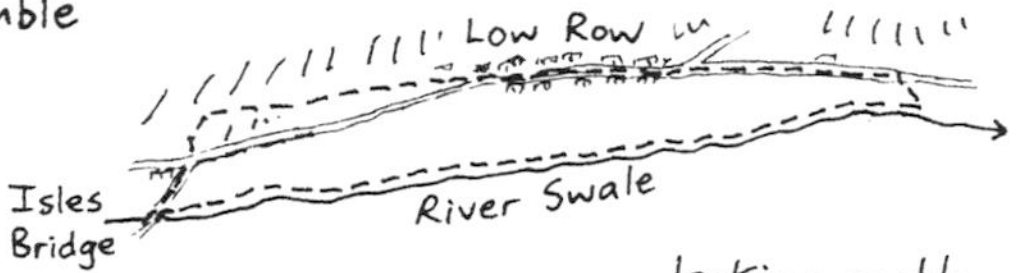

Park on or just off the roadside by the church and inn

THE WALK

From the inn head along the road to Reeth for ten minutes or so, and at a wood on the right look for a footpath sign to Isles Bridge. Here a path descends to the river and follows it upstream, clinging to its bank the whole of the way to Isles Bridge. Turn up the road to a junction, and only yards to the left climb an initially uninviting grass slope.

When the trees and brief path subside, go right along the top of a wall and a path returns, meeting a wider track which in turn joins the road through Low Row. Almost at once the road can be avoided by using the large expanse of grass alongside. It must finally be rejoined at the former school opposite the post office, from where the inn is only minutes further.

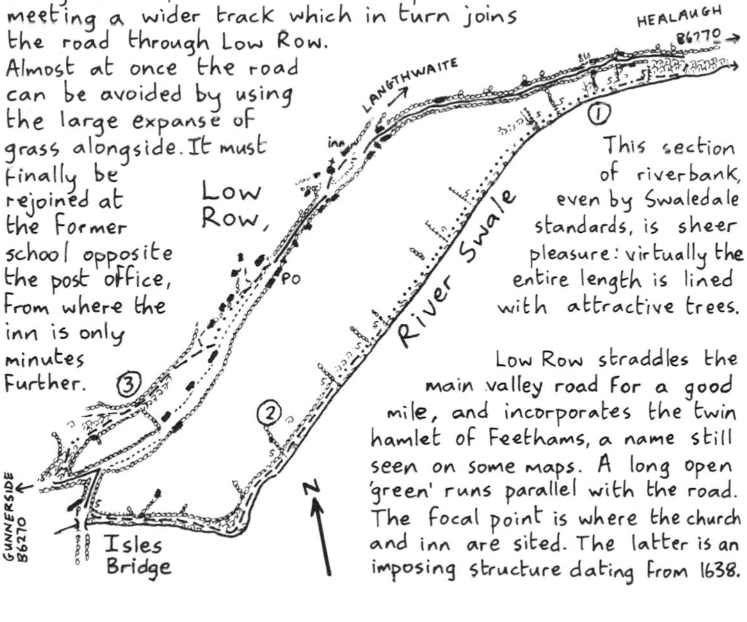

This section of riverbank, even by Swaledale standards, is sheer pleasure: virtually the entire length is lined with attractive trees.

Low Row straddles the main valley road for a good mile, and incorporates the twin hamlet of Feethams, a name still seen on some maps. A long open 'green' runs parallel with the road. The focal point is where the church and inn are sited. The latter is an imposing structure dating from 1638.

WALK 79

MUKER SIDE AND THWAITE

3½ miles

from Muker

Good views from low slopes, and two lovely villages

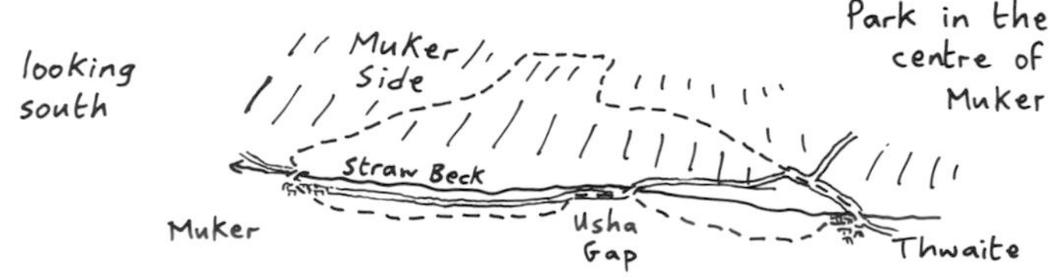
looking south
Muker Side
Park in the centre of Muker
Straw Beck
Muker
Usha Gap
Thwaite

THE WALK

Cross the bridge at the east end of the village and leave the road by an enclosed track rising slowly away to the right. The track soon doubles back to climb towards Muker Side. At a T-junction of walled tracks go right on a level section, and at the next junction turn sharp right to descend to a barn on a bend. Here vacate the imprisoning walls by a gate on the left. Cross two field-bottoms on a track passing an abandoned farm, and part way along the following field take a gate in the wall to slope down a field to a stile in the bottom-left corner. It leads to a footbridge after which a track runs out onto the road.

If there is a reasonable amount of water in the lively Cliff Beck under the footbridge, then a very short detour is recommended. Take a stile just after the bridge and descend the field to a stile onto the road at Scar Houses. Walk only a few yards to the right to see a charming waterfall on the same beck, just above the road. Retrace steps along the road to meet the track and then continue past the Hawes junction before dropping down into Thwaite.

Turn along the short lane in front of the shop, and at the end a Pennine Way sign points the way through a short ginnel and a couple of stiles into a field. Here the Way strikes left, but we continue roughly parallel with a beck on a sketchy path across four fields to reach a tiny bridge over another beck coming in from the left. Cross the field-bottom beyond, head past a barn to a stile from where a short enclosed path joins the road at Usha Gap. Go left to the farm and up its drive to a stile on the right. Cross to a stile near the far corner of the field, from where a string of obvious stiles lead across a host of field-bottoms to enter Muker just behind the inn.

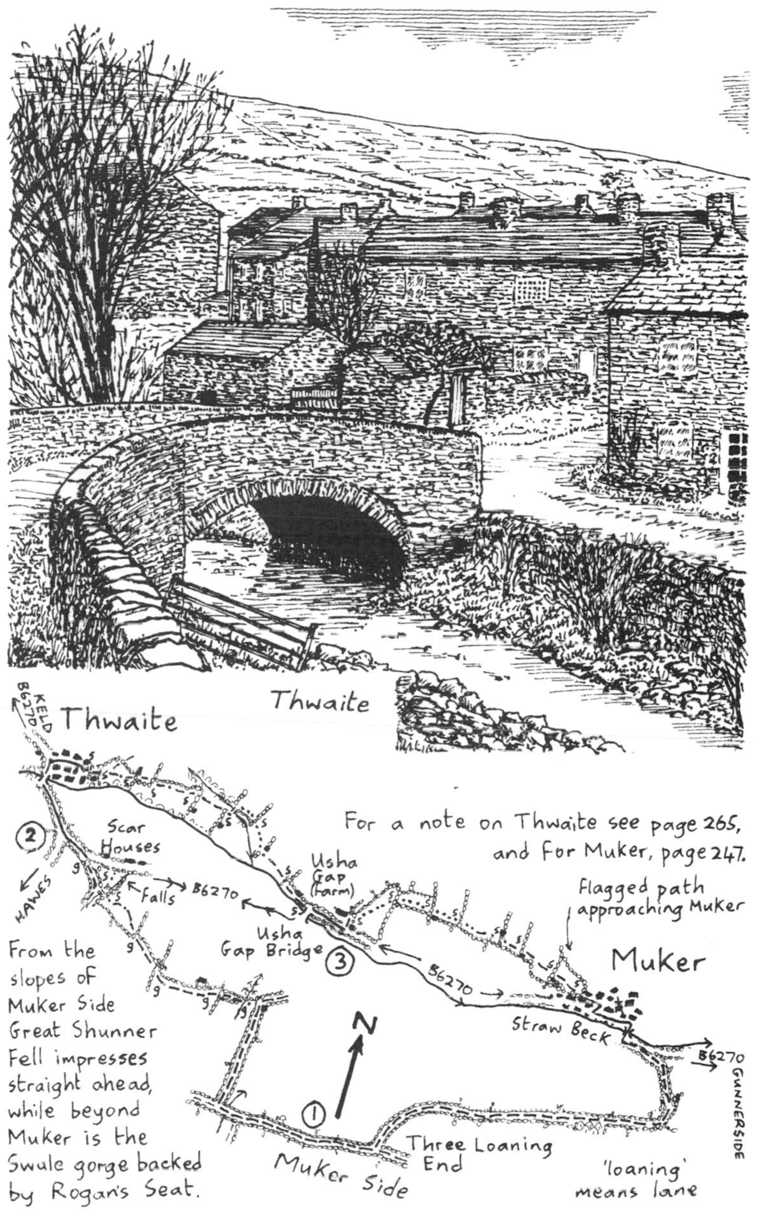
Thwaite
KELD B6270
Scar Houses
HAWES
Falls
B6270
Usha Gap (farm)
Usha Gap Bridge
Flagged path approaching Muker
Muker
B6270
Straw Beck
B6270
GUNNERSIDE
N
Three Loaning End
Muker Side
1
2
3

Thwaite

For a note on Thwaite see page 265, and for Muker, page 247.

From the slopes of Muker Side Great Shunner Fell impresses straight ahead, while beyond Muker is the Swale gorge backed by Rogan's Seat.

'loaning' means lane

WALK 80

ARKENGARTHDALE

5 miles

From Langthwaite

looking north-east

Whaw

Arkle Beck

Stang Bridge

Langthwaite

A valley walk with splendid views of this relatively little-known side valley

Parking in the village centre is limited, but there are several other places on the road above

THE WALK

Cross the bridge into the centre of Langthwaite and leave by a track on the left just after the shop. From a gate head across the field-bottom to a stile, then a sketchy path crosses two more fields to a house. Follow its drive down to join a wider drive, then head up it only a few yards to locate a path through the trees. It soon emerges, and two field-bottoms precede a large meadow which is crossed parallel with the beck to a stile onto a lane.

Cross straight over and up the lane opposite: this quietest of byways is followed for a considerable time, soon becoming unenclosed. It is vacated after a mile and a half by a stile on the left shortly after a left fork near some modern barns, and just before another farm. Four fields are crossed in a direct descent, before a path zig-zags through a colourful moor-like patch. On leaving it the minor lane in Whaw is joined.

Go left to the bridge, and without crossing it take a gate on the left and follow a farm-track through three fields to approach the beck. A generally sketchy path now continues through a number of fields and tree-lined sections, always with a stile near to the beck. On eventual arrival at a metal footbridge (having passed a wooden one several pastures back) cross it and go downstream to a stile onto a lane. Before taking the right-hand of the two gates opposite, a short detour up the lane is recommended to see a surviving powder-house, just over the wall on the right.

On returning to the gate a wide track leads to another gate, where it turns left: just opposite a house take a stile on the right. A short path joins a tarmac drive (the one to Scar House passed early in the walk) which is followed along its tree-lined way to emerge onto the road adjacent to the church. A left turn - complete with pavement - returns us through the rest of Langthwaite to the village centre.

The powder house, C.B. smelt mill

St. Mary's, Langthwaite

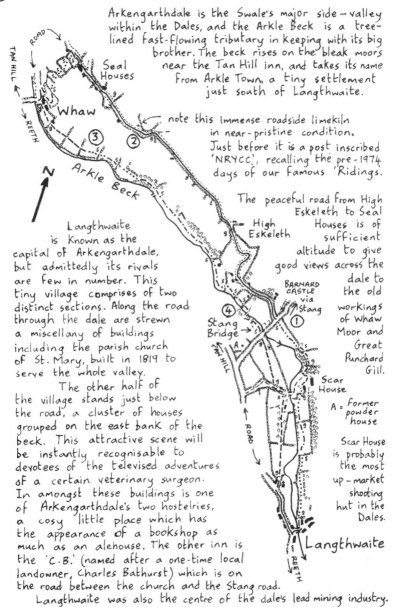

80

Arkengarthdale is the Swale's major side-valley within the Dales, and the Arkle Beck is a tree-lined fast-flowing tributary in keeping with its big brother. The beck rises on the bleak moors near the Tan Hill inn, and takes its name from Arkle Town, a tiny settlement just south of Langthwaite.

note this immense roadside limekiln in near-pristine condition. Just before it is a post inscribed 'NRYCC', recalling the pre-1974 days of our famous 'Ridings'.

The peaceful road from High Eskeleth to Seal Houses is of sufficient altitude to give good views across the dale to the old workings of Whaw Moor and Great Punchard Gill.

A = former powder house

Scar House is probably the most up-market shooting hut in the Dales.

Langthwaite is known as the capital of Arkengarthdale, but admittedly its rivals are few in number. This tiny village comprises of two distinct sections. Along the road through the dale are strewn a miscellany of buildings including the parish church of St. Mary, built in 1819 to serve the whole valley.

The other half of the village stands just below the road, a cluster of houses grouped on the east bank of the beck. This attractive scene will be instantly recognisable to devotees of the televised adventures of a certain veterinary surgeon. In amongst these buildings is one of Arkengarthdale's two hostelries, a cosy little place which has the appearance of a bookshop as much as an alehouse. The other inn is the 'C.B.' (named after a one-time local landowner, Charles Bathurst) which is on the road between the church and the Stang road.

Langthwaite was also the centre of the dale's lead mining industry.

WALK 81 — MARRICK PRIORY AND THE SWALE

6 miles — from Reeth

Easy walking with good lower valley scenery and surprise distant views on the return

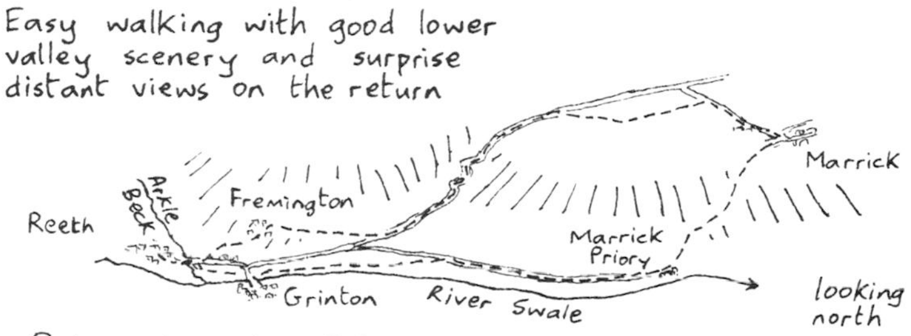
Marrick
Arkle Beck
Fremington
Reeth
Marrick Priory
Grinton
River Swale
looking north

Park in the centre of Reeth

THE WALK

Leave Reeth by the Richmond road, and a little after crossing the bridge over Arkle Beck take a wicket-gate on the right. After leaving some farm buildings behind, our path short-cuts the beck's confluence with the Swale and bears to the left, round a wall-corner to a wicket-gate and then straight ahead to a gate by Grinton Bridge. Cross straight over the road and a footpath clings to the riverbank until a stile admits onto a fenced lane. Turn right along this quiet byway to Marrick Priory, whose tower will have been in sight for quite some time.

At a cattle-grid by the priory the lane becomes a farm-track: here leave it and climb a path to the left to enter a wood. A marvellous flagged path heads up through it, and on leaving the wood remain with the right-hand wall as a sketchy path becomes a wide track to enter Marrick itself. At the first junction turn left up onto the through road, and then go left along it past a farm.

Soon after a small dip in the road look for a stile on the left, and follow a wall away. At a stile cross to the wall's other side and stay with it through several intervening stiles to join a road. A steep descent of this quiet lane ensues until just beyond a bend by a track to West Hag, a stile leads off to the right to begin the last lap. This consists of an invisible field-path which runs a level course making use of stiles and gateways and presenting no problems.

Fremington is reached when a narrow, enclosed path is joined just after an enclosed 'green lane' is crossed at right-angles. Head along the footpath onto a narrow lane, following it left and then right at the first opportunity. When it swings left to descend steeply, go straight along a track to a stile. A path accompanies a left-hand wall through a gateway to a stile, then heads half-right across the next field to a stile beyond which the final stile empties onto a road. Turn right to cross the bridge and re-enter Reeth.

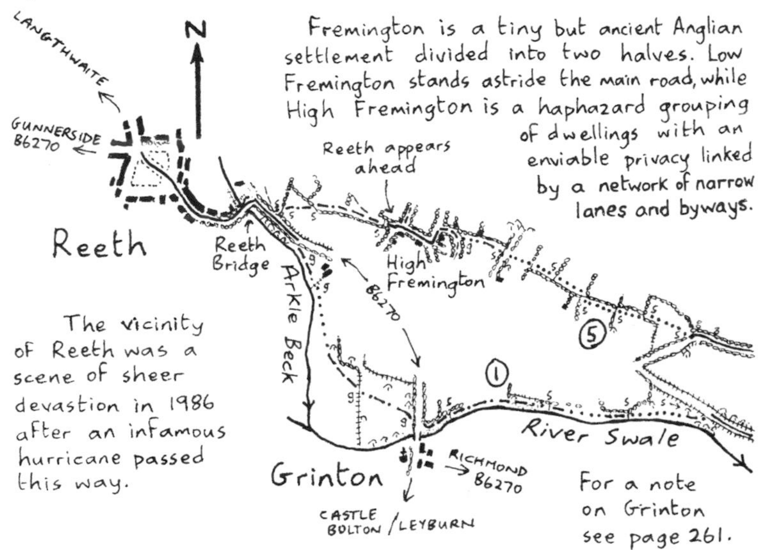
LANGTHWAITE
N
GUNNERSIDE
B6270
Reeth
Reeth appears ahead
Reeth Bridge
Arkle Beck
High Fremington
B6270
5
1
River Swale
Grinton
RICHMOND
B6270
CASTLE BOLTON / LEYBURN

Fremington is a tiny but ancient Anglian settlement divided into two halves. Low Fremington stands astride the main road, while High Fremington is a haphazard grouping of dwellings with an enviable privacy linked by a network of narrow lanes and byways.

The vicinity of Reeth was a scene of sheer devastion in 1986 after an infamous hurricane passed this way.

For a note on Grinton see page 261.

Reeth is popularly known as the capital of upper Swaledale, in effect the whole of that part of the dale within the National Park boundary. It boasts an enviable position on the lower slopes of Calver Hill, well above the Swale and the Arkle Beck. It is actually the latter of these two watercourses to which it shows allegiance, with neighbouring Grinton claiming the Swale. The village centrepiece is a large, sloping green, with the main buildings stood back on all sides.

There is a confident air about this one-time market town which radiates chiefly from the hoary inns and the shops alongside the green. Reeth caters indiscriminantly for dalesfolk and visitors alike, and is the ideal centre for a stay in the valley. Unfortunately parking limitations result in an untidy scene around the green in summer months. Inextricably linked with the lead mining days, Reeth was once much more populous. There is an absorbing folk museum here, while annual agricultural shows and festivals add to its local cultural attractions.

Marrick Priory

※ The top of the road is an excellent viewpoint, the setting of Reeth under Calver Hill being particularly well-displayed. Also well seen on the descent is Grinton, with its isolated youth hostel at Grinton Lodge high on the moor above the village.

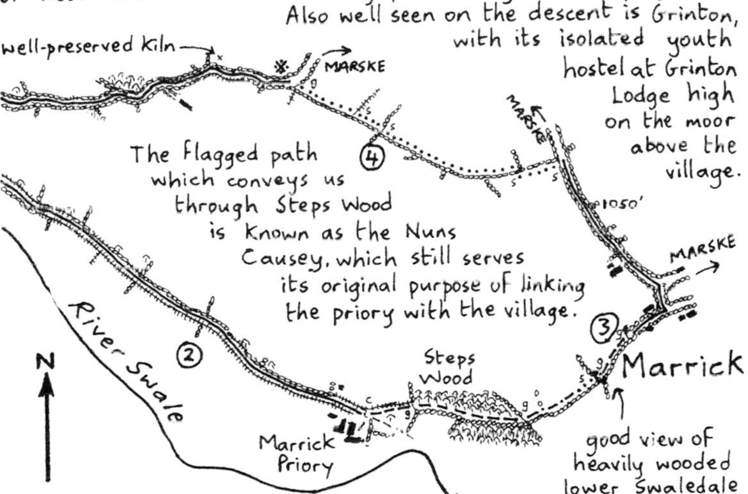
well-preserved kiln
※
MARSKE
MARSKE
4
The flagged path which conveys us through Steps Wood is known as the Nuns Causey, which still serves its original purpose of linking the priory with the village.
1050'
MARSKE
3
2
N
River Swale
Steps Wood
Marrick
Marrick Priory
good view of heavily wooded lower Swaledale

Marrick Priory, in its pastoral riverside setting was founded early in the twelfth century to house Benedictine nuns, and the larger part of the remains have been converted into a residential youth activity centre. Access is restricted to a gaze round the exterior. Marrick village stands high above at a breezy thousand feet up, and its better times were in the heyday of lead mining.

WALK 82 | BIRKDALE AND WHITSUNDALE

5½ miles | from Hoggarths

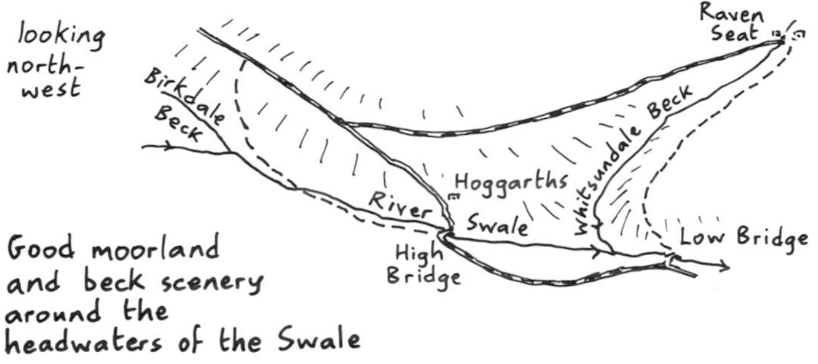
looking north-west
Raven Seat
Birkdale Beck
Whitsundale Beck
Hoggarths
River Swale
High Bridge
Low Bridge

Good moorland and beck scenery around the headwaters of the Swale

The farm of Hoggarths is a good mile past the Tan Hill junction west of Keld. There is parking for several cars just after the road crosses the Swale before climbing to the farm.

THE WALK

From the Keld side of the bridge (High Bridge) take the track running upstream, and just through a gate fork to the left between a stream and a wall. At a barn take a gate to its right and continue on a level course, soon leaving a wall behind and joining the beckside. Follow it to a stone arched bridge and then resume up the opposite bank. After having been deflected by trees up to a gate, go on to join a track at an assortment of buildings at Firs.

Take the track to maintain our upstream course, but when it swings left to become enclosed, continue along another track alongside the left-hand wall. It soon rises above the wall to suddenly end: bear left, nearing the wall again to a stile at the far end. From it climb half-right to an old cottage, and then follow its access track up to a gate. Once through, leave the track and accompany the wall to the left. A little up to the right is the unfenced B6270 road, and when the wall nears it climb to join it in the vicinity of a footpath sign.

Now turn right along the road - or its attendant verge - and within a few minutes a minor junction is reached. Here turn left along the peaceful and largely unfenced access road to its destination and terminus, Raven Seat. Enter the hamlet by a stone arched bridge then turn right up into a farmyard. Take a gate in the right-hand wall and then head downstream, parallel with Whitsundale Beck through several fields.

From a gate just beyond an attractive waterfall, climb half-left to a barn, continuing on a now-level course through several more pastures. Beyond a gate in a fence the path forks: take the right one to pass along the bottom side of a large crumbling enclosure. At a guidepost beyond continue on a level sheeptrod to avoid wet ground by the barns below, then descend to a gate at the next wall junction. A good track then drops down past a farm and over the Swale at Low Bridge to rejoin the B6270 Keld - Kirkby Stephen road.

Now turn right for a steady ten minutes along the road back to the next bridge, which is where the walk began.

Raven Seat is a tiny farming hamlet more than a little off the beaten track.

Unfortunately there is no public right-of-way to lonely Birkdale Tarn just above the road.

From the path one can gaze down into the deep wooded gorge of Oven Mouth.

The River Swale is formed by the meeting of Birkdale Beck and Great Sleddale Beck, and consequently our first mile is also the first mile of the Swale.

Whitsundale Beck is the first major tributary, the confluence being seen to good advantage from the road above, just before the walk ends.

Raven Seat
KIRKBY STEPHEN B6270
Falls
3
How Edge Scars
4
Oven Mouth
2
1525'
Hill Top
Birkdale
1
Firs
River Swale
Hoggarths
B6270
Whitsundale Beck
Eddy Fold
N
Smithy Holme
Falls
High Bridge
R. Swale
5
Kiln
Low Bridge
KELD B6270

WALK 83 — THE ENVIRONS OF GUNNERSIDE

5 miles — from Gunnerside

A walk of immense variety: lush meadows, high tracks and lead-mining remains.
Marvellous views of the main valley and Gunnerside Gill

looking north-west

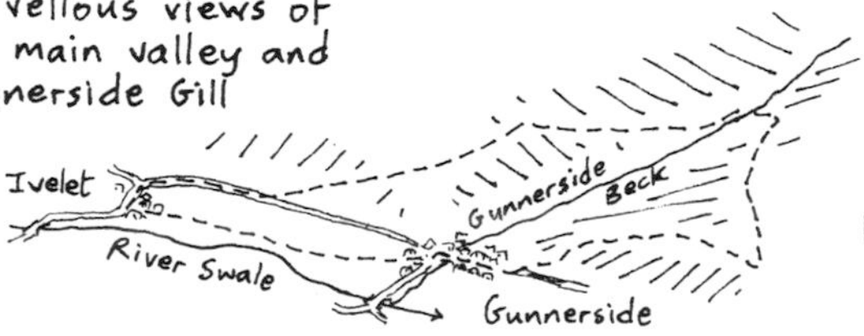

Park in the village centre

THE WALK

From the bridge in the village centre, depart along the lane to the right of the main up-dale road: it is identifiable by the tidy little green at the start of it. The lane soon ends at the school, and a gate to its right leads between modern housing to a gate into a field. The way now heads across countless meadows keeping generally level to arrive at a beck, crossing it by a tiny footbridge to emerge into the hamlet of Ivelet.

At the lane turn up to the right, bearing right at a junction, crossing a bridge and finally becoming level at the open hillside. After a short while take a wide track branching up to the left. It rises around the hill high above Gunnerside Gill, and though it can be seen climbing far ahead, we leave it at the first opportunity when a lesser track forks right to slope steadily down to the beck. On the opposite bank are the remains of lead workings, and a little further upstream cross the beck at a still-tall ruin on our bank. Just behind a smaller ruin over the beck, the main path up the gill is joined at a stile.

From the stile the path rises away from the beck, but before reaching a wall-corner turn right at a crossroads to begin the return to Gunnerside. The new path becomes sketchy as it rises to a narrow stile below a low ruin. Continue across the tops of two fields, emerging past a tiny section of wall and on to a wall-corner. Keep well above the wall and a path appears before joining a wide green track.

After going through a gateway the track passes several groups of farm buildings, and remains fairly level before meeting another track at a gate on the right. With Gunnerside far below, go through the gate and accompany this gentle byway on its steep but highly enjoyable descent back into the village.

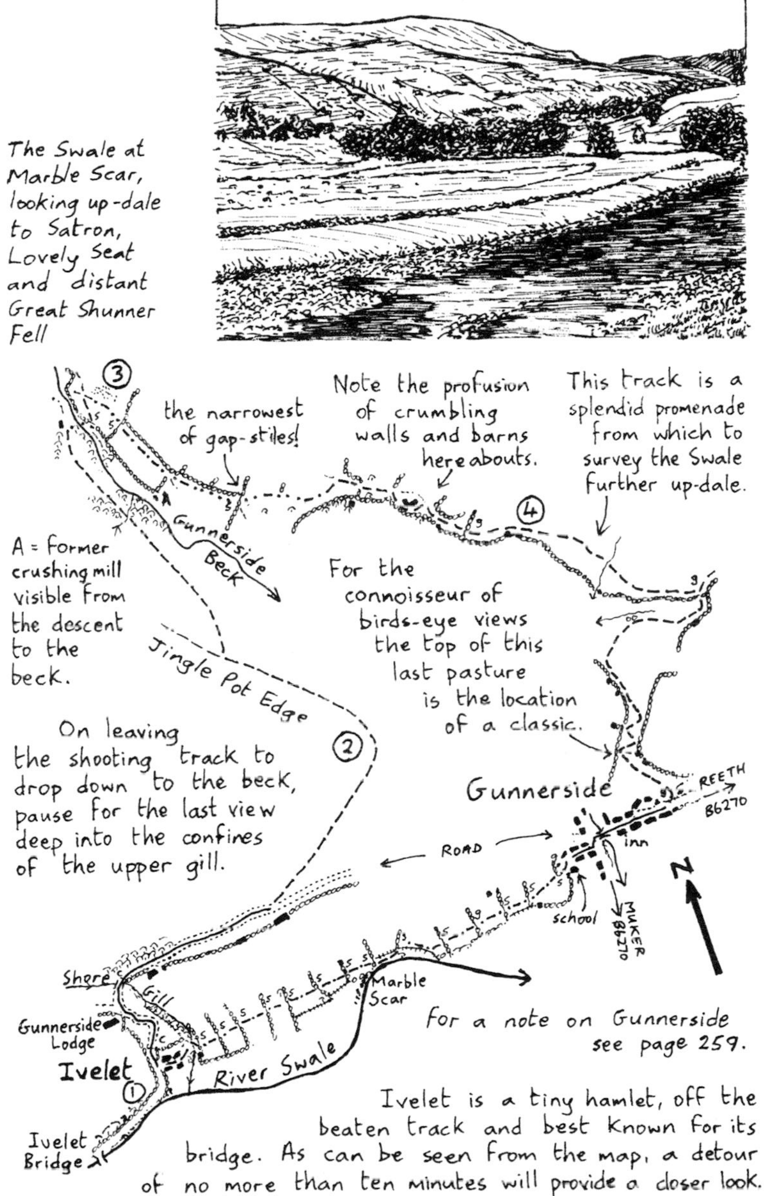
③
the narrowest of gap-stiles!
Note the profusion of crumbling walls and barns hereabouts.
This track is a splendid promenade from which to survey the Swale further up-dale.
④
A
Gunnerside Beck
A = former crushing mill visible from the descent to the beck.
For the connoisseur of birds-eye views the top of this last pasture is the location of a classic.
Jingle Pot Edge
②
On leaving the shooting track to drop down to the beck, pause for the last view deep into the confines of the upper gill.
Gunnerside
REETH
B6270
ROAD
inn
school
MUKER B6270
N
Shore Gill
Marble Scar
Gunnerside Lodge
Ivelet
①
River Swale
Ivelet Bridge

The Swale at Marble Scar, looking up-dale to Satron, Lovely Seat and distant Great Shunner Fell

For a note on Gunnerside see page 259.

Ivelet is a tiny hamlet, off the beaten track and best known for its bridge. As can be seen from the map, a detour of no more than ten minutes will provide a closer look.

WALK 84 **WHITCLIFFE SCAR AND THE SWALE**

7½ miles from Richmond

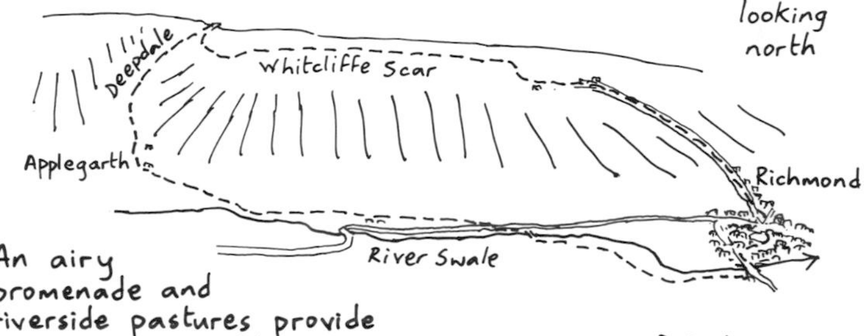
looking north
Deepdale
Whitcliffe Scar
Applegarth
Richmond
River Swale

An airy promenade and riverside pastures provide scenery as varied as anywhere further up-dale

The centre of Richmond has ample car-parking

THE WALK

Leave the top end of the Market Place along Finkle Street, turning left along Newbiggin and right along Cravengate. A little further on the road swings left, and here leave it by a long avenue, Westfields, rising straight ahead. It leaves the houses to become a quiet lane, remaining surfaced as far as Whitcliffe Farm. Now a track, remain on it until level with a farm on the left, and then climb the steep field to a fence at the top. Go left with it, up through a gateway, and then veer left to a fence running along the top of the eastern end of Whitcliffe Scar.

At an intervening wall we are conveyed to the scar side of the fence, and here we remain to reach the monument at Willance's Leap. Keep company with what is now a wall on the right, and our level path swings round with it, still above the Scar and then above a farm road in Deepdale. Eventually it is joined at its junction with a road, and we double back down the farm road as far as a cattle grid just short of East Applegarth. Take a stile just before it and descend by a well-collapsed wall, skirting the confines of Low Applegarth to a stile and gate in a fence. Just below it go left through a gateway, descending half-left through a gap in a wall, and similarly through a larger pasture to join a fence on the left. Passing a ruined barn continue down to a stile and thence onto the riverbank.

Two lengthy riverside pastures ensue, and although in neither does the unclear right of way appear to cling to the river, it seems more sensible and pleasant than to wander through the centre of the fields in aimless fashion. At the end of the second

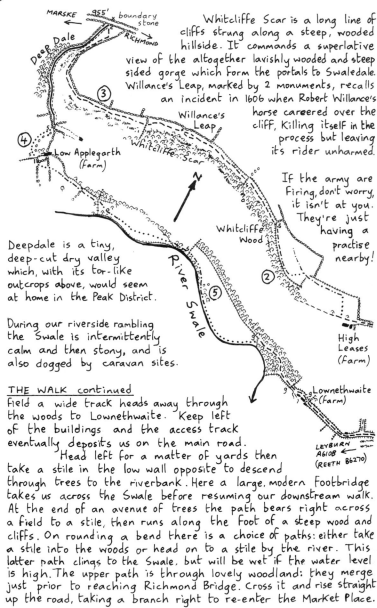

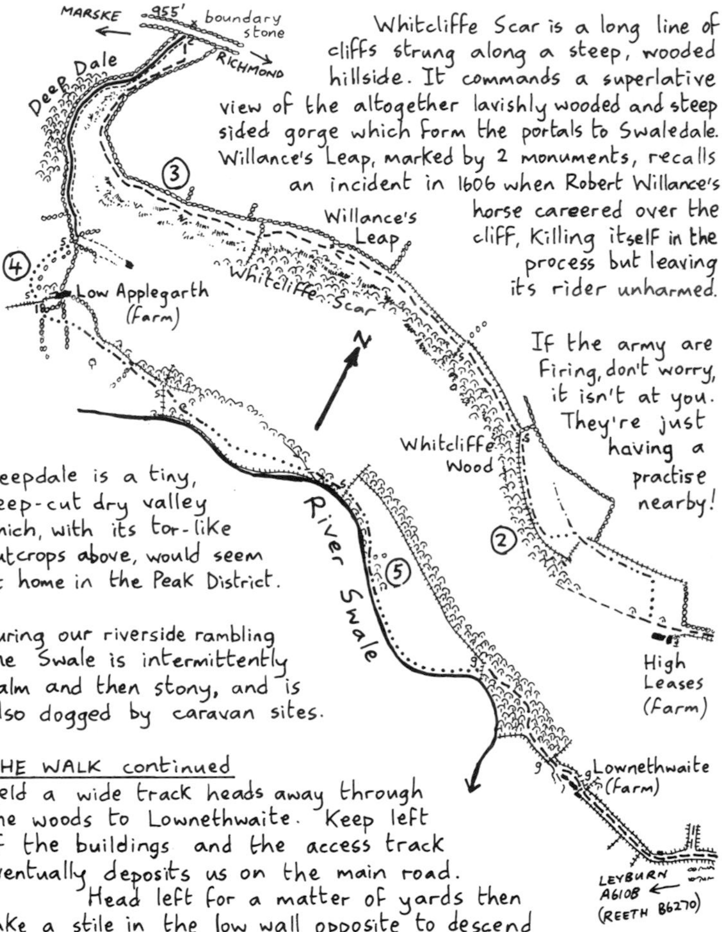

Whitcliffe Scar is a long line of cliffs strung along a steep, wooded hillside. It commands a superlative view of the altogether lavishly wooded and steep sided gorge which form the portals to Swaledale. Willance's Leap, marked by 2 monuments, recalls an incident in 1606 when Robert Willance's horse careered over the cliff, killing itself in the process but leaving its rider unharmed.

If the army are firing, don't worry, it isn't at you. They're just having a practise nearby!

Deepdale is a tiny, deep-cut dry valley which, with its tor-like outcrops above, would seem at home in the Peak District.

During our riverside rambling the Swale is intermittently calm and then stony, and is also dogged by caravan sites.

THE WALK continued

field a wide track heads away through the woods to Lownethwaite. Keep left of the buildings and the access track eventually deposits us on the main road.

Head left for a matter of yards then take a stile in the low wall opposite to descend through trees to the riverbank. Here a large, modern footbridge takes us across the Swale before resuming our downstream walk. At the end of an avenue of trees the path bears right across a field to a stile, then runs along the foot of a steep wood and cliffs. On rounding a bend there is a choice of paths: either take a stile into the woods or head on to a stile by the river. This latter path clings to the Swale, but will be wet if the water level is high. The upper path is through lovely woodland: they merge just prior to reaching Richmond Bridge. Cross it and rise straight up the road, taking a branch right to re-enter the Market Place.

Richmond is the gateway to Swaledale, although passing through it is the last thing to do. This is a truly remarkable town, steeped in history and retaining so much of its past, where other, less remote places have succumbed to the 20th century. Dominating the town is the castle, which stands on a rocky promontory high above the Swale. It was begun in 1071 by Alan Rufus, and the well-preserved ruins are now in the care of English Heritage and open to the public. Outstanding is the enormous 12th century keep, which watches over the whole town including, almost at its feet, the Market Place.

This equally-enormous feature shares double-bill with the castle, and has a multitude of uses. In the centre of its sloping cobbles is the church of the Holy Trinity with its 14th century tower. The building uniquely incorporates a row of shops, and houses the Green Howards Museum. Lined by shops and inns the Market Place is also used as a bus station as well as for its original purpose on Saturdays. A market cross is still very much in evidence.

Outside of the square, from which numerous wynds (narrow ways) radiate, is the parish church of St. Mary which includes a 14th century tower and 16th century stalls. Also in the vicinity is the impressively upstanding Grey Friars Tower, across the road from the Georgian Theatre. This fascinating place dates from 1788, and having been restored in the 1960's it now serves its original function once more.

The presence of the military around the town is due to the proximity of Catterick Camp. Also nearby are the Premonstratensian remains of Easby Abbey, dating from 1152.

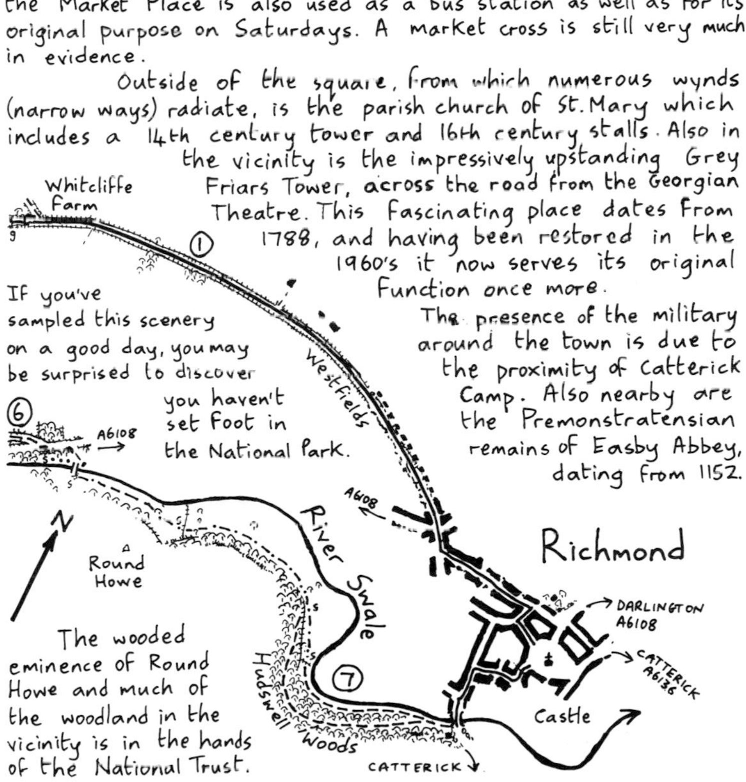
Whitcliffe Farm
1
Westfields
6
A6108
A6108
N
Round Howe
River Swale
Hudswell Woods
7
Richmond
DARLINGTON A6108
CATTERICK A6136
Castle
CATTERICK

If you've sampled this scenery on a good day, you may be surprised to discover you haven't set foot in the National Park.

The wooded eminence of Round Howe and much of the woodland in the vicinity is in the hands of the National Trust.

WALK	DATE	START	FINISH	WEATHER	COMMENTS
1					
2					
3					
4					
5					
6					
7					
8					
9					
10					
11					
12					
13					
14					

15					
16					
17					
18					
19					
20					
21					
22					
23					
24					
25					
26					
27					
28					

WALK	DATE	START	FINISH	WEATHER	COMMENTS
29					
30					
31					
32					
33					
34					
35					
36					
37					
38					
39					
40					
41					
42					

43					
44					
45					
46					
47					
48					
49					
50					
51					
52					
53					
54					
55					
56					

WALK	DATE	START	FINISH	WEATHER	COMMENTS
57					
58					
59					
60					
61					
62					
63					
64					
65					
66					
67					
68					
69					
70					

71					
72					
73					
74					
75					
76					
77					
78					
79					
80					
81					
82					
83					
84					

KEY TO THE MAP SYMBOLS

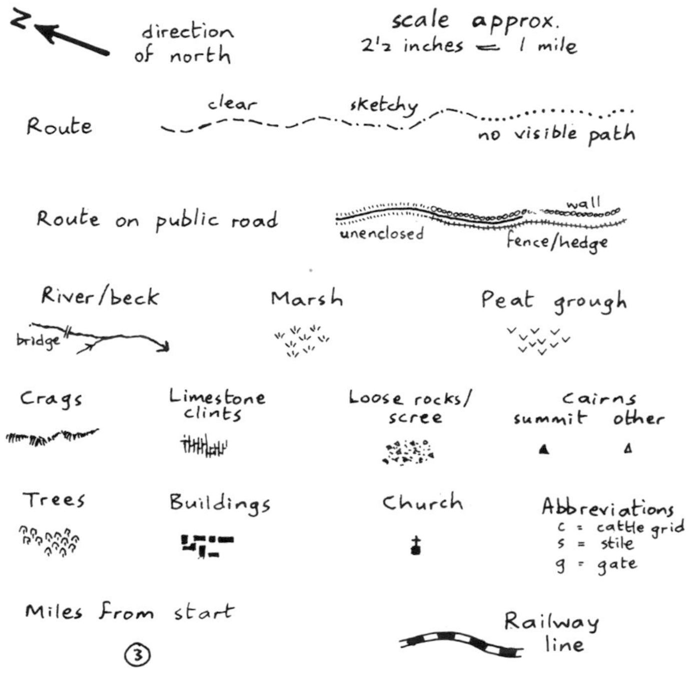

direction of north
scale approx.
2½ inches = 1 mile
clear
sketchy
Route
no visible path
Route on public road
wall
unenclosed
fence/hedge
River/beck
bridge
Marsh
Peat grough
Crags
Limestone clints
Loose rocks/ scree
Cairns
summit
other
Trees
Buildings
Church
Abbreviations
c = cattle grid
s = stile
g = gate
Miles from start
3
Railway line

THE COUNTRY CODE

Respect the life and work of the countryside
Protect wildlife, plants and trees
Keep to public paths across farmland
Safeguard water supplies
Go carefully on country roads
Keep dogs under control
Guard against all risks of fire
Fasten all gates
Leave no litter - take it with you
Make no unnecessary noise
Leave livestock, crops and machinery alone
Use gates and stiles to cross fences, hedges and walls